Fodor's

CITYGUIDE
HOUSTON

FODOR'S TRAVEL PUBLICATIONS

NEW YORK • TORONTO • LONDON • SYDNEY • AUCKLAND

WWW.FODORS.COM

A B C D

1

Courtney
WASHINGTON COUNTY
GRIMES COUNTY
Conroe
1486
Mostyn
149
1774
MONTGOMERY
1488
297
45
Chateau Woods
2979
362
Magnolia
Shenandoah
6
1488
Pinehurst
Oak Ridge North
Howth
Stage Coach
Decker Prairie
Woodlands
Hufsmith
Spring
290
Hempstead
Prairie View
Spring Creek
2978
Tomball
2920

2

359
290
6
Waller
Hockley
2920
Westfield
159
1887
WALLER COUNTY
Kohrville
249
Monaville
Cypress
290
6
1960
8
Aldine

3

Brazos River
331
359
362
529
Satsuma
Jersey Village
North Houston
249
Hardy Toll Road
1458
2855
HARRIS COUNTY
45
Pattison
San Filipe
Brookshire
90
Katy
6
610

Sealy
10
Addicks
BunkerHill Village
Houston
Frydek
1093

4

AUSTIN COUNTY
359
1463
1093
8
Bellaire
ALT 90
86
Simonton
Fulshear
723
610
521
Wallis
359
99
Sugarland
Stafford
288
Orchard
Brazos River
36
ALT 90
59
1092
Missouri City
2234
Richmond
Rosenberg
Dewalt

5

East Bernard
ALT 90
36
2759
Booth
6
Fresno
Beasley
Pleak
Arcola
60
Kendleton
59
FORT BEND COUNTY
762
Thompsons
521
Iowa Colony
360
Fairchilds
762
1161
Hungerford
Needville
1236
1994
BRAZOS BEND STATE PARK
762

6

102
Wharton
Guy
442
1462
Rosharon
521
288
1301
Damon
Bonney
961
60
Iago
3012
36
523
59
Mackay
Boling
Newgulf
Holiday Lakes
WHARTON COUNTY
442
Lane City
Pledger
1301
Varner Hogg Plantation
Baileys Prairie

7

Magnet
West Columbia
35
Angleton
1162
1728
1459
35
BRAZORIA COUNTY
288
288
2004
Colorado River
San Bernard River
Old Ocean
521
Richwood Village
1162
Sweeny
Brazoria
332
Clemville
Van Vleck
Allenhurst
521
Lake Jackson
332
1468
Bay City
457
Clute
288
Markham
2431
35
2611
Jones Creek
36
Freeport

8

MATAGORDA COUNTY
Cedar Lane
Churchill Bridge
PEACH POINT WMA
2918
1468
457
SAN BERNARD NATIONAL WILDLIFE REFUGE
1095
2853
2668
60
521
Sargent
Wadsworth

STREETFINDER

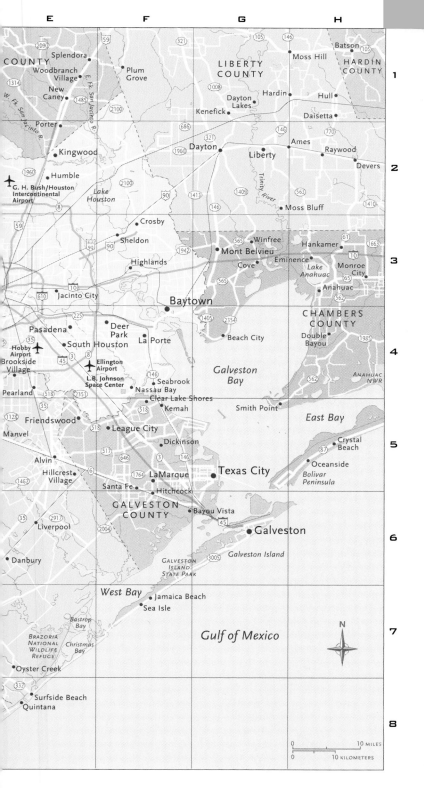

HOUSTON AREA AND VICINITY

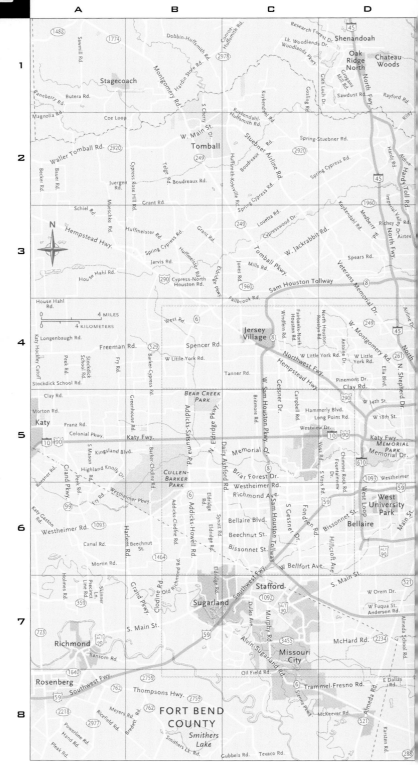

A   B   C   D

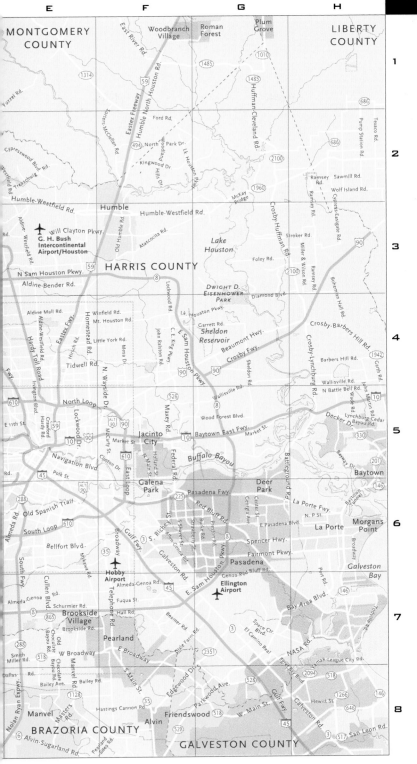

E   F   G   H

MONTGOMERY COUNTY

LIBERTY COUNTY

1

Woodbranch Village
Roman Forest
Plum Grove

East River Rd.
1485
1010

Eastex Freeway
1314

Humble North Houston Rd.

59

1485

Huffman-Cleveland Rd.

686

2

494
Ford Rd.
North Park Dr.

2100

686
Texaco Rd.
Pump Station Rd.

Cypresswood Blvd Rd.
Westfield Rd. Treaschwig

Kingwood Dr.

Lk. Houston Pkwy.

1960

Ramsey Rd.
Sawmill Rd.
Wolf Island Rd.

Cypress-Eastgate Rd.

Aldine
Humble-Westfield Rd.

Humble

Humble-Westfield Rd.

McKay Bridge

Crosby-Huffman Rd.

3

Rd.

Will Clayton Pkwy.
G. H. Bush Intercontinental Airport/Houston

Old Humble Rd.

Atascocita Rd.

Lake Houston

Foley Rd.

Stroker Rd.

Miller & Wilson Rd.

Ramsey Rd.

90

N Sam Houston Pkwy.

HARRIS COUNTY

59

8

DWIGHT D. EISENHOWER PARK

2100

Bohemian Hall Rd.

Aldine-Bender Rd.

Diamond Blvd.

4

Aldine Mall Rd.

Winfield Rd.
Mt. Houston Rd.

Lockwood Rd.

Lk. Houston Pkwy.

Garrett Rd.

Sheldon Reservoir

Beaumont Hwy.

Crosby-Barbers Hill Rd.

1942
Garth Rd.

Eastex Fwy.
Homestead Rd.
Hardy Toll Road
Aldine-Westfield Rd.

Hirsch Rd.

Little York Rd.
Mesa Dr.

John Ralston Rd.

C. E. King Pkwy.

E. Sam Houston Pkwy.

Crosby Fwy.

90
90
Sheldon Rd.

Crosby-Lynchburg Rd.

Barbers Hill Rd.

Wallisville Rd.

N Battle Bell Rd.
Wade Rd.

10

Tidwell Rd.

526

John Martin Rd.

5

North Loop

N. Wayside Dr.

Maxey Rd.

8
Wallisville Rd.

Wood Forest Blvd.

Decker Dr.

Lynchburg-Cedar Bayou Rd.

330

610

E 11th St.
Crawford
Lockwood Dr.
Hardy Rd.
Irvington Blvd.

ALT
90

59

90

McCarty St.

Jacinto City

10
Baytown East Fwy.

Market St.

Barkley Dr.

Baytown

201

10

Navigation Blvd.

Market St.

Holland St.
N. Main St.

Federal Rd.

Buffalo Bayou

Battleground Rd.

146

Clinton Dr.

610
East Loop

Polk St.

45
ALT 90

Galena Park

Pasadena Fwy.

225

Deer Park

La Porte Fwy.
N. P St.

Morgans Point

6

288

Old Spanish Trail

Almeda Rd.

610
South Loop

Bellfort Blvd.

35
Broadway

Gulf Fwy.

Galveston Rd.

S. Richey
S. Shaver St.
Allen Genoa Rd.

Burke Rd.

Red Bluff Rd.

Preston Rd.
Strawberry Rd.

Center St.
Georgia Ave.

8

Spencer Hwy.

Fairmont Pkwy.

E Pasadena Blvd.

La Porte

Broadway

Galveston Bay

7

South Fwy.

Cullen Blvd.

Mykawa Rd.

Hobby Airport

Almeda-Genoa Rd.

45

Pasadena

Genoa Red Bluff Rd.

Ellington Airport

Port Rd.

146

Bay Area Blvd.

146

Almeda-Genoa Rd.
8
863
Schurmier Rd.

Telephone Rd.

Fuqua St.

Beamer Rd.

3

Space Ctr. Blvd.

NASA Rd. 1

Armand Bayou

Brookside Village

Old Chocolate Bayou Rd.
Brookside Rd.

Hall Rd.

El Camino Real

Clear Lake

League City Rd.

Pearland

W Broadway

E Broadway

Dixie Farm Rd.

2351

528

Egret Bay Blvd.

2094

518

Smith Miller Rd.
282

518

Chocolate Bayou Rd.

Manvel Rd.

S. Main St.

Hewitt St.

1266

146

Dallas
Bailey Ave.
Bailey Rd.

1128

Edgewood Dr.

Parkwood Ave.

528

Gulf Fwy.

646

8

Nolan Ryan Expwy.
Manvel

Masters Rd.

Hastings Cannon Rd.

35

Friendswood
518

W. Main St.

45

Galveston Rd.
3
517
San Leon Rd.

6
Alvin-Sugarland Rd.

Pearland Sites Rd.

Alvin
528

BRAZORIA COUNTY

GALVESTON COUNTY

3

1

West Rd.
Longenbaugh Rd.
West Rd.
Jersey Village
Fairbanks-North Houston Rd.
North Houston-Rosslyn Rd.
Tomball Pkwy.
W Mt. Houston Rd.
Antoine Dr.
Huffmeister Rd.
529
6
290
8
Spencer Rd.
Windfern Rd.

2

Keith Harrow Blvd.
W Little York Rd.
N Eldridge Pkwy.
Tanner Rd.
Brittmore Rd.
W Sam Houston Tollway
Hempstead Hwy.
Gessner Dr.
Northwest Fwy.
W Little York Rd.
Pinemont Dr.
W Mangum Rd.
Clay Rd.
Clay Rd.
Clay Rd.
Campbell Rd.

3

Groschke Rd.
Addicks-Satsuma Rd.
Patterson Rd.
N Eldridge Pkwy.
Bear Creek Park
Springwoods Park
Kempwood Dr.
Hammerly Blvd.
Long Point Rd.
290
Silber Rd.
Katy Fwy.
Westview Dr.
Spring Valley
Hilshire Village
10 90

4

Cullen-Barker Park
Dairy Ashford Rd.
Memorial Dr.
Briar Forest Dr.
Westheimer Rd.
8
Briarpark Dr.
Hedwig Village
Bunker Hill Village
Piney Point Village
Hunters Creek Village
Voss Rd.
Buffalo Bayou
S Voss Rd.
Fountainview Dr.
Chimney Rock Rd.

5

Westheimer Pkwy.
6
Addicks-Clodine Rd.
Addicks-Howell Rd.
Winkleman Rd.
Eldridge Rd.
Richmond Ave.
Alief Clodine Rd.
Bellaire Blvd.
Brays Bayou
Sam Houston Tollway
S Gessner Dr.
Harwin
Fondren Rd.
Westpark Dr.
59
Bellaire Blvd.
Bissonnet St.
S Rice Ave.
Chimney Rock Rd.

6

Boss Gaston Rd.
Old Richmond Rd.
Synott Rd.
Eldridge Rd.
Eldridge Rd.
Beechnut St.
Bissonnet St.
59
Keegans Bayou
Brays Bayou
Fondren Rd.
Creekbend Dr.
W Bellfort Ave.
Hillcroft Ave.
Chimney Rock Rd.
W Airport Blvd.

7

Old Richmond Rd.
Voss Rd.
ALT 90
Oyster Creek
Sugarland
W Airport Blvd.
Stiles Ln.
Southwest Fwy.
Greenbriar Dr.
Mula Rd.
1092
Stafford Rd.
Stafford
ALT 90
Brand Ave.
Dulles Ave.
Ave. E
Murphy Rd.
Staffordshire Rd.
Texas Pkwy. Rd.
Independence Blvd.
S Main St.
Fondren Rd.
Hillcroft Ave.
W Fuqua Dr.
Blue Ridge Rd.

8

59
Sweetwater Blvd.
Palm Royale Blvd.
Brazos River
Williams Trace
Lexington Blvd.
Alvin-Sugarland Rd.
Oil Field Rd.
Cartwright Rd.
1455
Missouri City
Glen Lakes Ln.
McHard Rd.
Mustang Bayou

0   2 MILES
0   2 KILOMETERS

STREETFINDER

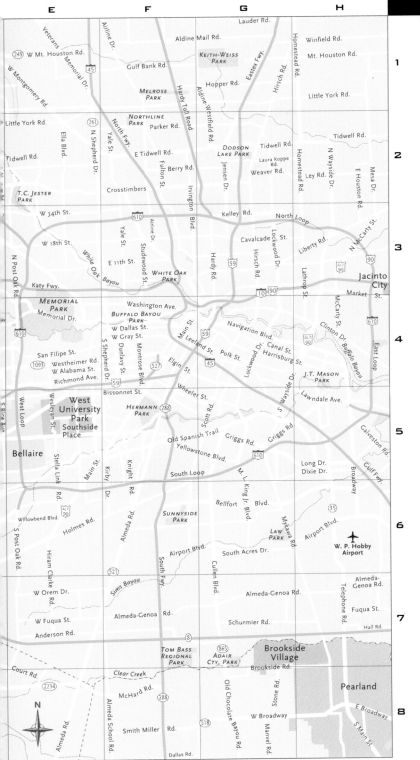

	E	F	G	H	

Veterans
(249) W Mt. Houston Rd.
W Montgomery Rd.
Memorial Dr.
Airline Dr.
(45)
Gulf Bank Rd.
Aldine Mail Rd.
Lauder Rd.
KEITH-WEISS PARK
Essex Fwy.
Hopper Rd.
Hirsch Rd.
Homestead Rd.
Winfield Rd.
Mt. Houston Rd.
Little York Rd.

1

Little York Rd.
Ella Blvd.
(261)
N Shepherd Dr.
Yale St.
North Fwy.
Hardy Toll Road
MELROSE PARK
NORTHLINE PARK
Parker Rd.
Aldine-Westfield Rd.
DODSON LAKE PARK
Tidwell Rd.
Laura Koppe Rd.
Weaver Rd.
Homestead Rd.
Ley Rd.
N Wayside Dr.
E Houston Rd.
Mesa Dr.
Tidwell Rd.
Tidwell Rd.

2

T.C. JESTER PARK
E Tidwell Rd.
Fulton St.
Berry Rd.
Jensen Dr.
Crosstimbers

Irving Blvd.

W 34th St.
N Post Oak Rd.
Yale St.
Airline Dr.
Studewood St.
(610)
E 11th St.
W 18th St.
White Oak Bayou
Katy Fwy.
WHITE OAK PARK
Hardy Rd.
Kelley Rd.
Cavalcade St.
Lockwood Dr.
Hirsch Rd.
North Loop
Liberty Rd.
Lathrop St.
(59)
(10) (90)
Market St.
N McCarty St.
ALT (90)
Jacinto City

3

MEMORIAL PARK
Memorial Dr.
(610)
Washington Ave.
BUFFALO BAYOU PARK
W Dallas St.
W Gray St.
San Filipe St.
(1093)
Westheimer Rd.
W Alabama St.
Richmond Ave.
N Shepherd Dr.
Dunlavy St.
Montrose Blvd.
(527)
Main St.
(59)
Leeland St.
Elgin St.
(45)
Navigation Blvd.
Polk St.
Canal St.
Harrisburg St.
Lockwood Dr.
Clinton Dr.
Buffalo Bayou
J.T. MASON PARK
(610)
East Loop

4

Bissonnet St.
West Loop
West University Park
Southside Place
Wesleyan St.
HERMANN PARK
(288)
Wheeler St.
Scott Rd.
Old Spanish Trail
Yellowstone Blvd.
Griggs Rd.
Griggs Rd.
Wayside Dr.
Lawndale Ave.
(610)
Calveston Rd.
Gulf Fwy.

5

Bellaire
S Rice Ave
Stella Link Rd.
Main St.
Kirby Dr.
Knight Rd.
South Loop
Long Dr.
Dixie Dr.
Broadway

Willowbend Blvd.
S Post Oak Rd.
ALT (90)
Holmes Rd.
Almeda Rd.
SUNNYSIDE PARK
Airport Blvd.
Bellfort Blvd.
M. L. King Jr. Blvd.
South Acres Dr.
Cullen Blvd.
LAW PARK
Mykawa Rd.
Airport Blvd.
(35)
W. P. Hobby Airport

6

Hiram Clarke Rd.
(521)
South Fwy.
Sims Bayou
Airport Blvd.
Almeda-Genoa Rd.
Telephone Rd.
Almeda-Genoa Rd.
W Orem Dr.
W Fuqua St.
Almeda-Genoa Rd.
Schurmier Rd.
Fuqua St.
Hall Rd.

7

Anderson Rd.
Court Rd.
(2234)
TOM BASS REGIONAL PARK
(8)
Clear Creek
McHard Rd.
(288)
Almeda School Rd.
ADAIR CTY. PARK
(865)
Old Chocolate Bayou Rd.
(518)
Smith Miller Rd.
Dallas Rd.
Stone Rd.
W Broadway
Manvel Rd.
Brookside Village
Brookside Rd.
Pearland
E Broadway
S Main St.

8

N

THE LOOP, WEST AND SOUTHWEST

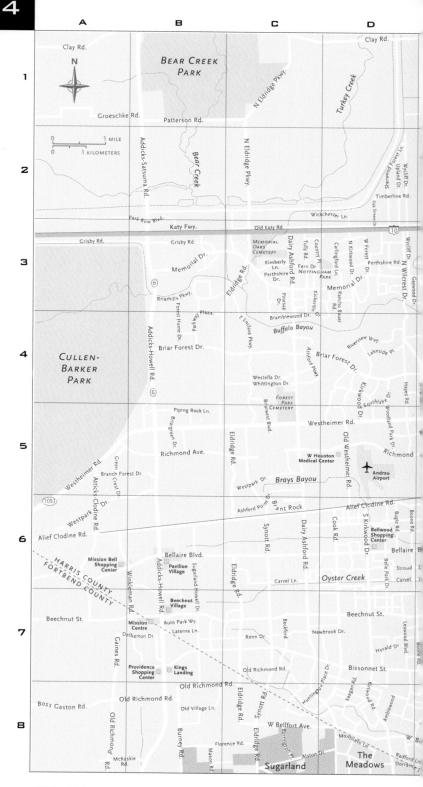

4

A   B   C   D

Clay Rd.

N

BEAR CREEK PARK

N Eldridge Pkwy.

Clay Rd.

Turkey Creek

Groeschke Rd.

Patterson Rd.

Bear Creek

N Eldridge Pkwy.

Forest Ln.
Wycliff Dr.
Upland Dr.
Pommard

0   1 MILE
0   1 KILOMETERS

Timberline Rd.

Park Row Blvd.

Katy Fwy.

Old Katy Rd.

Wickchester Ln.

Oak Street Dr.

10

Grisby Rd.

Grisby Rd.

MEMORIAL OAKS CEMETERY

Dairy Ashford Rd.

Tully Rd.

Country Pl

Carlingford Ln.

N Kirkwood Dr.

W Forest Dr.

Perthshire Rd.

N Wilcrest Dr.

Gaywood Dr.

Memorial Dr.

Eldridge Rd.

Kimberly Ln.
Perthshire Dr.

Fern Dr.
NOTTINGHAM PARK

Memorial Dr.

Briarhills Pkwy.

Forest Home Dr.

Way Plaza.

Pineasp Dr.

Kickerillo

Rancho Bluer Rd.

Bramblewood Dr.

Buffalo Bayou

CULLEN-BARKER PARK

Addicks-Howell Rd.

Briar Forest Dr.

E Enclave Pkwy.

Ashford Pkwy.

Briar Forest Dr.

Riverview Way.

Lakeside Pl

6

Westella Dr.
Whittington Dr.

Kirkwood Dr.

Southlake

Hayes Rd.

Piping Rock Ln.

FOREST PARK CEMETERY

Briarwest Blvd.

Westheimer Rd.

Woodland Park Dr.

Briargreen Dr.

Richmond Ave.

Eldridge Rd.

Old Westheimer Rd.

Richmond

Westheimer Rd.

Green Crest Dr.

Branch Forest Dr.

W Houston Medical Center

Andrau Airport

1093

Atticks-Clodine Rd.

Westpark Rd.

Westpark Dr.

Brays Bayou

Brant Rock

Ashford Point Dr.

Alief Clodine Rd.

Boone Rd.

Bugle Rd.

Alief Clodine Rd.

Synott Rd.

Dairy Ashford Rd.

Cook Rd.

S Kirkwood Dr.

Bellwood Shopping Center

Bellaire Bl

HARRIS COUNTY
FORTBEND COUNTY

Mission Bell Shopping Center

Winkleman Rd.

Bellaire Blvd.

Addicks-Howell Rd.

Pavilion Village

Sugarland-Howell Dr.

Eldridge Rd.

Carvel Ln.

Oyster Creek

Belle Park Dr.

Stroud

Carvel

Beechnut Village

Beechnut St.

Beechnut St.

Leawood Blvd.

Boone Rd.

Mission Centre

Auto Park Wy.

Laterna Ln.

Renn Dr.

Beckford

Newbrook Dr.

Herald Dr.

Gaines Rd.

Delbarton Dr.

Providence Shopping Center

Kings Landing

Old Richmond Rd.

Bissonnet St.

Kirkwood Rd.

Keegan Rd.

Huntington Place Dr.

Old Richmond Rd.

Eldridge Rd.

Synott Rd.

Bunkington

Boss Gaston Rd.

Old Richmond Rd.

Old Village Ln.

Burney Rd.

Mason Rd.

Eldridge Rd.

W Bellfort Ave.

Barrington Pl.

Alston Dr.

Monticeto Ln.

The Meadows

Radford Ln.
Dorranche

W Bl

McKaskie Rd.

Florence Rd.

Sugarland

STREETFINDER

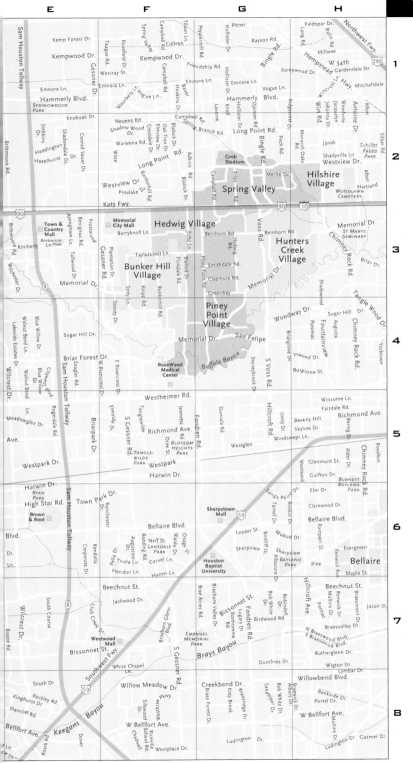

	E	F	G	H

Northwest Fwy.

Kemp Forest Dr.

Kempwood Dr.

Spring Valley

Campbell Rd.

Colleen

Tilson Ln.

Pepperrell Rd.

Pitner

Hollister

Rayson Rd.

Feldspar Dr.

Bolin Rd.

Lang Rd.

Millwee

Hempstead Hwy.

W 34th

1

Kempwood Dr.

Teague Dr.

Rosefield Dr.

Kempwood Dr.

Campbell Rd.

Friendship Rd.

Hollister

Hollister Rd.

Bingle Rd.

Kempwood Dr.

Wincrest In. Hwy.

Woodvine

Jacquelyn Dr.

Johanna Dr.

Gardendale Dr.

Mitchelldale

Westray St.

Gessner Dr.

Emnora Ln.

Emnora Ln.

Emnora Ln.

Emnora Ln.

Vogue Ln.

Afton

Antoine Dr.

290

Emnora Ln.

Moorberry Ln.

S Vogue Ln.

Bauer

Hoskins Dr.

Hammerly Blvd.

Hollister Rd.

Wirt Rd.

SPRINGWOODS
PARK

Hammerly Blvd.

Lavene

Knol

Ojeman Rd.

Schiller
FREED Rd.

Silber Rd.

Knoboak Dr.

Neuens Rd.

Campbell Rd.

Spring Branch Rd.

Long Point Rd.

Pech Rd.

Ridgecrest Dr.

Janak

Monarch Oaks

Shadyvilla Ln.

Westview Dr.

2

Stebbins
Dr.

Shadow Wood
Dr.

Shadowdale Dr.

Haddington Dr.

Hazelhurst Dr.

Warwana Rd.

Blalock Rd.

Oak Tree Dr.

Elmview Dr.

Crestdale Dr.

Witte

Adkins

Long Point Rd.

Spring

Grob
Stadium

Fries Rd.

Merlin Dr.

Hartland

Afton

Hilshire
Village

WOODLAWN
CEMETERY

Westview Dr.

Bunkerhill Dr.

Pinelake Dr.

Campbell Dr.

Blalock Dr.

Spring Valley

Katy Fwy.

90

90

10

Town &
Country
Mall

Memorial
City Mall

Hedwig Village

Beinhorn Rd.

Voss Rd.

Beinhorn Rd.

Memorial Dr.

ST MARYS
SEMINARY

BENDWOOD
PARK

Brittmoore Rd.

Kimberly

Anthingham Ln.

Bengaus Rd.

Frostwood

Plantation Dr.

Gessner Rd.

Barryknoll Ln.

Echo Ln.

Hedwig Rd.

Hunters
Creek
Village

Chimney Rock Rd.

3

Winchester Dr.

Tallwood Dr.

Taylorcrest Ln.

Smithdale Rd.

Shadywood

Briar Dr.

Memorial Dr.

Bunker Hill
Village

Flindale Dr.

Blalock Dr.

Piney Point Rd.

Claymore Rd.

Tangle Wood Dr.

8

Knipp Rd.

Bunkerhill Rd.

Greenbay

Stoney Dr.

Sugar Hill Dr.

Piney
Point
Village

Woodway Dr.

Sugar Hill Dr.

Augusta

Chimney Rock Rd.

Yorktown

4

Blue Willow Dr.

Walnut Bend Ln.

Seagler Rd.

E Rivercrest Dr.

W Rivercrest Dr.

Memorial Dr.

San Felipe

Potomac

Fountainview

Lakeside
Estates Dr.

Briar Forest Dr.

RoseWood
Medical
Center

Buffalo Bayou

S Voss Rd.

Stoneybrook Dr.

Briargrove Dr.

Inkwood Dr.

Burgoyne St.

Wilcrest Dr.

Clopeck Blvd.

Blue Willow
Dr.

Walnut Bend

Rogerdale Rd.

Sam Houston Tollway

Elmside Dr.

Tanglewilde

Jeanetta

Westheimer Rd.

Winsome Ln.

Fairdale Rd.

Richmond Ave.

Meadowglen Dr.

Briarpark Dr.

S Gessner Rd.

Richmond Ave.

Ocee St.

Fondren Rd.

Dunvale Rd.

Beverly Hill

Skyline Dr.

Bering Dr.

5

Ave.

TANGLE-
WILDE
PARK

BLOSSOM
HEIGHTS
PARK

Westglen

Hillcroft Rd.

Windswept Ln.

Westward

Chimney Rock Rd.

Royalton

Westpark Dr.

Westpark

Glenmont St.

Alder Dr.

Harwin Dr.

Gulfton Dr.

BURNETT
BAYLAND
PARK

Harwin Dr.

RYAN
PARK

Town Park Dr.

Sand's Point Dr.

Elm Dr.

6

High Star Rd.

Ranchester
Dr.

Sharpstown
Mall

Rockin Dr.

Tarrel Dr.

Clarewood Dr.

Brown
& Root

59

Bellaire Blvd.

Rampart St.

Blvd.

Corporate Dr.

Kendalia

Bellaire Blvd.

Bairedale

Augustine Dr.

Reding Rd.

Neff St.

Walda St.

Osage St.

LANSDALE
PARK

Leader St.

Bintliff Dr.

Mobud Dr.

Pine

Evergreen

Bellaire

Dr.

Triola Ln.

Carvel Ln.

Sharpview

SHARPVIEW
BAYLAND
PARK

Renwick Dr.

Maple St.

Ln.

Hendon Ln.

Hazen Ln.

Houston
Baptist
University

Sharpview
Albacore Dr.

Wilcrest Dr.

South Course

Club Creek Dr.

Beechnut St.

Jackwood Dr.

Brae Acres Rd.

Braeburn Valley Dr.

Bissonnet St.

Fondren Rd.

Robindell
Dr.

Hillcroft Ave.

Beechnut St.

Renwick Dr.

Mullins Dr.

Pontiac

Braesvalley Dr.

Jason St.

Braeswood Dr.

7

Boone Rd.

Westwood
Mall

Braeburn Blvd.

S Gessner Rd.

Lugary Dr.

Bob White
Dr.

Bonhomme
Rd.

Birdwood Rd.

N Braeswood Blvd.

S Braeswood Blvd.

Bissonnet St.

EMANUEL
MEMORIAL
PARK

Brays Bayou

Rutherglenn Dr.

White Chapel

Dumfries Dr.

Wigton Dr.

Lymbar Dr.

8

59

South Dr.

Rockley Rd.

Willow Meadow Dr.

Creekbend Dr.

Braes Forest Dr.

Kitty Brook

Braesridge Dr.

Swingmoor Dr.

Bob White Dr.

Willowbend Blvd.

Braeswick Dr.

Albury Dr.

Kinghurst Dr.

Pkwy.

Bankside Dr.

Portal Dr.

8

Stancliff Rd.

Sillwood
Dr.

Braesmeadow
Dr.

W Bellfort Ave.

W Bellfort Ave.

Bellfort Ave.

Keegans Bayou

Dover

Riceville
School Rd.

Chadwell

Westplace Dr.

Ludington Dr.

Ludington Dr.

Mullins Dr.

Gasmer Dr.

Sam Houston Tollway

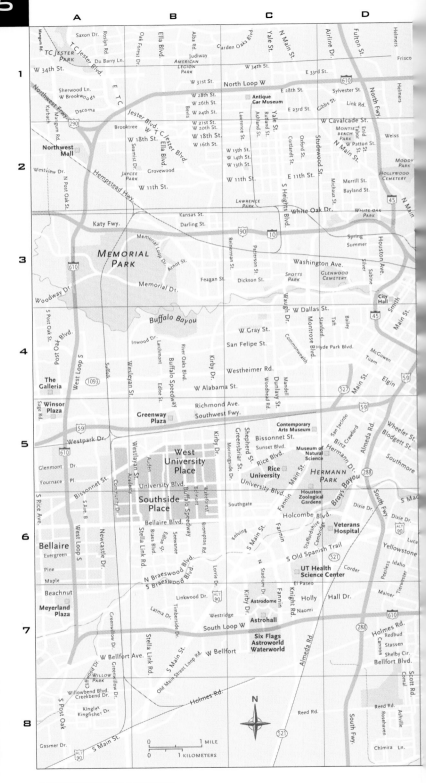

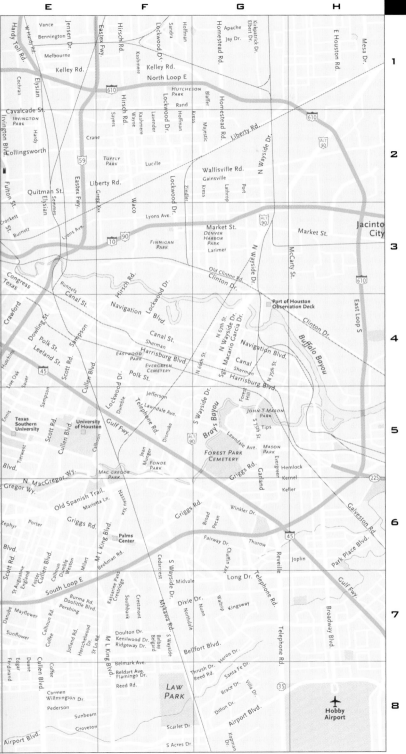

6

	A	B	C	D

1

Brittmore Rd.
Claymoore Park Dr.
Clay Rd.
Quincannon
Shadowdale Dr.
Triway Ln.
Kemp Forest
Teague Rd.
Kempwood
Rosefield Dr.
Spring Valley Rd.
Spring Rock
Campbell Rd.
Blalock
Morning View
Colleen

2

Kersten Dr.
Norton
Alcott
Emnora
Hammerly Blvd.
Gessner Rd.
Westray
Emnora
Palo Pinto
Kenwood
Moolberry Ln.
Eagle Rock
Elmgate
Elmview
Blalock
Lazy Spring
Hoskins
Bauer

3

Brittmore Rd.
SPRINGWOODS PARK
Sam Houston Tollway
Stebbins Dr.
Townhurst
Tiger Trail
Knoboak Dr.
Barwood
Shadow Bend Dr.
Conrad Sauer
Timber Oak Dr.
NOB HILL PARK
Knoboak Dr.
Shadow Wood
Warwana Dr.
Crestdale
Elmview
Oak Tree
Blalock
Yupondale
Benbow
Campbell

4

Eddystone Dr.
Hazelhurst Dr.
Shadow Oaks
Shadowdale Dr.
Conrad Sauer
Westview
Gessner Rd.
Witte
Cedardale
Pinelake
Long Point Rd.
Confederate
Blalock
Cedar Post
Oak Tree Dr.
Long Branch
Bunkerhill Rd.
Adkins Rd.
EXIT 758A
EXIT 758B

5

Lasso
EXIT 755
Town & Country Mall
EXIT 757
Katy Freeway
90
10
HEDWIG VILLAGE
Gayford
Denise Dr.
Magdalene Dr.
Merrdel Rd.
Echo Ln.

6

Queensbury Ln.
BENDWOOD PARK
Attingham Dr.
Benignus Rd.
Frostwood Dr.
Barryknoll
Riedel
Kimberly
Electra
Taylorcrest rd.
ElectraDr.
Kimberly Ln.
Perthshire Rd.
Kimberly Ln.
Cobblestone
Taylorcrest
Flintwood
Bunkerhill Rd.
Blalock
Flintdale Rd.
Wilchester Dr.
E. Gaywood Dr.
Hallie
Tallwood
Frostwood
Boheme Dr.
Plantation Rd.
Strey Ln.
Knipp

7

Boheme Dr.
Memorial Dr.
Paul Revere Dr.
Vanderpool Ln.
Gessner
Warrenton Dr.
Stoney Ck.
BUNKER HILL
Greenbay Hollow
Monica Ln.
Boheme Rd.
Hermitage Ln.
Briar Dr.
Briar Hill Dr.
Sam Houston Tollway
Pine Forest
Briarpark Dr.
Briarpark Dr.
Hibury Dr.
Durrette Dr.
Longleaf Ln.
Knipp
Mayerling Dr.
Memorial Dr.
Riverview

8

Walnut Bend Ln.
Blue Willow Dr.
Valley Forge Dr.
Seagler Rd.
Briarbrook Dr.
W. Rivercrest Dr.
E. Rivercrest Dr.
Bayou Brook
Briar Forest Dr.
Memorial
S. Piney Point
Lakeside Estates Dr.
Willcrest
Briar Forest Dr.
Delmonte Dr.
Chevy Chase Dr.
Olympia Dr.
Tanglewilde

BUNKER HILL, PINEY POINT, AND MEMORIAL AREA COMMUNITIES

A   B   C   D

1

3000 FEET
1 KILOMETER

Magnum
La Monte Dr.
Hewitt Dr.
Chantilly Ln.
Clebe Rd.
Donna Bell Ln.
La Monte Ln.
Althea Dr.
Chippendale Rd.
Piney Woods
Rosslyn Rd.
Oak Forest Dr.
W. 43rd
Ella Blvd.
Golf Dr.
Sue Barnett
Alba Rd.
W. 42nd
W. 41st
Fisher
Wakefield
Brinkman
T.C. JESTER PARK
Judiway
Du Barry Ln.
OAK FOREST PARK

N

2

W. 34th St.
Gardendale
Mangum Rd.
Sherwood Ln.
Brookwoods
Vollmer Rd.
Ascot Ln.
Dacoma
W. T C Jester Blvd.
Lou Ellen Ln.
Ansbury
610
W 34th
W 31st
Stonecrest
North Loop West
W 28th
W 26th
N. Durham
290
Northwest Fwy.

3

Karbach
Hempstead Hwy.
W. Governors Cir. E
E. T C Jester Blvd.
Brooktree
Lazybrook
Willowby
Tannehill
Droxford
Seamist
W. 18th
Helberg Park
Ella Blvd.
W. T C Jester Blvd.
W 22nd
W 20th
W 16th
Beall
Dian

4

Story
N. Post Oak
W. 12th St.
610 W. 11th St.
Jaycee Park
Cindy Ln.
Grovewood
W. 12th St.
W. 11th St.
Hurst
Toledo
W 14th
Wynnwood
Shirkmere
Shelterwood
Sherwood
Worthshire
T. C. Jester Blvd.

5

Beth El Cemetery
EXIT 11B
10 90
EXIT 11A
EXIT 763
Chatsworth
Portwest Dr.
Pine Haven
N. Post Oak Rd.
Old Katy Rd.
Washington
Katy Fwy.
EXIT 764
Arabelle
Cohn
Kansas
Petty
Larkin
EXIT 765A Cornish
Nolda
Maxie

6

Memorial Dr.
N. Post Oak Rd.
Woodway Dr.
W. Memorial Loop Dr.
MEMORIAL PARK GOLF COURSE
MEMORIAL PARK
Houston Arboretum and Nature Center
Picnic
Memorial Dr.
E. Memorial Loop Dr.
Haskell
Arriot
Crestwood
Terrace
Westcott
Schuler
Washington
Rose
Blossom
Feagan
Birdsall
Asbury
Detering

7

S. Post Oak Ln.
Longmont
610
Hollyhurst
Post Oak Park Dr.
Willowick
Inverness
Inwood
RIVER OAKS COUNTRY CLUB
Lazy Ln.
Pine
Inwood
Pelham
Stanmore

8

Sage Rd.
McCue Rd.
S Post Oak Blvd.
West Loop South
Post Oak Park Dr.
Briarglen
Bancroft
Suffolk
Drexel
San Felipe
West Ln.
Weslayan St.
Del Monte
Chevy Chase
Olympia
Piping Rock
Timber Ln.
Maconda
River Oaks Park
Larchmont
Claremont
River Oaks
Bellmeade
MARY ELLIOT PARK
Ella Lee Ln.
REBECCA MEYER PARK
Locke Ln.
Ferndale
Kipling
Kirby Dr.
Dickey
Westheimer Rd
Revere
Westheimer Rd.

STREETFINDER

E   F   G   H

1

W. Crosstimbers
Garden Oaks
Blueberry
W 38th
Yale
Crosstimbers
Oxford
Europa
N. Main St.
Cortlandt
E 40th
E 38th
Correll
EXIT 52B
E. Crosstimbers
Basswood
Fulton
Bauman
Roswell
Appleton
Helmers
Yorkshire
Wainwright
Westford
Bennington
Bennington
Frisco

N. Shepherd Blvd. (Spur 261)

2

W 34th
W 32nd
W 30th
EXIT 15
Ashland
N. Shepherd Dr.
N. Lawrence
EXIT 16
Cortlandt
Columbia
E 33rd
E 32nd
E 28th
E 26th
Aurora
E 24th
Airline Dr.
Sylvester
Link Rd.
EXIT 51
610
EXIT 178/C
Melbourne
Caplan
North Loop East
Kelley
Fairbanks
Graceland
Sue

3

E 20th
E 18th
E 16th
E 14th
Ashland
Alliston
Herkimer
Alexander
N. Durham
N. Shepherd Dr.
Yale
Michaux
MONTIE BEACH PARK
N. Main St.
Tabor
Northwood
Cordell
North Frwy.
EXIT 50
Fulton
Canadian
Cavalcade
Frawley
Weiss
Patton
Edison
Irvinton Blvd.

4

LAWRENCE PARK
W 12th
W 10th
W 8th
Yale
Cortlandt
Columbia
Beverly
Studewood
Michaux
W. Melwood
Pizer
Cottage
Pecore
Merrill
Watson
Julian
Highland
Woodland
Florence
EXIT 49B
45
HOLLYWOOD CEMETERY
Fulton

5

LAWRENCE PARK
W 6th
EXIT 765B
EXIT 766
Nolda
Eigel
Koehler
Eli
Durham
Bonner
Yale
E 6th
EXIT 767
E 4th
10 90
White Oak Dr.
Usener
STUDE PARK
Katy Frwy.
EXIT 767
WOODLAND PARK
White Oak
Spring
Crockett
Sawyerdale
Summer
White
Sabine
Colorado
Houston Ave.
Holly
N. Main
EXIT 48A/B
Everett
Keene
Freeman
Fletcher
Boundary

6

Roy
Rose
Parker
Shepherd Dr.
Snover
Patterson
Jackson Hill
Feagan
Wichmann
Studemont
BUFFALO BAYOU PARK
Memorial Dr.
Center
Oliver
GLENWOOD CEMETERY
Center
Washington
Hemphill
Sabine
Silver
Memorial Dr.
EXIT 47A
SABINE PARK
Allen Pkwy.
Hicks
Edwards
Dart
Bagby
10 90
EXIT 768B
Prairie
Texas

7

Kirby Dr.
Chilton
W Dallas
W Clay
W Gray
Peden
S Shepherd Dr.
Rosine
Rochow
Peveto
W Bell
W Clay
W Dallas
W Saulnier
Andrews
Ruthven
W Gray
W Webster
Valentine
Arthur
Baldwin
Rusk
Walker
McKinney
Dallas
Polk
Bell
Leeland
Pease
Jefferson
Calhoun
45
North Frwy.

8

an Felipe
Huldy
diana
airview
Harold
Elmen
Woodhead
Driscoll
Mc.Duffie
Dunlavy
Yupon
Commonwealth
Waugh
Mandell
Kipling
Hawthorne
Yoakum
Mulberry
W. Alabama
MAGNOLIA CEMETERY
Bomar
Van Buren
Montrose
Willard
W. Drew
Peden
Hyde Park Blvd.
Crocker
Whitney
Stanford
Garrot
Westheimer
Courtlandt
Hawthorne
527
Genessee
Mason
Taft
Helena
Bagby
Brazos
Smith
Louisiana
Milam
Travis
Main St.
Fannin
Anita
Elgin
Francis
Berry
San Jacinto
Caroline
Austin
La Branch
Crawford
Webster
Hadley
Chenevert
McGowen
EXIT 45B
59

NORTHWEST

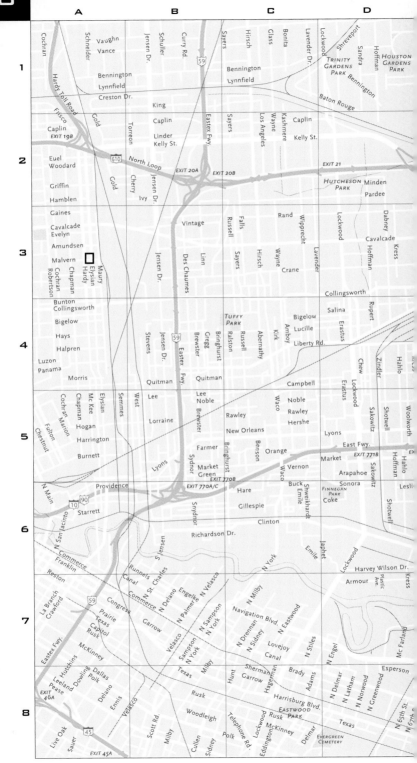

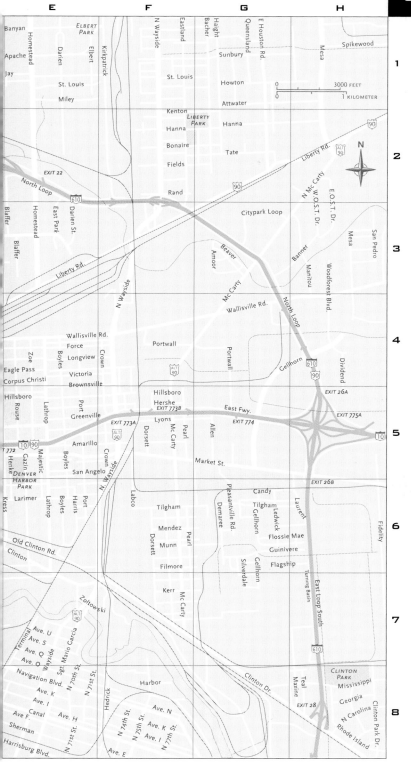

E   **F**   **G**   **H**

Banyan

Homestead

ELBERT PARK

Elbert

Kirkpatrick

N Wayside

Eastland

Haight Bacher

Queensland

E Houston Rd.

Mesa

Spikewood

Apache

Darien

St. Louis

Sunbury

Jay

St. Louis

St. Louis

Howton

Miley

Kenton

LIBERTY PARK

Attwater

0   3000 FEET

0   1 KILOMETER

Hanna

Hanna

Liberty Rd.

90

ALT 90

N

Bonaire

Tate

EXIT 22

Fields

Rand

90

N McCarty

W.O.S.T. Dr.

E.O.S.T. Dr.

North Loop

610

Citypark Loop

Mesa

San Pedro

Blaffer

Homestead

East Park

Darien St.

Beaver

Amoor

Banner

Manitou

Woodforest Blvd.

Blaffer

Liberty Rd.

N Wayside

McCarty

Wallisville Rd.

North Loop

Wallisville Rd.

Force

Longview

Crown

Portwall

Portwall

Gellhorn

610

90

Dividend

Zoe

Boyles

Victoria

Eagle Pass

Corpus Christi

Brownsville

90

EXIT 26A

Hillsboro

Rouse

Lathrop

Port

Greenville

Hillsboro

Hershe

EXIT 773B

East Fwy.

EXIT 775A

EXIT 773A

ALT 90

Lyons

McCarty

Pearl

Allen

EXIT 774

10

T 772

Henke

10 90

Majestic

Gazin

Amarillo

Boyles

Crown Wayside

N

Dorsett

Market St.

DENVER HARBOR PARK

San Angelo

Larimer

Lathrop

Boyles

Harris

Port

Laboc

Candy

Pleasantville Rd.

Demaree

Tilgham

Gellhorn

Ledwick

Laurent

EXIT 26B

Fidelity

Kress

Old Clinton Rd.

Clinton

Dorsett

Tilgham

Mendez

Munn

Pearl

Flossie Mae

Gellhorn

Guinivere

Silverdale

Flagship

Filmore

Kerr

McCarty

East Loop South

Turning Basin

610

Zoltowski

ALT 90

Ave. U

Terminal

Ave. S

Sgt. Mario Garcia

N 70th St.

N 71st St.

Clinton Dr.

CLINTON PARK

Mississippi

Ave. Q

Ave. O

Wayside

Navigation Blvd.

Ave. K

Ave. I

Hedrick

Harbor

Ave. N

Teal

Maxine

EXIT 28

Georgia

N Carolina

Rhode Island

Clinton Park Dr.

Canal

Ave. F.

Ave. H

N 74th St.

N 75th St.

N 31st St.

Ave. K St.

Sherman

Ave. I

N 77th St.

Harrisburg Blvd.

Ave. E

EAST END

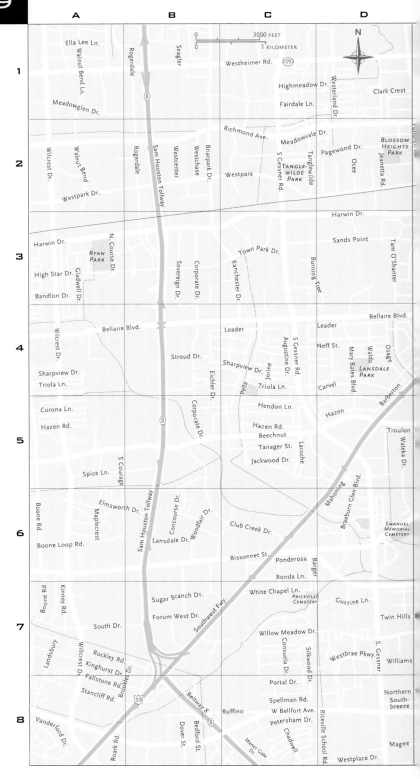

STREETFINDER

E   **F**   **G**   **H**

1

Westheimer Rd. 109

W Alabama Ave.

Crossview Dr.
Dunvale Rd.
Highmeadow Dr.
Stoneybrook
Hillcroft Ave.
Unity Dr.
Fresh Meadows Dr.
BRIAR-MEADOW PARK
Greenridge
Fountainview
Winsome
Fairdale
Chimney Rock Rd.
McCullough
Richmond Ave.
Beverly Hill Ln.
ANDERSON PARK
Schumacher
Beverly Hill Ln.

Fondren Rd.
Daffodil Ave.
Pagewood Ln.
Windswept
Westglen
Skyline Dr.
Windswept Ln.
59
Star Ln.
Pagewood

Lipan

2

Westpark (Alief Rd.)

Harwin Dr.
Glenmont St.

Bellerive
Bonhomme
Savoy Dr.
Rookin
Sands Point
Hornwood
Rookin
Westward
Rampart
Gulfton
Renwick Dr.
Alder Dr.
BURNETT BAYLAND PARK
Royalton

3

Clarewood Dr.
Elm
Moonmist Dr.
Clarewood Dr.
Dashwood

Demoss

Bellaire Blvd.

Lugary
Southwest Fwy.
Mahoning
Cannock
Leader
Mobud Dr.
Roos Rd.
Triola
Mobud Dr.
Braeswick Dr.
Roos Rd.
Sharpview
Althacre Rd.
Bluhill
Sandpiper
Hillcroft Ave.
Ashcroft Dr.
Rampart
Edgemore Dr.
Jessamine
Renwick Dr.
Alder Dr.
Bissonnet
Evergreen
Chimney Rock Rd.
Aspen
Ferris

4

59
Fondren Rd.

Langdon Ln.
Pine St.

BELLAIRE

Brae Acres Rd.
SHARPSTOWN PARK
Braeburn
Bonhomme Rd.
Bissonnet
Cypress
Beechnut
Bob White
Mc Avoy
Grape Dr.
Braewick
Dunlap Dr.
Indigo St.
pontiac
Mullins Dr.
Hazen
Holly St.
Edith St.
Carew
Indigo St.
Jackwood St.
Atwell Dr.
Braesmont
Mimosa
Ferris

5

Bayou
Lugary Dr.
Wanda Ln.
Birdwood
Reamer
Kuldell Dr.
Braesvalley Dr.
N Braeswood Blvd.
S Braeswood Blvd.
Braesheather

6

Braeswood Blvd.
Larkwood Dr.
Bayou Bridge
Bob White Dr.
Rutherglenn Dr.
Dumfries Dr.
Ashcroft Dr.
Mullins Dr.
Valkeith Dr.
Yarwell Dr.
Wigton

Dr.
Valley Hills
Braesridge
Sandpiper
Wigton Dr.
Lymbar Dr.
Willowbend Blvd.
Lymbar Dr.
WESTBURY PARK
Stillbrooke Dr.
Atwell
Oasis
Chimney Rock
Cedarhurst
Endicott Ln

7

Creekbend Dr.
Fondren Rd.
Bob White Dr.
Albury Dr.
Braewick
Dunlap
Ashcroft
Bankside Dr.

Portal Dr.

Dr.
Braes Forest Dr.
Kitty Brook Dr.
Braesridge
Quail Meadow Dr.
Pembridge Dr.
W Bellfort Ave.
Sandpiper Dr.
Fairmont
Hillcroft Ave.
McKnight
Beaudry Dr.
Landsdowne Dr.
Burlinghall Dr.
Spellman
Burdine
Gaymoor
S Willow Dr.
Gasmer

8

Ludington Dr.
Cartagena
Ludington Dr.

SOUTHWEST HOUSTON AND BELLAIRE

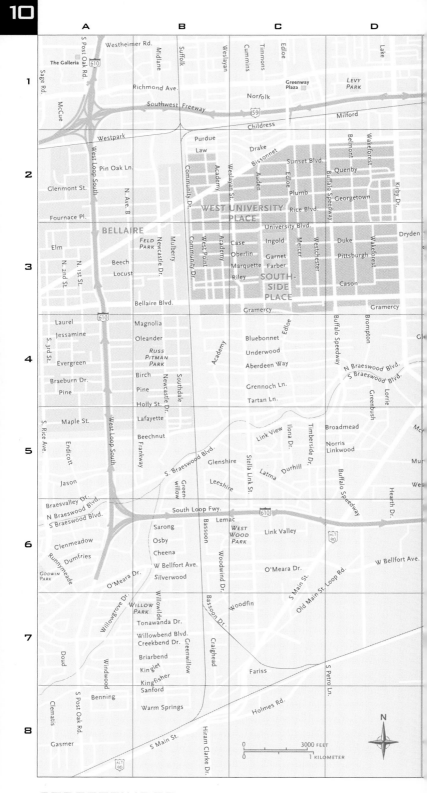

E F G H

1

Greenbriar
S Sheperd Dr.
Colquitt
Richmond Ave.
Branard
Graustark
Yoakum
Colquitt
521
Cleburne
59
Elgin
Hutchins
Holman
Southwest Freeway
59
Dunlavy
Mandell
Millford
Montrose
Yoakum
Wheeler
Dowling
Live Oak
Eagle
Delano
Banks
North Blvd.
South Blvd.
Bissonnet
Fannin
San Jacinto
Austin
Crawford
Blodgett
Southmore
Prospect
Ruth

2

Albans
Sunset Blvd.
Dunstan
Rice Blvd.
Kent
(Pvt.)
Stockton
Main St.
Fannin
Sunset Blvd.
Binz
Almeda Rd.
South Freeway
Rosedale
Southmore
Live Oak
Sampson
Sauer
Ennis
Texas
Southern
University
Greenbriar
Wilton
HERMANN
PARK
Hermann Loop
288
University
of Texas
Health Center
Rice University
Zoo Circle Dr.

3

Morningside
University Blvd.
Swift
Montclair
Southgate
Mc Clendon
Holcombe Blvd.
Zoo
N. MacGregor Way
Texas
Medical
Center
Bates
Holcombe Blvd.
Grand Blvd.
N. MacGregor Way
BRAYS BAYOU
HIKE & BIKE TRAIL
S. MacGregor Way
N. Parkwood
Ardmore
Charleston
Tampa
Bowling
Dixie Dr.

4

Kelving
Glenhaven
S Braeswood Blvd
Cecil
Staffordshire
Cambridge
Shields Ave.
Veterans
Administration
Hospital
Old Spanish Trail
ALT
90
Peerless
Luca
Lozier
Tiewester
Yellowstone
Ward
Idaho
S Main St.
Old Spanish Trail
Greenbriar
Fannin
521
Grand Blvd.
Alice
Corder
Ardmore
South Fwy.
288
University
of Texas
Health Science
Center
Hepburn

5

Nee
Kirby Dr.
N. Stadium Dr.
Astrodome
estridge
Fannin
Knight Rd.
El Paseo
Holly Hall St.
Naomi
Almeda Rd
EXIT 38C
EXIT 38A
South Loop Fwy.
Springhill
Tiewester
Corder
Amos
Seabrook St Rd.
Holly Hall St.
Scott St.
Rebecca St.
610

6

Interchange Dr.
Kirby Dr.
610
EXIT 1B
EXIT 1B
Astroworld
Knight Rd.
Fannin
Magnet
Bassett
Canyon St.
Holmes Rd.
Redbud
Stassen
Woodward
Corinth
Shelby
Bellfort Rd.
SUNNYSIDE
PARK
Brandon
Gladstone
Mc Kinley
Danube
Davenport
Cross Point Ave.

7

Holmes Rd.
521
288
South Freeway
Reed Rd.
Alvin
Corral
Scott Rd.
Ferdinand

8

Almeda Rd.
Buffum
Rosenhaven
Sunbeam
Chimira
Ashville Dr.
Chesterfield Dr.
Asheville Dr.
Wilmington Ave.
Barberry Dr.

SOUTHEAST /SOUTHWEST

A B C D

1

EXIT 45A

McIlhenny
Delano McGowan
Sauer Sampson
Rosalie Canfield Napolean

Scott Rd.
Milby
Callie
Tuam
Anita

Ernestine
S Lockwood
Dumble

Baird
Fourcade

Bell

Collier

Polk

Villa de Matel

Jefferson

EXIT 44A

Holman
Nettelton
Elgin
Simmons
Reeves
Winbern
Alabama
Holman
Alabama

Gulf Fwy.
Munger
Broadmoor
Elliott
Telephone Rd.

Des Jardines
Dismuke
Sunnyland

45

2

Cleburne
Texas
Southern
University
Tierwester
Sampson

Cullen Blvd.
Rockwood

University
of Houston

M. L. King Jr. Blvd.

Jean
Munger
Knoblock
Lidstone

Eskridge

S Jensen

Sylvan

Blodgett
Wentworth
Arbor
Wichita

Wheeler
Calhoun

FONDE
PARK

EXIT 42

Southmore

N MacGregor Way

MACGREGOR
PARK

ALT
90

Telephone Rd.

BRAYS BAYOU
HIKE & BIKE TRAIL

S MacGregor Way

M. L. King Jr. Blvd.

Produce Row
Brock Ave.

Wheeler

3

Parkwood
Roseneath
Fernwood
Griggs
Charleston

Old Spanish Trail

Arvilla
Marietta

Nassau

Beekman

Brock Ave.
Erby

Penwood

S Wayside

Real
Askew

ALT
90

Eppes

La Salette
Zephyr
Scott
Dixie
Porter
Sherwood
St. Augustine
Perry
England
Goforth
Foster
Hull
Cullen Blvd.

865

Calhoun

Balkin

Grace Ln.

Perry
Enyart

M. L. King Blvd.

Griggs Rd.
Browncroft
Keystone

South Loop Fwy.

BROOKLINE
PARK

610

Belk

4

Yellowstone
Ward

Idaho
Alice
Faulkner
Goforth
Eastwood
New York

Dumble
Weston

Milart

Southcrest

Cherryhill Ave.
Cloveridge Ave.
Iron Rock Ave.
Cavalier Ave.
Midvale Ave.

Cedarcrest

Rupley Cir.
Maudlin

S Wayside
Northdale

Heiser
Luce
Ledbetter
Joyner

5

St. Augustine
England

Holmes Rd.

South Loop Fwy.

610

Malmedy
Rapido
Burma Rd.
Doolittle

Southridge

Crestridge

Southmont Ave.
Southlea Ave.

Southbank

Crestmont
Silsbee

Kirbyville St.

Mykawa Rd.

EXIT 36A

865

Pershing

Southtown

6

Theresa
Mayflower St.
McLean
Redbud Mc St.
Briscoe
Sunflower
Stassen

Bellfort Rd.

Van Fleet

Lingonberry
Rd.
Teton

Calhoun Rd.
Coffee

Darnay
Jutland Dr.

Doulton Dr.
Willowglen

Herschelwood

St. Lo Road

Doolittle
Pershing
Van Fleet

Doulton Dr.
Kenilwood Dr.
Ridgeway Dr.

Crestmont
Belgard
Belbay

S Wayside

Northdale

Roxbury

7

Ferdinand St.
Edgar
Duane
Brinkley Ave.
Larkspur St.
Mallow St.

Delilah
Cullen Blvd.
Coffee

Bellfort Rd.

Jutland Dr.

Westover Ave.
Larkspur St.
Clover St.

Reed Rd.

Noel

M. L. King Blvd.

Flamingo Dr.

Belcrest Ave.
Westover Ave.

Southbank

Reed Rd.

Schevers

Southcrest

Vasser

City
Prison
Farm

Westover

Crosswell
Mykawa Rd.

Carmen

Wilmington Ave.

8

865

Higgins
Pederson

Sunbeam
Rickey
Groveton

St. Lo
Tenehia

Groveton
Lakefield Dr.

SIMS BAYOU
PARK

Airport Blvd.

Clearway
Dr.

LAW PARK
Scarlet

Linnet Ln.

Chickedee
Gallinule Ln.

Blue Heron
Ln.

STREETFINDER

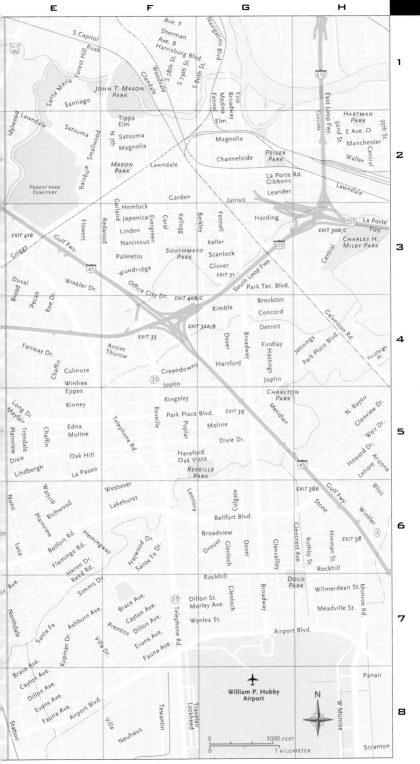

E   **F**   **G**   **H**

1

S Capitol
Rusk
Ave. F
Sherman
Ave. B
Harrisburg Blvd.
Forest Hill
Santa Maria
Santiago
JOHN T. MASON PARK
Glendale
Woodvale
Navigation Blvd.
S 80th St.
S 74th St.
S 82nd St.
Frio
Broadway
Medina
Fennel
East Loop Fwy.
92nd St.
95th St.
Central
610
HARTMAN PARK
E Ave. O
Manchester

2

Lawndale
Satsuma
Rainbow
Rosewood
N 7th
Tipps
Elm
Satsuma
Magnolia
Elm
Magnolia
Channelside
PEISER PARK
La Porte Rd.
Gibbons
Leander
Waller
Lawndale
Concrete
MASON PARK
Lawndale

FOREST PARK CEMETERY

Garden
Junius

3

EXIT 41B
Griggs
Gulf Fwy.
Flowers
Redwood
Garland
Hemlock
Japonica
Linden
Narcissus
Palmetto
Woodridge
Evergreen
Coral
Kellogg
SOUTHMAYD PARK
Berkley
Fennell
Keller
Scanlock
Glover
EXIT 31
Harding
610
EXIT 30B/C
255
La Porte Fwy.
CHARLES H. MILBY PARK
Central

4

Duval
Broad
Pecan
Roe Dr.
Winkler Dr.
Fairway Dr.
Chaffin
Culmore
Winfree
Eppes
45
Office City Dr.
EXIT 40B/C
Woodridge
Arnim
Thurow
EXIT 33
EXIT 32A/B
Greendowns
Joplin
Kimble
Dover
Broadway
Hartford
Hastings
Findlay
Brockton
Concord
Detroit
Joplin
South Loop Fwy.
Park Ter. Blvd.
Jennings
Park Place Blvd.
Galveston Rd.
Rockleigh Pl.

5

Long Dr.
Mayfair
Trendale
Plainview
Dixie
Lindbergh
Kinney
Chaffin
Edna
Moline
Oak Hill
La Paseo
Telephone Rd.
Reveille
Kingsley
Park Place Blvd.
Poplar
Moline
Dixie Dr.
Hereford
Oak Vista
REVEILLE PARK
EXIT 39
CHARLTON PARK
Meridian
45
N. Bayou
Glenview Dr.
Weir Dr.
Howard Dr.
Lenore
Arizona

6

Nunn
Luce
Waltrip
Richwood
Plainview
Bellfort Rd.
Flamingo Rd.
Heron Dr.
Reed Rd.
Westover
Lakehurst
Haywood Dr.
Santa Fe Dr.
Hemingway
Leonora
College
Bellfort Blvd.
Broadview
Drouet
Glenloch
Dover
Glenvalley
Glencrest Ave.
Stone
EXIT 36B
Gulf Fwy.
Ruthby St.
Hinman St.
EXIT 38
Rockhill
Bliss
Winkler
3

7

Ave.
Northdale
Simms Dr.
Santa Fe
Kopman Dr.
Ashburn Ave.
Brace Ave.
Cayton Ave.
Prentiss
Dillon Ave.
Evans Ave.
Fauna Ave.
Villa Dr.
35
Telephone Rd.
Rockhill
Dillon St.
Morley Ave.
Wynlea St.
Glenloch
Broadway
DOLO PARK
Airport Blvd.
Wilmerdean St.
Meadville St.
Monroe Rd.

8

Brace Ave.
Cayton Ave.
Dillon Ave.
Evans Ave.
Fauna Ave.
Airport Blvd.
Station
Villa
Tewantin
Neuhaus
WILLIAM P. HOBBY AIRPORT
Travelair
Lockheed
N
Panair
W Monroe
Scranton

0   3000 FEET
0   1 KILOMETER

UH, SOUTH HOUSTON, HOBBY AIRPORT

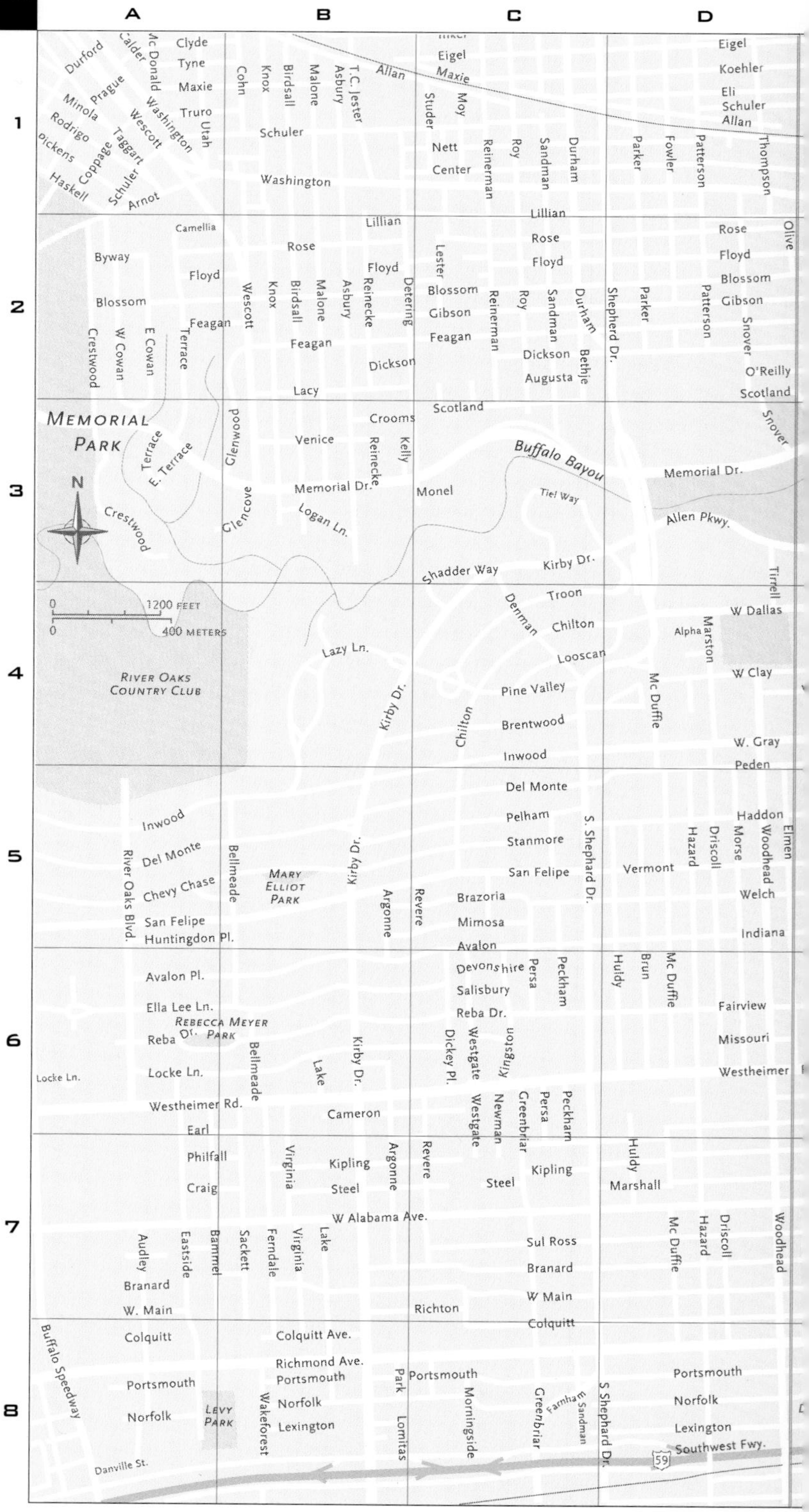
A
B
C
D
1
2
3
4
5
6
7
8
Durford
Calder
Mc Donald
Clyde
Tyne
Maxie
Truro
Utah
Washington
Wescott
Prague
Minola
Rodrigo
Pickens
Haskell
Coppage
Taggart
Schuler
Arnot
Cohn
Knox
Birdsall
Malone
Asbury
T.C. Jester
Allan
Maxie
Eigel
Moy
Studer
Nett
Center
Schuler
Washington
Reinerman
Roy
Sandman
Durham
Parker
Fowler
Patterson
Thompson
Eigel
Koehler
Eli
Schuler
Allan
Camellia
Byway
Blossom
Floyd
Feagan
Crestwood
W Cowan
E Cowan
Terrace
Wescott
Knox
Birdsall
Malone
Asbury
Reinecke
Rose
Feagan
Lacy
Lillian
Floyd
Dickson
Detering
Lester
Blossom
Gibson
Feagan
Reinerman
Roy
Sandman
Durham
Bethje
Lillian
Rose
Floyd
Dickson
Augusta
Shepherd Dr.
Parker
Patterson
Snover
Rose
Floyd
Blossom
Gibson
O'Reilly
Scotland
Olive
Memorial
Park
Terrace
E. Terrace
Glenwood
Glencove
Crestwood
N
Venice
Crooms
Reinecke
Kelly
Memorial Dr.
Logan Ln.
Scotland
Monel
Buffalo Bayou
Tiel Way
Memorial Dr.
Allen Pkwy.
Snover
0
1200 FEET
0
400 METERS
River Oaks
Country Club
Shadder Way
Kirby Dr.
Troon
Denman
Chilton
Looscan
Lazy Ln.
Kirby Dr.
Chilton
Pine Valley
Brentwood
Inwood
Mc Duffie
Alpha
Marston
Tirrell
W Dallas
W Clay
W. Gray
Peden
Inwood
Del Monte
Chevy Chase
San Felipe
Huntingdon Pl.
River Oaks Blvd.
Bellmeade
Mary
Elliot
Park
Kirby Dr.
Argonne
Revere
Del Monte
Pelham
Stanmore
San Felipe
Brazoria
Mimosa
Avalon
S. Shephard Dr.
Vermont
Hazard
Driscoll
Morse
Woodhead
Elmen
Haddon
Welch
Indiana
Avalon Pl.
Ella Lee Ln.
Rebecca Meyer
Dr.
Park
Reba
Locke Ln.
Locke Ln.
Westheimer Rd.
Bellmeade
Lake
Kirby Dr.
Devonshire
Salisbury
Reba Dr.
Persa
Peckham
Huldy
Brun
Mc Duffie
Dickey Pl.
Westgate
Kingston
Fairview
Missouri
Westheimer
Cameron
Westgate
Newman
Greenbriar
Persa
Peckham
Earl
Philfall
Craig
Virginia
Kipling
Steel
Argonne
Revere
Steel
Kipling
Huldy
Marshall
W Alabama Ave.
Audley
Eastside
Bammel
Sackett
Ferndale
Virginia
Lake
Sul Ross
Branard
W Main
Mc Duffie
Hazard
Driscoll
Woodhead
Branard
W. Main
Richton
Colquitt
Buffalo Speedway
Colquitt
Colquitt Ave.
Richmond Ave.
Portsmouth
Portsmouth
Norfolk
Levy
Park
Wakeforest
Norfolk
Lexington
Park
Lomitas
Portsmouth
Morningside
Greenbriar
Farnham
Sandman
S Shephard Dr.
Portsmouth
Norfolk
Lexington
Southwest Fwy.
59
Danville St.

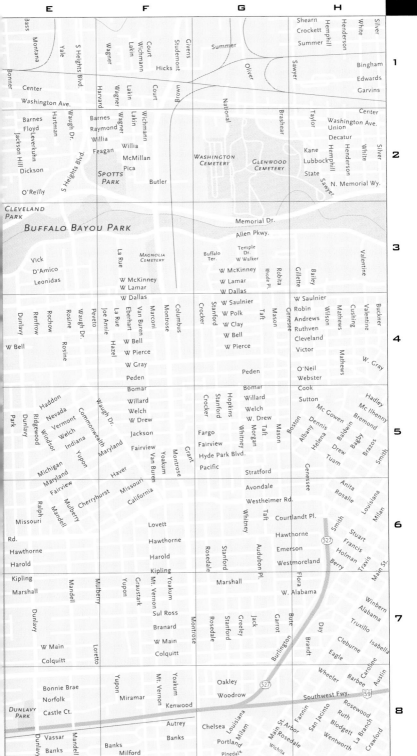

RIVER OAKS, UPPER KIRBY DISTRICT, MONTROSE

A B C D

1

2

3

4

5

6

7

8

Crockett
Summer
Winter
Sabine
Colorado
Trinity
Bingham
Hickory
Edwards
Dart
Holly
Beachton
Elder
EXIT 768B
Glaser
Myrtle
Harrington
Keene
Main St.
Brooks
Burnett
Naylor
Elysian
Hardy
Mc Kee
Atlas
Conti
Providence
Baytown East Fwy.
Rothwell
William
N Nance
Sterrett

Center
Washinton
Ash
Dewey
Trinity
Colorado
Sabine
Lubbock
State
W. Capitol
Memorial Dr.
Houston Ave.
Riesner
Girard
Franklin
Artesian
Meek
Bagby
Girard
EXIT 768A
Girard
10
90
Sheawood
ALLENS
LANDING
PARK
N. San Jacinto
Allen
Baker
Top
Mc Kee
Mc Gowen
N
Race
Rains
Washington Ave.
SESQUICENTENNIAL
PARK
Commerce
Franklin

EXIT 47A
SABINE
PARK
Allen Pkwy.
Sabine
SAM
HOUSTON
PARK
Clay
Dallas
Brazos
Bagby
Brazos
TRANQUILITY
PARK
HERMANN
SQUARE PARK
Smith
Louisiana
Milam
Travis
Prairie
Texas
Capitol
Rusk
Walker
Congress
Preston
Caroline
Austin
Ruiz
Jackson
Chenevert
Hamilton

W Saulnier
Arthur
Robin
Andrews
Ruthven
Cleveland
Baldwin
Bagby
Brazos
45
Howe Fuller
Andrews
Ruthven
Main St.
Fannin
Polk
Clay
Bell
Leeland
Pease
San Jacinto
McKinney
Lamar
Dallas
La Branch
Crawford
Jackson
HOUSTON
CENTER
GARDENS
Chenevert
Hamilton
Southwest Freeway
59
Chartres
Emanuel
Hutchins
Rusk
Walker
McKinney
Lamar
Dallas
Polk
Dowling
St. Charles
Live Oak
Nagle
Preston
Prairie
Texas
Capitol

Jefferson
Calhoun
Pierce
Smith
Louisiana
Milam
Travis
Gray
Webster
Hadley
North Fwy.
45
EXIT 46B
Bell
Leeland

Main St.
Fannin
San Jacinto
Dennis
Drew
Tuam
Anita
Rosalie
Elgin
Stuart
Mc Ilhenny
Caroline
Austin
McGowen
La Branch
Crawford
Jackson
Chenevert
Hamilton
59
Chartres
Emanuel
Hutchins
Bastrop
Mc Ilhenny
Hadley
Pease
EXIT 46A Jefferson
Calhoun
Pierce
Gray
Webster
Gulf Fwy.

Stuart
Francis
Holman
Austin
La Branch
Crawford
Alabama
Truxillo
Isabella
59
Almeda Rd.
Chenevert
Cleburne
Chartres
Wheeler
Rosewood
Mosely
Chenevert
Southwest Fwy.
EMANCIPATION
PARK
Chartres
Emanuel
Hutchins
Bastrop
Holman
Dowling
Berry
Winbern
St. Charles
Alabama
Truxillo
Isabella
Cleburne
Tuam
Anita
Rosalie
Elgin
Live Oak
Francis
Nagel
Delano
Ennis
McGowen
Dennis
Anita
Rosalie
Sauer
Velasco
Live Oak
Nagel
Delano
Gray
45
Webster
Trulley
Hadley
Mc Ilhenny
Sauer
Brailsfort
Briley
Burkett
Brailsfort
Tierwester
Roberts
Bremond
McGowen
Dennis
Drew
Tuam
Nettleton
Anita
Rosalie
Beulah
Sampson
Francis
Simmons

STREETFINDER

E F G H

Opelousas
Leona
Lyons Ave.
West
McCall
Conti
Lyons Ave.
Schwartz
Stonewall
Snydor
Bayou
Meadow
Crove
Market
Green
Moses
Providence
Worms
Benson
Vernon
Sondick
Providence
Providence
Maury
Mary
West
Providence
59
Buck
Providence
Buck
Buck
EXIT 770A/C
Crete
Buck
Hare
McLeary
Acres
10
90
EXIT 771A
Waco
Buck
Hare
Gunter
Coke
Waco
Nimrod
Emile

1

EXIT 769C
10
90
Maury
Semmes
Mary
McCall
59
EXIT 770B
Baer
Gillespie
Syndor
Bayou
Crove
Gregg
Cage
Bringhurst
Press
Cline
Emile

Southwest Freeway
McCall
Clark
Grayson
Cline
Cline
Baron
Melva
Clinton Dr.
Richardson Dr.
Cage
Hirsch
Ida
Emile

2

West
Felix
East
Roanoke
Bryan
Shiloh
Foote

0   1200 FEET
0   400 METERS

Lottman
Ann
S Jensen
McAlpine
N St. Charles
Naple
Kennedy
N Nagle
Middle
Engelke
Runnels
Franklin
Canal
McAlpine
Commerce
N Live Oak
N Paige
N. Velasco
Lemke
Foley
Ball
Freund
N

3

Congress
St. Charles
Nagle
Delano
Paige
Middleton
Garrow
Roberts
Preston
Hawkins
N Delano
N Ennis
N Palmer
Engelke
Runnels
Saltus
Canal
McAshan
Commerce
N York
N Hutcheson
N Everton
N Milby
Lovejoy
Bering
N Dreman
N Estelle
N Sidney
N Jenkins
Burch
Rotman
Fox
Navigation Blvd.
Crites
N. Jenkins
N Eastwood
Schroeder
Hagerman
Canal
Blanche
Ct.
Lockwood
Suburban

4

Delano
Paige
Ennis
Palmer
Velasco
Roberts
S. Sampson
S York
Preston
Harrisburg Blvd.
Texas
Capitol
S Sampson
S York
Hutcheson
Everton
Milby
Ross
Kendall
Dreman
Crace
Garrow
Wilmer
Hunt
Estelle
Sidney
Jenkins
N. Eastwood
Super
Hagerman
N. Eastwood
Canal
Brady
Sherman

5

Palmer
Velasco
Roberts
S. Sampson
S. York
Clay
Denver
Polk
Denver
Bell
Leeland
Miller
Milby
Hussion
Keating
Milby
Rusk
Walker
McKinney
St. Joseph
Lamar
Woodleigh
Dallas
Oakhurst
Sidney
N. Eastwood
Polk
Fashion
Harrisburg Blvd.
Lockwood
Rusk
Walker
McKinney
Park
Forest
Burr
Stiles
Bryan
EASTWOOD
PARK
Tonwood

6

Roberts
Sampson
Pease
Jefferson
Coyle
Tharp
Scott Rd.
Edmundson
Miller
Miller
Pease
Jefferson
Coyle
Cullen Blvd.
Ingeborg
Sidney
Clay
Bell
Leeland
Pease
Jefferson
Coyle
Harby
Fashion Rd.
Ernestine
Woodside
Eddington
Bell
Curtin
Park
Oakland
Dumble
Gustay
Bell
Leeland
Stimson
Martin
Hauser

7

Webster
Hadley
EXIT 45A
Tharp
Winchester
McIlhenny
Bremond
McGowen
Athens
Gulf Freeway
45
Pease
Jefferson
Dumble
Monroe
Lawson
Pearson
Elliott
Fourcade
Elliott
Wesley
Mable
Baird
Mulford
Telephone Rd.
Elliston

8

Canfield
Napoleon
Scott Rd.
Lucinda
Milby
Callie
Tuam
Anita
Rosalie
Leek
Cullen Blvd.
Dennis
Drew
University
of Houston
Maplewood
EXIT 44A
Hicksfield
Scharpe
Munger
Diez
Lawson
Godwin
Lombardy

	A	B	C	D

1
Milford, Purdue, South Blvd., Westchester, Buffalo Speedway, Belmont, Wroxton — Milford, North, Wakeforest, Dincans, Kirby Dr. — North Blvd., Bartlett, South Blvd., Bissonnet, Wroxton, Albans, Greenbriar, Shepherd St. — Milford, North Blvd., South Blvd., Wilton, Hazard, Wilton, Wroxton, Albans

2
Albans, Sunset Blvd., Nottingham, Robinhood, Rutgers, Plumb, Tangley, Belmont, Lafayette — Sunset Blvd., Nottingham, Quenby, Robinhood, Plumb — Sunset Blvd., Nottingham, Quenby, Robinhood, Tangley, Dunstan, Bolsover, Kevin, Morningside, Whitely — Sunset Bl., Tangley, Dunstan, Bolsover, Rice Blvd., Wilton

3
Georgetown, Rice Blvd., Jarrard — Georgetown, Rice Blvd., Milton, Jarrard, University Blvd., Wake Forest, Charlotte, Annapolis, Fordham, Lake — WEST UNIVERSITY PLACE — Fenwood, Pemberton, Barbara — Rice Blvd., Times Blvd., Amherst, University Blvd., Shakespeare, Dryden Rd., Swift, School — Dryden Rd.

4
Sewanee, Westchester, Rutgers, Buffalo Speedway, Vanderbilt, Carnegie, Belmont, Duke — Brompton, Wakeforest, Kirby Dr. — Carolina, Pittsburgh, Centenary, Arbuckle, Talbott, W. Cason, Werlein, Annapolis — Addison, Watts, Goldsmith, Southgate, Wordsworth, Mc Clendon, Mac Arthur, Kevin, Greenbriar, Montclair, Bellgreen — Swift, Addison, Stockton, Mc Clendon, Mac Arthur, Sheridan

5
Bradford, Gramercy, Bellefontaine, Maroneal, E. Glenhaven Blvd. — Bellaire Blvd., Brompton, Gramercy, Bellefontaine, S. Bluebonnet — Holcombe Blvd., Dorrington, Bellefontaine, Maroneal, E. Glenhaven Blvd., Morningside, Kevin, S. Bluebonnet — Dorrington, Kelving, Greenbriar, S. Main St., Shamrock Dr., Braeswood

6
Sewanee, Bluebonnet, Underwood, Dumbarton, Aberdeen Wy., Merrick, Drummond, Grennoch Ln., Oakwood, Buffalo Speedway — N. Braeswood Blvd., S. Braeswood Blvd., Tilden — Underwood — Brays Bayou

7
Durness Wy., Tartan Ln., Glen Arbor Dr. — Winslow, Conway, Stanton, Prescott, Ashwood, Chiswell, Lorrie Dr., Fairhope — Braesmain — S. Old Spanish Trail, Kirby Dr., La Concha Ln.

8
Bevlyn, Timberside, Buffalo Spdwy, Baughn, Durhill, Elmridge — Castlewood, Broadmead, Deal Dr., Gannett Dr., Norris Dr., Linkwood Rd., Murworth Dr., Greenbush, Hatton, Bluegate, Lorrie Dr., S. Main St., ALT 90 — Lantern Point Dr. — N. Stadium Dr., McNee, Murworth Dr., Astrodome

STREETFINDER

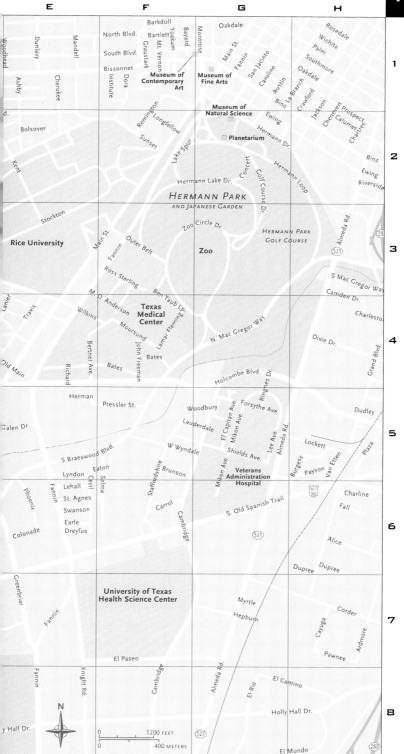

E

Woodhead
Dunlavy
Mandell

North Blvd.
Barkdull
Bartlett
Yoakum
Bayard
Montrose
Oakdale
Rosedale
Wichita

South Blvd.
Mt. Vernon
Graustark
Palm
Southmore

Ashby
Cherokee
Bissonnet
Dora
Institute
Museum of Contemporary Art
Museum of Fine Arts
Main St.
Fannin
San Jacinto
Caroline
Austin
La Branch
Oakdale
Crawford
Jackson
Chenevert
Prospect

d.
Bolsover
Remington
Longfellow
Sunset
Museum of Natural Science
Ewing
Hermann Dr.
Calumet
Chartres
1

Kent
Lake Spur
Planetarium
Binz
Ewing
Riverside
2

Concert
Golf Course Dr.
Hermann Loop
Binz

Hermann Lake Dr.
HERMANN PARK
AND JAPANESE GARDEN

Stockton
Zoo Circle Dr.
HERMANN PARK GOLF COURSE
Almeda Rd.
28
3

Rice University
Main St.
Fannin
Outer Belt
Zoo
521

Ross Sterling
S Mac Gregor Way

Lanier
Travis
M. D. Anderson
Ben Taub Lp.
Camden Dr.
Charlesto.

Wilkins
Texas Medical Center
Moursund
Lamar Fleming
N. Mac Gregor Way
Dixie Dr.
Grand Blvd.
4

Old Main
Richard
Bertner Ave.
John Freeman
Bates
Bates

Herman
Pressler St.
Holcombe Blvd.
Ringnes Dr.

Galen Dr.
Woodbury
Lauderdale
El Capitan Ave.
Milkon Ave.
Forsythe Ave.
Lee Ave.
Almeda Rd.
Dudley
Lockett
Plaza
5

S Braeswood Blvd.
W Wyndale
Shields Ave.

Lyndon
Eaton
Cecil
Selma
Staffordshire
Brunson
Milkon Ave.
Burgess
Payson
Van Etten

Phoenix
Fannin
Lehall
St. Agnes
Swanson
Veterans Administration Hospital
Charline
Fall
6

Colonade
Earle
Dreyfus
Carrol
Cambridge
S. Old Spanish Trail
521
Alice
Dupree

Greenbriar
University of Texas Health Science Center
Dupree

Fannin
Myrtle
Hepburn
Corder
Cayuga
Ardmore
7

El Paseo
Pawnee

Fannin
Knight Rd.
Cambridge
Almeda Rd.
El Rio
El Camino

N
0 1200 FEET
0 400 METERS
521
Holly Hall Dr.
8

y Hall Dr.
El Mundo
288

A **B** **C** **D**

1

Almeda Rd.
South Fwy.
Hutchins
Blodgett
Wentworth
Arbor
Rosedale

Dowling
Cleburne
Eagle
Live Oak
Barbee
Wheeler
Rosewood
Ruth
Ennis

Truxillo
Isabella
Velasco
Sauer
Briley
Berry
Winbern
Alabama
Truxillo
Cuney
Cleburne

Nettleton
Nalle
Holman
Sampson
Simmons
Reeves
Sanders
Alabama
Canfield
Napoleon
Nettleton
Tierwester
Cobb
Sampson

2

Palm
Southmore
Dowling
Oakdale
Prospect
Calumet
Binz
Live Oak
Live Oak

Wentworth
Arbor
Delano
Rosedale
Wichita
Palm
Ennis
Palmer

Wheeler
**Texas
Southern
University**
Blodgett
Wentworth
Arbor
Rosedale
Sauer

Attucks
Canfield
Eagle
Rosewood
Ruth
Susan Ann
Canfield
Ru

Tierwester

3

N. Calumet
S. Calumet
Riverside Dr.
Brays Bayou

RIVERSIDE
PARK
Oakdale
Sampson
Prospect
Calumet
Binz
Ewing
N. Mac Gregor Way
Burkett

Wichita
Palm
Southmore
Burkett

Grantwood
Scott Rd.
Went
Arbor
Roseda
Wichita
Palm
Gertin

4

South Fwy
Ardmore
Milburn
Shenandoah
Bowling Green
Charleston
Ozark
Sedalia
Tampa
Dixie Dr.
(288)

Oakmont
S. Mac Gregor Way
N. Parkwood
Del Rio
Ozark
Charleston
Tampa

Brays Bayou Hike and Bike Trail
N. Parkwood
S. Parkwood
Rio Vista
Swank
N. Parkwood
Griggs Rd.
Odin Ct.

Scott Rd.
Julius
Kuhiman
Charleston

5

Holcombe Blvd.
Ardmore
Sedalia
Bowling Green
Kelton
Kilgore
Natchez
Raleigh
(ALT 90)

Dixie Dr.
Allegheny
Peerless
Del Rio
Burkett
Lozier
Illinois
Culberson
Zephyr

Tierwester
Meriburn
Old Spanish Trail

Scottcrest
Tolnay
Tristan
Dupe
Dixie
Porter

6

Alice
(288)

Daphne
Luca
Stearns
Cadillac
Winton
Tierwester
Ward

Alsace
Cosby
Luca
Florinda
Daphne
Alberta

Zephyr
Sherwood Dr.
St. Augustine
Conley
England
Sidney
Balkin
Hull
Short
Perry
Goforth
Fros

7

South Fwy.
Peerless

Wyoming
Idaho
Alice
Southlawn
Tierwester
Faulkner
Lehall
Amos
Dreyfus
Amos
Corder

La Salette
Scott Rd.
Driftwood
Beachwood
Sherwood Dr.
Idaho
Alice
Southlawn
Faulkner

St. Augustine
Yellowstone
Conley
England
Sidney
Goforth
Foster
Eastwood
Cullen Bl

8

N
Springhill

Tierwester
Nathaniel Brown
Mt. Pleasant
Seabrook
Noah
Mainer
Lydia
Goodhope
La Salette

Corder
Mt. Pleasant

| 0 | | 1200 FEET |
| 0 | | 400 METERS |

Dreyfus
London
(865)
Holmes Rd.

STREETFINDER

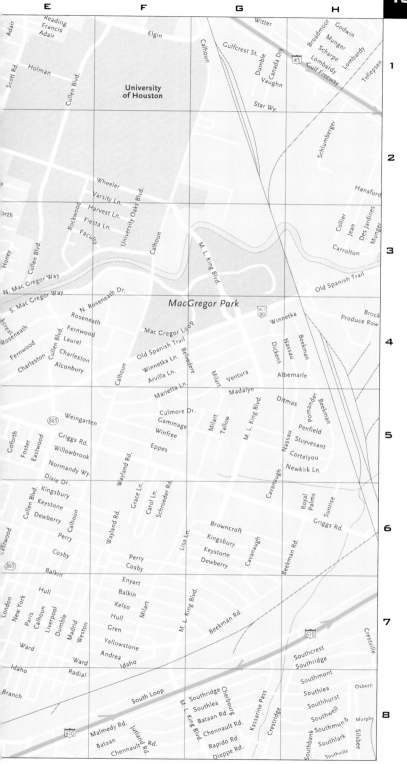

UNIVERSITY OF HOUSTON AREA

FROM THE EDITORS OF

TexasMonthly ®

MANY MAPS • WHERE & HOW

FIND IT ALL • NIGHT & DAY

ANTIQUES TO ZIPPERS

BARGAINS & BAUBLES

ELEGANT EDIBLES • ETHNIC EATS

STEAK HOUSES • BISTROS

DELIS • TRATTORIAS

CLASSICAL • JAZZ • COMEDY

THEATER • DANCE • CLUBS

COCKTAIL LOUNGES

COUNTRY & WESTERN • ROCK

COOL TOURS

HOUSECLEANING • CATERING

GET A LAWYER • GET A DENTIST

GET A NEW PET • GET A VET

MUSEUMS • GALLERIES

PARKS • GARDENS • POOLS

BASEBALL TO ROCK CLIMBING

FESTIVALS • EVENTS

DAY SPAS • DAY TRIPS

HOTELS • HOT LINES

GET A LAWYER • GET A DENTIST

PASSPORT PIX • TRAVEL INFO

HELICOPTER TOURS

DINERS • DELIS • PIZZERIAS

BRASSERIES • TAQUERÍAS

BOOTS • BOOKS • BUTTONS

BICYCLES • SKATES

SUITS • SHOES • HATS

RENT A TUX • RENT A COSTUME

BAKERIES • SPICE SHOPS

SOUP TO NUTS

Fodor's

CITYGUIDE
HOUSTON

FODOR'S TRAVEL PUBLICATIONS

NEW YORK • TORONTO • LONDON • SYDNEY • AUCKLAND

WWW.FODORS.COM

FODOR'S CITYGUIDE HOUSTON

EDITOR
Christina Knight

EDITORIAL CONTRIBUTORS
Edie Carlson-Abbey, Cathy Casey, David Garcia, Erica Goros, Melissa Howard, Miranda Jones, Julie Martin, Patricia Martin, Jarrett McGehee, Kristen Necessary, Jennifer Olsen, Gina Petrelli, Nita Rainwater, Randal Rauscher, Lauren Rose, Theresa Scroggins Price, Erin Siudzinski, Edith Sorensen

MAPS
David Lindroth Inc., *cartographer*; Bob Blake, *map editor*

DESIGN
Fabrizio La Rocca, *creative director*; Allison Saltzman, *text design*; Tigist Getachew, *cover design*; Jolie Novak, *senior picture editor*; Melanie Marin, *photo editor*

PRODUCTION/MANUFACTURING
Angela L. McLean

COVER PHOTOGRAPH
Jack Hollingsworth Photography (skyline view from Tranquility Park)

COPYRIGHT

First Edition

ISBN 0–679–00622–2

ISSN 1533–0494

SPECIAL SALES

Fodor's Travel Publications are available at special discounts for bulk purchases for sales promotions or premiums. Special editions, including personalized covers, excerpts of existing guides, and corporate imprints, can be created in large quantities for special needs. For more information, contact your local bookseller or write to Special Markets, Fodor's Travel Publications, 280 Park Avenue, New York, NY 10017. Inquiries from Canada should be directed to your local Canadian bookseller or sent to Random House of Canada, Ltd., Marketing Department, 2775 Matheson Boulevard East, Mississauga, Ontario L4W 4P7. Inquiries from the United Kingdom should be sent to Fodor's Travel Publications, 20 Vauxhall Bridge Road, London SW1V 2SA, England.

PRINTED IN THE UNITED STATES OF AMERICA

10 9 8 7 6 5 4 3 2 1

CONTENTS

METROPOLITAN LIFE

On a bad day in a big city, the little things that go with living shoulder-to-shoulder with a few million people wear us all down. But the special pleasures of urban life have a way of keeping us around town—and thankful, even, for every second of stress. The field of daffodils in the park on a fine spring day. The perfect little black dress that you find for half price. The markets—so fabulously well stocked that you can cook any recipe without resorting to mail-order catalogs. The way you can sometimes turn a corner and discover a whole new world, so foreign you can hardly believe you're only a few miles from home. The never-ending wealth of possibilities and opportunities.

If you know where to find it all, the city cannot defeat you. With knowledge comes power. That's why Fodor's has prepared this book, with the editors at Texas Monthly. It will put phone numbers at your fingertips. It'll take you to new places and remind you of those you've forgotten. It's the ultimate urban companion—and, we hope, your new best friend in the city.

It's the Houstonwise shopaholic, who always knows where to find something, no matter how obscure. We've made a concerted effort to bring hundreds of great shops to your attention, so that you'll never be at a loss, whether you need a special birthday present for a great friend or some obscure craft items to make Halloween costumes for your kids.

It's the restaurant know-it-all, who's full of ideas for every occasion—you know, the one who would never send you to the slick chain joint where the tortillas taste like cardboard and the steaks don't taste like anything at all. In this book we'll steer you around the corner, to a cozy little place with five tables, a chalkboard menu, and the family matriarch in the kitchen.

It's a hip barfly buddy, who can give you advice when you need a charming nook, not too noisy, to take a friend after work. Among the dozens of bars and nightspots in this book, you're bound to find something that fits your mood.

It's the sagest culture vulture you know, the one who always has the scoop on what's on that's worthwhile after dark. In these pages, you'll find dozens of jazz clubs, concert venues, and arts organizations.

It's also the city whiz, who knows how to get you where you're going, wherever you are.

It's the best map guide on the shelves, and it puts all the city in your briefcase or on your bookshelf.

Stick with us. We lay out all the options for your leisure time—and gently nudge you away from the duds—so that you can truly enjoy your Houston life.

YOUR GUIDES

No one person can know it all. To help get you on track around the city, a stellar group of local experts are sharing their wisdom.

Texas Monthly magazine plugged Fodor's directly into everything going on around Houston. Winner of eight National Magazine Awards, it has chronicled life in Texas since 1973 and is every Texan's last word on the Texas scene. Music, the arts, travel, restaurants, museums, and cultural events—the *Texas Monthly* staff has all the bases covered.

Edie Carlson-Abbey is a proud "naturalized Texan" and has been a Houston resident since 1976. She has enjoyed the growth and change of Houston's cuisine scene for those many years and has been writing about food since the late 1980s.

Patricia Martin has lived in Houston and been associated with Rice University as a historian and administrator for thirty years. She also directed Rice's book and magazine publishing Program in the early 1980s. She is the author of two children's books, numerous academic publications, and has written extensively about food and travel for various magazines, including *My Table, Houston City Magazine,* and *Ultra.*

A native Houstonian, **Theresa Scroggins Price** relishes the opportunity to show off her hometown. As a freelance writer, she considers restaurant reviews the best gig of all. She hasn't cooked a meal in ages because of the great Houston restaurant scene.

Edith Sorenson is a Houston-based writer who has spent the last few years writing about entertainment, food, film, and pets for print and on-line publications.

HOW TO USE THIS BOOK

The first thing you need to know is that everything in this book is arranged by category and by alphabetical order within category.

Now, before you go any farther, check out the city maps up front. Each map has a number, in a black box at the top of the page, and grid coordinates along the top and side margins. On the text pages, nearly every listing in the book is keyed to one of these maps. Look for the map number in a small black box preceding each establishment name. The grid code follows in italics. For establishments with more than one location, additional map numbers and grid codes appear at the end of the listing. To locate a museum that's identified in the text as **7** *e-6*, turn to Map 7 and locate the address within the e-6 grid square. To locate restaurants that are nearby, simply skim the text in the restaurant chapter for listings identified as being on Map 7.

Where appropriate throughout the guide, we name the neighborhood or town in which each sight, restaurant, shop, or other destination is located. We also give you complete opening hours and admission fees for sights, and reservations, credit-card, closing hours, and price information for restaurants.

At the end of the book, in addition to an alphabetical index, you'll find directories of shops and restaurants by neighborhood.

Chapter 7, City Sources, lists essential information and resources for residents—everything from vet and lawyer-referral services to caterers worth calling.

We've worked hard to make sure that all of the information we give you is accurate at press time. Still, time brings changes, so always confirm information when it matters—especially if you're making a detour.

Feel free to drop us a line. Were the restaurants we recommended as described? Did you find a wonderful shop you'd like to share? If you have complaints, we'll look into them and revise our entries in the next edition when the facts warrant. So send us your feedback. Either e-mail us at editors@fodors.com (specifying *Fodor's CITYGUIDE Houston* on the subject line), or write to the *Fodor's CITYGUIDE Houston* editor at Fodor's, 280 Park Avenue, New York, NY 10017. We look forward to hearing from you.

Karen Cure
Editorial Director

chapter 1

RESTAURANTS

Throughout the 90s, Zagat and others reported that Houston led the nation in chef-owned restaurants and that Houstonians were more likely to eat out than anyone else. The diversity and high quality of restaurants in this city leads people to forego their own kitchen and take advantage of eating out at every opportunity. Although most enjoy a few treasured spots, and can't go too long without a beloved dish, there is such variety that finding something new or different is easy. The days of Tex-Mex dominance are long gone. The influence of foreign produce and spices popularized by immigrant groups, intriguing ideas for local culinary institutions, and a desire to keep a competitive edge have all helped local restaurateurs develop great food at a reasonable price that is readily available.

Houstonians bring a Latin leisure to meals—at lunch and dinner they want to be seated immediately and then linger at the table (although the more popular restaurants may not accommodate a drop-in customer). Each neighborhood has backyard burger joints worth patronizing, but the cuisine of almost every ethnic group on earth is served somewhere in the city. Nearly every segment of town has its favorite Thai, Indian, Latin American, and Japanese restaurants as well as outstanding burger, Tex-Mex, and Italian eateries. From the burgeoning Downtown scene, to quirky Montrose, to the eclectic Heights and into the strip center world of the suburbs, the restaurant business is booming. And, more and more restaurants accommodate, if not welcome, children. Enjoy!

general information

RESERVATIONS

Most popular restaurants in Houston do not take reservations, but allow you to call before you leave to "get your name on the list." Although this tactic can levy a slight advantage over other patrons, it does not guarantee immediate seating when you arrive. Large groups of six or more, however, should call ahead so the restaurant can prepare tables before you arrive. The "no reservations" policies of most Houston eateries discourage walk-ins, but conveniently encourage them to have a drink at the bar while they wait.

SMOKING/ NO SMOKING

Most restaurants in Houston have smoking sections (although they seem to be getting smaller by the day). The rule is that the smoking section must not interfere with the dining area unless that area is devoted primarily to the sale of alcoholic beverages. Smoking is usually allowed at outside dining areas.

TIPPING

Tipping in Texas follows the near-universal formula of 15% as baseline gratuity. Additional compensation depends on your judgment of the service and overall experience. A simple guideline for calculating the tip is to double the 8.25% tax item on the check.

PRICE CATEGORIES

Restaurant price categories are based on the average cost of a dinner that includes appetizer, entrée, and dessert (no beverages).

CATEGORY	COST*
$$$$	over $45
$$$	$30–$45
$$	$18–$30
$	under $18

*per person, excluding drinks, service, and sales tax (8.25%)

restaurants by cuisine from american to vietnamese

AMERICAN

13 b-3
BISTRO LANCASTER
Breakfast, lunch, and dinner can be had at this small restaurant in the Lancaster Hotel downtown. All the basic breakfast fare, lunches of soups, salads, or a fish special, and dinner of grilled salmon or beef tenderloin will hit the spot. This is a favorite spot for a pretheater meal in a classy atmosphere. *701 Texas Ave., Downtown, 713/228–9500. AE, D, DC, MC, V. $$$–$$$$*

13 b-3
CLIVE'S: THE GRILLE
Once the posh granddaddy in the theater district, Clive's is nowadays slightly more casual to accommodate the ever-burgeoning downtown scene. This is still a standing favorite of theatergoers who appreciate the friendly, efficient service that gets them to the show on time. A dynamic mural of Houston is the centerpiece of the clubby haunt. There's not much in the way of "nouvelle," but you do take part in the creation of your entrée. Choose your meat—from beef tenderloin, to rack of lamb, to Gulf snapper—and select a sauce such as wild mushroom, rosemary garlic, or béarnaise. Your entrée is cooked to your liking—char-grilled, pan-seared, or oven roasted. *517 Louisiana, Downtown/Theater District, 713/224–4438. AE, DC, MC, V. Closed Sun. No lunch Sat. $$–$$$*

7 g-7
FOX DINER
The funky patio, the fuchsia door, and the wily fox painted on the white box-of-a-building hint at surprises inside. Sure enough, confetti-painted floors, pink walls, the red room, and a faux folk art aquarium greet you within. The new American menu is a festival of food showing passion for and enjoyment of cooking and fine, but not fancy, dining. From macaroni and cheese to pork loin sandwiches with chow-chow (a mus-

tardy condiment with veggies that you can buy at any grocery store) to roasted Pacific salmon, the kitchen delights the offbeat crowds from Downtown, the revitalized Fourth Ward, and River Oaks. Although it's called a diner and they do serve fried chicken and King Ranch casserole, the gourmet menu, conservative servings, and upscale prices suggest a gentrified kitchen. First-class sandwiches and elegant salads are easier on the wallet. *905 Taft, Montrose, 713/523–5369. AE, D, MC, V. No smoking. No lunch Sat. No dinner Sun. $$*

3 d-5
JAX GRILL
A "grill" in the true sense of the word, this is the place to bring your friends and family for good food and a fun atmosphere. Even though the food probably can't be categorized as the best in town, it's tasty and a variety is ready for the choosing: burgers, crawfish étouffée, tacos, chicken-fried steak, fresh vegetables, and a dessert not to be missed, Jax Sack. It's an edible chocolate sack filled with pound cake and white chocolate mousse, topped with chocolate chips, strawberries, blueberries, and drizzled with caramel. Yum! *6510 S. Rice Ave., Rice University Village, 713/668–3606. Reservations required for large parties. AE, D, MC, V. $$*

7 b-8
OUISIE'S TABLE
Whether you want to lunch with the ladies, partake with your parents, or feast with your friends, Ouisie's gracious, country-lodge setting on the edge of River Oaks is hard to beat. So is her food. A huge chalkboard posts daily specials and a list of food and wine pairings. If you're really in a comfort food mode, try macaroni and cheese, with penne pasta and not even a dab of Velveeta, topped with herbed breadcrumbs. Also satisfying are crab cakes and fried oysters with jalapeño tartar sauce. *3939 San Felipe, at Willowick, River Oaks, 713/528–2264. Reservations essential. AE, D, DC, MC, V. No smoking. Closed Sun.–Mon. $$*

7 e-8
REMINGTON GRILL
Set in the luxurious St. Regis Hotel, this is the spot for special occasions or, better yet, an expense account meal. Although the food doesn't always meet

expectations, the overall experience is worth it. The atmosphere is intimate and sophisticated and draws interesting-looking hotel guests and dressed-up locals. Entrées include grilled tuna, horseradish-crusted salmon, and steaks. The generosity lies in the 14 vegetable side orders. *1919 Briar Oaks La., Galleria/Post Oak, 713/403–2631. AE, D, MC, V. $$–$$$$*

AMERICAN CASUAL

10 *a-8*
ANNIE'S HAMBURGERS
"Thou shalt not whine" is posted near the menu, and here you'll have no reason. You may shed a nostalgic tear, however, when you bite into old-time burgers—no guacamole or goat cheese toppings, just juicy meat on a white bread bun. The real joy, though, is Annie's breakfast. These are morning meals like grandma used to make— saucer-sized biscuits with cream gravy; platter-sized pancakes; waffles; French toast; even breakfast tacos—with prices from the good ol' days. The menu specials are "Take it or Leave it," and a recent add-on suggests an ever-growing band of those who happily "take it." Annie's green awnings against a dark wood exterior are a welcoming sight on the rather tired South Post Oak strip. *10821 S. Post Oak, Southwest, 713/729–9861. Reservations not accepted. No credit cards. $*

3 *e-4*
AVALON DRUG CO. AND DINER
This River Oaks institution with its old-style soda fountain is a favorite for all. In addition to its traditional American breakfasts, it also serves greasy hamburgers and sandwiches. The food may not be the best in town, but it's fun to eat at the counter with your kids. *2417 Westheimer Rd., River Oaks, 713/527–8900. AE, MC, V. No dinner. $*

10 *c-1*
3285 Southwest Fwy., West University Place, 713/838–2500.

3 *f-4*
BACKSTREET CAFÉ
Salad lovers will find a lot to be happy about here as will anyone who enjoys good comfort food in a charming set-ting. The shaded patio is a great spot to enjoy special chicken dishes, meat loaf, and mushroom soup. *1103 S. Shepherd Dr., River Oaks, 713/521–2239. AE, D, MC, V. $$–$$$*

12 *g-5*
BARNABY'S CAFÉ
This snug little diner is a friendly neighborhood hangout offering a range of dishes from salads to out-of-the-ordinary sandwiches, hamburgers, and meat loaf with garlic mashed potatoes. The food is consistently good, and service is quick. *604 Fairview St., Montrose, 713/522–0106. AE, D, MC, V. $*

12 *c-5*
1701 S. Shepherd, River Oaks, 713/520–5131.

3 *e-4*
BECK'S PRIME
This place boasts that the richness of their food is proof they don't cut corners. You can expect high-calorie, high-cholesterol consumption, but boy, it's worth it. Bare-bones counter service or drive-through serves up arguably our town's best burgers—big, juicy, and custom-made, served on yellow egg buns, with your choice of condiments, cheeses, and doneness. The menu includes leaner options like a remarkably good swordfish sandwich, grilled vegetables, a pretty good veggie burger, and a couple of adequate salads. It's convenient fast food, but it's made with the best of ingredients. The experience isn't complete until you've indulged in Beck's too-thick-for-a-straw jamocha, chocolate, or strawberry shake. Thankfully, you can order a dessert portion of only 4 ounces. All locations have plenty of outdoor seating. *2902 Kirby Dr., Upper Kirby District, 713/524–7085. Reservations not accepted. AE, DC, MC, V. $*

3 *d-4*
2615 Augusta, Galleria/Post Oak, 713/266–9901.

3 *d-5*
BUBBA'S TEXAS BURGER SHACK
The name fits the atmosphere, but that doesn't stop all types of Houstonians from feasting on one of Houston's best burgers. Surprisingly, they also serve a champagne brunch on Sundays. *5230 Westpark Dr., West University Place, 713/661–1622. DC, MC, V. $*

2 b-5

CLAY'S RESTAURANT

Soccer families who spend weekends at Bear Creek Park take note: a couple of miles west on Clay Road is the perfect place to while away the time between games. Workers in the west Houston "energy corridor" have long enjoyed lunches of Clay's burger baskets heaped with fries. The expanded menu, awesome backyard, and enough picnic tables for a family reunion are now attracting the masses on the weekends. There are tables and booths inside—you just never see anyone sitting there. *17717 Clay Rd., Katy/Bear Creek, 281/859–3773. AE, D, DC, MC, V. $*

13 b-4

JAMES CONEY ISLAND

James Coney Island is an institution, and many Houstonians make picking up a dog with all the fixings a weekly ritual. History tells us that Tom and James Papadakis, Greek immigrant brothers, flipped a coin to decide whose name would appear on the hot dog restaurant. The family sold the chain in 1993, and its new owner closed the original location on Walker Street. There are a total of 21 locations all over town. There's plenty of room for seating. *1142 Travis St., Downtown, 713/652–3819. Reservations not accepted. AE, D, MC, V. $*

10 a-2

PRINCE'S HAMBURGERS

A trip back to the 1950s is what you and your family will experience when you come here, along with a great burger. Kids' meals are served in cardboard models of classic cars and jukeboxes line the walls. *3899 Southwest Fwy., West University Place, 713/626–9950. AE, D, DC, MC, V. $*

7 b-2

ROZNOVSKY'S HAMBURGERS

Only a handful of places in town evoke memories and anecdotes from old-timer Houstonians, and this is one of 'em. The location has changed but the reputation remains with picnic-plaid curtains intact. The menu offers chicken-fried steak sandwiches and hot dogs, but come for the burgers, the kind you eat with juice dripping down your arm. For serious appetites, there's the double double cheeseburger (two meats, two cheeses). Wash it down with Coke or better, a Lone Star beer. If decor is what you're looking for, move on. But if ambience is what you want, this place is full of it. Ask anyone. *3401 West T.C. Jester, North, 713/957–1100. No credit cards. Closed Sun. No dinner Sat. $*

BARBECUE

3 f-4

DREXLER'S BAR-B-QUE

Does the name ring a bell? Clyde Drexler's mom and family score big in the Third Ward shadows of Downtown at this barbecue place, too sparkling-clean to be called a joint. From the kitchen, though, parade homemade hot links, smoked meats, and peppery sauce to please the pickiest purist. Sandwiches are served, rightfully, on white bread, and sides are the church-picnic-type beans and potato salad. When a big game isn't on the tube, the jukebox pipes out the sounds of R&B, soul, and zydeco. Without the basketball star, the crowds would still come. But with decor by Clyde—memorabilia from Phi

---

GOTTA GO

The "must try" list for anyone wanting to be a true Houstonian:

Americas (Latin)
This true showcase is a must-see for restaurant lovers.

Goode Company Bar-B-Q (Barbecue)
Texas BBQ and Texas memorabilia make this a necessity for natives and new arrivals.

James Coney Island (American Casual)
This Houston institution has expanded to 21 locations. The not-so-healthy cheese from a gun and tasty chili are trademarks.

Ragin Cajun (Cajun/Creole)
Louisiana imports even agree that during crawfish season there is no better place to get a steamy bucket of mudbugs. Plenty of necessities like napkins and bibs are provided.

Nino's (Italian)
This granddaddy of down-home Italian food has provided delicacies for more than 23 years. Next door are Vincent's and Grappino's, making this part of Montrose a testament to the dining success of the Mandola family.

Slamma Jama and Clutch City days—you feel proud to share a hometown with such good people. *2020 Dowling St., Third Ward, 713/752–0008. AE, D, DC, MC, V. Closed Sun.–Mon. $*

14 *b-1*
GOODE COMPANY BAR-B-Q
If it's Goode, it's great, and that's why native Houstonians take out-of-state guests here for a taste of Texas. Authentic barbecue with tip-top sides is served cafeteria-style in the Texas-touting interior. Seating is family-style at long tables indoors or at the outdoor picnic tables, with country & western tunes as backdrop. Enjoy longnecks or lemonade while eating slow-smoked anything-and-everything. Jalapeño-cheese bread and a bowl of dipping sauce make a great meal, but sorry, you'll have to order some meat to get the sauce. Vegetarians go for the monster-sized baked potatoes. Sides like jambalaya and pinto beans are good, but the pecan pie is legendary. Goode's great food, good prices, and straightforward service make it seem easy to fit into Texas. *5901 Kirby Dr., at Bartlett, West University Place, 713/522–2530. Reservations not accepted. AE, D, DC, MC, V. $*

6 *e-5*
8911 Katy Fwy., at Campbell Rd., Memorial/Spring Branch, 713/464–1901.

7 *d-7*
OTTO'S BARBEQUE AND HAMBURGERS
Serving up burgers and barbecue since 1951, Otto's most unique formula is for its brisket. The barbecue is a favorite of former president George Bush, and his personal greetings and photos are proudly hung on the family den–like walls. Take your tray and try and find a table. . If you're craving one of Otto's tasty burgers, use the Memorial Drive door, rather than the Reineke Street entrance. *5502 Memorial Dr., Memorial, 713/864–2573. Reservations not accepted. D, DC, MC, V. Closed Sun. $*

BRAZILIAN

4 *h-5*
RODIZIO GRILL
Carnivores, here is your fantasyland—a Brazilian-style steak house where the grilled meats don't stop coming until you say so. Every effort has been made to make this a total Brazilian experience—the staff, the decor, the bar drinks, the music. For less than $20, you can sample or indulge in a dozen selections of beef, poultry, pork, and seafood. Servers, dressed as "gauchos," present long skewers of meats, fresh off the rotisserie, to your table. Then, they carve off a hunk, if it pleases you. Also included are an appetizer platter and a mega-sized salad bar. The Houston venue is one of six locations nationwide. *5851 Westheimer, Galleria, 713/334–7400. Reservations essential. AE, D, DC, MC, V. $$*

4 *d-4*
SAMBA CAFÉ
Pot roast, steak and onions, grilled chicken, black beans, and collard greens do not sound exotic, but at Samba Café, these are the tastes of Brazil. Customers' conversations are predominantly in Portuguese, so you know this is the real stuff. Think of these meals as South American home-style cooking. The house specialty, rich and tasty *feijoada* (assorted platter of thinly sliced meats) proves black beans are the universal soul food when sided by collard greens and delicate rice. *Churrascos mixto* is a hefty sampler of grilled meats—tender sirloin, succulent chicken, and zesty sausage. Flan lovers crave Samba's coconut creation. Come Friday or Saturday nights after 8 and you will find a festive spot complete with jazz combo. *1854 B Kirkwood, Southeast, 281/558–0830. AE, D, MC, V. No smoking. Closed Mon. $*

CAFÉS

5 *b-5*
CAFÉ EXPRESS
These sleek fast food eateries are brought to you by the Café Annie folks. Sometimes the queue to order can be dauntingly long, but the wait allows time to change your mind a few times. Just when you've decided on a virtuous soup and salad, someone walks by with a sizzling burger and someone else with a tantalizing dessert. With plenty of patio seating and sleek bars featuring spirits and caffeine, these popular venues are popping up all over town. *3200 Kirby (and other locations), Upper Kirby District, 713/522–3994. AE, D, DC, MC, V. $*

5 *c-2*

KALDI CAFÉ

Tucked away in the heart of the historic Heights district in an antique shop, this arty diner is a favorite brunch spot for locals and those looking for good food "the morning after." They also serve fine coffees and have recently started serving lunch and dinner. *250 W. 19th St., Heights, 713/802–2246. D, MC, V. Closes 3 PM Sun. $–$$*

CAJUN/CREOLE

12 *h-6*

BRENNAN'S

Now thirty-something, this sophisticated, New Orleans–imported institution's longevity attests to its quality. The elegant setting and gracious service are equally fine for a romantic dinner or a large party celebrating somebody's something. Longtime patrons and newcomers gravitate to Brennan's Southern hospitality for power lunches or jazz brunches. Visit the classics like the 3-3-3 soups—gumbo, turtle, and mushroom soups served in three small bowls. Crawfish enchiladas, warm spinach salad, and peppercorn-crusted steak with generous sides are all done dependably deliciously. Pecan-crusted fish of the day and Louisiana-true gumbo set the standard for creole/Cajun cuisine. Straying from tradition is a risk—some dishes hit, some miss. Surprisingly, they can't seem to do justice to crab cakes. Bread pudding (dizzy with whiskey), soufflées, and bananas Foster are legendary. Any minor glitches or signs of being a hair behind the times are readily dismissed when spending an idyllic evening or Sunday morning in the lovely courtyard. Jacket required for dinner only. *3300 Smith, South Downtown, 713/522–9711. Reservations essential. AE, D, DC, MC, V. $$$$*

4 *h-5*

COPELAND'S
OF NEW ORLEANS

Attempting to evoke a New Orleans atmosphere on Houston's Richmond strip, Copeland's owners whip up hurricanes, pipe in zydeco and jazz, and decorate with purple and gold. Their food reflects founder Al Copeland's strength—a sure hand with spices. He is also the man behind Popeye's Fried Chicken. Best bets include the fried seafood such as oysters, crawfish, and catfish, sautéed crab claws, crab cakes, crawfish étouffée (when in season), and the addictive hush puppies. Less intriguing are shrimp pasta and blackened snapper. Expect conviviality and a casual party mood. *6353 Richmond Ave., Richmond Strip, 713/953–9448. AE, D, DC, MC, V. $$*

4 *h-5*

PAPPADEAUX
SEAFOOD KITCHEN

Another Pappas gold mine, this Cajun kitchen puts out consistently good food to consistently satisfied crowds. Bring the kids; bring the folks; bring the whole gang because there is plenty of seating in these cavernous spots. While you wait (and you will), enjoy beverages on the pretty patios reminiscent of French Quarter courtyards, but twice the size. Despite the noise level, Pappadeaux remains remarkably popular because the seafood is tasty, the portions are huge, and the prices are fair. One more reason for customer loyalty: the seafood fondue. *6015 Westheimer, Galleria/Post Oak, 713/782–6310. Reservations not accepted. AE, MC, V. $$*

6 *a-5*

10499 I–10 West, Town & Country, 713/ 722–0221.

5 *b-5*

RAGIN CAJUN

Welcome to "NooAwlins" on Richmond. As if it were an endearing joint on Bourbon Street, the walls are covered with photos and bumper stickers, and the counter is bordered with yearbooks from the colleges of Louisiana. During crawfish season, the place is packed with mudbug lovers from open to close. An array of po' boys, including oyster, shrimp, and catfish, are wonderful, messy sandwich concoctions of fish, shredded lettuce, and zesty red sauce. Long tables park you elbow-to-elbow with displaced Cajuns looking for a fix of *boudin* (Cajun sausage), shrimp étouffée, and bayou-style gumbo. On a clear day, tables are set for sidewalk dining—choice seating indeed. *4302 Richmond Ave., Galleria/Post Oak, 713/623–6321. Reservations not accepted. AE, D, DC, MC, V. Closed Sun. $*

13 c-2
TREEBEARDS
Eating on the cheap never tasted so good. In the second oldest building in Houston, throngs of Downtown suits, politicos, and construction workers line up for generous servings of "urban Southern cooking." The farmers' market mural on the building's south side pays tribute to Houston's heritage; the successes of the kitchen pay homage to Louisiana cookin'. Red beans and rice with sausage, shrimp étouffée, jambalaya, gumbo, meat loaf, and all the sides are served cafeteria-style. The dense, rich butter cake alone would cause a run on the market (square, that is), so Treebeards offers three additional Downtown locations, including Christ Church Cathedral. You'll have to navigate lunchtime traffic because dinner is only served on Fridays. *315 Travis, Market Square, Downtown, 713/228–2622. Reservations not accepted. AE, DC, MC, V. Closed Sat.–Sun. Lunch only. $*

13 c-3
1117 Texas, Christ Church Cathedral, Downtown, 713/229–8248.

13 b-3
1100 Louisiana, Downtown, 713/752–2601.

CARIBBEAN

3 d-3
CAFÉ RED ONION
As traffic roars away out front on Highway 290, you might have to queue up to be seated in the bare bones, strip center storefront that is Café Red Onion. There's nothing very fancy offered, but attention is paid to color and presentation, as well as taste. You'll get two menus, one of specialty items that carry a Caribbean flair and the other of more typical Mexican fare: fajitas, enchiladas, and tacos. Try a little of both: roasted red pepper soup with chunks of chicken, beef fajitas, fried plantain with sour cream, and fish (snapper) tacos. *12041 Northwest Fwy., at 43rd St., Northwest, 713/957–0957. Reservations not accepted. AE, D, DC, MC, V. No smoking. Closed Sun. $–$$*

10 g-2
REGGAE HUT
Images of the late, great patron saint of reggae, Bob Marley, smile down on the mismatched tables and chairs in this little joint tucked next to a Caribbean grocery store on Almeda. Terrific jerk chicken (chicken rubbed with a variety of spices), so tender it falls from the bone, shouldn't be missed. Surround it with crisp plantains (a starchy fruit from the banana family), salted and peppered with hot sauce, red beans and rice, and sweet "coco" bread. And, by all means, don't forget Jamaica's Red Stripe beer, specially priced on Wednesdays. Red snapper stewed in a brown sauce, garlic crab legs, or curried shrimp are worthy alternatives to the jerk chicken. *4814 Almeda, Medical Center, 713/524–2905. AE, D, DC, MC, V. No smoking. Closed Sun. $–$$*

CHINESE

2 d-2
EMPRESS
This jewel of Champions still reigns strong for regal dining. Tucked in a corner of an expansive, mazelike shopping center in this country club area, Empress holds court with white glove service, a gracious dining room, and an eclectic semi-Chinese menu. Asian and European influences add sophistication notches above typical chow mein. Expect the bill to reflect those notches. Pacific Rim dishes are as good as the renditions of old standards. As is (owner) Scott Chen's trademark, exquisite presentations prevail, like shrimp-and-avocado salad, or mixed seafood in white wine and lemon sauce, or boneless chicken tenderloin with ginger and fennel. *5419-A Farm Road 1960 W, Champions, 281/583–8021. AE, D, MC, V. Closed Sun. No lunch Sat. $$–$$$*

9 e-4
FUNG'S KITCHEN
A bright neon welcome, an expansive dining area, and a menu with more than 350 selections are crowd-pleasing, if not overwhelming. Hungry diners, Asian and Anglo, line up for the excellent seafood selections. Two preparations of oysters on the half shell—one steamed in garlic and another topped with black bean sauce—may be the best bivalves in town and the cheapest at $7.50 a dozen. The extensive menu includes boar, venison, duck, ostrich, and classic favorites like Mongolian beef and Kung Pao chicken. One entrée highlight is sautéed eggplant, with shrimp stuffing in black bean sauce. Waiters sometimes seem pressed to handle the throngs, but even

that can't deter from fine-tasting fare. *7320 Southwest Fwy., Southwest, 713/779–2288. AE, D, DC, MC, V. $–$$$$*

CONTEMPORARY

14 *c-2*
BENJY'S
The chic, spare setting of this casual spot in the Village belies the exuberance of its eclectic cuisine. Hints of Italian, fine wood oven–baked pizzas, and dabs of the Southwest, like sides of roasted corn cakes, coexist remarkably well with Asian-influenced choices like snow-crab spring rolls. Sometimes the pairings get too imaginative, but overall the food is sprightly and interesting. The brunch menu is equally impressive. Service is notably friendly, and the cozy upstairs bar is a cool hangout in which to continue conversations. *2424 Dunstan, Rice University Village, 713/522–7602. AE, DC, MC, V. No smoking. Closed Mon. No lunch Sat. $$–$$$*

12 *f-8*
BOULEVARD BISTROT
With a welcoming bar and sidewalk dining, the Bistrot qualifies as a pleasant Montrose hangout. Ingenious wall decor—chalkboards with elaborate artwork that changes seasonally—indicates creative forces at work. Indeed, award-winning, nationally recognized chef Monica Pope stirs up memorable, New American meals. Wild mushroom risotto and pistachio-crusted salmon (with tangy mandarin orange sauce) are two of her recurring hits on the one-page menu. Some folks wouldn't touch a beet salad with a 10-ft baguette, but hers is legendary with *frisée* (chicory vegetable), *cambozola* (creamy cheese), caramelized walnuts, and orange vinaigrette. For a divine finish to a meal, order the sour-cherry chocolate bread pudding if it's featured. *4319 Montrose, Montrose/Museum District, 713/524–6922. Reservations essential. AE, D, DC, MC, V. Closed Mon. No dinner Sun. $$*

12 *e-4*
DAILY REVIEW CAFÉ
This casual Fourth Ward eatery proves that, in Houston, comfort food and urbanity can coexist. The menu's appeal is as broad as the crowd is diverse—from buzz-cut hip young things to Downtown blue-suits. Entrées are imaginative twists on traditional favorites, like the chicken potpie perked up with shaved fennel and carrots in very rich, soulful cream sauce. The menu changes, but the favorites are perpetual. The zesty Mediterranean salad plate includes eggplant, orzo, currants, pine nuts, lemon couscous, tabbouleh, and tomato salad, and equally rewarding is the creamy quiche of roasted tomatoes, mushrooms, and sage. The penne with tender spicy meatballs is a knockout. Fresh cinnamon-raisin bread keeps diners smiling through the meal. Great for casual and al fresco dining, this spartan café delivers efficient service, admirable variety, and a hip approach to decor. Go early to avoid a wait. *3412 W. Lamar St., at Dunlavy, Montrose, 713/520–9217. AE, D, MC, V. No dinner Sun.–Mon. $–$$*

13 *c-4*
DEVILLE AT THE FOUR SEASONS HOTEL
From maître d' to server, attention to your enjoyment is given unobtrusively in this hushed, but friendly dining room. The upscale atmosphere is perfect for an important business lunch, a special family occasion, or when you simply want to have a conversation (without shouting) during a meal. Stop in for lunch or before the theater. Smoked yellow pepper gazpacho with salmon ceviche is a good way to start the meal. Pan-seared Chilean sea bass shows off the exceptional skills of the chef, and the desserts can be memorable. *1300 Lamar, Downtown, 713/652–6250. AE, D, MC, V. No lunch Sat. No dinner Sun. $$$$*

7 *a-7*
JAGS
Society caterer Jackson Hicks plays to anyone who pays at his lunch-only restaurant in the dramatic, high-ceilinged atrium of the Decorative Center. The well-turned-out and their decorators come for the special ambience and service, as well as Hicks's food. No credentials are checked at the door, however; anyone can enjoy his crab *blinis* (small, yeast-raised buckwheat pancakes), salmon with cucumber salad, and health-conscious salads and sandwiches—presented, of course, with proper panache. Yeasty orange rolls please both the best and the less well-dressed. *5120 Woodway, Galleria/Post Oak, 713/621–4766. Reservations essential. AE, D, DC, MC, V. Lunch only. Closed Sat.–Sun. $$*

12 e-6
MARK'S

Come exalt the creative cuisine at chef Mark Cox's sanctuary along this funky strip of lower Westheimer. This one-time church serves its parishioners well, albeit in a fairly noisy atmosphere. Your voice will join the alleluias, though, and your conversion will be complete once you try the richly flavored red-pepper bisque with seafood and the grilled medallions of veal over risotto with asparagus and a morel-shiitake mushroom sauce. Desserts run from light sorbets to more sinful temptations. As for pew selection, avoid the west-side addition if your hearing has diminished or your voice doesn't carry. *1658 Westheimer, at Dunlavy, Montrose, 713/523–3800. Reservations essential. AE, D, DC, MC, V. $$*

12 g-8
REDWOOD GRILL

Relax in a comfy booth, bask in the glow of terra-cotta–hued walls, nibble gratis half-moon biscuits, and watch the dressed-up ladies and gentlemen gather. Redwood offers a three-course prethe-ater menu for around $30—a great deal given the inviting setting and the imaginative food. Seafood is an excellent choice at Redwood, whether the fresh snapper with tempura coating, the juicy seared scallops in tarragon sauce, or the perfectly baked salmon with pistachio crust. The Grill's peppercorn-crusted filet mignon—well, it sets the standard. Lighter options are equally delicious and creative, like Nantucket blue spinach salad with blueberries and blue cheese. A favorite finish is scoops of creamy mango and raspberry sorbets. All in the quiet crowd are smiling at meal's end. *4611 Montrose, Museum District, 713/523–4611. Reservations essential. AE, D, DC, MC, V. No smoking. $$–$$$*

6 a-5
RIVIERA GRILL RADISSON SUITE HOTEL

Without the benefit of a good location, Riviera thrives on its solid reputation for luxurious meals. Within the Radisson at Town & Country Mall, the attractive garden room befits the Mediterranean menu. Chef John Sheely changes the menu seasonally, but you can expect remarkable appetizers and grilled entrées with imaginative sides. After one visit, customers spread the word. Favorite recent appetizers include the spicy-sweet calamari in honey-and-red-pepper crust. Memorable entrées include superb pepper-crusted Chilean sea bass atop a ragout of roasted tomatoes, olives, and capers; and sun-dried tomato polenta topped with seared shrimp, asparagus, and wild mushrooms. Chocoholics beware: the bitter-sweet chocolate torte looks tame, but is rich enough to satisfy a small crowd. Beyond the culinary delights, Riviera grants guests the rare experience of a leisurely meal. *10655 Katy Fwy., Memorial/Spring Branch, 713/974–4445. Reservations essential. AE, MC, V. Closed Sun. $$$–$$$$*

10 a-1
RUGGLES GRILLE 5115

Located in the Saks Fifth Avenue store at the Galleria, this is a favorite lunch spot for shoppers. Good choices are the spicy shrimp tostada with *queso* (cheese) fresco and guava *habañero* (hot pepper) or the salmon with artichokes, caviar, and walnut vinaigrette. For your entrée, try the snapper or the duck breast served with honey-glazed barbecue mango sauce. *5115 Westheimer, Galleria, 713/963–8067. AE, D, MC, V. Closed Sun. $$–$$$*

6 f-8
SCOTT CHEN'S

Turn your sights inward, to avoid the parking lot view, and be rewarded with a tranquil setting of rich paneling and wine cellar ambience. Scott Chen has perfected his yen to join the best of East and West with this pricey, ambitious menu. Pretty presentations paired with culinary skill result in sure-to-please dishes. Try the salad of sliced avocado with arugula, blue cheese, and apples in caper oil. Follow with grilled oysters with crabmeat, ginger, and oyster sauce, or grilled sea bass with sweet chile sauce. For those calorie counters, taste the light tempura shrimp, which gives you the freedom to indulge in a dessert of creamy chocolate walnut cheesecake. *6540 San Felipe, at Voss, Tanglewood, 713/789–4484. AE, D, DC, MC, V. Closed Sun. $$$–$$$$*

12 f-7
TONY RUPPE'S

In the mish-mash neighborhood that is the Montrose/Museum District, Tony Ruppe's provides a lovely two-story space with seating that's intimate, but doesn't have you in on your neighbors' conversation. Seafood selections successfully focus on the *s*'s: salmon, snapper, swordfish, sea bass, shrimp, and sushi tuna. Try the pan roasted sea bass on eggplant Parmesan or charred swordfish with eye-watering horseradish mashers. The three *r*'s worked well too, in the rocket, romaine, and radicchio salad. Red meat eaters are not denied a place at the table, either: beef tenderloin, lamb chops, and veal chop add to the variety on this inventive menu. *3939 Montrose Blvd., Suite C, Montrose, 713/ 852–0852. AE, DC, MC, V. Closed Sun. $$$–$$$$*

CONTINENTAL

7 b-8

ANTHONY'S RESTAURANT

This is a creation of well-known Houston restauranteur Tony Vallone, and it's a hit. With the menu changing daily, every visit can be a new experience, from snapper stuffed with shrimp to ravioli of duck to warm chocolate midnight cake. *4007 Westheimer Rd., River Oaks, 713/961–0552. Reservations required weekends. AE, D, MC, V. Closed Sun. No lunch weekends. $$$–$$$$*

7 a-7

LA RÉSERVE

As formal as your great-aunt's parlor, although more lavish, the Omni's resplendent dining room still conveys an inviting warmth. Service is friendly and maintains a measured pace. Sink into a corner banquette and watch the evening unfold. From the imaginative kitchen come visually delightful arrangements of salads and entrées. Some dishes approach perfection— pyramid of charcoal-grilled vegetables with goat cheese cream in bell pepper sauce, and rack of lamb with cumin-flavored mousse and roasted garlic potatoes. Heart-healthy red snapper, flavorful on a bed of artichokes, new potatoes, and tomatoes, or pan-seared Texas sea bass in an amusing costume of crisp potato scales are also worthy choices. Very special desserts include chocolate soufflé, which should be ordered from the start. You will leave utterly content. *4 Riverway, at Woodway, Galleria/Post Oak, 713/871–8181. Reservations essential. AE, D, DC, MC, V. Closed Sun.–Mon. $$$–$$$$*

5 b-5

MAXIM'S

Picture a grand special-occasion– expense-account dining room, and you've captured this Houston landmark, owned and personally managed for 50 years by the Bermann family. Bending only slightly to trends, Maxim's continues to please its pampered regulars with oysters Rockefeller and Mornay, generous Gulf shrimp cocktails, and grilled or sautéed trout and snapper, often dabbed with a butter or cream sauce. Prime lump crabmeat may adorn nearly any course except dessert, but it's best served alone in browned butter. Yes, crepes suzette, cherries jubilee, and baked Alaska remain on this dessert list. Appropriately, Ronnie Bermann maintains a fine wine cellar. *3755 Richmond Ave., Greenway Plaza, 713/877–8899. Reservations essential. AE, D, DC, MC, V. Closed Sun. No lunch Sat. $$$*

12 b-3

RAINBOW LODGE

You'll feel miles away from the frantic Memorial Drive corridor as you dine in

---

HOUSTON'S LANDMARK RESTAURANTS

These locales are part of Houston and its history:

Brennan's (Cajun/Creole)
Jack Nicholson and Shirley MacLaine had their first date here in the movie, "Terms of Endearment." Many others have enjoyed the Sunday brunch for more than 30 years.

Maxim's (Continental)
Now a pregame stop for upper-crust Rockets fans, Maxim's has also provided pampering for power lunches for more than 50 years.

Ninfa's (Tex-Mex)
Many agree that Houston Tex-Mex started here. The original Ninfa's east side location provides the atmosphere many Mexican restaurants have unsuccessfully tried to mimic.

Otto's Barbeque and Hamburgers (Barbecue)
Serving up burgers and barbecue since 1951, Otto's describes itself "as much a part of Houston's landscape as the Bayou itself." Otto's is also a favorite hangout of former president Bush.

this beautiful old home on the banks of Buffalo Bayou. The lush setting is wildly popular for suitors popping the question and for many a bridal portrait. The dining room has somber hunting trophies mounted on the walls, but the rustic elegance and outdoor landscape and wildlife are naturally soothing. On the Gulf Coast menu, you will find whatever is fresh and in season—game, seafood, and various pastas and homegrown salads. For its fine, gourmet meals, Rainbow Lodge is perfect for special occasion dining. *1 Birdsall St., at Memorial Dr., River Oaks, 713/861–8666. Reservations essential. AE, D, DC, MC, V. Closed Mon. No lunch Sat. $$$–$$$$*

12 *b-6*
RIVER OAKS GRILL
It's just a neighborhood restaurant, but the neighborhood happens to be River Oaks. The paneled dining room with brass accents and a piano bar evokes a popular club. The velvety lobster bisque is without peer, but oysters Rockefeller or lump crabmeat are other good appetizer options. Fillet of beef stuffed with Roquefort, steak *au poivre* (crushed pepper) with port-wine sauce, and rack of pork loin with mustard sauce are all options for the heavy eater. Veal *piccata* (seasoned sautéed veal served with lemon juice and chopped parsley) dressed with capers and a roasted vegetable napoleon with mozzarella are the lighter selections. *2630 Westheimer, at Kirby, River Oaks, 713/520–1738. AE, D, DC, MC, V. Closed Sun. $$–$$$*

4 *e-5*
ROTISSERIE FOR BEEF AND BIRD
For two decades, Rotisserie has lured Houstonians to Wilcrest for elegant, unique dining. As surely as the rotisserie turns, hawk-eyed owner Joe Mannke keeps up the quality at this tradition-anointed place. The chef and sommelier welcome you into a fireside, early American country setting with meals representing rich heritage. Expectations are quickly raised with gratis salmon pâté and unusually good rolls, then sustained by entrées of wild game, prime beef, and fresh seafood. Treat yourself to one of Mannke's special dinners, like the annual fall Harvest Dinner featuring the "agricultural bounty of the Lone Star State" from wines to produce, to fish and game. Jacket recommended. *2200 Wilcrest, at Westheimer, Memorial/Spring Branch, 713/977–9524. Reservations essential. AE, D, DC, MC, V. No smoking. Closed Sun. $$$*

5 *a-4*
TONY'S
Houston's toniest spot, the glossy bastion of high society, is a hubbub of activity and more fun than you might expect. Tony's is refined and priced to the sky, but not stuffy. Servers and diners alike seem to enjoy themselves. To be sure, Tony's is hopping with the bejeweled and tanned, but you'll likely find dressed-down diners as well. From the plush setting to the complimentary treats (pâté to start; cookies and chocolates to end), you'll feel privileged indeed. Velvety lobster bisque and the Ashley salad of spinach, pears, Gorgonzola, and blueberries are favorite starters. For entrées, consider these inspirations: halibut bouillabaisse with mushrooms, asparagus, and crab; pan-seared snapper with lobster medallions; and cheese-filled caramelli pasta in truffle sauce. Even with the big-deal aura, you may experience a random slip in service, and nitpickers will wish for more space between tables. *1801 Post Oak Blvd., Galleria/Post Oak, 713/622–6778. Reservations essential. AE, D, DC, MC, V. Closed Sun. No lunch. $$$$*

CUBAN

4 *h-6*
CAFÉ PIQUET
In a nondescript Bissonnet strip center sits this Cuban food haven—or is it heaven? For a small, mama-y-papa business, the selection is impressively varied, and reliably satisfying. The menu is in Spanish and English, and likewise, diners are heard conversing in both languages. The authentic items are lightly fried chicken, pork, beef, and seafood, but for the cholesterol-wary, the perfectly grilled or roasted versions are equally tasty. Try the shrimp creole and Cuban-style sandwiches for a real taste of Havana. Black bean aficionados rave about this sumptuous side dish, which is served with all meals, along with rice and plantains. Home-style cooking and service is the credo and one you will appreciate. *6053 Bissonnet, at Alder, Bellaire, 713/664–1031. MC, V. No smoking. Closed Mon. $*

DELICATESSENS

5 *a-4*

EATZI'S MARKET AND BAKERY

If life is a celebration, EatZi's is where you pick up the party food. Technically, yes, EatZi's is a restaurant, or at least they've reserved a small portion of its domain for diners. Make your way through the crowds in front of the salad wall, grill, deli, bakery, meat and seafood counter, produce aisle, or ready-made take-out cooler. Choices abound, from buying a prepared meal to fixing one from scratch from the array of meats, breads, and produce you'll find. You can also build a great deli sandwich and eat it here. After you pick up your order, find a seat at a table. *1702 Post Oak Blvd., Galleria/Post Oak, 713/629–7660. AE, D, DC, MC, V. No smoking. $*

10 *c-4*

EDLOE STREET DELI

Practically an extension of suburban West University kitchens, Janet Carter Wilson's cozy deli–dining room has been serving family-friendly fare since the 1970s. Regulars praise her Mexican food—enchiladas, quesadillas, and burritos—and her burgers are irresistible. Deli favorites include home-style pimento-cheese, egg-salad, and chicken-salad sandwiches, potato salad, tortilla soup, and toothsome desserts—carrot cake, cheesecake, mud pie, key lime pie, and brownies. Wilson's take-out casseroles provide instant entrées for many a neighborhood dinner party, and her chicken enchiladas are a West U. Christmas Eve tradition. *6119 Edloe St., West University Place, 713/666–4302. AE, D, MC, V. Closed Sun. No dinner Mon.–Tues. $*

12 *d-6*

PAULIE'S

This casual, sunny, and serene deli–bakery offers a pleasant setting for lunch, afternoon tea or lemonade, an early dinner, or fetching a take-out meal. Specialties include *panini* (hefty sandwiches on grilled country bread) and a terrific salad of shell pasta combined with artichoke hearts, shredded spinach, red peppers, black olives, and feta cheese in a pesto dressing. The staff prepares excellent soups, salads, and pasta dishes. The fettuccine Alfredo smoked salmon is one favorite, but most diners admit they are eagerly waiting to finish their meal with a decorative, iced shortbread cookie, shaped and iced appropriate to the season. Owned and operated by the friendly Petronella family, this spot just across from Lanier Middle School has become an instant hit without overcrowding—a blessing indeed. *1834 Westheimer, at Driskill, Montrose, 713/807–7271. Reservations not accepted. MC, V. Closed Sun. $*

ECLECTIC

12 *h-7*

FUSION CAFÉ

The owners of the restaurant have their mothers to thank (and so do you). The down-home recipes of their three mothers—one Jamaican, one Louisiana Cajun, one East-Texas Southern—are what make up the menu. Take comfort in their versions of lusty oxtail stew, spicy jerk chicken, tender pork chops smothered in brown gravy, crisp-fried chicken, with or without waffles, and red beans and rice—all served with a choice of well-seasoned vegetables. Add a tall glass of "sweet tea" or a bottle of Jamaican Red Stripe and you'll still spend less than $10, leaving you with no reason to pass up the divine crumb-crusted sweet potato pie or pineapple-carrot cake. A casual atmosphere and diverse patrons mark this interesting midtown corner. *3722 Main St., at Alabama, Montrose, 713/874–1116. Reservations not accepted. AE, D, DC, MC, V. No smoking. $*

12 *f-6*

URBANA

A streamlined modern design, a stylish streetside patio, and funky background tunes aptly fit Urbana, John Puente's contribution to the hip Montrose scene; in fact, he named it with urban Texans in mind. Urbana's food matches the upbeat expectations, beginning with wild-mushroom quesadillas or grilled Portobello mushrooms and rounds of goat cheese drizzled with balsamic vinaigrette. Recommended entrées include chicken breast in garlic cream that comes stacked with asparagus, avocado salsa, and tortilla crisps, quail with jalapeño-cheese grits, and buffalo meat loaf spiced with *cascabel* (hot pepper) chile catsup. Generous salads, topped with salmon, tuna, or chicken, make excellent lunch fare. Eat early or outside if you aren't enlivened by happy-crowd noise bouncing off hard surfaces. *3407 Montrose Blvd., at Hawthorne, Montrose, 713/521–1086. Reservations essential. AE, D, DC, MC, V. $$*

ENGLISH

12 *f7*
BLACK LABRADOR PUB

There's a collegiate, almost Ivy League, feel to this pub, practically on the campus of the University of St. Thomas. Maybe it's the vine-covered walls of the patio, or the gigantic chessboard with playable pieces out front, or the patrons reading books and newspapers. A serious bar, an expansive fireplace, and comfy booths cajole you to relax. The menu here is downright vibrant with soups, salads, burgers, and even Tex-Mex to complement the English specials. The Tour of Britain is a sampler of shepherd's pie, bangers and mash (sausage and potatoes), fish and chips, and baked beans. Everything here goes great with a pint of brew. *4100 Montrose, Montrose, 713/529–1199. Reservations not accepted. AE, DC, MC, V. $$*

FRENCH

4 *d-5*
BISTRO PROVENCE

French bistro fare—a rare commodity in Houston—is admirably prepared and served in these intimate, wood-beamed dining rooms operated in far west Houston by the Georges Guy family. Satisfy your longings for authentic pâtés, escargots in garlic butter, stuffed mussels or mussel soup, and rich *confit* (salted meat simmered in its own juices) of duck or rabbit. Absolute musts include Provençal stews like *boeuf a la bourguignonne* (beef braised in red wine and garnished with small mushrooms and white onions) at either site. The Westheimer setting offers more seafood selections and a generous space, but the small Memorial hideaway feels pleasingly cozy on cool evenings. Outstanding rustic breads and pizzas issue from the wood-burning oven, and reasonably priced French wines offer another plus. No reservations are needed, but expect a wait on weekend evenings. *11920-J Westheimer, at Kirkwood, Memorial/Spring Branch, 281/497–1122. AE, MC, V. No smoking. Closed Sun. $$*

4 *d-3*
13616 Memorial, Memorial/Spring Branch, 713/827–8008.

5 *a-4*
CAFÉ PERRIER

Known for its quality cuisine and special presentations, this restaurant is a popular spot for large groups. With its piano bar and copper-topped bar, Café Perrier has a stream of regular customers at its door for lunch and dinner. *4304 Westheimer, Galleria/Post Oak, 713/355–4455. AE, D, MC, V. Closed Sun. $$–$$$$*

7 *f-8*
LA COLOMBE D'OR

This charming, sophisticated restaurant occupies the first floor of a turn-of-the-century mansion whose upper floors have been converted into a small luxury hotel by longtime owner Steve Zimmerman. A natural choice for special occasions, its kitchen usually rises to meet such a challenge and at times even reaches the sublime, depending on the current chef. Forget about budgets and calories and succumb to classic preparations and presentations of lobster, lamb, prime cuts of beef, and vegetables. Expect the elaborate desserts to be—what else?—rich. *3410 Montrose, Montrose, 713/524–7999. Reservations essential. AE, D, DC, MC, V. $$$$*

GERMAN

4 *f-5*
RUDI LECHNER'S RESTAURANT

This Bavarian stalwart has a loyal following that comes for the convivial atmosphere and a pleasing German-Austrian menu. Owner Rudi Lechner has been hosting celebrations for 20 years in his handsome dining room in Woodlake Square. Wiener schnitzel, goulash, and grilled sausage samplers provide authenticity, whereas grilled salmon and chicken with mushrooms in Marsala sauce satisfy less adventurous appetites. Month-long Oktoberfest brings in chicken-dancers of all ages, but live Alpine music is performed every Friday and Saturday, all year long. *2503 S. Gessner, Memorial/Spring Branch, 713/782–1180. AE, DC, MC, V. $$*

GREEK

`10` e-1
MYKONOS ISLAND RESTAURANT

Do you like your food forthright? The only fusion happening here is English language and Greek food, and that's why Mykonos Island has been around for years. In the Greenbriar/Shepherd triangle, where 6 months is a good run, this family-operated tavern stands firm with a loyal clientele. You happily accept the basic decor, red booths and green potted plants, and somewhat lackadaisical service when calamari, moussaka, *dolmas* (stuffed grape leaves), and snapper are this good. Frequent menu references to "mama" and the many Greek customers confirm this is the classic real deal. *2181 Portsmouth, West University Place, 713/523–4114. AE, D, DC, MC, V. Closed Sun. $*

`12` f5
NIKO NIKO'S

Once a sidewalk stand like you see on the streets of Athens, Niko Niko's has grown into a café. Opa! Complete with wooden booths and order-up window, this is Greek fast food, and it's baklavas above its burger and taco cousins. Value-conscious feta-lovers pack the house for the hefty menu selections at lean prices. The gyros and Greek salads may be the best in town, but daily specials and grilled seafood dishes are worth your while and your money, too. On Montrose, when you see the blue awnings, nudge your steering wheel, and you'll be at the front door. There is much-needed additional parking across the street. *2520 Montrose, Montrose, 713/528–1308. Reservations not accepted. AE, D, MC, V. $*

INDIAN

`4` c-4
ASHIANA

With an elegant atmosphere, Ashiana is an Indian jewel. The kitchen specializes in north Indian Moghlai cuisine, and the staff is happy to recommend meals for novices. Tandoori meats (marinated, spiced, and broiled in traditional clay ovens) are tender and mildly spicy. Plenty of vegetarian selections are offered like *daal Ashiana*—creamy lentils with garlic, tomatoes, onions, and light spices. They also do a fine *saag paneer* (spinach with

cheese in tomato cream sauce). Tucked in a ho-hum strip center, this spacious, attractive restaurant stands out from its brethren. *12610 Briar Forest, Katy, 281/679–5555. AE, D, DC, MC, V. $$*

`5` a-4
BOMBAY PALACE

It's not quite palatial, but Bombay Palace's large dining room, decorated in pastels and starched linens, does regally invite both Indian natives and non-natives to enjoy a special repast. Lamb is strongly recommended—*saag gosht* (lamb chunks in a savory spinach sauce or in a browned onion, garlic, and ginger reduction)—as is *gosht patiala* (chicken with basmati rice and saffron) and several seafood specialties. *Chana masala* (garbanzos with onions, tomatoes, and tamarind), peas *pulao* (a rice dish), and warm *kulcha* (breads) make a fine foil for main courses. Cool *kheer* (creamy rice pudding) provides an equally classic finish. The extensive luncheon buffet draws raves. *3901 Westheimer, at Weslayan, Galleria/Post Oak, 713/960–8472. Reservations essential. AE, DC, MC, V. $$*

`4` h-5
INDIA'S

A long-standing purveyor of Indian food, India's attracts those who swear by its chicken *tikka masala* (cutlet marinated in fortified wine), saag paneer, and warm kulcha. Others come for the tandoori (cooked in a huge clay oven) dishes, curries such as the lamb *vindaloo* (extremely spicy dish marinated in vinegar), vegetable *samosas* (pastries filled with lentils), and crisp lentil *pappadums* (crackerlike bread made from lentils). Vegetarians have several options, and the lunch buffet always lures a Galleria-area crowd. Service ranges from intrusive to indifferent, which may be an incentive to opt for the buffet. *5704 Richmond Ave., Galleria/Post Oak, 713/266–0131. AE, D, DC, MC, V. $$*

`5` b-5
KHYBER NORTH INDIAN GRILL

An inviting brick and glass interior with an open kitchen sets this Indian restaurant apart from many of its lackluster competitors, but its food and attentive owner, Mickey Kapoor, really give it the edge. Lamb is the meat to order, whether grilled on a kabob or slowly melded with onions, tomatoes, ginger, and traditional spices in a *bhuna* (peanuts, cinnamon, and ginger) curry. Other grilled meats, curries, and side dishes also merit favorable mention—more favorable than the seafood. Expect northern Indian cuisine to be lighter and less hot, but more sophisticated, than its southern counterpart. *2510 Richmond Ave., Upper Kirby District, 713/942–9424. $$*

14 *c-3*
SHIVA
The reason why devotees of this dining room find its dark, beaded-curtain interior eccentrically attractive may escape some, but the appeal of French-trained chef Ricki Oberoi's light touch with traditional Indian fare is more obvious. A generic lunchtime buffet offers the perfect opportunity to sample his treatment of standard tandoori, curries, and stews, as well as unusual (and often complex) vegetarian combinations. Soothing yogurt salad and sweet rice or cottage-cheese desserts offer perfect contrasts. Evening dining provides a similar array via menu service. *2514 Times Blvd., Rice University Village, 713/523–4753. AE, D, DC, MC, V. $*

5 *h-7*
TAJ MAHAL
Long before the city exploded with Indian restaurants—north Indian, south Indian, vegetarian, low-calorie, you-name-it—Houstonians trekked to this unimposing strip site on the Gulf Freeway for tasty, inexpensive house specialties. Taj Mahal's tandoori chicken, tikka masala, saag paneer, and daal still equal those dishes at more fashionable spots; and the breads, notably onion kulcha and *keema naan* (leavened bread filled with minced meat), approach perfection. Lightly battered and fried vegetable *pakora* (vegetable fritter) makes a fine starter, and the *makhni* (tomato gravy) or vindaloo curries will please curry lovers. A bargain-priced buffet draws a hungry lunch crowd. *8328 Gulf Fwy., at Bellfort Ave., East Side, 713/649–2818. AE, D, DC, MC, V. Closed Mon. $*

ITALIAN

4 *d-3*
ACHILLES ITALIAN RESTAURANT
Trendy new eateries aside, this venerable place remains a west Memorial favorite. Every neighborhood should be so fortunate to have an Italian kitchen like this—polished, friendly service, white linens, and a limited, but robust menu. You won't find much creativity, but classic versions of lasagna, *osso buco* (braised veal shank), cannelloni, and veal Parmesan are consistently good. Achilles is lively enough for enjoying a special occasion—be it even just getting out of the house. *14120 Memorial Dr., Memorial/Spring Branch. 281/558–0615. AE, DC, MC, V. $$*

5 *b-5*
CARRABBA'S
Once a place where 45-minute waits were considered short, Carrabba's maintains a thriving, but more tolerable, level of business. (Yes, you will wait for a table on the weekend.) The name has been franchised, but both Kirby and Woodway locations remain with the original owner, Johnny Carrabba. Thank goodness for that. A pioneer in the open kitchen concept, Carrabba makes you feel part of the family and part of the show. And what a show it is—both the meal and the people-watching. The wood-burning oven churns out stellar pizzas and focaccia. Pastas are varied from simple *picchi pacchu* (tomato and basil) to sublime *rigatoni campagnolo* (Italian sausage, peppers and *caprino* (goat cheese in a tomato sauce). Heartier appetites are rewarded with Italian classics like lasagna and manicotti or grilled entrées, like tenderloin, fish, and chicken. *3115 Kirby Dr., between Richmond and W. Alabama, Upper Kirby District, 713/522–3131. Reservations not accepted. AE, D, DC, MC, V. $$*

4 *g-4*
1399 S. Voss, at Woodway, Tanglewood, 713/468–0868.

14 *c-3*
COLLINAS
This modest bare-bones spot packs 'em in all around town for well-prepared Italian fare at low prices. Collinas is a favorite neighborhood joint where pizza goes slightly upscale, but not to the point of pretension. *Greca* pizza (Greek-style)—pepperoni, roma tomatoes, black olives, feta cheese, onions—is so good, you'll be tempted to toss plates. And the crowd is rowdy enough to join you. The Italian *muffaleta* (a gigantic meat- and cheese-stuffed sandwich dressed with olive relish) originated in New Orleans, but is well-known throughout the Gulf

Coast. Beer and wine is served, but you can bring your own wine for a small corking fee. *2400 Times Blvd., at Morningside, Rice University Village, 713/526–4499. Reservations not accepted. AE, D, DC, MC, V. Closed Sun. $*

10 *c-1*

3333 Richmond Ave., between Timmons and Weslayan, Greenway Plaza, 713/621–8844.

4 *f-3*

12311 Kingsride La., Memorial/Spring Branch, 713/365–9497.

12 *f6*

DA MARCO

In its beginning in March 2000, this restaurant was nominated as one of the best around. Its flavorful food, regional wine selection, and warm atmosphere make for a special evening out. Some of the most favorite dishes are porcini risotto, sea bass, and tagliatelle. *1520 Westheimer, River Oaks, 713/807–8857. AE, D, MC, V. Closed Sun. $$–$$$*

12 *h-6*

DAMIAN'S

High-set windows, romantic lighting, and walls crowded with framed photos, posters, and artwork give a cozy feel to Damian's, situated many blocks south of downtown—too far for walking but a quick commute by car. The slightly formal atmosphere is nonetheless welcoming, the waitstaff well informed and competent. This kitchen really cares—any place that ensures, midwinter, that the tomatoes in tomatoes *caprese* are ripe and juicy (and served with fresh mozzarella and basil), is focused on high quality. You can expect the very best in pastas, too: try the spaghetti *alla carbonara* (rich with bacon and garlic) or linguine with seafood. Veal dishes shine also, as do the seafood entrées. *3011 Smith St., at Elgin, Montrose, 713/522–0439. Reservations essential. AE, DC, MC, V. $$$*

4 *e-5*

FRED'S ITALIAN CORNER

West University residents and medical center workers have relished this secret spot for years, and not because of the ambience. They come for the food. Many a displaced medical center worker pines for a Fred's fix. Booth benches line two walls with miniature tables squeezed in between. Menus are scattered about the beverage area, but after one visit, you won't need a menu. Place your order at the counter with Fred, in full chef regalia, who sits on a barstool at the cash register. Then vie for any available seat. Large groups don't fit well at lunch. Momentarily, a waiter brings your spaghetti or lasagna or pizza, and you thank your lucky stars for the real deal. There's not an ounce of frou-frou to be found. Dinner is full service and less hectic. *10555-B Westheimer, Medical Center, 713/978–5055. AE, D, DC, MC, V. No smoking. Closed Sun. No lunch Sat. $*

5 *a-2*

FUZZY'S PIZZA

What's so great about Fuzzy's that a President—George Bush, of course—would proclaim his loyalty nationwide? The consensus is that the pizza is practically perfect, most of the time. You can have your crust—thick or thin—and eat it, too, with toppings to please all parties. The ingredients are fresh and generously applied, like a spry tomato sauce, Canadian bacon, zesty Italian sausage, and all your other favorites. Vegetarians will love the spinach pizza, and singles will appreciate the pizza-by-the-slice option. Ordered with a notably good Greek salad, one slice of pie is a substantial lunch at these insanely popular spots. Read my lips: no nouvelle cuisine, just good eating. Sports lovers will appreciate the big-screen TV tuned into the big games of the day. *823 Antoine, Memorial/Spring Branch, 713/682–8836. Reservations not accepted. AE, MC, V. $*

9 *f-1*

2727 Fondren, Memorial/Spring Branch, 713/787–5200.

10 *d-2*

5925 Kirby, West University Place, 713/522–6677.

7 *b-8*

GROTTO

The crowd is the junior beautiful set, and no wonder . . . these are Tony Vallone's less formal New Italian eateries. Ribald murals set the mood for feasting and frivolity, but these meals would be great in a dark closet. Although tables are crowded and jammed into every possible space, the savory meals compensate for ultracoziness. Take, for instance, plump oysters *mimmo* (infant) crisply encased in Italian breading as your appetizer. Move on to seafood ravioli topped with shrimp and crab claws or chicken *francese* (prepared with artichoke hearts and mushrooms). Snare a bite of your friend's *risotto primavera* (pasta full of yellow squash, zucchini, and porcini mushrooms). For the full experience and maximum table time, indulge yourself with rich desserts. Dress is casual, but you'll want to look your best. *3920 Westheimer, at Weslayan, River Oaks, 713/622–3663. AE, D, DC, MC, V. $$*

6 *f-7*
6401 Woodway, at Voss, Tanglewood, 713/782–3663.

12 *d-4*
LA GRIGLIA
Dramatic decor, open kitchen, imaginative and dependable food, and fair prices make this River Oaks favorite a touchstone among Houston's many fine affordable restaurants. This place fills by 7 PM, so arrive early or prepare to enjoy the scenery for a while. It's a pleasant wait if you like watching good-looking people watching each other. The bawdy murals of large fish suggest that seafood might be quite a catch. So try seafood cheesecake, maybe the richest appetizer in town, and worth every calorie, or smooth, silky shrimp bisque. Soft-shell crabs and fillet of red snapper are excellent entrées. The creative kitchen also excels with grilled meats and pastas. As a Vallone establishment, La Griglia, pronounced *gril-ya*, draws a snappy casual crowd. *2002 W. Gray, River Oaks, 713/526–4700. AE, D, DC, MC, V. $$*

12 *f-6*
LA MORA CUCINA TOSCANA
In the heart of the Montrose district, with all manner of strangeness surrounding it, sits La Mora, a gem of a restaurant. Before you're even seated you will have choices to make: seating in the snug, romantic front room, or back in the sometimes noisy atrium with its soaring, glass-topped roof. The menu offers much more difficult choices, though. For starters, try the smoked mozzarella with sweet peppers and garlic-and-herb-sautéed mushrooms or the hearty pasta and bean soup. You can't go wrong with a main course of rotisserie-roasted pork loin with sage, garlic, and rosemary pancetta or veal scaloppini in lemon butter sauce. *912 Lovett, Montrose, 713/522–7412. AE, D, DC, MC, V. $$*

12 *h-6*
LA STRADA
The funkier Westheimer location is a place for seeing and being seen, as much as for eating—especially at Sunday brunch, when young Houstonians strut their stuff. The food is far from secondary, however, and includes a wide array of interesting pasta dishes to go along with stellar bellinis (champagne with peach nectar). Seafood also fares well in these kitchens, and the desserts beg to be shared. The outside-the-Loop La Strada on San Felipe comes off the slicker of the two, if no quieter. Visit La Strada to combine food and fun, not to read while you dine alone. *322 Westheimer, Montrose, 713/523–1014. AE, D, DC, MC, V. $$*

7 *a-8*
5161 San Felipe, Galleria/Post Oak, 713/850–9999.

13 *c-3*
MIA BELLA TRATTORIA
Set in a charming old building downtown, executive chef–owner Youssef Nafaa's fare of contemporary Italian sometimes takes on a Mediterranean influence. A business lunch favorite is the *insalata di rossini de pollo* (grilled chicken, basil, sun-dried tomatoes, and pasta salad atop field greens). Evening guests (Tuesday dinners are "all candlelit") usually prefer the rainbow trout with its vegetable sauté. *320 Main St., Downtown, 713/237–0505. AE, DC, D, MC, V. $$–$$$*

12 *f-4*
NINO'S
This granddaddy of Houston restaurants was one of the first to bring fine, reasonably priced Italian cooking to the city. In its heyday, a 90-minute wait was acceptable for the "down-home Italian" delicacies like focaccia, calamari, and risotto. Now, thankfully, crowds are much more manageable and waits are minimal. Still, Nino's appetizers and entrées can go head on with tonier places in town. Owner Vincent Mandola keeps updating the menu but retains the classics that put him on the map. Start with *antipasto misto* (marinated and roasted vegetables), then enjoy wood-fired rotisserie lemon-garlic chicken with mashed potatoes for inspired comfort food. Pasta and veal lovers may have tough decisions, but guaranteed satisfaction. Next door are Vincent's, a more casual

spillover spot, and Grappino's, a wine and cigar bar with snacks. Think of it as Mandola's Montrose-area food and spirits court. *2817 W. Dallas, Montrose, 713/522–5120. AE, D, DC, MC, V. Closed Sun. No lunch Sat. $$*

13 c-3
OSTERIA D'ALDO
In the burgeoning Downtown, Aldo offers this cozy wine cellar–like dining room and a menu that takes tapas in an Italian direction. The lovely three-story white building has architectural touches like a green spire on the roof and a corner entrance that opens into a dark, cool, and candlelit venue. A policeman was witnessed using his flashlight to see his plate. The food, though, is far from dim. All items are less than $10, but you will need at least two items to make a meal. Lighter appetites will appreciate the tidbit portions, and all will appreciate the deft hand in the kitchen. A sampling of the menu includes fried artichoke hearts, red-pepper soup with cheese crostini, snapper with salsa *verde* (green), and beef tenderloin meatball (baseball-sized) over red peppers. *301 Main St., Downtown, 713/224–2536. AE, D, DC, MC, V. Closed Sun. No lunch Sat. $$*

10 d-3
PREGO
At this surefire spot for Italian food with flair, meals are consistently soul-satisfying—reason enough for the lunch crowds. The Rice Village location is convenient, and with the spiffy interior as backdrop, the imaginative fare really shines. Salads are fine; entrées are super. The grilled Portobello mushroom salad and a good bread basket start you off well. Add rich, spicy poblano-and-red-pepper soup, and you have a good meal indeed. The rotisserie turns out attractive meat dishes like mustard-crusted lamb chops. The pasta is also enticing, from the jalapeño fettuccine with grilled chicken, black beans, tomato, and cilantro to sophisticated ravioli with veal, cremini mushrooms, and dried apples in Marsala wine sauce. For a simpler meal, try the grilled-chicken pizza. Efficient service lets diners relax . Prego just gets better each visit. *2520 Amherst, at Kirby Dr., Rice University Village, 713/529–2420. Reservations essential. AE, MC, V. $$–$$$*

9 h-1
SIMPOSIO
On the menu, the owner promises an authentic Italian celebration. The kitchen and staff deliver. With the first morsel, appetizers will win you over. Simple antipasti of grilled scallops with baby lettuces will make you wonder why scallops don't taste this tender and luscious everywhere. Carpaccio with wild mushrooms, shaved Parmesan, and mixed greens is another fine starter. Chef Alberto Baffoni will prepare most anything on request, but who needs anything more special than rich, stewlike osso buco; creamy risotto generously mingled with salmon and asparagus; or roast duckling in pineapple-flavored reduction. The faux terra-cotta walls and comfortable banquettes are as welcoming as the hostess and waiter. On a Richmond corner that seemed to have a Velcro sign (for the many tried-but-failed operations), this lauded dining room has firm staying power. *5591 Richmond Ave., Richmond Strip, 713/532–0550. Reservations essential. AE, D, MC, V. No lunch Sat.–Sun. $$*

12 e-2
STAR PIZZA II
Tucked into the trail end of Heights Boulevard, Star Pizza II is a going concern for lunch and dinner. The small parking lot often has as many cars waiting for take-out as for eat-in customers. It's funky inside, with worn furnishings, low ceilings, and a heavily tattooed server or two. But you'll likely have a good time with the crowd ranging from young to old. Lunch buffet offers a salad bar and hot slices. At all hours you can have very fine pizza available in both New York and Chicago styles. *140 S. Heights Blvd., Heights 713/869–1241. Reservations not accepted. AE, D, MC, V. $*

6 f-5
UGO'S ITALIAN GRILL
Bravissimo! for this little treasure offering terrific Italian food, reasonable prices, and warm hospitality. High praises go to the comfortable atmosphere as well as laudable classics and touches of innovation. Happy customers return often for memorable lasagna with homemade pasta, zesty sausage, and Bolognese sauce. A house specialty is porcini-stuffed ravioli tossed with olive oil, garlic, basil, julienne vegetables, and sun-dried tomatoes sprin-

kled with feta cheese. Kids and adults love the pizzas and the bread, with marinara dipping sauce on request. Ugo's enjoys a high volume of regulars, for good reason. *8800 Katy Fwy., Memorial/Spring Branch, 713/365–0101. AE, D, DC, MC, V. $–$$*

10 *c-1*
3879 Southwest Fwy., West University Place, 713/572–3100.

JAPANESE

9 *a-1*
CAFE JAPON
Houstonians choose this pleasant, unpretentious place partially because of the extensive selections, readable menus, and comfortable settings. Appetizers are especially fine. Diners who venture beyond standard tempura are rewarded with *ika teriyaki* (grilled squid), vegetable *udon* (noodle soup), crab and shrimp spring rolls, or *hamachi kama* (yellowtail). For true sushi lovers, this place may be a bit too Americanized—sushi is precut and served on plates, silverware is supplied in lieu of chopsticks, and service is brisk. *11312 Westheimer, Katy, 281/531–9100. AE, D, DC, MC, V. $$*

9 *c-1*
KANEYAMA JAPANESE RESTAURANT
The sushi is always fresh, the service is unfailingly gracious, and the warm, airy feel of the dining room suits the Japanese menu. Families celebrate in the tatami rooms, couples opt for the bar, and singles chat easily with the chefs at the sushi counter. Enjoy skewers of chicken *yakitori* (small pieces of grilled then skewered chicken) broiled in a sweet, spicy sauce, or delicately fried shrimp tempura. Sample a few items off the extensive sushi menu of raw, grilled, smoked, and cooked seafood selections, traditional and exotic. After a bowl of heart-warming and heart-healthy miso soup, you'll agree this is soul food, Japanese-style. *9527 Westheimer, Memorial/Spring Branch, 713/784–5168. AE, D, DC, MC, V. $$*

12 *b-8*
MIYAKO
Pretty, pleasant Miyako pleases novices and veterans alike. The brave vets sidle up to the bar to devour expertly prepared sushi and *sashimi* (sliced raw fish served with condiments). The bar attracts friendly singles and duos alike. For those not-yet indoctrinated in raw fish, bento boxes are the training wheels version of Japanese fare: included is miso soup, salad, cooled meat with teriyaki sauce, tempura vegetables, and fried rice. Rolls and hand rolls come in various combinations of fish and seasonings or you can create your own version. Miyako regularly has crunchy giant clam, not often found elsewhere. Plenty of very good beef, chicken, and seafood appetizers and entrées please the sushi-wary diner. The Kirby location is open and airy; the Westheimer location, the granddaddy, is smaller with light and dark woods. All locations provide gracious service for groups and individuals. *3910 Kirby Dr., at Hwy. 59, Glenway Plaza, 713/520–9797. Reservations not accepted. AE, DC, MC, V. $$*

9 *g-1*
6345 Westheimer, at Hillcroft, Galleria/Post Oak, 713/781–6300.

9 *a-1*
NARA
In this small, serene, stylishly spare setting, knowledgeable young staffers advise you on the best sushi and the perfect sake (warm or chilled). Chef Donald Chang excels at Japanese fusion cuisine, blending East and West in such novel creations as tacos filled with tempura fried shrimp accented with miso-tinged guacamole. He spices up scallops with a sauté of jalapeños, onions, and garlic, then walks on the mild side with broiled salmon in brown ginger sauce. Miso soup and vegetable tempura come with entrées. Good sushi selections are presided over by a cordial, helpful sushi chef. Try the *maki rolls* (sushi rolls), like the rock n' roll version consisting of tempura shrimp, smelt roe, and cucumber, or the fine *tonka roll* (spicy yellowtail, salmon, and avocado). An extensive selection of sake is a smooth finish and worth the trip out to Westheimer. *11124 Westheimer, at Wilcrest, 713/266–2255. AE, D, DC, MC, V. Closed Sun. $$*

13 *b-2*
SAKE LOUNGE
In a dramatic corner setting that provides sweeping views, Sake Lounge is a great place for dinner before taking in a movie at the adjacent Angelika Theater

or for a drink afterward. Quite the buzz when it opened with Bayou Center in 1998, it's having to compete with more downtown openings these days. Its sushi is impeccably fresh; enjoy some at your table or at the bar—with sake, of course. Sashimi, tempura, and noodle dishes also rate a mention; but Western palates can find equal satisfaction in more familiar meat, seafood, and salad offerings. Note the good wine and beer variety. Sake's decor and fusion cuisine will transport you at least as far as California, if not all the way to Japan. *550 Texas Ave., Downtown, 713/228–7253. Reservations not accepted. AE, D, DC, MC, V. $$*

KOREAN

6 *d-4*

KOREA GARDEN

In this ethnically rich north Spring Branch area, where a taqueria is next door to an Oriental supermarket, Korea Garden provides a second home for Koreans and a pleasant change of pace for all food lovers. Helpful servers take fine care of the clientele, especially novices. Intimate booths feature built-in grills for cook-your-own dishes. The item of choice is classic Korean *bulgogi* (paper-thin, marinated beef, pork, chicken, and squid). While you chat, leisurely grill the meat to your liking, then wrap it in fresh ruffly lettuce and dress it in an array of condiments, like Chinese radish, spicy zucchini, seaweed, mushrooms, salty soybean paste, and pickled cucumbers. The results are grand with each distinct bite. Go with a group to share the cooking, eating, and fun. *9501 Longpoint, West, 713/468–2800. AE, D, DC, MC, V. No smoking. $*

LATIN

7 *a-8*

AMERICAS

Whether you come to savor the intriguing Pan-American menu or to ogle the fanciful decor, you can't go wrong. Waitstaff happily give a visual tour of the architecture showcasing mosaic tile trees and wacky lighting fixtures. Sample the tapas in the quarry-style bar downstairs or sweep loftward for a table surveying a delightful eyeful. Addictive, complimentary, crisp-fried plantains with *chimichurri* (pesto-like) sauce start off the meal, and since entrées come with a plateful of seasonal vegetables, go easy on the appetizers. Black bean soup and roasted-corn mousse rolled in smoked Chilean salmon are satisfying starters. Succumb to choice beef with the popular *churrasco* tenderloin, butterflied and basted in chimichurri sauce. Forego any virtue remaining by overindulging in luscious *tres leches* cake (yellow cake soaked in three milks, topped with meringue), a benchmark version of that delicacy. *1800 Post Oak Blvd., between San Felipe and Westheimer, Galleria/Post Oak, 713/961–1492. Reservations essential. AE, D, DC, MC, V. Closed Sun. $$$–$$$$*

9 *c-1*

CHURRASCOS

The house is always packed at these South American hot spots (Churrascos and America's [*see above*] have the same ownership), which are favorites for entertaining and family outings. Amid the beams and stucco walls, you will feel like guests in the dining room of a busy hacienda. If service is sometimes sketchy, gratis plantain chips and tender entrées are well-nigh perfect. Surrender to the Churrascos-practiced Latin way with beef—savory, signature tenderloin—or pork, sautéed with lime, roasted peppers, and scallions. Allow yourself to be lured by seafood—yucca-crusted butterfly shrimp with jalapeño tartar sauce or grilled salmon over avocado-pepper cream sauce, just to name a few. Or dine sensibly, but bountifully, on the renowned grilled vegetable platter. Churrascos's guests do not leave without dessert, where bread pudding all but soars and tres leches cake sets the standard. The Cordua family brought South American cuisine to Houston, and the citizens are ever grateful. *9705 Westheimer, Montrose, 713/952–1988. Reservations essential. AE, D, DC, MC, V. Closed Sun. $$–$$$*

12 *e-6*

2055 Westheimer, Upper Kirby District, 713/527–8300.

13 *c-3*

RUGGLES BISTRO LATINO

Well-respected restaurateurs Bruce and Susan Molzan have staked out their claim for a share of the exploding downtown scene with this Latin-flavored bistro. Clever potato-wrapped crab quesadillas, as well as oyster nachos with habañero mayonnaise display a successful merging of Pan-American tastes. Beef tenderloin with chimichurri sauce, optionally enhanced with crab, tops their entrée menu, but specials like simply grilled pompano may tickle your fancy instead. Without doubt, the tropical rum drinks will leave you smiling, as will larger-than-life desserts. The generous dining room, attractively finished to resemble a cantina, suffers from low lighting at night. *711 Main St., Downtown, 713/227–9141. Reservations essential. AE, D, DC, MC, V. Closed Sat.–Sun. $$–$$$*

10 *e-3*
SABROSO GRILL
Sabroso, meaning delicious, aptly describes the food at this South American venue. The colorful interior makes for festive dining, and the front patio extends a great vantage point for Village people-watching. The Grill offers good Latino dishes: crisp plantains with creamy cilantro dipping sauce; rich, cheesy, grilled shrimp quesadillas; plump veggie burritos; and spicy fish tacos loaded with greens. Spectacular nachos—fried plantain chips, onion, tomato, corn—are unlike any version you've had before. Service here is relaxed, so don't come in a hurry. Lively taped music adds to the hassle-free environment. *5510 Morningside, Rice University Village, 713/942–9900. AE, D, DC, MC, V. $*

BEST PATIOS

Houstonians will often brave the heat to sit at any one of these delightful patios:

Beck's Prime (American Casual)
The Augusta Street location has a canopy of trees that provide plenty of shade for burger-hungry patrons.

Black Labrador Pub (British)
An oversize chessboard set in a patio surrounded by ivy-covered walls is reason enough to enjoy a pint outside.

Blue Agave (Tex-Mex)
Margaritas are best enjoyed on either of the two covered patios. Although most patios are equipped with lawn furniture, Blue Agave has substantial tables and chairs that allow for finer outside dining.

Café Noche (Mexican)
The artistic masses in the Montrose area pack the outdoor seating for Sunday brunch.

MEXICAN

7 *e-8*
BERRYHILL HOT TAMALES
It's too citified to be a taquería, but Berryhill can dish out some *muy buena comida* (very good meals). Although tamales are the title dish and very good in their own right, especially the spinach and chicken verde (with green sauce), the real treat here are Baja tacos with spicy grilled catfish, loaded with greens and tomatoes, wrapped in soft corn tortillas. Also worth a taste are chicken enchiladas verde, impressive for the slow, savory burn. Amenities include fresh salsas, great prices, and a bare-bones atmosphere. *2639 Revere, at Westheimer, River Oaks, 713/526–8080. Reservations not accepted. AE, D, MC, V. $*

7 *a-8*
1717 Post Oak Blvd., Galleria/Post Oak, 713/871–8226.

12 *f-5*
CAFÉ NOCHE
Plenty of outdoor dining is the main draw here, but primo Mexican cuisine keeps crowds coming back for more. Groups vie for a coveted patio table. Steering clear of the cliché cantina look, the interior is nicely uncluttered with dramatic paintings and sculptures by local artists. The menu presents Tex-Mex favorites and authentic regional options. In particular, ceviche (big chunks of salmon, snapper, and shrimp in a zesty marinade) gets high marks. Traditionalists launch into the tamale plate with fat pork tamales in verde sauce or the substantial nachos. Adventurers will love *pork mojo* (tender medallions sautéed in creamy garlic sauce) or *chile en nogada* (lightly fried poblano chile stuffed with chicken, beef, pork, apples, and currants). Sunday brunch is a $12 bargain with made-to-order omelets and buffet selections of spicy links, eggs, ceviche, and taco makings, not to mention waffles and desserts. One peculiarity here is the mandatory 18% tip for weekend reservations. *2409 Montrose Blvd., between Westheimer and Fairview, Montrose, 713/529–2409. AE, DC, MC, V. $$*

10 *f-2*
EL PUEBLITO CAFÉ
Alto! This colorful café looks like countless other Mexican restaurants, but the food will stop you in your tracks. El

Pueblito's slogan, "Rica Comida," means rich food, but this kitchen proves you *can* get your Tex-Mex fix without mounds of cheese and greasy chips. The first treats are the table salsas—one fresh-made tomato version, the other a novel fruit salsa of pineapples, garlic, and peppers. Standouts on the menu include vivid quesadillas *vegetariana* (starring sautéed spinach and mushrooms) and tacos *marinos* (with grilled snapper and that pineapple salsa). The homemade tortillas and side rice and beans are *muy deliciosas* (very delicious), also. Servers are notably friendly, and the atmosphere is like a fiesta. The wagon wheel porch might seem hokey at first, but since you found love at first bite, it grows on you. *1423 Richmond Ave., Montrose, 713/520–6635. AE, D, MC, V. No smoking. $*

10 d-1
EL TIEMPO
The hacienda exterior and packed parking lot conjure kitschy expectations. But with good food, good drink, and good fun, it's not the same ol' enchilada. The name means "the time," so expect a good one at this boisterous place from the Laurenzo family—children of maven Mama Ninfa. The family photos remind you of the family that first brought tacos *al carbon*, precursors to fajitas, to Houston. The patio, complete with waterfall, is pretty, and the dining room is rustic, cantina-style. Fajitas are of every delicious sort imaginable—shrimp, quail, pork ribs, even lobster. Guacamole is homemade chunky-style. Even quesadillas are a novelty with lump crabmeat and bacon. For lighter appetites one spicy snapper taco à la carte is a pleasing meal in itself. For those who love industrial strength margaritas, this version is edgy enough to raise eyebrows. Portions (and prices) are *mas grande* (very large). *3130 Richmond Ave., at Audley, between Kirby Dr. and Buffalo Speedway, Upper Kirby District, 713/807–1600. AE, D, DC, MC, V. $$*

13 d-3
IRMA'S RESTAURANT
Although the Tex-Mex and Mex-Mex food is worth a visit to this Warehouse District institution, the real lure is its hospitable owner, Irma Galvan. Don't turn down her offer of the best homemade lemonade in town—then dig into a plate of enchiladas, spicy chiles relleno, or chicken and pork tamales. An always-crowded lunch hour suggests your waiting until after 1 for quicker service. Irma herself displays color aplenty, but her whimsical decorating poses worthy competition. *22 N. Chenevert, Downtown, 713/222–0767. AE, DC, MC, V. Closed Sat.–Sun. $*

6 f-5
LAS ALAMEDAS
The grand hacienda of Las Alamedas is a landmark on the Katy Freeway. You'll quickly forget the proximity to the roadway because the vast interior with tile accents seems right out of Monterrey, and the back dining room overlooks a peaceful wooded ravine. The beautiful setting hosts wedding receptions, and the free appetizer buffet and notable margaritas at happy hour draws afterwork celebrants. The menu is upscale Mexican cuisine, and the kitchen is sometimes uneven, but generally very good. Two splendid entrées are tacos *de cochinita pibil* (chunks of pork simmered in *achiote* sauce) and *huachinango a la azteca* (red snapper stuffed with corn mushrooms in poblano sauce). Brunch lovers will want to sample the bounteous feast here. The service is smooth and friendly, and attire is business casual leaning toward dressy. *8615 Katy Fwy., Memorial/Spring Branch, 713/461–1503. Reservations essential. AE, D, DC, MC, V. $$–$$$*

13 e-3
MERIDA
Under longtime ownership of the Acosta family, this authentic Mexican kitchen dishes up typical Tex-Mex fare, including some of the best flour tortillas in town, but specializes in Yucatecan dishes. Sample a *panucho* (corn tortilla stuffed with black beans, roast pork, and marinated onions), *salbut* (open-faced tortilla piled with roast pork, onions, lettuce, and tomatoes), and empanada (deep-fried corn turnovers filled with spicy beef) to discover tastes from *far south of the border*. The outstanding Mexican breakfast features classic *menudo* (hearty tripe soup) and a variety of egg dishes from *huevos rancheros* (fried eggs and ranchero sauce over tortillas) and *chilaquiles con huevo* (crisp-fried tortillas simmered with tomato sauce, eggs, chiles, onions, and cheese) to Yucatecan *huevos a la Motulena* (crispy tostadas topped with just about

everything in the kitchen). Mexican-American families, yuppies in starched jeans, and policemen make up the usual crowd. *2509 Navigation, Neartown, 713/227–0260. Reservations not accepted. AE, D, DC, MC, V. $*

10 *c-1*
100% TAQUITO

Seen the taco trailers popping up around town? One of the trailers has moved indoors across Highway 59 from Compaq Center. Inside 100% Taquito, you still feel the outdoors with murals of Mexico City streets, facades of windows and doors, concrete floor, and a high, unfinished ceiling. Past the inventory of sodas, bottled water, and *cervezas* (beer) stacked along the wall is the tin-roofed trailer with "order" and "pick-up" windows. As the menu announces, this is not Tex-Mex but authentic Mexican tacos (smaller, with onions and cilantro, not lettuce and cheese), quesadillas (tacos with cheese, not tortilla sandwiches), and *sopes* (thick tortilla pizzas). The prevalence of Spanish speakers attests to its bona fide Mexican flavors. With tons of outdoor seating, here is a perfect lunch or pre-event spot that is very good, very cheap, and quite unique. *3245 Southwest Fwy., at Buffalo Speedway, West University Place, 713/665–2900. Reservations not accepted. AE, D, MC, V. No smoking. $*

7 *a-3*
OTILIA'S

Spring Branchers may not want this secret out, but this unpretentious converted drive-in serves great Mexican food. The old fast-food exterior belies the skilled kitchen serving "100% Mexican, no Tex-Mex." Worth the visit are tacos *potosinos* (soft corn tortillas sautéed in chile *guajillo*, rolled around white cheese and onions, snuggled next to fiery potatoes and carrots). A traditional Yucatán dish, cochinita pibil, consists of tender baked pork with red onions and green chiles. For breakfast lovers—*venga!* Choose the *huevos divorciados* (two eggs, over easy, "divorced" by beans, one topped with red sauce, the other with green sauce). Fine *chilaquiles* (scrambled eggs mixed with tortilla bits and cheese served with bacon, beans, and salsa) please many patrons. Schedule a nap after this breakfast. Service is simple and friendly. *7710 Longpoint, between Antoine and Wirt Rd., Memorial/Spring Branch,*

713/681–7203. Reservations essential. AE, D, DC, MC, V. $

9 *g-3*
PICO'S MEX-MEX

Families, couples, Bellaire area residents, and cross-town devotees come here for authentic traditional and contemporary Mexican cuisine. It seems there's always a party going on—birthdays, reunions, and even baby showers—with mariachi accompaniment. Loyalists will tell you this simple cantina, complete with Christmas lights and fountains, is the best real Mexican food in town. Who could argue when eating *camarones adobados* (poblano-stuffed, bacon-wrapped shrimp)? Others rave about the *chiles en nogada* (poblano pepper stuffed with shredded pork, raisins, almonds, covered with walnut sauce, sprinkled with pomegranates)? Some would just as soon eat breakfast here all night long, which you can. Still, many a weary mom has ended her week here with a well-deserved goldfish bowl–sized margarita. This place pleases most, if not all. *5941 Bellaire Blvd., Bellaire, 713/662–8383. Reservations not accepted. AE, D, DC, MC, V. $$*

7 *d-8*
TACO MILAGRO

Don't be fooled by the order-at-the-counter routine; this River Oaks taquería is several cuts above the ordinary Tex-Mex joint, as befits a creation of superchef Robert Del Grande, of Café Annie (*see* Southwestern, *below*) and Café Express fame (*see* Cafés, *above*). Top quality is apparent from the array of house-mixed salsas to the real lime-juice margaritas and at all points between. Expect an imaginative twist on classics: shrimp or chicken tamales with a soufflé-like masa wrap; chiles relleno stuffed with cheese, pecans, and apricot bits; enchiladas filled with barbecued pork. The colorful setting offers pleasant seating inside, at the bar, or on the palm-lined patio. *2555 Kirby Dr., at Westheimer, River Oaks, 713/522–1999. Reservations not accepted. AE, D, DC, MC, V. $*

10 *e-1*
TAQUERÍA LA TAPATIA

Don't be fooled by the facade of this popular Mexican restaurant. This restaurant has a reputation for being one of the best taquería chains in Houston. In addition to the traditional enchilada platters, try the Mexican sandwiches or the shrimp tacos. Night owls take note: they're open until 5 AM on weekends. *1749 Richmond Ave., Upper Kirby District, 713/521–3144. AE, D, MC, V. $*

9 *f-3*

6413 Hillcroft, Bellaire, 713/995–9191.

9 *h-1*

5541 Richmond, Richmond Strip, 713/787–9680.

9 *c-2*

3965 S. Gessner, Memorial/Spring Branch, 713/266–4756.

9 *g-3*
TILA'S
The much-anticipated revival of this well-loved '80s hangout is softer, cozier, and quieter than the old Montrose spot. A high ceiling, a remnant of the previous service station occupant, lends a spacious air to the comfortable setting with striking artwork on the walls. On the tables you'll find sophisticated city food. For starters, tortilla soup impresses with its chipotle pepper punch. The kitchen gets upscale with spicy pork tenderloin in basil-mint pesto, stuffed with endive and cheeses, finished with light wine demi-glace; and with salmon *borracho* (paper-thin slices of salmon marinated in tequila, with a spicy cilantro-lime sauce and capers). As for the litmus test, Tila's perfect traditional margaritas go well with salsa fresca, a bucket of tortilla triangles, and crisp plantain rounds. Maneuvering to the limited parking at the Shepherd/Allen Parkway curve is a bit tricky. *1111 S. Shepherd, River Oaks, 713/522–7654. AE, D, DC, MC, V. $$*

MIDDLE EASTERN

12 *d-8*
AL DIWAN
The menu at this restaurant offers greater variety than many Middle Eastern spots. The house hors d'oeuvres platter is likely to tantalize any group as a starter, particularly its *labneh* (yogurt cream cheese). That sauce goes equally well with a mixed-grill entrée, featuring lamb and well-seasoned homemade sausages. Don't miss the meal-sized salad with dates, nuts, and olives. Be prepared to be patient with unskilled servers. Check out the unusual selection of decent wines. A talented belly dancer

performs occasionally at dinner. *2128 Portsmouth, Montrose, 713/529–4199. AE, D, DC, MC, V. Closed Sun. $$*

9 *g-1*
CAFE LILI LEBANESE GRILL
The Bejjani family keeps customers smiling at this bright little counter operation in another Westheimer strip center. Decor is your basic vinyl, but who cares when the Lebanese food is fine, prices are harmless, and proprietors are so darn friendly. Besides, who wouldn't be happy with an order of *moujadara* (lentils and rice topped with caramelized onions) or smoky, satisfying *baba ghannouj* (baked eggplant and sesame dip)? Most dishes are well seasoned—witness the tabbouleh (cracked wheat and parsley salad) and the grilled kabob combo consisting of chicken breast, beef tenderloin, and beef sausage. Cooking the old country way, a familial atmosphere, and no-frills setting have earned a faithful following. *5757 Westheimer, Suite 112, Galleria, 713/952–6969. AE, D, DC, MC, V. Closed Sun. $*

14 *c-3*
DIMASSI'S MEDITERRANEAN CAFÉ
Graceful arches and deep hues complement what may be the most colorful display of food on a cafeteria line in town. Although it is a cafeteria, the atmosphere is peaceful and unrushed. The eclectic mix of Rice students, business duos, and West U. ladies-who-lunch selects from dozens of sides, salads, and entrées on the colorful line. You can combine tabbouleh, *fattosh* (toasted bread salad), hummus, baba ghannouj, and *tahini* (oily paste made from ground sesame seeds) in the sampler platter. For about $8, the luncheon vegetarian sampler provides good value and numerous choices. *2401 Times Blvd., Suite A, West University, 713/978–7770. Reservations not accepted. AE, D, DC, MC, V. No smoking. $*

10 *a-1*

5064 Richmond, Upper Kirby District, 713/439–7481.

PERSIAN

9 *f-1*
GARSON RESTAURANT
Devotees of Middle Eastern cuisine savor Persian delights in this attractive,

contemporary setting. Things get off to a good start with complimentary pita, feta cheese, and crunchy vegetables; and the stews and grilled meats typical of Persian cuisine that follow live up to expectations. A skewered combination of beef and chicken, served with grilled tomatoes, onion, and peppers, pleases many tastes, as do grilled quail, well-prepared lamb chops, and a thick stew made of beef and eggplant. For an exotic ending, sample the rich Persian ice cream or sip hot mint tea. *2926 Hillcroft, Southwest, 713/781–0400. Reservations essential. AE, D, MC, V. $$*

PERUVIAN

9 *f-3*

SUPER RICO

For a warm introduction to the fusion of cultures in Peru, try this small diner in a multicultural strip center off the Southwest Freeway. In meager surroundings, you will find a "super rich" menu of wonderfully varied Peruvian seafood, chicken, beef, and soups. A specialty, *ceviche mixto* (snapper, shrimp, calamari, and octopus) is citrusy and piquant and should not be missed. *Chupe de camarones*, a traditional chowderlike soup, brims with shrimp and rice. Also recommended is *picante de marisco* (a creamy, peppery seafood stew served with rice). The owner treats all like honored guests, so expect a leisurely, memorable meal. *6121 Hillcroft, Sharpstown, 713/271–3056. AE, D, MC, V. Closed Mon. $*

SEAFOOD

4 *d-5*

DENIS' SEAFOOD HOUSE

Once an easy-in, easy-out West-sider's favorite, Denis' reels in a packed house on weekends—and for good reason. Denis does seafood Cajun-creole–style with the freshest fish available. A wall-sized chalkboard broadcasts what is available, and you can expect your Gulf Coast regulars as well as numerous imports. Snapper, salmon, catfish, trout, mahimahi, or fresh catch-of-the-day are prepared as you like with your favorite toppings, such as Pontchartrain (shrimp, scallops, crawfish, and mushrooms in wine roux) or Courtboullion (shrimp, crawfish, and oysters in tomato roux). Appetizers are easier on

the wallet and offer a terrific sampling of the kitchen's talents. Like any good Cajun joint, the beers are ice cold and party drinks are abundant. One complaint: there's not much waiting area for the overflowing crowd. *12109 Westheimer, West, 281/497–1110. Reservations not accepted. AE, D, DC, MC, V. $$*

10 *d-1*

GOODE COMPANY SEAFOOD

On the abandoned tracks on Westpark, this old railroad car packs in the passengers. The draw? Tasty, plentiful, and cheap seafood. For starters, *campechana de mariscos* (shrimp, crab, and avocado with spicy red sauce) served in a soda fountain glass with tortilla chips is a standout. Impeccably cooked entrées include mesquite-grilled flounder, smoky shrimp verde, and trout amandine. Po' boys are sandwiches loaded with tender, corn-battered or grilled shrimp, catfish, oysters, or a combo of two. Entrées are usually large enough to save for lunch the next day or to split in two (for a small fee). Don't let the wait discourage you; it's worth it. *2621 Westpark, at Kirby Dr., West University Place, 713/523–7154. Reservations not accepted. AE, D, DC, MC, V. $–$$*

9 *f-1*

KING FISH MARKET

Along the Richmond strip outside the Loop, you'll find plenty of places ready to tempt you inside with promises they can't keep. King Fish Market promises fresh seafood, prepared well, and delivers. Crab bisque is pleasingly rich without the heaviness that's often a trait of this soup. Grilled snapper "on the half shell" is simple and fine—just-done meat sizzling in half its skin. For the palate seeking more complexity, try sesame-seared Hawaiian *onaga* (red snapper). The roasted garlic-ginger sauce makes its presence known without stealing the show, and the bacon-wrapped sea scallops and crispy lobster spring roll are fine side companions. *6356 Richmond Ave., Galleria/Post Oak, 713/974–3474. Reservations essential. AE, DC, D, MC, V. $$–$$$*

5 *a-4*

MCCORMICK & SCHMICK'S

This prestigious seafood chain recently dropped anchor in tony new Uptown Park, just north of the Galleria. An immediate success, McC & S relies on the freshest of seafood—more than 30 varieties daily—flown in from around the globe, but primarily from the Pacific Northwest. More than 12 kinds of pristine oysters are available each day, their taste and safety worth every dollar of the hefty price tag. Houstonians are quickly adding Oregon petrale sole, Columbia River sturgeon, Alaskan king salmon, and Hawaiian onaga to their lists of favorite fish; deservedly, steamed Dungeness crab may soon knock lobster from its pedestal. An imaginative array of wines, beers, and scotches completes the menu. McC & S's handsome mahogany-lined interior "talks Texan" from framed memorabilia to stained-glass armadillo sconces. Reservations or not, expect a wait most nights. *1151 Uptown Park Blvd., at West Loop, Galleria/Post Oak, 713/840–7900. AE, D, DC, MC, V. $$$*

9 *a-1*

THE SEAFOOD SHOPPE

Some like it hot and some like it fresh. The Seafood Shoppe likes it both ways. The dining room and staff are hospitable enough, but it's the Cajun-style menu with fair prices that converts customers to fans. True to Bayou flavors, most items are low-grade spicy, like the savory shrimp creole (with a side of awesome green beans). Most servings are bountiful. Don't miss the sweet potato fries or the fresh-squeezed cherry lemonade. *10555-B Westheimer, Katy, 713/978–5055. AE, D, DC, MC, V. $$*

SOUTHWESTERN

7 *a-8*

CAFÉ ANNIE

This star in Houston's constellation of award-winning restaurants outshines all thanks to celebrity chef Robert Del Grande. Beautiful people sweep through the dining room—a subdued setting with subtle Texas touches and dramatic florals that rival the beautiful food presentations. The new Southwestern inventions approach brilliance with a bit of ancho chile jam in mussel soup; diced up salmon with pickled red onions; fillet of beef roasted with coffee beans. Very high expectations are invariably met. Understated elegance, undeniable hospitality, uptown prices, and fine food make Annie a popular choice for a special night out. One complaint—and it is a rare one—the kitchen may be a bit too

fast for indulging in this repast. *1728 Post Oak Blvd., Galleria, 713/840–1111. Reservations essential. AE, D, DC, MC, V. No smoking. Closed Sun. No lunch Sat. $$$$*

12 *d-4*

MESA GRILL

Decorated attractively in Santa Fe–style, Mesa features food that reflects New Mexico as clearly as it does Mexico. The complimentary sweet potato chips, served with both a typical salsa and an outstanding smoky-flavored one, may fill you before you can sample the trendy enchiladas or adobe pie casserole. Sunday brunch buffet is a good opportunity to get a fix on their Southwestern combinations, and, if the weather is good, the patio tables provide one of the city's most pleasant al fresco settings. *1971 W. Gray, River Oaks, 713/520–8900. AE, D, DC, MC, V. $$*

10 *e-2*

RAVEN GRILL

Raven is a favorite of the neighborhood with its outdoor patio and somewhat interesting wine list. Dishes range from enchiladas to grilled cheese sandwiches to grilled vegetables. Although the food is thought to have a slight blandness to it, this is still a pleasant, reliable place to bring the entire family. *1916 Bissonnet, Museum District, 713/521–2027. AE, MC, V. $–$$*

4 *e-5*

RIO RANCH

Mosey out west for cowboy cuisine in a Hill Country ranch house. This rambling sister outpost to Café Annie offers relaxed dining in a Texas setting. Steaks come wood-grilled, smoky, and tender as you please. Chicken boasts campfire flavor, with andouille sausage and crawfish to boot. Knife-and-fork burgers and chile-crusted quail share the menu with city-slicker-pleasing salads and grilled red snapper. Rio Ranch serves a laudable ranch-style brunch as well. The inexpensive buffet features border-style breakfast plus all your favorites: waffles, omelets, meats, and sweets. Most appealing, the Ranch has the perfect front porch on which to sip smooth margaritas next to the pretty man-made Rio. *9999 Westheimer, Southwest, 713/952–5000. AE, D, DC, MC, V. $$*

12 f-6
RUGGLES GRILL

Why do crowds repeatedly return to Ruggles' loud, packed dining room? For the food! The wait at this bustling Montrose institution, even with reservations, is notorious. The New Southwestern menu compensates with wild mushroom soup with thyme and barbecued chicken quesadillas that are worth waiting for. Entrées are platter-sized wonders surrounded by seasonal vegetables. Try the seared snapper with shrimp and avocado, or the pecan-crusted salmon fillet with crab, corn, and horseradish sauce. The vegetable platter is always inspired with selections like wild rice with raisins and puréed butternut squash. Escape the customary boisterous crowd by lunching or brunching in this old, sun-filled house. Brunch dishes range from full entrées to egg dishes served with gratis rolls and muffins. *903 Westheimer, at Montrose, Montrose, 713/524–3839. Reservations essential. AE, MC, V. Closed Mon. $$*

12 g-8
SIERRA GRILL

Competent servers will pamper you through a memorable meal in this handsome Southwestern venue. Reminiscent of Taos, New Mexico, the dining room and the dishes combine influences from Southwest and Native American cuisine with Texas twists. Renowned chef and owner Charlie Watkins creates a changing, but always innovative and remarkable, menu. Interesting and tasty starters like blue-cornmeal oysters, bisque of sweet corn, and smoke-roasted salmon will have you wishing for more. Touted for wondrous seafood, the kitchen also turns out noteworthy meats such as pork chops with jalapeño mint and grilled chicken with goat cheese and chipotle sauce. Finally, sides like sweet potato tamale sometimes steal the show. Although the dishes are complex, the atmosphere is warm and casual. *4704 Montrose, Museum District, 713/942–7757. Reservations essential. AE, D, MC, V. No lunch. $$–$$$*

13 c-2
TRAVIS CAFÉ

Tucked into one of the best restored buildings in old Downtown, tiny Travis Café was named the "best Downtown restaurant" by one Houston publication in 1999. With limestone walls, pine floors, and an iron roof–covered sidewalk, the decor conjures up visions of the Texas Hill Country, but the food offers a far more cosmopolitan mix. Appetizers of pot stickers filled with smoked trout and black beans, a dip livened with bacon and fire-roasted onions, or a quesadilla enfolding cheeses, sweet peppers, corn, and black beans may be enough to satisfy you. However, you might want to save room for one of the irresistible entrées—a hefty roast beef sandwich, Southwest Caesar wrap stuffed with grilled chicken, or lively el Diablo pasta. This charming Nodo addition is convenient for lunch and postperformance dining. *208 Travis, between Congress and Franklin, Downtown, 713/223–4073. Reservations not accepted. AE, D, MC, V. $$*

SPANISH

14 c-3
MI LUNA

Spanish is "in," and Mi Luna was one of the first to capitalize on the trend when it opened in Rice Village in 1998. Hot and cold tapas dominate the menu, which suits the restless, always-dieting young crowd. They are served family-style, so your group can share and order more as you choose. Mussels steamed in wine and garlic, shrimp in olive oil, and various other meats and vegetables, often accompanied by *manchego* (hard sheep's milk cheese), roasted peppers, and olives, are some of the selections. Give the slightly sweet Moroccan *bistilla* (filo-pastry dish) a try. All that variety washes down easily with good, yet inexpensive, Spanish red wine or sangria. *2441 University Blvd., Rice University Village, 713/520–5025. AE, D, DC, MC, V. $–$$*

13 c-3
SOLERO

Once a lone ranger in the now-hip Downtown nightlife, Solero is a traditional tapas restaurant decorated in modern funk. Comfortably seated in an upholstered booth, you may dither a bit over choices. Accept the menu's invitation to nibble until you can nibble no more. Among the assorted snacks are piquant roasted-red-pepper soup with bits of corn and tortillas; sliced manchego cheese with tart apple slices; pan-fried snapper cakes; spicy grilled chorizo with mozzarella and garlic-seasoned potatoes. The tapas concept works well for lunch and pre- or postperformance dining, or for a swanky night that's easy on the belt and the budget. A well-heeled, under 40 crowd is particularly drawn to this lovingly restored 1882 building with fashionably high ceilings. *910 Prairie, Downtown, 713/227–2665. Reservations not accepted. AE, D, MC, V. Closed Sun. $$*

13 *c-2*
TASCA KITCHEN AND WINE BAR
The verdict is in for this chic tapas restaurant and wine bar: it's one of Downtown's best diners. Menu, bar, patrons—everything is cool and clever at Tasca. Start with the "Boat," a long silver platter of six chef's appetizer choices. Then order more as the spirit moves you. Try salmon carpaccio, chorizo with flaming brandy Torres, or goat cheese dumpling with *sambal* (mixture of brown sugar, chiles, and salt) chile oil. The pleasant, but noisy, setting of exposed wood beams, old brick walls, and booths is appropriate for the jazz music in the background and the long, appealing bar. This is a good spot for pre- or postperformance light meals, and if you stick with the tapas menu, you dine well for fewer bucks. *908 Congress, Downtown, 713/225–9100. AE, D, MC, V. Closed Sun. No lunch Sat. $$*

STEAK

3 *c-6*
C&H STEAK COMPANY
Residents in the southwest suburbs, headed toward Sugar Land, can thank their lucky stars and the Pappas bunch, Chris and Harris, for an impressive dining outpost. The out-of-Africa motif, exuberant service, and fine fare impart a sophisticated air. Although the staff is dressed to the nines, diners have the choice of following suit or not. Portions are overwhelming—pure Pappas—and so is the quality and taste. The menu is typical steak house fare with excellent sides and enough alternatives, such as veal, salmon, and crab cakes, to please non-beef eaters. The tempting dessert menu includes an extensive list of cognacs and cigars. *12000 Southwest Fwy., Meadows Place, 281/277–9292. AE, MC, V. $$–$$$$*

9 *h-1*
CAPITAL GRILLE
Make no mistake: That's "capital" as in "capitalism," as you'll quickly note from the well-heeled crowd flocking to this steak house, part of a national chain that originated in Providence. Tailored to a Texas clientele and designed to look like an old-money club, Capital Grill features large portraits of heroes, from Houston's Jesse Jones to France's Napoléon. The starred prime beef stands imperiously on its own merit, but rises to culinary heights grilled au poivre and served with cognac sauce. The lobster-and-crab cakes, generous side dishes, fine wine list, and smooth-as-silk martinis also bear mentioning, as does the skilled waitstaff. *5365 Westheimer, at Yorktown, Galleria/Post Oak, 713/623–4600. Reservations essential. AE, D, DC, MC, V. $$$*

9 *g-1*
PAPPAS BROS. STEAKHOUSE
"Prime" is the operative word at this popular steak house—prime beef, a prime setting, and a clientele primed for coddling, conversation, and cholesterol. The Steakhouse, poshest of the Pappas's restaurant dynasty, gains a clubby look from dark wood, cushy booths, and phones at the tables. A room is reserved for aficionados of cigars and strong drinks, and the brothers' smoother-than-silk martini may be the best appetizer in town (starters are superb, but superfluous because entrées and sides are gargantuan). Thumbs up to a tomato-and-mozzarella salad (big enough to share) and to fork-tender New York strip steak with peppercorn sauce. Creamy mashed potatoes and giant fried onion rings provide delicious accompaniments to fillets, cooked to medium-rare perfection. Broiled salmon with shrimp and crab are pure delights. Expect a wait, even with reservations, and coat-and-tie is preferred. *5839 Westheimer, at Bering, Galleria/Post Oak, 713/780–7352. Reservations essential. AE, MC, V. $$$–$$$$*

2 *d-3*
RESA'S PRIME STEAKHOUSE AND PIANO BAR
Refreshingly refined, yet relaxed, this Champions-area institution still lures fans out—way out. The decor is straight out of the '70s—from a dimly lighted interior to the cigarette machine by the entrance—but the kitchen turns out

some of the best steaks and seafood in the 'burbs. Starters include wedge of iceberg lettuce with ranch dressing and shrimp cocktail with rémoulade. Fillets and New York strips are juicy, well-marbled, and cut-with-a-fork tender. Seafood specials like halibut with shrimp-and-crabmeat stuffing are delicious. A lovely piano bar and a charming owner, Resa Kelly, add pleasant touches. One oddity—no-smoking seating is by request only. *14641 Gladebrook Dr., at Farm Road 1960, Champions, 281/893–3339. Reservations essential. AE, DC, MC, V. $$$*

7 b-8
SULLIVAN'S STEAKHOUSE

Part of a small chain that forged its initial link in Austin, Sullivan's quickly became a strong contender in Houston's "sweepsteaks," catering to significant meat-eaters willing to pay well for aged Angus beef, high-quality side dishes, and bottles of vintage red. Filet mignon and prime rib vie for best-of-house, with the bone-in KC strip another favorite. Be sure to request the superb horseradish sauce with the slab of rib. Mashed potatoes, crunchy with more of that horseradish, creamy spinach, broiled mushrooms, and broccoli with hollandaise fill out the sides list, but you may already have "filled out" with the complimentary iceberg salad, drizzled with a blue cheese vinaigrette. Ironically, dark woods, art deco fixtures, vintage boxing pictures, and a jazzy '40s soundtrack create a young-at-heart atmosphere. *4608 Westheimer, Galleria/Post Oak, 713/961–0333. AE, D, DC, MC, V. Closed Sun. No lunch. $$$*

6 a-5
TASTE OF TEXAS

With Texana to the max, this expansive place is as much about pride as prime beef. The entry looks like a sprawling ranch house, and the lobby evokes longings for evenings on the front porch, complete with rockers. So relax, you will wait a while for your table. Once seated, beaming young servers will dish out Southern hospitality along with fine meals. A trip to the salad bar, notable for really fine breads and homemade jellies, sets the stage for good things to come. Famous for its steaks, the kitchen also offers chicken, lobster, and shrimp grilled "just the way you like it"—guaranteed. Side dishes for entrées include hearty tortilla soup and fat, crisp asparagus as well as the usual baked potato or

wild rice. Out-of-state guests get a kick out of this place, and you get fair prices, to boot. *10505 Katy Fwy., West, 713/932–6901. Reservations not accepted. AE, D, DC, MC, V. No lunch Sat.–Sun. $$*

12 b-7
VALLONE'S

Retro steak house fare with millennium prices describes this Vallone venture. In keeping with that shtick, rock-n-roll songs from the '60s to present play at just-the-right volume; and red leather banquettes keep the River Oaks customers cozy. For starters, iceberg wedge salad doused in blue cheese dressing, hearty Texas 1015 onion soup, and lump crabmeat cakes with a gentle rémoulade sauce are prime choices. For entrées, perfectly cooked filet mignons and melt-in-your-mouth sake beef medallions leave no doubt as to their pedigree. The kitchen does surf as well as turf. Seared sea bass, in crab essence with champagne sauce, is beyond reproach. The clientele and spiffy staff seem cliquish, but all comers receive outstanding food and first-class service. *2811 Kirby Dr., River Oaks, 713/526–2811. Reservations essential. AE, D, DC, MC, V. No lunch. $$$*

TEX-MEX

12 f-4
BLUE AGAVE

The deliberately tacky decor, including year-round Christmas lights, may delight or distract you, but turn your attention instead to Blue Agave's Tex-Mex food with a twist, provided by chef–owner Charlie Watkins, also of Sierra Grill. Begin with calamari (yes, calamari), then choose from among excellent enchiladas—beef, chicken, cheese, artichoke, and spinach—or order a combination of your favorites. Good barbecued baby-back ribs and pecan-crusted trout veer from the usual fare. The margaritas, *frijoles borrachos* (flavorful beans seasoned with tomatoes, chiles, bacon, and beer) and house-made flan rank high in their respective categories. Sample premium tequilas from the ample bar. *1340 W. Gray, Montrose, 713/520–9696. Reservations essential. AE, DC, MC, V. No lunch Sat. $$*

12 b-6
CHUY'S

If you see a big red fish with shades on, you're in the right place. Every night is a party catered with exceptional food for the post-baccalaureate crowd. This Austin-grown Tex-Mex legend draws patrons from all walks of life. At Chuy's, where the King (Elvis, of course) is patron saint, eclectic is the norm and decor is anything that can hang on a wall. The mission here is to feed you well and keep you happy. Try the "big as yo face" burritos, the Elvis Special (a Tex-Mex sampler platter), or the 9-1-1 Hot Plate (with hunka burnin' green chile sauce), and most likely, you'll join the groupies. Margarita-heads get their Chuy's fix with the regular, the swirl (swirls of strawberry), or the dot (a dot of strawberry). *2706 Westheimer, River Oaks, 713/524–1700. Reservations not accepted. AE, D, DC, MC, V.* $

9 *f-1*   *Kirby*
6328 Richmond Ave., Richmond Strip, 713/974–2322.   *Hillcroft +*
                B.Hwy. Fontaine
10 *d-1*

GOODE COMPANY HAMBURGERS AND TAQUERÍA

Here is true fusion cuisine—Tex-Mex, all-American burgers and fries, and big trail-drive breakfasts. One of Jim Goode's trio near Kirby/Westpark, this very casual spot draws the crowds for lunch and dinner, and even greater hordes for weekend breakfast. Read the menu on the wall as you wait in line to place your order. Burgers and fries are um-um good, but don't stop there. Fajitas, enchiladas, catfish, even grilled quail are as tasty as any place in town, and they come with savory Spanish rice, beans, and guacamole. The real treasure here is the breakfast. Come as you are (and they do) for heapin' helpings of *huevos rancheros* (fried corn tortillas topped with fried sunny side up eggs and covered with a layer of salsa) *migas* (scrambled eggs cooked with tomatoes, onion, and fried tortillas), or pecan waffles. (A favorite Sunday ritual is to order inside, jostle for a patio table, and settle down with the paper.) Once again, Goode had a great idea. *4902 Kirby Dr., at Westpark, West University Place, 713/520–9153. Reservations not accepted. AE, D, DC, MC, V.* $

4 *b-3*

LUPE TORTILLAS

Families flock to Lupe's because the kids can play in the Texas-size sandbox with enough toys to avoid fitful tug-of-

wars, while parents sip beverages on the patio. To the rare childless diners, the wait can seem interminable. The silly Spanglish menu, with descriptions like "eez preety goood," offers remarkably good chalupas, tacos al carbon, fajitas, and all your favorite Tex-Mex. Lupe's gets very crowded on Fridays and Saturdays. *318 Stafford, Katy, 281/496–7580. Reservations not accepted. AE, D, DC, MC, V. No lunch Sat.–Sun.* $–$$

12 *c-8*
2414 Southwest Fwy., West University Place, 713/522–4420.

12 *c-7*

MISSION BURRITOS

Californians call them wraps, but Texans love these burritos, especially at this fun adobe-style fast-food stop. The mission here is to customize burritos with fresh, high-quality ingredients. The patio makes a fine place to sit while savoring a huge vegetarian burrito. The MAC—Muy Awesome Chicken—burrito is outstanding, stuffed with char-grilled fowl, pinto or black beans, roasted tomato salsa, avocado, and more. *Picas* (stuffed jalapeños) pack a punch, and don't bypass the tacos—the chicken version with mixed cheeses in white-corn tortillas is terrific. If there's no parking when you arrive, have *paciencia* (patience). People move quickly in this shrine to the burrito. *2245*

COOL FOR KIDS

Houston families flock to these restaurants for good food and a comfortable atmosphere for their children:

Chuy's (Tex-Mex)
A kid's menu, crayons, kid-friendly cups, and many decorative oddities can occupy a child's time here.

Clay's Restaurant (American Casual)
Soccer moms bring their kids here for burgers they both love. Sandbox included.

Goode Company Hamburgers and Taquería (Tex-Mex)
Jim Goode could form his own T-ball league with his younger patrons alone. There's plenty of options here for the young and picky.

Lupe Tortillas (Tex-Mex)
Plenty of toys are in the sandbox, and there's even good food.

W. Alabama, between Greenbriar and Kirby Dr., Upper Kirby District, 713/529–0535. AE, D, DC, MC, V. $

13 f-3
NINFA'S
Legendary Ninfa Laurenzo started her empire here with tacos al carbon, green sauce, and Ninfaritas. Today, there's a Ninfa's in every neighborhood, but only one original Ninfa's, and naturally, it's the best. Most Ninfa's serve pretty good Tex-Mex, but Ninfa's on Navigation remains the inspirational source. The modest building, colorful interior, open kitchen (long before that was the trend), the señoras making tortillas, and eclectic crowd of the well-heeled and the well-worn create an evocative environment. Here is the true Tex-Mex that is our bread of life. *2704 Navigation Blvd., at Canal St., East End, 713/228–1175. AE, D, DC, MC, V. $–$$*

9 f-1
PAPPASITO'S CANTINA
Ask Houstonians their favorite place for Mexican food and Pappasitos will claim the majority vote, by far. What's so great about it? Monstrous servings of reliably good Tex-Mex with family budget tabs may be the leading cause of affection. Add a boisterous atmosphere, good service, and a likely encounter with someone you know, and this cantina has all the makings a crowd-pleaser. Don't be a chain snob; join the fun. *6445 Richmond Ave., at Hillcroft, Richmond Strip, 713/784–5253. AE, MC, V. $$*

12 c-8
Little Pappasitos Cantina, 2536 Richmond Ave., Upper Kirby District, 713/520–5066.

10 g-1
SPANISH VILLAGE
Long before every holiday had lights, Spanish Village kept Christmas lights twinkling year round (a bright spot on down-at-the-heels Almeda Road). Mention Spanish Village to any longtime—40 years minimum—Houstonian, then wait for the memories to pour forth. Floor-to-ceiling Polaroid pictures document generations who have celebrated here. The heavy tile tables that have been there forever are now pricey folk art. The Tex-Mex food is still good and the margaritas are legendary, but don't order one without food. *4720 Almeda Rd., Medical Center, 713/523–2861. AE, D, DC, MC, V. Closed Sun.–Mon. $–$$*

THAI

4 d-3
BLUE ORCHID
Pretty pink touches, mirrored columns, and leafy plants create a gracious setting for spicy Thai and Vietnamese fare. As easy on the wallet as on the eye, lunch at this west Houston favorite is a real bargain. For less than $8, you get a crunchy cabbage salad with chicken and shrimp, two additional crispy shrimp, two delicate Vietnamese spring rolls, choice of entrée, plus rice or noodles. For the gentler palates, the kitchen obligingly tempers the firepower of many Thai dishes. You must request no MSG, though. Come evening, twinkling lights outside, candlelight inside, and an ambitious menu transform the place for serene dining. *14004 Memorial Dr., West Downtown, 281/870–8636. AE, DC, MC, V. Closed Sun. $*

12 f-4
GOLDEN ROOM
Set on the north edge of the Montrose district, the barn-red exterior of Golden Room stands out among its less fortunate neighbors. The cozy interior is welcoming, with banquettes lining one wall, and deep green walls accented with gold touches. Try starting with fresh spring rolls, chockablock full with grilled chicken and vegetables, or refreshing grilled shrimp salad with spicy lime sauce—the iceberg lettuce isn't exactly upscale, but it works anyway. Zesty garlic sauce makes for a notable ginger chicken, and for the calorie counters, consider steamed snapper done up with chopped ginger, carrots, and jalapeños. *1209 Montrose Blvd., Montrose, 713/524-9614. AE, DC, D, MC, V. No smoking. Closed Sun. $–$$*

12 b-8
MAI THAI
Mai Thai is an elegant little restaurant nestled into a companionable grouping of Asian restaurants on Kirby, just off the Southwest Freeway. If you want a quiet, comfortable spot to enjoy lunch or dinner, you'll be hard pressed to find a nicer place to dine. The menu offers what you would expect: *satay* (skewers of grilled beef or chicken), *mee krob* (crisp fried noodles), red, green, and yellow curries, *thom yum goong* (the classic lemongrass, lime-based Thai soup), *phad Thai* (Thai fried noodles), sticky rice with mango, and high-octane Thai iced coffee. Any choice is a good one. *3819 Kirby*

Dr., Central, 713/522–6707. AE, D, DC, MC, V. No smoking. Closed Sun. $$

10 *d-2*
NIT NOI

Nit Noi's two locations rank among Houston's sleekest and most favored Thai restaurants. The dining rooms are spacious, and the elegant dishes are known for their blending of fresh ingredients. Crisply fried spring rolls, enhanced with a fruity sweet-and-sour sauce, stand out among the starters; vegetarian dumplings, rich with mushroom stuffing, also deserve a tasting. A sure hand with spices marks the main courses from steamed red snapper to spicy pork with basil, chiles, and vegetables to the ubiquitous, but excellent, phad Thai. For the ultimate in Thai comfort food, slurp a bowl of chicken soup with coconut milk and lemongrass. *2426 Bolsover, Rice University Village, 713/524–8114. AE, D, DC, MC, V. $$*

6 *f-8*
6395 Woodway, Memorial/Spring Branch, 713/789–1711.

10 *c-3*
SAWADEE THAI RESTAURANT

Is there such a thing as a neighborhood, family Thai restaurant? Of course there is, and at Sawadee you can expect to see your West U. neighbors enjoying themselves, kids in tow, in a well-lighted, serviceable space. Vegetable soup is mouthwatering with its lemongrass infused broth. Thai standards like mee krob, beef satay, shrimp curry, pork *panaeng* (pork with sweet curry cooked in a coconut milk base, kaffir and lemon leaves), and phad Thai boast fresh ingredients and are ably prepared and nicely presented. As with most Asian menus, Sawadee's offers plenty for the vegetarians in the crowd, substituting tofu and eggplant for meat. *6719 Weslayan, between Bellaire and Stella Link, Bellaire, 713/666–7872. Reservations not accepted. AE, D, MC, V. No smoking. $–$$*

9 *a-1*
THAI CAFÉ

Those outside the Beltway have enjoyed this lovely café for more than 15 years. With soft rose tones, dark woods, and white linens, Thai Café is attractive enough for special occasions and quiet meals but neighborly enough for regulars. Choice appetizers are steamed

dumplings (with minced pork, crabmeat, and vegetables) served open-faced with a vinegary, sweet and spicy soy sauce. The extensive menu features terrific curries, great clay pots, and numerous seafood and vegetarian options. Lunch specials bring in a full house. *10928 Westheimer, at Wilcrest, Memorial/Spring Branch,713/780–3096. Reservations not accepted. AE, D, DC, MC, V. Closed Sun. No lunch Sat. $*

12 *d-7*
THAI PEPPER

Long before Thai cuisine was popular, Thai Pepper was luring diners to the savory, spicy, addictive tastes of Thailand. This longtime favorite, off South Shepherd, welcomes couples and small groups into its rich interior. The dark woods, white linens, and candlelight are peaceful and pleasant, even if you do strain to see the menu. Soft spring rolls and satay measure up fine as benchmark appetizers. But the talented kitchen shines with Triple Spicy Fish (hot chile sauce turns snapper into a mouth- and eye-watering feast) and Drunk Noodles (scallops, basil, onions, and mushrooms). All dishes can be ordered mild, medium, or hot. Only masochists order anything "hot." *2049 W. Alabama, at S. Shepherd, Montrose, 713/520–8225. AE, DC, MC, V. No lunch Sat.–Sun. $*

7 *b-3*
VUNG THAI

Here's a cheery spot on the dreary feeder of the 610 and 290 spaghetti bowl. The lemon-lime color scheme isn't the only thing brightening this little place. Yum Apple Salad is peppy—a crunchy confetti mix of sliced green apples, chicken, shrimp, red onions, toasted cashews, and coconuts. Basil chicken is a spicy sauté with onions, mushrooms, bell peppers, and enough basil for a sweet finish. Staple appetizers, like steamed dumplings and beef satay, measure up fine. In a hard-to-get-to location (call for directions), friendly service and dependable fare fills the tables. *1714 W. Loop North, Northwest, 713/868–3551. AE, MC, V. No smoking. Closed Sun. $*

VEGETARIAN

6 *d-5*
A MOVEABLE FEAST

If your preference is a healthy vegetarian diet, this is your place. You'll find your basic veggie burgers and Tex-Mex dishes plus "Southern-style" chickenless fried chicken. The herb salad dressing is a favorite of regular customers. *9341 Katy Fwy., Memorial/Spring Branch, 713/365–0368. AE, DC, D, MC, V. $*

7 *d-8*

2202 W. Alabama, Montrose, 713/528–3585.

12 *c-7*
BABA YEGA
This cozy institution not only serves great vegetarian fare, but you can get your dose of herb remedies at the adjoining shop. The staff is an eclectic mix, adding to the atmosphere of the old house's setting. *2607 Grant St., Montrose, 713/522–0042. AE, D, DC, MC, V. $*

VIETNAMESE

13 *c-5*
KIM SON
Many generations come to worship at this Downtown shrine to Vietnamese cuisine. If the commute is too daunting, you can likely find a smaller version in your part of town. The mother location attracts wedding parties and other big gatherings, but have no fear. Those groups party upstairs while the lovely, main floor dining room is reserved for everyone else. The most popular item on the vast menu is the "Vietnamese fajitas," flank steak strips grilled with lemongrass and served with rice paper wrappers and a plate piled high with lettuce, mint, cilantro, and slices of pineapple, carrot, and cucumber. Wrap it up, pour on the fish sauce, and join the fan club. *2001 Jefferson St., at Chartres, Downtown/Theatre District, 713/222–2461. AE, D, DC, MC, V. $–$$*

10 *d-2*
MISS SAIGON CAFÉ
This Rice Village café is a light, pretty place to stop with a friend or two; the little tables can hardly seat more. The stripped-down basics still show, but the space is charming nonetheless, with clay pot–colored walls covered with artwork for sale. Among standard Vietnamese fare, the spring rolls are more than adequate with peanut sauce and perilously hot pepper sauce. Not-so-standard fare is especially good, like the grilled pork sand-

wich on toasted baguette. Vermicelli dishes show extra care: the roots of sprouts are snipped, and the char-grilled pork is trimmed of fat. Seriously sweet, iced Vietnamese coffee will keep you revved for a good while. Both the ambience and the food prepared by the French-trained chef are a step above the fluorescent lighting and Chinese crossover menus of so many Asian restaurants. Cozy and attractive, it draws a good crowd, including starving Rice students and profs. *5503 Kelvin, at Times Blvd., Rice University Village, 713/942–0108. AE, MC, V. No smoking. Closed Sun. $*

12 *f-6*
MO MONG
Dubbed "nuevo Vietnamese" by multicultural Houstonians, Mo Mong's owners have managed to create a dramatic minimalist dining room in a two-story building behind the old Tower Theater, and inventive cuisine to match. Rewards for those locating the half-hidden spot include inspired vegetable dumplings in ginger-chile-soy sauce, spring rolls bulging with tofu, mint, and crisp veggies, and succulent Nha Trang oysters (a dish named after a beach in Vietnam). Mama Khang's fish, Saigon curry, chicken in a pungent lemongrass sauce, and Indochine fried rice with shrimp and sausage are praised, as are the helpful staff at the downstairs bar. *1201 Westheimer, Montrose, 713/524–5664. AE, D, DC, MC, V. $$*

4 *f-5*
NAM
All the good Vietnamese places are not clustered Downtown or on Bellaire. Outside the Loop, but inside the Beltway, is this casual, friendly old-timer. Long popular with folks out west, Nam delivers pretty platefuls of light, colorful fare in a tranquil setting. Maybe it's the goldfish in the aquarium or the healthy food, but you leave feeling more balanced than when you came. Start well with shrimp-and-scallion crepe topped by assorted crunchy greens including mint and cilantro. Hot-and-sour vegetable soup is tart with lemongrass, but sweetened with pineapple chunks. Terrific *bun xao mem* (soft rice noodles with shrimp, chicken and peanuts) or zesty lemongrass chicken are infallible entrées. *2727 Fondren, at Westheimer, Memorial/Spring Branch, 713/789–6688. AE, D, DC, MC, V. $*

chapter 2

SHOPPING

The lure of air-conditioning in a hot climate paired with almost unrestricted urban sprawl has made Houston a mall-oriented town, although there are a few shopping districts that require open-air strolling. You can also rely on seemingly endless strip centers for quick-stop shopping, whether you're looking for a pair of luxury shoes or a few bags of dog food. At the center of every neighborhood is a mall, complete with a food court, several dozen stores, and perhaps some sort of entertainment—an arcade, a movie theater, and, in the case of the Galleria, an ice-skating rink.

The Galleria, the first mall to become a tourist destination in Houston, has been a thriving enterprise from the beginning. It's grown from the original ice-rink building with a skylight based on the "everything's bigger in Texas" principle to include multiple, increasingly lavish buildings. Teenagers roam between the ice rink and the Sharper Image; ladies who lunch make the most of their afternoon at Neiman Marcus, Tootsie's Galleria, and Saks; casual shoppers head to Banana Republic, Macy's, and Crate & Barrel to look for bargains or purchase must-haves at Tiffany & Co., Dolce & Gabbana, and Polo.

shopping areas

DEPARTMENT STORES

9 b-5
AUCHAN HYPERMARKET
This high-ceiling warehouse serves as a "hyper" grocery store. Its wide aisles and glaring fluorescent lights showcase everything from Zebco fishing gear to Veuve Clicquot champagne. 8800 W. Sam Houston Pkwy., Southwest, 281/530–9855.

2 d-1
DILLARD'S
The Chanel counter sets the tone for the cosmetics department, and other departments also lead with chic names. You'll pay premium prices for the best brands, but throughout the store less elite merchandise, such as Liz Sport women's wear, is offered at reasonable prices. 1201 Lake Woodlands Dr., Woodlands Mall, The Woodlands, 281/363–9300.

2 g-8
19010 Gulf Fwy., Baybrook Mall, Clear Lake/Bay Area, 281/486–0700.

2 f-3
20131 Highway 59 N, Deerbrook Mall, North, 281/540–1612.

3 b-7
16517 Southwest Fwy., First Colony Mall, Sugar Land/Fort Bend, 281/980–8300.

2 d-3
12000 North Fwy., Greenspoint Mall, North, 281/875–5900.

10 a-1
4925 Westheimer Rd., Galleria, Galleria/Post Oak, 713/622–1200.

6 a-5
800 W. Sam Houston Pkwy. N, Town & Country Mall, Memorial/Spring Branch, 713/464–1851.

4 b-5
2600 Hwy. 6, West Oaks Mall, Southwest, 281/558–4431.

2 c-3
7925 FM 1960 W, Willowbrook Mall, FM 1960 area, 281/890–9200.

13 b-4
FOLEY'S
Foley's stores carry a bit of Ellen Tracy and Calvin Klein for flash, although the real deal is midrange goods at reasonable prices. Back-to-school season creates a major mob scene at all Foley's, and sensible brides register here. 1110 Main St., Downtown/Theater District, 713/405–7035.

2 f-7
12200 Gulf Fwy., Almeda Mall, South Houston/Hobby Airport, 713/943–4300.

2 f-3
20131 Hwy. 59 N, Deerbrook Mall, North, 281/540–9250.

2 d-3
12000 North Fwy., Greenspoint Mall, North, 281/875–7300.

6 c-5
900 S. Gessner, Memorial City Mall, Memorial/Spring Branch, 713/461–0400.

7 *a-3*

9800 Hempstead, Northwest Mall, Memorial/Spring Branch, 713/683–5300.

9 *e-4*

7500 Bellaire Blvd., Sharpstown Shopping Center, Sharpstown, 713/776–7300.

4 *b-5*

2600 Hwy. 6 S, West Oaks Mall, Southwest, 281/531–3700.

2 *c-3*

7920 FM 1960 W, Willowbrook Mall, FM 1960 area, 281/955–4300.

2 *d-1*

1201 Lake Woodlands Dr., Woodlands Mall, The Woodlands, 281/362–6100.

10 *a-5*

JCPENNEY

This unfussy chain has long been known for work clothes, inexpensive housewares, and reliable appliances. In the mid-'90s, the venerable retailer added fashion, like Arizona Jeans, and a strong Web presence to update its image and attract new customers. *4700 Beechnut, Meyerland Plaza, 713/666–3861.*

7 *a-3*

9800 Hempstead, Northwest Mall, Memorial/Spring Branch, 713/681–5441.

6 *a-5*

800 W. Sam Houston Pkwy. N, Town & Country Mall, Memorial/Spring Branch, 713/973–1092.

2 *f-7*

12200 Gulf Fwy., Almeda Mall, South Houston/Hobby Airport, 713/944–9100.

4 *b-5*

2600 Hwy. 6 S, West Oaks Mall, Southwest, 281/558–2991.

10 *a-1*

LORD & TAYLOR

Pleasant salespeople and plenty of open space combine to make your experience seem luxe, yet the prices aren't in the stratosphere. Men and women both can consider this a safe place to splurge on a significant jacket or just one pair of irresistibly vogue shoes. *5061 Westheimer, Galleria/Post Oak, 713/627–8100.*

2 *c-3*

7925 FM 1960, Willowbrook Mall, FM 1960 area, 281/970–7900.

10 *a-1*

MACY'S

From the famed Cellar to the china shop, Macy's provides a nice mix of high-end and midrange clothes, leather goods, and kitchenware. Shoe sales and cosmetic counter specials are always a draw. *2727 Sage, Galleria/Post Oak, 713/968–1985.*

10 *a-1*

NEIMAN MARCUS

Nothing says oil money like Neiman's legendary holiday catalogue—famed for gifts like his-and-her helicopters—and the store's shoe sales are legendary. Comb through racks of designer goods, or test your fortune and figure on Givenchy, Christian Lacroix, and Mischka Couture. The low-key salon and café are, discretely, places to see and be seen. *2600 South Post Oak, Galleria/Post Oak, 713/621–7100.*

6 *a-5*

10615 Town & Country, Town & Country Mall, Memorial/Spring Branch, 713/984–2100.

10 *a-1*

SAKS FIFTH AVENUE

Swank as all get-out, the Houston Saks features the first Clarins Institute spa in the United States, a gleaming wood bar perfect for people-watching, Prada and Gucci boutiques, and couture salons. Ready-to-wear includes Calvin Klein and Versace and little-bitty lacy nothings from La Perla. The wide, well-polished white-tiled aisles of Saks are a walkway between two sections of the Galleria, and one imagines that, daily, credit card limits are met. *5115 Westheimer, Galleria/Post Oak, 713/627–0500.*

6 *a-5*

800 W. Sam Houston Pkwy. N, Town & Country Mall, Memorial/Spring Branch, 713/827–6300.

2 *c-3*

SEARS ROEBUCK

The "Softer Side of Sears" campaign has lured more shoppers to this durable department store, but most customers are loyal for low-priced clothing and housewares and a solid selection of tools and automotive services. *7920 FM 1960 W, Willowbrook Mall, FM 1960 area, 218/955–4700.*

2 *d-3*
12000 North Fwy., Greenspoint Mall, North, 281/874–7200.

6 *c-5*
900 S. Gessner, Memorial City Mall, Memorial/Spring Branch, 713/984–5600.

2 *g-8*
19010 Gulf Fwy., Baybrook Mall, Clear Lake/Bay Area, 281/486–3174.

2 *d-1*
1201 Lake Woodlands Dr., Woodlands Mall, The Woodlands, 281/362–3000.

6 *d-5*
TARGET
Weekends and weeknights, the register lines are packed with folks who ran in for tube socks and a garden hose, and ended up loading a red plastic shopping cart with cute casual clothes, decorative appliances, clever knickknacks, and video games. 9429 Katy Fwy., Hedwig Village, Memorial/Spring Branch, 713/464–9461.

7 *b-8*
4323 San Felipe, River Oaks, 713/960–9608.

2 *f-5*
12001 East Fwy., Pasadena/Southeast, 713/451–2111.

14 *c-7*
7801 Main, Astrodome/Old Spanish Trail, 713/795–4735.

3 *c-2*
13250 Northwest Fwy., North, 713/939–7878.

9 *b-1*
10801 Westheimer, Memorial/Spring Branch, 713/782–9950.

2 *c-4*
10701 Jones Rd., FM 1960 area, 281/890–8440.

2 *e-3*
4701 FM 1960 W, FM 1960 area, 281/444–0600.

9 *e-4*
7051 Southwest Fwy., Sharpstown, 713/771–8321.

2 *f-7*
10000 Kleckley Dr., South Houston/Hobby Airport, 713/941–3800.

4 *b-6*
6800 Hwy. 6, Southwest, 281/568–9290.

2 *b-4*
6955 Hwy. 6, Katy/Bear Creek, 281/550–8955.

2 *a-5*
19955 Katy Fwy., Katy/Bear Creek, 281/647–9191.

3 *d-2*
13250 Northwest Fwy., North, 713/939–7878.

9 *e-1*
WAL-MART
Few establishments in Houston proper say Southern like Wal-Mart. Discount clothes, major brand appliances, toys, and automotive supplies are all offered at pleasing prices. Bonus: several stores are open way past bedtime, so busy people can get a tube of grout, new towels, or fresh clean cotton underwear in emergencies. 2727 Dunvale, Richmond Strip area, 713/977–2099.

3 *d-2*
13484 Northwest Fwy., North, 713/690–0666.

2 *f-5*
13750 East Fwy., Pasadena/Southeast, 713/453–5018.

2 *d-3*
10411 North Fwy., North, 281/999–9920.

4 *e-1*
10750 Westview Dr., North, 713/984–2773.

2 *d-3*
3275 FM 1960 W, FM 1960 area, 281/440–4482.

2 *c-3*
7075 FM 1960 W, FM 1960 area, 281/893–2207.

4 *b-7*
14550 Beechnut, Southwest, 281/561–0866.

3 *a-1*
7080 Hwy. 6 N, Cy-Fair, 281/855–1604.

MALLS & SHOPPING CENTERS

2 *f-7*
ALMEDA MALL
Foley's and JCPenney are anchors at this southwest center. Unique shops include an Avon boutique and Game Express.

12200 Gulf Fwy., Almeda Mall, South Houston/Hobby Airport, 713/944–1010.

2 g-8
BAYBROOK MALL
Shoppers can stop in for cotton slacks at Mervyn's, or spend more for the same at Eddie Bauer. Visit specialty shops like Merle Norman makeup and Godiva chocolates when you want to take time to pamper yourself, or run into Dillard's when you need to do all your shopping in one fell swoop. 19400 Gulf Fwy., Friendswood, Clear Lake/Bay Area, 281/488–4627.

2 f-3
DEERBROOK MALL
Anchor stores Dillard's, Foley's, JCPenney, Macy's, and Sears compete with more than 100 stores. An AMC 24 Theatre offers another way to spend money or time on the weekends. 20131 Hwy. 59 N, Humble, North, 281/446–5300.

3 b-7
FIRST COLONY MALL
Spring of 1996 saw the already rapidly expanding far southwest shopping options increase by several orders of magnitude. This million-square-ft mall is home to droves of smaller stores along with department stores such as Dillard's, Foley's, JCPenney, and Mervyn's. 16535 Southwest Fwy., at Hwy. 6, Sugar Land/Fort Bend, 281/265–6123.

10 a-1
GALLERIA
Since the grand, grand opening in 1970, the Galleria has grown to include complexes II and III, but you can stroll in air-conditioned comfort all the way from the first anchor store, Neiman Marcus, to Macy's (which opened in 1986, extending the mall's southwest corner to Sage Street). The Galleria's almost 300 stores spread over three floors provide an almost overwhelming shopping experience. Socialites shop at high-end stores (Tiffany & Co., Spritzer Fashion and Furs) but share food courts with those patronizing middle-of-the-road retailers (Banana Republic, Casual Corner). The indoor ice rink offers both public skate times and lessons. Valet parking is available near Neiman Marcus. Most lots, however, are free. 5075 Westheimer, Galleria/Post Oak, 713/622–0663.

2 d-3
GREENSPOINT MALL
It's a big mall—1.5 million square ft—and maybe too big. JCPenney and Foley's hold on as anchor stores, and there are a number of boutique spaces that are often either just closed or opening soon. You can usually find a bookstore, or a jewelry store, etc; it's just that you can't count on the same bookstore or jewelry store or what-have-you from visit to visit. 200 Greenspoint Mall, Hwy. 75 at Gears Rd., off Beltway Exit 8, North, 281/875–4201.

6 c-5
MEMORIAL CITY MALL
If your shopping depends on Taco Bell, giant pretzels, and fresh-squeezed lemonade, then Memorial's vast food court will win you over. Anchor stores include Foley's and Sears. The pet store, Petland, often carries hedgehogs and prairie dogs and other small mammals. We can't suggest you take such a pet home, but the pet shop is near the Sony Memorial Theater, so you can stop in to ooh and ahh before seeing a film in the fairly grand cinema. Stores present a lot of duplication, that is, there's more than one store selling faux Native American gewgaws, more than one store selling plastic hair accessories and fake henna tattoos, and so on, but the traffic is heavy enough to support all the merchants. 1000 Katy Fwy., at Gessner, Memorial/Spring Branch, 713/932–0076.

10 a-5
MEYERLAND PLAZA
Compared to Houston's other malls, Meyerland Plaza is inside out. There is no indoor, air-conditioned center. Borders Books and Music, Super Kmart, Bed, Bath and Beyond, and other stores face outward, forcing you to walk or drive from door to door. Unattached satellite stores include Steinmart and Old Navy. 4700 Beechnut, Meyerland, 713/664–1166.

13 b-3
THE PARK SHOPS
Two blocks of Downtown Houston provide Downtown workers access to both long afternoons of shoe shopping and quick lunchtime trips for clothes, books, sporting goods, or gifts. In true mall form, this Downtown center has an elaborate fountain. 1200 McKinney, Downtown/Theater District, 713/759–1442.

9 *e-4*

SHARPSTOWN SHOPPING CENTER

Houston's first indoor mall has always kept up with the times. The elegant boutiques that were added during the '80s boom have slowly been replaced by stores catering to the neighborhood's growing population of African-Americans, Asians, and Hispanics, but through all the changes and expansion, Foley's and Montgomery Ward are stalwarts. *7500 Bellaire Blvd., Sharpstown, 713/777–2393.*

6 *a-5*

TOWN & COUNTRY MALL

Although blue laws are long gone, this mall is still slow on Sunday. Many stores don't open at all, and those that do start closing around 4 PM. On weekdays and Saturday, the mall is designed for the taste and pace of the middle-aged and senior homeowners nearby. There is no screaming arcade, no food court clotted with awkwardly flirting teens, and few of the mobile sunglass huts and pager carts parked in the aisles of most malls. Instead, this sedate shopping center features gift shops, a half-dozen jewelers, and the comforting Southern designs of Frontera Furniture. Saks is no longer at Town & Country, but Neimans and the more practical JCPenney remain anchor stores. *800 W. Sam Houston Pkwy. N, Memorial/Spring Branch, 713/468–2113.*

7 *a-7*

UPTOWN PARK

Fine restaurants are the major draw here, but many of the attractive faux European village facades house high-end clothing and accessory stores. *1100 Uptown Park Blvd., Galleria/Post Oak, 713/840–8474.*

4 *b-5*

WEST OAKS MALL

Along with department stores such as Dillard's, Foley's, JCPenney, Mervyn's, Palais Royal, and Sears, and 100-odd specialty stores, West Oaks Mall has a fatfree.com store. Stock up on fat-free treats to make up for all the Chick-Fil-A waffle-cut fries you ate while shopping. *1000 West Oaks Mall, Westheimer at Hwy. 6, Southwest, 281/531–1332.*

9 *c-6*

WESTWOOD MALL

Between Sharpstown Mall's ability to adapt and thereby attract traffic, and the development of First Colony Mall and its surrounding strip centers, Westwood has become something of a zombie mall. The movie theater is long closed, but people who need to pick up shoes and what-have-you on the way home from work find it useful. *9700 Bissonnet, Sharpstown, 713/777–8285.*

2 *c-3*

WILLOWBROOK MALL

Why go inside the Loop when you can find Ann Taylor, Eddie Bauer, Lord & Taylor, Williams-Sonoma and more specialty shops in this suburban center? The anchor stores, Dillard's, Foley's, JCPenney, Sears, and Montgomery Ward, cover the basics. *7925 FM 1960 W, FM 1960 area, 281/890–6255.*

OUTDOOR SHOPPING CENTERS

Most of the time, the phrases "Let's go shopping" and "Let's go to the mall" are interchangeable. However, there are a few spots where shoppers can stroll from store to store under blue skies and break for latte at open-air cafés. The crescent-shaped original buildings of River Oaks Shopping Center and rows of Washingtonian palm line Gray, from Shepherd to Driscoll. High-end retail stores such as Talbots, Jaeger, the Cotton Club, and Origins skin care are side-by-side with a paint-your-own pottery store, the Black-Eyed Pea restaurant, and a Starbucks. Highland Village, on Westheimer between Weslayan and Suffolk, has "snack" options ranging from the Grotto, Tony Vallone's third venture, to biscotti and cooked coffee at Starbucks. Shopping is exquisite in Highland. The stylish storefronts define a look and feel best described as "American Express platinum."

For a funkier outdoor experience, try 19th Street, between Yale and Ashland. This stretch of historic Heights has a few boutiques selling antiques and quaint modern crafts, and a few discount stores along the lines of Sand Dollar and the Fire Sale.

SHOPPING NEIGHBORHOODS

9 *d-3*

HARWIN

Warehouse stores, strip centers, and minimalls line the former business park street. Traffic is awful, parking is difficult, and you never know exactly what you'll find. Such complications are balanced by bargain goods ranging from human-hair wigs to tool sets. Various stores offer no-name merchandise, knockoffs, and the real McCoy. *Harwin, from Hillcroft to S. Gessner.*

7 *b-8*

HIGHLAND VILLAGE

The plus: a more laid-back atmosphere than the nearby Galleria. The minus: shoppers must brave Houston weather while strolling from store to store. Pottery Barn, Joan & David, Max Lang custom jewelry, Williams-Sonoma, Tootsie's, and a couple dozen higher-end stores populate the deliberately quaint strip centers lining Westheimer just inside the Loop. *4000 block of Westheimer, between Weslayan and Suffolk.*

14 *c-3*

RICE UNIVERSITY VILLAGE

Stalwarts like the 5&10 Variety and Kahn's Deli add charm to a shopping neighborhood that has grown to include a Gap, a Limited, and several upscale restaurants in recent years. *Bordered by Sunset Blvd., University Blvd., Kirby, and Greenbriar.*

specialist shops

ANTIQUES

auction houses

6 *f-8*

HART GALLERIES

Many of us grew up with Mom slipping off to Hart Gallery auctions, but this old dog knows all the new tricks. Estate items from high-end neighborhoods like Tanglewild, pieces from well-known national collections, and local consignments are sold by day, by live auction, and through on-line auctions. *2301 S. Voss, Galleria/Post Oak, 713/266–3500.*

14 *e-8*

PEYTON-SMITH AUCTION GALLERIES

English antiques and upper-level estate sale fancies are the hook. A steady stream of consignment objects keeps the bidders queuing up for Monday night auctions. *8937 Knight Rd., Astrodome/Old Spanish Trail, 713/797–0399.*

2 *h-7*

SIMPSON'S GALLERIES

Many have accidentally bid over their budget on one-of-a-kind finds like massive Continental antiques, exquisite lacquered mantle clocks, or 19th-century American primitive oils, but few have regretted the deals. *4001 S. Main, Downtown/Theater District, 713/524–6751.*

flea markets & antiques centers

9 *f-1*

A-1 FLEA MARKET

Part of Houston's charm is the entrepreneurial spirit that allows a "chain" flea market to flourish. Why get up early to hit suburban garage sales when you can spend a late morning strolling through your local neighborhood A-1? *3511 Hillcroft, Richmond Strip, 281/221–6814.*

2 *f-5*

717 Maxey Rd., Pasadena/Southeast, 713/451–4434.

9 *g-2*

COMMON MARKET

Fake IDs that wouldn't fool an elementary school hall monitor and a staggering amount of inferior jewelry take up an awful lot of space in this sprawling complex. But within the warren of buildings, tents, and even a couple of railway boxcars, Houstonians of every stripe shop for Depression glass, Mexican patio furniture, hand-thrown pottery, and the latest cute critter collectibles. *6116 Southwest Fwy., Galleria/Post Oak, 713/780–0070.*

12 *e-1*

HEIGHTS STATION ANTIQUES

Although the shops are open seven days a week, the dealers seem to find time to slip off to the country and gather furniture and kitchen goods from turn-of-the-century farms. *121 Heights Blvd., Heights, 713/868–3175.*

12 *d-6*

RIVER OAKS ANTIQUE CENTER

The building is a former discount sporting goods shop, but today's contents are from the best homes. To soften sticker shock, salespeople assure "We are negotiable, and we do have quality merchandise." Indeed. Fine furnishings with a hand-rubbed glow reflect light from stemware, crystal light fixtures, chandeliers, china, silverware, and other early 20th-century luxury goods. Rare and sometimes unique items include original Tiffany pieces and Lalique works. *2030 Westheimer, Montrose, 713/ 520–8238.*

12 *g-5*

TEXAS JUNK CO.

Despite an effort to stock Texana and cowboy collectibles, this is more junk than anything else. Go for garage sale goods in vast quantity. *215 Welch, Montrose, 713/524–6257.*

3 *c-3*

TRADE MART

Those shopping for antiques in a hurry can pop into this 70,000-square-ft mall for a quick fix of china, glassware, collectibles, or cunning end tables. Shoppers can comb through the hundred-odd dealer booths for genuinely rare finds, like ready-to-build electronics kits from the '50s. *2121 W. Sam Houston Pkwy. N, North, 713/467–2506.*

11 *c-4*

TRADING FAIR II

This large, well-organized, and efficient market has a few things from the 19th century and quite a few from the last few decades. American collectibles trends can be tracked by a stroll down Trading Fair aisles. *5515 South Loop E, South Houston/Hobby Airport, 713/731–1111.*

collectibles

7 *a-4*

ANTIQUE CENTER OF TEXAS

You can go home again, or at least back to the desktop Indy 500 of your youth with David's vintage Matchbox cars. *1001 West Loop N, Memorial/Spring Branch, 713/688–4211.*

7 *a-4*

CARL'S CLOCKS

Anyone who wants to really know what time it is can keep up to the minute in stunning style with one of this shop's mesmerizing American or European timepieces. Many are so decorative it's difficult to remember they have a function. *1001 West Loop N, Memorial/Spring Branch, 713/688–4211.*

6 *a-5*

DRAGONFIRE

Carefully costumed Madame Alexander Dolls, fuzzy bears, and earlier, more detailed Breyer horses will sate any inner-child. *800 W. Sam Houston Pkwy. N, Town & Country Mall, Memorial/Spring Branch, 713/722–7915.*

12 *e-6*

FLASHBACK FUNTIQUES

Live the retro life with pop machines, juke boxes, and two-tone furnishings from the '40s and '50s. *1627 Westheimer, Montrose, 713/522–7900.*

10 *d-6*

TRAINSOURCE TEXAS

Trains of every age and every gauge are lovingly displayed here. *3264 South Loop W, Astrodome/Old Spanish Trail, 713/ 662–0809.*

furniture

12 *b-6*

BROWNSTONE GALLERY

Weirdly funky for such a high-end establishment, the Brownstone makes furnishing your first mansion easy. Their style is anything extraordinary. Massive Spanish ironworks, clubby red leather suites, and painfully delicate French chairs are all deemed fit for the dazzling showroom. *2803 Westheimer, Montrose, 713/523–8171.*

12 *d-5*

COLIN GIBBINS ANTIQUES

Colin himself is a direct import, and assuages homesickness by surrounding himself with country crockery, textiles, cupboards, and other furniture from the United Kingdom. *2215 Woodhead, Montrose, 713/524–4011.*

6 c-7

THISTLE ANTIQUES
The Memorial neighborhood surrounding this store is finally developing a dignity fitting the formidable English, French, and other Continental pieces sold here. *12472 Memorial Dr., Memorial/Spring Branch, 713/984–2329.*

ART SUPPLIES

4 b-7

HOBBY LOBBY CREATIVE CENTERS
Foam shapes, doll faces, glitter, tempera paints, and other tools of the home crafter are a tribute to the creativity and enthusiasm of everyone from Girl Scout troop leaders to drag queens. *14639 Beechnut, Southwest, 281/564–6391.*

2 f-3

2325 FM 1960 W, FM 1960 area, 281/444–4770.

3 b-7

12680 Fountain Lake Circle, Sugar Land/Fort Bend, 281/240–2122.

3 d-2

13470 Northwest Fwy., North, 713/460–9999.

2 c-3

10955 FM 1960 W, FM 1960 area, 281/894–9798.

3 a-2

4705 Hwy. 6 N, Katy/Bear Creek, 281/550–6411.

6 c-5

10516 Old Katy Rd., North, 713/467–6503.

10 a-5

8715 West Loop S, Meyerland, 713/665–2666.

4 c-5

MICHAEL'S
Holiday season, any holiday season, is a big deal at these arts-and-crafts emporiums. Along with selling dried flowers, wire ribbon, and faux-finish kits, many locations provide a dependable framing shop. *12556 Westheimer, Southwest, 281/558–1088.*

2 c-3

7616 FM 1960 W, FM 1960 area, 281/894–4955.

2 f-3

2206 FM 1960 W, FM 1960 area, 281/580–2882.

3 d-2

13238 Northwest Fwy., North, 713/690–4117.

10 c-2

3904 Bissonnet, Rice University Village, 713/662–0913.

4 b-6

6823 Hwy. 6 N, Katy/Bear Creek, 281/463–9826.

6 f-8

1430 S. Voss, Galleria/Post Oak, 713/952–8004.

12 f-5

TEXAS ART SUPPLY
Serious artists and only minimally committed hobbyists alike can count on the knowledgeable staff to help them find everything from oil pastels to puff paints. Even those of us who can't draw a straight line enjoy sorting through the fanciful pens and stationery. *2001 Montrose, Montrose, 713/526–5221.*

9 f-1

2237 S. Voss, Galleria/Post Oak, 713/780–0440.

2 g-8

1507 Baybrook Mall Dr., Baybrook Mall, Clear Lake/Bay Area, 281/486–9320.

12 f-5

UTRECHT ART SUPPLY CENTER
You could equip a studio with Utrecht brand paint, art, and drafting supplies, but in case that's not your aim, the shelf space is shared by other brands, too. *1618 Westheimer, Montrose, 713/522–0525.*

BEADS

14 c-3

THE BEAD SHOP
Since the '60s, this Rice Village spot has been the source for glass, wood, stone, metal, and plastic beads and the tools for making custom jewelry. They'll string your beads and sell you a how-to text on the art. *2476 Times Blvd., Rice University Village, 713/523–9350.*

BEAUTY

fragrances & skin products

`12` c-6

AVEDA LIFESTYLE STORE

Botanical beauty products, and even candles, organized in Aveda's tasteful khaki and blue packaging are sold at better salons, but there's something deliciously decadent about stocking up on spiced skin lotion in a store that has no other purpose. *2920 Westheimer, Galleria/Post Oak, 713/622–8332.*

`14` c-3

BATH & BODY WORKS

Generous types can stop in for gifts. The self-indulgent can spoil themselves with shopping bags full of everything that makes a tub foamy and fragrant and silky lotions for after toweling off. *2414 University Blvd., Rice University Village, 713/520–7370.*

`2` c-3

5307 FM 1960 W, FM 1960 area, 281/895–7760.

`10` a-1

5075 Westheimer, Galleria, Galleria/Post Oak, 713/993–9566.

`6` c-5

900 Gessner, Memorial/Spring Branch, 713/467–6489.

`2` d-3

12300 North Fwy., Greenspoint Mall, North, 281/874–9226.

`2` c-3

THE BODY SHOP

Current trends in aromatherapy are always represented in the soap sets and oils offered by this durable boutique, and there's a fruit-basket of flavors to moisturize your lips with. None of the all-natural products have been tested on animals. *7925 W. FM 1960, Willowbrook Mall, FM 1960 area, 281/890–8243.*

`2` d-3

12000 North Fwy., Greenspoint Mall, North, 281/875–5228.

`9` e-4

7500 Bellaire Blvd., Sharpstown Shopping Center, Sharpstown, 713/774–5998.

`2` d-1

1201 Lake Woodlands Dr., Woodlands Mall, The Woodlands, 281/367–4616.

`2` g-8

19010 Gulf Fwy., Baybrook Mall, Clear Lake/Bay Area, 281/286–0206.

`10` a-1

CRABTREE & EVELYN

No Anglophile can resist the fussy, softly scented goods sold by this ode to the days when women gave their long locks 100 strokes each evening, and changed the shelf paper during spring cleaning. *5015 Westheimer, Galleria I, Galleria/Post Oak, 713/871–0922.*

`12` d-4

ORIGINS

The company's ever-growing line of botanical skin care products, cosmetics, soaps, shampoos, and even toothpaste are all presented in custom wrapping that strikes a perfect note of eco-friendliness and elegance. The Sensory Therapy lotion meant to relieve stress is both a modern-day Vicks Vapo-Rub and a miracle cure. *2005 W. Gray, River Oaks, 713/807–8600.*

`10` a-1

ULTA

Some very stylish women saunter into this ordinary-looking strip-center chain for discount prices and an almost overwhelming selection. The long list of hair-care names includes Paul Mitchell, Bed Head, Sebastian, and KMS. Makeup choices range from Ulta's own line to L'Oreal and Maybelline. And there's still more: Ferre and redoubtable department store perfume favorites, and towering rows of skin-care products and manicure tools. *5130 Richmond, Galleria/Post Oak, 713/621–9160.*

`6` c-5

10405 Katy Fwy., Memorial/Spring Branch, 713/722–8590

`2` c-3

7530 FM 1960 W, FM 1960 area, 281/894–7182

`4` b-5

2392 S. Hwy. 6, Southwest, 281/531–7997.

hair care

`12` d-6

MADELON

Along with styling a tight-knit coterie of Inner-Loopers, Madelon occasionally does duty as a Houston Grand Opera

Hairdresser. In 1999 she moved into a larger location, which still features Aveda products, handmade jewelry, soaps, and gifts by local artists. Her new luxury feature is the hair-wash massage table: there's no more breaking your neck to bend back into the sink, your spine maintains a comfortable line. The salon is booked months in advance for the annual Hair Ball in May, a goofy, high-dollar fundraiser for Lawndale Art & Performance Center. *2521 Hazard, Montrose, 713/524–7283.*

10 *a-1*

NATURE'S WAY DAY SPA & SALON

An emphasis on eco-friendly treatments does not prohibit hair coloring. They use Aveda, of course. *5000 Westheimer, Galleria/Post Oak, 713/629–9995.*

8 *b-1*

REGENIA'S

The less fashion-forward needs of children and senior citizens are met, and the salon sees women who need molded and wrapped styles that can stand up to Houston's heat. The salon also offers conditioning and hair growth treatments. *9420 Jensen, North, 281/278–9047.*

2 *f-8*

SHEAR PLEASURE

The good ol' gal in you will find an undeniable appeal to enjoying urban indulgences like facials and a massage in a salon run by a woman with a beauty parlor name, Darleen. *904 S. Friendswood Dr., Clear Lake/Bay Area, 281/482–3381.*

7 *a-7*

TOVA HAIR STUDIO & DAY SPA

Luxury is stressed at this day spa, and although the personal care options for men and women can be enjoyed one at a time, spending a full day for the whole deal is suggested. *1409 S. Post Oak, Galleria/Post Oak, 713/439–1414.*

12 *c-5*

URBAN RETREAT

Power pampering for businesswomen and plenty of packages for groups built the business in the beginning. Mud, oxygen treatments, and massage continue to provide relaxation, in half-hour increments, for upper-level manage-

ment from all over the city. *2329 San Felipe, River Oaks, 713/523–2300.*

BICYCLES

4 *d-5*

BIKE BARN

Every Bike Barn location looks like a large, impersonal dealership, yet they're all focal points for clubs. *12118 Westheimer, Southwest, 281/558–2234.*

2 *h-7*

2422-B Bay Area Blvd., Clear Lake/Bay Area, 281/480–9100.

14 *b-3*

5935 Kirby, Rice University Village, 713/ 529–9002.

4 *b-7*

7083 Hwy. 6, Southwest, 281/463–2200.

7 *c-8*

BIKESPORT

With strong lighting and an alarmingly clean workshop, this hard-core bike shop is reminiscent of a European sports car garage, which suits the clientele just fine. *2909 Jonel St., Upper Kirby District, 713/850–0250.*

14 *h-1*

DANIEL BOONE CYCLES

Relentless gentrification in the blocks surrounding Boone's has done nothing to alter the neighborly look and feel of this friendly shop. All types of bikes, full service with a smile, and plenty of free advice have been Boone's hallmarks since back when only kids wanted a bike for Christmas. *5318 Crawford, Medical Center, 713/526–7011.*

10 *b-5*

PLANETARY CYCLES

Cyclists seeking something out of the ordinary can count on Planetary for recumbent bikes, folding commuter models, and other novel locomotion. *4004 S. Braeswood, Astrodome/Old Spanish Trail, 713/668–2300.*

9 *f-6*

SOUTHWEST SCHWINN

This family store does a brisk business in sales and maintenance of Kestrel, GT, and Dyno and caters to racers. *6607 Braeswood, Meyerland, 713/777–5333.*

6 *d-4*

1000 Campbell Rd., Memorial/Spring Branch, 713/464–8277.

12 *b-2*

WEST END BICYCLES
Specializing in mountain bikes and conveniently near Memorial Park's trails, West End has one more kicker: it's attached to an art gallery. 5427 Blossom, Heights, 713/861–2271.

BOOKS

general

10 *d-3*

BARNES & NOBLE
A massive selection and grande lattes make this chain a popular weekend hangout for singles and families alike. 3003 W. Holcombe Blvd., Astrodome/Old Spanish Trail, 713/349–0050.

6 *c-7*

12850 Memorial Dr., Memorial/Spring Branch, 713/465–5616.

9 *e-1*

7626 Westheimer, Richmond Strip Area, 713/783–6016.

10 *a-1*

5000 Westheimer, Galleria/Post Oak, 713/629–8828.

4 *b-5*

2450 Hwy. 6, Southwest, 281/293–8699.

2 *d-1*

1310 Lake Woodlands Dr., The Woodlands, 281/363–0271.

2 *f-7*

B. DALTON BOOKSELLER
Map and game-cards are often emphasized almost as much as books, but some stores offer student specials for kids who bring in proof of good grades. 11510 Gulf Fwy., Almeda Mall, South Houston/Hobby Airport, 713/944–9310.

10 *a-1*

5085 Westheimer, Galleria, Galleria/Post Oak, 713/960–8191.

2 *g-8*

19400 Gulf Fwy., Baybrook Mall, Clear Lake/Bay Area, 281/488–3327.

6 *c-5*

1000 Katy Fwy., Memorial City Mall, Memorial/Spring Branch, 713/464–2951.

2 *c-3*

7920 FM 1960 W, Willowbrook Mall, FM 1960 area, 281/890–6097.

2 *f-3*

20131 Hwy. 59 N, Deerbrook Mall, North, 281/446–4970.

4 *d-3*

BLUE WILLOW BOOKSTORE
This gentle suburban bookstore has a reasonable selection and service that massive chains can't match. 14532 Memorial, Montrose, 281/497–8675.

12 *c-7*

BOOKSTOP
Houston's flagship, in a converted movie palace, has wide aisles and a peaceful coffee bar in the former balcony. 2922 S. Shepherd, Upper Kirby District, 713/529–2345.

2 *d-3*

2215 FM 1960 W, FM 1960 area, 281/580–0195.

2 *g-8*

1513 W. Bay Area Blvd., Clear Lake/Bay Area, 281/554–6630.

2 *c-3*

9668 FM 1960 Bypass, North, 281/548–1551.

10 *d-1*

15415 Southwest Fwy., Sugar Land/Fort Bend, 281/242–7400.

10 *a-5*

BORDERS BOOKS & MUSIC
Sprawling display tables up front offer bargain books. Towering best-seller displays are the next level in. Then there are rows and rows of excruciatingly categorized sections. 4700 Beechnut, Meyerland Plaza, Meyerland, 713/661–2888.

9 *d-1*

9633-A Westheimer, Richmond Strip, 713/782–6066.

3 *b-7*

12788 Fountain Lake Circle, Sugar Land/Fort Bend, 281/240–6666.

14 *c-1*

BRAZOS BOOKSTORE
Proprietor Karl Killian makes life easy for literary types—his selection of fiction, criticism, and hard-to-find magazines is complemented by regular readings and inventive events. 2421 Bissonnet, Rice University Village, 713/523–0701.

12 *h-7*

MAIN STREET BOOKS

Although African-American literature, history, and other nonfiction are the focus, this family-oriented Downtown shop is a good resource for any parent and carries a selection of social studies examining all cultures. *4201 Main, Downtown/Theater District, 713/524–2524.*

12 *b-6*

RIVER OAKS BOOKSTORE

The shop carries new and used, and because of the old guard neighborhood, the selection has a strong emphasis on military, Texana, and hunting and fishing texts. *3270 Westheimer, River Oaks, 713/ 520–0061.*

13 *c-4*

WALDENBOOKS

On family mall trips, the bookish kid always makes a beeline for Waldenbooks. The chain also does well during holiday mall frenzies. *One Houston Center, Downtown/Theater District, 713/951–0041.*

2 *g-8*

19400 Gulf Fwy., Baybrook Mall, Friendswood, Clear Lake/Bay Area, 281/ 488–2330.

2 *d-3*

12000 North Fwy., Greenspoint Mall, North, 281/875–0381.

7 *a-3*

9800 Hempstead, Northwest Mall, Memorial/Spring Branch, 713/682–2237.

2 *c-3*

7920 FM 1960 W, Willowbrook Mall, FM 1960 area, 281/469–1901.

2 *d-1*

1201 Lake Woodlands Dr., Woodlands Mall, The Woodlands, 281/364–1061.

4 *b-5*

2600 Hwy. 6, West Oaks Mall, Southwest, 281/558–2585.

antiquarian

14 *h-3*

BOOK COLLECTOR

Leather-bound books are sold to aficionados of Napoleonic and Civil War history and to those looking to decorate with books by the yard. *2347 University Blvd., Rice University Village, 713/661–2665.*

14 *c-1*

DETERING BOOK GALLERY

Hardwood floors and high, narrow windows provide a fitting atmosphere for the rare, out-of-print, and antique books in the gallery. *2311 Bissonnet, Rice University Village, 713/526–6974.*

14 *c-3*

OUT-OF-PRINT BOOKSTORE

A brisk, businesslike exterior and well-ordered interior belie the staff's emphasis on browsing and pondering, and you'll need that time. A truly beautiful selection of exquisite books includes Texas topics such as the petroleum industry and now-collectible editions of pop classics like Nancy Drew. *2450 Times Blvd., Rice University Village, 713/ 526–8616.*

specialty

If you're looking for foreign-language books, note that most chain bookstores have a Spanish section and, occasionally, Chinese books. Sometimes you find Spanish editions of popular books alongside the English versions.

14 *c-3*

AQUARIAN AGE BOOKSHELF

Really, this is half bookstore, half tapes, crystals, gewgaws, and other New Age fetish items. *5603 Chaucer, Rice University Village, 713/526–7770.*

9 *h-4*

BEREAN CHRISTIAN STORE

Books are only the beginning. This is really a minimall of all things Christian. The book section includes bibles of every stripe, theology, religious coloring books, and theme fiction for all ages. A good three-quarters of the space is devoted to videos, CDs, tapes, gifts, and more. *5410 Bissonnet, Bellaire, 713/663–6115.*

10 *b-1*

BODY, MIND & SOUL

To nurture your soul, they carry very hefty physical books about metaphysical studies and everything for the astrologer, including charting software. *4344 Westheimer, River Oaks, 713/993–0550.*

13 *b-5*

BROWN BOOKSTORE
Engineers are always happy browsing through the shrink-wrapped technical manuals and government publications carried at this technical bookstore. *1517 San Jacinto, Downtown/Theater District, 713/652–3937.*

12 *b-6*

COKESBURY BOOKSTORE
Staid pastors and solemn church ladies trust Cokesbury for serious, conventional Christian texts and church supplies. *3502 W. Alabama, Upper Kirby District, 713/621–1755.*

12 *f-6*

CROSSROADS MARKET BOOKSTORE
No one seems to mind that most of the commerce in this gay bookstore involves cards, gifts, magazines, and pastries from the coffee shop. *1111 Westheimer, Montrose, 713/942–0147.*

4 *e-5*

MAJORS SCIENTIFIC BOOKS
All over town, engineers, medical researchers, and graduate students hear this from their local bookstore clerk: "We don't carry that. You might try Majors downtown." *7205 Fannin, Downtown/Theater District, 713/799–9922.*

12 *e-7*

MENIL COLLECTION BOOKSTORE
After a stroll through the Menil galleries, pop across the street for two-dimensional take-home images of African and contemporary art. Folk and outsider artworks and jewelry are also tendered. *1520 Sul Ross, Montrose, 713/521–9148.*

14 *c-1*

MURDER BY THE BOOK
Trend reports say independent bookstores are in peril, but the Murder folks are too busy expanding their store and their mailing list of loyal customers to notice. They cater to fans of mystery, crime, and every possible subset thereof with readings and book signings. The store's even hosted a mystery cruise. *2342 Bissonnet, Rice University Village, 713/524–8597.*

2 *c-3*

NAUVOO BOOKS
With a colorfully light attitude, this Mormon boutique quips: "Your one-stop shop for LDS (Latter-Day Saints) products." *15816 Champion Forest Dr., Cy-Fair, 281/370–3730.*

15 *g-5*

SHRINE OF THE BLACK MADONNA
African-American families rely on this reading room, cultural center, and place of worship. Some of the Shrine's annual events feature nationally known guests. *5309 Martin Luther King Blvd., Astrodome/Old Spanish Trail, 713/645–1071.*

13 *b-3*

U.S. GOVERNMENT BOOKSTORE
You might expect the dry government publications and copies of various forms and charts, but you may be surprised to find narratives of military history. Citizen hopefuls can bone up on immigration and naturalization requirements. *801 Travis, Downtown/Theater District, 713/228–1187.*

comics

9 *f-1*

BEDROCK CITY
Both locations are crowded on Wednesday when the new issues arrive. If you can't make delivery day, put your name on a list, and the clerks will hold your favorite titles for you. *6517 Westheimer, Galleria/Post Oak, 713/780–0675.*

2 *d-3*

2204 FM 1960 W, Suite B, FM 1960 area, 281/444–9763.

1 *a-1*

THIRD PLANET
Higher brows who insist on the latest graphic novels shop elbow to elbow with serious collectors combing the bins for raw early superhero comics, trading cards, and posters. Decorate your comic reading room with action figures, games, and other trademark tchotchkes. *2718 Southwest Fwy., Montrose, 713/528–1067.*

used

12 c-8

ALL-BOOKS
Along with collectibles such as Civil War and World War II histories, Texana, and art books, the collection in this tidy white house includes books about mushrooms. *2126 Richmond, Montrose, 713/522–6722.*

9 h-4

BOOK RACK
The air is scented with the slight must of mountains of books read on vacation and novels considered required reading at local schools. *4024 Bellaire, Astrodome/Old Spanish Trail, 713/666–9511.*

3 h-6

COLLEEN'S BOOKS
Thoughtful organization and a seemingly endless section of Texana make this iconoclast's venture several steps above the average used bookstore. *6880-C Telephone Rd., South Houston/Hobby Airport, 713/641–1753.*

12 f-5

HALF-PRICE BOOKS
Smart students pick up required reading here, sometimes getting quality annotations in the bargain. Genre fiction, self-help, and bestsellers past are all easy to find. *2410 Waugh Dr., Montrose, 713/520–1084.*

2 c-3

4865 FM 1960 W, FM 1960 area, 281/583–9992.

14 c-3

2537 University Blvd., Rice University Village, 713/524–6635.

4 d-5

11920 Westheimer, Southwest, 281/558–4968.

2 g-8

18111 Egret Bay Blvd., Clear Lake/Bay Area, 281/335–1283.

4 b-5

3203 Hwy. 6 S, Southwest, 281/265–0900.

4 b-3

PAPERBACK EXCHANGES
A two-for-one trade-in deal makes addiction management easy, and romance, western, thriller, and sci-fi fans take full advantage. *14469 Memorial, Memorial/Spring Branch, 281/596–7323.*

4 b-6

6422 N. Hwy. 6, Katy/Bear Creek, 281/859–1045.

2 d-2

5010 Louette Rd., Cy-Fair, 281/379–3689.

9 h-4

5213 Bellaire, Bellaire, 713/668–8892.

4 b-6

6674-B S. Hwy. 6, Katy/Bear Creek, 281/530–4688.

CAMERAS

12 c-7

CAMERA CO/OP
Pro and amateur photographers and everyone who values good lenses find this selection of cameras and accessory equipment unmatched. *3514 S. Shepherd, Montrose, 713/522–7837.*

9 g-1

HOUSTON CAMERA EXCHANGE
Almost constant television advertising celebrates the shop's used camera division even though quick cash for used Nikons is only a small part of the business. Names you know as well as brands like Bogen, Tamron, and Pentax are in stock. *5900 Richmond, Galleria/Post Oak, 713/789–6901.*

9 h-1

SOUTHWESTERN CAMERA
You can set yourself up with a classic boxy Hasselblad, any number of lenses, lights, reflectors, film for any light or speed, and a scanner. Or you can snap up a digital camera. *5371 Westheimer, Galleria/Post Oak, 713/960–9904.*

7 e-5

500 N. Shepherd, Heights, 713/880–2505.

2 g-7

133 W. Bay Area Blvd., Clear Lake/Bay Area, 281/332–5990.

CANDLES

3 b-1

ASPEN GLOW
All you need to give your home a warm, flickering glow and soothing scents can be found here. *7979 N. Eldridge Pkwy., Traders Village, North, 281/890–2488.*

3 *b-1*

BURNING DESIRES

Find the cure for the fluorescent glow of your office, or light your home with oil lamps, floating candles, lava lamps, black lights, strobe lights, and more. You may not have enough light to read, but you'll be able to meditate or make romance until the cows come home. *14620 FM 529, at Huffmeister, Cy-Fair, 281/859–5822.*

2 *d-2*

TAPER CAPER
CANDLE SHOP

Men may feel out of place among the Yankee, Trapp, and Fitz & Floyd candles, colonial and holiday candlesticks, and tapestries. Women bent on getting unique gifts feel right at home. *222 Gentry, Spring, 281/288–7558.*

3 *b-7*

WICKS-N-STICKS

The '60s never died at Wicks-n-Sticks. Although the name remains the same, the wares have shifted from sand candles and ice-cube candles to contemporary scented pillars. *16535 Southwest Fwy., First Colony Mall, Sugar Land/Fort Bend, 281/494–1717.*

2 *g-8*

19010 Gulf Fwy., Baybrook Mall, Clear Lake/Bay Area, 281/486–8709.

2 *d-1*

1201 Lake Woodlands Dr., Woodlands Mall, The Woodlands, 281/298–9425.

10 *a-1*

5075 Westheimer, Galleria, Galleria/Post Oak, 713/627–0919.

2 *c-3*

7920 FM 1960 W, Willowbrook Mall, FM 1960 area, 281/807–5700.

CLOTHING
FOR CHILDREN

8 *e-8*

ANGEL'S THINGS

No grandparent can resist the well-tailored, storybook kiddie clothes offered by this shop. *800 S. Wayside Dr., East End, 713/926–6292.*

7 *a-8*

CHILDREN'S COLLECTION

Adults aren't the only ones angling for best dressed by shopping at this Post Oak boutique. Sturdy overalls and colorful wash-and-wear cotton blends may be okay on the average playground, but some youngsters are expected to have a better look on the seesaw, swings, and slides of their tony neighborhood park. *1717 Post Oak Blvd., Galleria/Post Oak, 713/622–4415.*

6 *c-7*

CHOCOLATE SOUP

Children and tot clothing are sold here at factory outlet prices. Although the prices are designed to draw the budget-conscious, like most Memorial strip center stores, Chocolate Soup's interior feels utterly boutique. *12850 Memorial, Memorial/Spring Branch, 713/467–5957.*

6 *f-7*

COTTON TOTS

You give in on the sugar. You give in on the fast food. You can maintain at least one of your parenting promises by sending your kids to school in natural fibers. *6401 Woodway, Galleria/Post Oak, 713/785–8686.*

12 *e-6*

2055 Westheimer, Ste. 125, Montrose, 713/526–8686.

7 *b-7*

GAP KIDS

Who knew khaki was cute? Suit up your small fry in casual-Friday clothing cut down to their sizes. *4056 Westheimer, River Oaks, 713/963–9311.*

4 *b-3*

600 W. Sam Houston Pkwy. N, Memorial/Spring Branch, 713/464–3243.

14 *c-1*

6225 Kirby, Rice University Village, 713/942–9225.

6 *c-5*

900 Gessner, Memorial/Spring Branch, 713/467–2495.

10 *a-1*

5175 Westheimer, Galleria/Post Oak, 713/965–9929.

6 *f-8*

1675 Voss, Galleria/Post Oak, 713/783–1750.

12 *d-4*

GYMBOREE

Strong simple colors and durable designs are the Gymboree statement. *2012 W. Gray, River Oaks, 713/529–9095.*

6 c-7

12850 Memorial, Memorial/Spring Branch, 713/468–4847.

6 c-5

900 Gessner, Memorial/Spring Branch, 713/464–7199.

6 c-5

LIMITED TOO

When teal is in for adults, you'll see the same shade on youngsters dressed at this junior version of teen and twentysomething fashion staples of The Limited, The Limited Express, and Structure. 1000 Katy Fwy., Memorial City Mall, Memorial/Spring Branch, 713/464–5559.

10 a-1

5085 Westheimer, Galleria/Post Oak, 713/621–6330.

10 a-1

LITTLE LORDS & LADIES

You might wonder just how far high school rebellion would go when a kid's been subjected to such fussy dressing, although it's hard to think of anything but how perfect and adorable they look in Little Lord and Lady ruffles and bows. The shop also has a children's hair salon. 6100 Westheimer, Galleria/Post Oak, 713/782–6554.

6 f-7

SECOND CHILDHOOD

Each August, harried moms say a blessing for this dependable source of quality school clothes at outlet prices. 1438 S. Voss, Galleria/Post Oak, 713/789–6456.

CLOTHING FOR WOMEN/ GENERAL STORES

classic & casual

2 c-3

ANN TAYLOR

Career women owe a great deal to Ann Taylor's structured, somewhat conservative, and still ego-boosting stylish slacks, suits, and slick after-five ensembles. 7920 W. FM 1960 W, Willowbrook Mall, FM 1960 area, 281/469–6792.

2 d-1

1201 Lake Woodlands Dr., The Woodlands, 281/298–6394.

2 g-8

19400 Gulf Fwy., Baybrook Mall, Clear Lake/Bay Area, 281/280–8331.

12 d-4

1992 W. Gray, River Oaks, 713/526–7153.

6 c-7

12850 Memorial, Memorial/Spring Branch, 713/973–1196.

10 a-1

5085 Westheimer, Galleria/Post Oak, 713/627–3722.

14 c-3

5515 Kelvin, Rice University Village, 713/521–0981.

4 b-3

BANANA REPUBLIC

Dress to match your sport utility vehicle with styles from this sophisticated sector of the Gap enterprise. Look for slim black suits, leather coats, and filmy neck scarves. Sometimes it goes overboard on the single color highlighted in any given season—who bought the bright purples of fall 2000? 600 W. Sam Houston Pkwy. N, Memorial/Spring Branch, 713/461–6057.

2 c-3

7925 FM 1960 W, FM 1960 area, 281/894–9587.

10 a-1

5015 Westheimer, Galleria, Galleria/Post Oak, 713/621–4451.

14 c-3

2400 University Blvd., Rice University Village, 713/523–4730.

10 b-1

3922 Westheimer, River Oaks, 713/963–0320.

6 c-5

CASUAL CORNER

Women with entry-level office jobs can find serious work suits at soothing prices. 1000 Katy Fwy., Memorial City Mall, Memorial/Spring Branch, 713/468–2689.

9 e-4

7500 Bellaire Blvd., Sharpstown Shopping Center, Sharpstown, 713/776–9567.

7 a-3

9930 Hempstead, Memorial/Spring Branch, 713/688–1378.

7 a-8

ESTHER WOLF

The same set of women shows up in both the society pages and at Esther Wolf's. The lingerie department's "bra lady" can do more for you than any plastic surgeon. *1800 Post Oak, Galleria/Post Oak, 713/622–1331.*

9 e-4

FOXMOORE

This low-key chain stocks sweaters, slacks, and simple suits. *7500 Bellaire Blvd., Sharpstown, 713/271–8661.*

7 g-1

4500 North Fwy., Northline Mall, North, 713/697–2885.

14 c-3

J. LAIRD

Proprietress Fae Laird (you'll have to ask her about the J) stocks her boutique with a little bit of this and a little bit of that. If your own instincts can't pull something together, then count on Fae to find pieces that work together for you. *2509 Rice Blvd., Rice University Village, 713/526–7179.*

2 g-8

THE LIMITED

This durable mall standard is trendy central, always ready with the colors and cuts for each season. Hair accessories, sunglasses, cute socks, and other details are stocked near the checkout. *19400 Gulf Fwy., Baybrook Mall, Friendswood, 281/488–4955.*

10 a-1

5085 Westheimer, Galleria, Galleria/Post Oak, 713/961–5301.

6 c-5

1000 Katy Fwy., Memorial City Mall, North, 713/932–7009.

6 a-5

800 W. Sam Houston Pkwy. N, Town & Country Mall, Memorial/Spring Branch, 713/461–9711.

4 b-5

2600 Hwy. 6, West Oaks Mall, Southwest, 281/556–6032.

2 c-3

7920 FM 1960 W, Willowbrook Mall, FM 1960 area, 281/890–6680.

4 b-5

LIMITED EXPRESS

The Limited's younger, ever trendier little sister has fashionable clothes cut in unforgiving sizes and summer dresses showing lots of skin. *2700 S. Hwy. 6, Southwest, 281/531–0033.*

6 c-5

1000 Katy Fwy., Memorial City Mall, Memorial/Spring Branch, 713/464–5559.

2 d-1

1201 Lake Woodlands Dr., Woodlands Mall, The Woodlands, 281/298–7611.

10 a-1

5085 Westheimer, Galleria/Post Oak, 713/621–6330.

2 g-8

19400 Gulf Fwy., Baybrook Mall, Clear Lake/Bay Area, 281/286–4796.

13 b-3

PALAIS ROYAL

If it is at all possible to sell pastels and softer shapes, Palais Royal will. When the fashionistas simply will not allow peach and robin's egg and the like, then Palais Royal goes with the flow and brings in somber colors. *917 Main, Downtown/Theater District, 713/658–1182.*

14 c-3

3902 Bissonnet, Rice University Village, 713/660–7711.

2 f-5

431 Uvalde, Pasadena/Southeast, 713/450–1551.

7 c-2

1345 W. 43rd St., North, 713/686–3436.

6 c-5

1000 Katy Fwy., Memorial City Mall, Memorial/Spring Branch, 713/461–6617.

6 f-8

6550 Woodway, Galleria/Post Oak, 713/467–5647.

9 e-4

7500 Bellaire Blvd., Sharpstown Shopping Center, Sharpstown, 713/777–5571.

2 d-3

12300 North Fwy., Greenspoint Mall, North, 281/875–1144.

2 *c-3*

5407 FM 1960 W, FM 1960 area, 281/440–1620.

2 *c-3*

7920 FM 1960 W, Willowbrook Mall, FM 1960 area, 281/890–8229.

2 *f-7*

11510 Gulf Fwy., Almeda Mall, South Houston/Hobby Airport, 713/944–5050.

9 *a-1*

10957 Westheimer, Southwest, 713/782–1084.

3 *d-2*

6696 Antoine, North, 713/682–6520.

7 *b-4*

530 N.W. Hempstead, Memorial/Spring Branch, 713/681–5881.

9 *f-8*

11251 Fondren, Meyerland, 713/995–5443.

10 *d-6*

10201 Main, Astrodome/Old Spanish Trail, 713/667–5601.

9 *e-4*

7500 Bellaire Blvd., Sharpstown, 713/777–5571.

12 *e-3*

901 N. Shepherd, Heights, 713/880–9808.

11 *f-4*

7100 Gulf Fwy., South Houston/Hobby Airport, 713/645–6033.

4 *b-6*

6863 Hwy. 6 N, Katy/Bear Creek, 281/345–7979.

4 *b-5*

2600 Hwy. 6, West Oaks Mall, Southwest, 281/531–4494.

4 *d-7*

11939 Bissonnet, Southwest, 281/561–9465.

4 *e-5*

10957 Westheimer, Memorial/Spring Branch, 713/782–1084.

14 *c-3*

RASPBERRY ROSE

If you have a hard time navigating the wide selection of unique and romantic clothing and accessories, the staff will be happy to help you create a personal style. 2434 Rice Blvd., Rice University Village, 713/529–2260.

10 *a-5*

TALBOTS

Preppy in Houston? Yes, it can be done. This chain sells plenty of red, white, navy, plaid, and nothing daring. 4700 Beechnut, Meyerland Plaza, Meyerland, 713/667–9900.

contemporary

14 *c-3*

URBAN OUTFITTERS

From pre-worn-looking jeans to crocheted tops your grandmother would have never made for you, this trendy chain supplies the college student's wardrobe, and working adult's playwear. Check the quality of the stitching before paying for fun fashion that will fall apart fast. 2501 University Blvd., Rice University Village, 713/529–3023.

10 *a-1*

WET SEAL

The fine group of enablers who staff this store allows you to dress like Sarah Jessica Parker without spending the amount of money her stylists do. 5075 Westheimer, Galleria, Galleria/Post Oak, 713/840–7657.

designer

10 *a-1*

A. TAGHI

If you have the money, you can choose conservative styles and shoes such as Bruno Magli and Bally or make a more aggressive statement with Versace Classic and Dolce & Gabbana. 5116 Westheimer, Galleria/Post Oak, 713/963–0884.

10 *a-1*

BEBE

Slim-Fast and Pilates gave us size 2 and then size 0 (!) figures. Bebe provides crop tops, stretch fabrics, and sheers to show off hard-won shapes. Even grown-up Texas women have fun with these scanty and often trashy designs. In 1998, it appeared that every single female in Houston bought a pair of short jeans with a 5-inch cuff of oriental fabric; Bebe's sold most of them. *5015 Westheimer, Galleria/Post Oak, 713/622–2113.*

10 *a-1*
BETSEY JOHNSON
Looking for something with a splash of hot pink? Feathers? Just want high-end funk? Betsey Johnson provides fanciful dress-up for girls with grown-up budgets. The mostly rayon fabrics will last as long as the trend-of-the-moment does. *5015 Westheimer, Galleria/Post Oak, 713/963–9550.*

12 *d-4*
BISOU BISOU/ B.B.1 CLASSIC
Mostly skintight and skin-baring clothes is what the well-dressed waif will stock up on here in mesh and crepe. The prices aren't bad at all. A store with deals like a nylon/Lycra bias-cut slip dress for less than $100 is a store deserving loyalty. *2001 W. Gray, River Oaks, 713/942–7565.*

6 *f-7*
ELIZABETH ANTHONY COLLECTION
Selections range from a-touch-too-chic-for-the-office to dressed-to-the-nines outfits. Nothing outré, however. *1395 S. Voss, Galleria/Post Oak, 713/467–4646.*

14 *c-3*
J. HAMPTON
Men and women who need to travel at the speed of fashion drape themselves in Dina Bar-el, Wayne Rogers, Versace Classic, A'nue, JhaneBarnes, and other youthful looks. *2433 University Blvd., Rice University Village, 713/523–9443.*

7 *b-8*
JOAN & DAVID
Joan & David's minimalist lines and gray-toned palette ensure you're always elegant and never overdressed. Shoes, scarves, belts, and even jewelry are also available to complete the look. *4045 Westheimer, River Oaks, 713/963–9848.*

7 *b-8*
TOOTSIE'S
This boxy, high-ceilinged store is like a Target of couture, and that's a good thing. Shop in casual comfort for amazing clothing and accessories from designers like Richard Tyler, Moschino, Helmut Lang, and more. *4045 Westheimer, River Oaks, 713/629–9990.*

10 *a-1*
5075 Westheimer, Tootsie's Galleria, Galleria, Galleria/Post Oak, 713/439–0076.

discount & off-price

9 *e-1*
CLOTHESTIME
The goods on the racks can be judged by a simple rule: there's an inverse ratio between fashion and quality. Stylish after-five dresses might not be so well made, but Clothestime's super-cheap sportswear is durable. *7539 Westheimer, Richmond Strip, 713/978–7017.*

12 *d-6*
2055 Westheimer, Montrose, 713/528–0771.

10 *a-5*
9927 S. Post Oak Blvd., Meyerland, 713/728–1082.

14 *c-3*
2517 University Blvd., Rice University Village, 713/942–9929.

6 *d-5*
9401 Katy Fwy., Memorial/Spring Branch, 713/467–4277.

3 *c-2*
5762 Hollister, North, 713/690–2336.

3 *c-2*
DRESS BARN
This is the perfect place to pick up clothes for fickle teens, colorful sportswear, and ordinary, cut-rate nine-to-five ensembles. *5762-½ Hollister, North, 713/690–6161.*

10 *a-1*
5140 Richmond, Galleria/Post Oak, 713/963–9844.

13 *b-3*
1200 McKinney, The Park Shops, Downtown/Theater District, 713/650–6762.

2 *c-3*
7714 FM 1960 W, FM 1960 area, 281/469–6922.

9 *e-4*
LERNER SHOP
Chunky and roomy sweaters and dresses that go from work, to school, to the kids' school, and then out to eat are

easy to find. The chain often stocks coordinated outfits. *7500 Bellaire, Sharpstown, 713/776–3134.*

6 *c-5*

1000 Katy Fwy., Memorial City Mall, Memorial/Spring Branch, 713/461–8079.

7 *a-3*

9800 Hempstead, Memorial/Spring Branch, 713/686–4101.

4 *e-4*

800 W. Sam Houston Pkwy. N, Memorial/Spring Branch, 713/973–9520.

6 *c-5*

LOEHMANN'S

The holy grail! It's not unusual to find well-known names for a third of their usual price, and seasoned shoppers boast of scoring astounding bargains like a current Fendi bag for practically nothing. Fear not. The legendary group dressing room is long gone. You can try things on in privacy. *9347 Katy Fwy., Memorial/Spring Branch, 713/932–8011.*

9 *e-5*

7455 Southwest Fwy., Sharpstown, 713/777–0164.

3 *b-7*

OFF 5TH

Thanks to the mysteries of retailing, you can often find the same clothes still selling at Saks Fifth Avenue in the outlet store at 40% to 70% below original retail. And Off 5th is more than an outlet. If you find the perfect Ungaro pants in size 8 and need a 6, salespeople will call other Off 5th stores to search for your size and have them shipped direct. *12610 Fountain Lake Circle, Sugar Land/Fort Bend, 281/277–6700.*

2 *e-3*

ROSS DRESS FOR LESS

Many women who would prefer to spend their clothing budget on cocktail dresses and sportswear rely on Ross for serviceable dress-code attire. Whether your office requires conservative dresses with stockings only, or allows less formal slacks, you'll find your nine-to-five uniform here. *4645 FM 1960 W, FM 1960 area, 281/583–0391.*

2 *f-7*

12200 Gulf Fwy., Almeda Mall, South Houston/Hobby Airport, 713/944–3990.

3 *a-1*

7081 Hwy. 6 N, Cy-Fair, 281/859–3996.

2 *c-2*

T.J. MAXX

A little bit of digging can pay off in a big way. Clothes are jammed into racks with only a bare minimum of organization, but a thorough shopper can pick up La Perla bras, Woolrich jeans, and clothes for every occasion at terrific discounts. *10717 Jones Rd., FM 1960 area, 281/955–9876.*

resale

12 *g-7*

BLUE BIRD CIRCLE

Sometimes it's difficult to believe that such a large, clean, well-organized store can have such excellent bargains. Most of the clothes here (men's, women's, and children's) come from upper-crust closets. *615 Alabama, Montrose, 713/528–0470.*

7 *b-8*

DORENE'S RE-FINERY

Shop for designers up to and including Chanel, but do it the inexpensive way. After all, if you're only attending one gala, no one will notice if you wear last year's designs, and the difference between the price of a new designer suit and a resale designer suit is enough to buy a ticket for a benefit luncheon. *4745 Westheimer, River Oaks, 713/629–5818.*

12 *f-6*

THE GUILD RESALE SHOP

This church charity shop has a hodgepodge of clothing, toys, furniture, and sports equipment, and a few long racks of wonderful clothes. *1203 Lovett Blvd., Montrose, 713/529–0995.*

7 *e-3*

SAND DOLLAR THRIFT STORE

Although location, ambience, and most wares mark this as a bottom-rung resale shop, Sand Dollar frequently has a rich selection of late '50s and early '60s dresses in mint condition. *1903 Yale, Heights, 713/868–4940.*

7 *h-5*

2300 N. Main, Heights, 713/229–0266.

5 *h-5*

7018 Harrisburg Blvd., East End, 713/923–1461.

unusual sizes

2 h-5
THE AVENUE
You already know one of your best bets is a flowing top over loose pants, but this store has some other options in store for you, too. *12140 East Fwy., Pasadena/Southeast , 713/453–0339.*

12 d-4
1544 West Gray, River Oaks, 713/ 521–7844.

14 c-3
LANE BRYANT
Never mind the attractive and well-made clothes suitable for plus-size sisters. The in-store ads alone make Lane Bryant worth the trip. Every wall features big black-and-white shots of big models looking gorgeous. *2521 University Blvd., Rice University Village, 713/528–3711.*

4 e-4
800 W. Belt Dr., Memorial/Spring Branch, 713/461–7295.

9 e-4
7500 Bellaire Blvd., Sharpstown Shopping Center, Sharpstown, 713/270–0800.

2 d-3
12000 North Fwy., Greenspoint Mall, North, 281/875–0485.

2 c-3
7925 FM 1960 W, FM 1960 area, 281/ 955–5036.

2 f-7
12200 Gulf Fwy., Almeda Mall, South Houston/Hobby Airport, 713/944–0110.

4 b-5
2600 Hwy. 6, West Oaks Mall, Southwest, 281/497–2149.

7 a-3
9930 Hempstead Rd., Memorial/Spring Branch, 713/681–4671.

10 a-5
4700 Beechnut, Meyerland Plaza, Meyerland, 713/432–7764.

10 a-1
MACY'S WOMAN
Indulge in the full-bore department store experience with cosmetic counters, coffee shops, and accessories without having to handle annoying one-digit-size clothes. *2727 Sage, Galleria/Post Oak, 713/968–1985.*

6 c-5
PETITE SOPHISTICATE
Being short-waisted is not a fashion flaw. In fact, when you can find a store with clothes cut for you, the effect is a perfect silhouette. If you're under 5'4", whether size 2 or double-digits, Petite Sophisticate has clothes in your proportions. *1000 Katy Fwy., Memorial City Mall, Memorial/Spring Branch, 713/465–6037.*

10 a-1
5132 Richmond, Galleria/Post Oak, 713/ 622–2131.

10 a-1
TALL ETC.
Interesting, isn't it? Supermodels get to be on E! in the very, very latest, and yet you have a hard time simply finding a decent suit. This is your answer. Although the store doesn't stock haute names, Tall Etc. can put you in stylish clothes cut for your build. *5880 Westheimer, Galleria/Post Oak, 713/974–4955.*

vintage

12 d-4
BAUBLES & BEADS
Those of us not blessed with wealthy aunts to hand down barely worn fine clothing turn to the consignment racks at this oh-so-helpful store. Many locations offer alterations. *1945 W. Gray, River Oaks, 713/524–4100.*

14 c-1
2437 Bissonnet, Rice University Village (men's only), 713/522–5645.

6 d-5
9715 Katy Fwy., Memorial/Spring Branch, 713/468–3544.

3 b-8
3613 Hwy. 6, Sugar Land/Fort Bend, 281/ 980–7600.

9 c-1
9600 Westheimer, Woodlake Square, Richmond Strip, 713/785–2646.

12 f-6
STEP BACK VINTAGE FASHIONS
The padded shoulders of the '80s are long gone, but Joan Crawford–style shoulders are still in vogue. You can also find unique formal wear here. *1212 Westheimer, Montrose, 713/522–7997.*

12 *e-7*

TIMELESS TAFFETA

Fill your closets with jersey cocktail dresses from the '40s, poofed skirts from the '50s, and formals from most of the 20th century. *1657 Westheimer, Montrose, 713/529–6299.*

12 *e-y*

WAY WE WORE

This clothing and costume shop has yesterday's clothes for the idiosyncratic dresser and those who need a special look for a festive occasion. *2602 Waugh, Montrose, 713/526–8910.*

12 *f-6*

WEAR IT AGAIN, SAM

A savvy staff makes vintage shopping more fun by creating humorous window displays. *1411 Westheimer, Montrose, 713/523–5258.*

CLOTHING FOR WOMEN/SPECIALTY STORES

furs

7 *a-8*

RICHARD PETERS FURS

If you want sable in the Southwest, stop on in, and don't mess around with any muffs or car coats. Go for full-length fur. *1801 Post Oak Blvd., Galleria/Post Oak, 713/965–0696.*

10 *a-1*

SAKOWITZ

There are plenty of reasons to have a fur even though you live in a semitropical climate. Most of those reasons, full-length, dense of pile, and blissfully soft, are in climate-controlled housing at Sakowitz. *5026 Westheimer, Galleria/Post Oak, 713/622–7947.*

handbags & gloves

10 *a-1*

COACH

The '90s saw Coach add colors to the long-standing line of sturdy, durable, and unfussy bags. The Galleria boutique offers a full selection, from the standard notebook clutch up to big, bright, modern handbags. *5075 Westheimer, Galleria/Post Oak, 713/877–8737.*

7 *a-7*

FENDI

Anyone who takes to globetrotting should be sure to set off with a Fendi bag. The collection is known for luxe leathers and faux skins, and all goods feature the cunning Fendi F logo. Not all the bags here are leather, but they're all absolutely fabulous. *5015 Westheimer, Uptown Park, Galleria/Post Oak, 713/961–1111.*

leather

10 *a-1*

MODERNO

Forget buckskin, piping, and fringe. This boutique carries styles suitable for cyberfantasies like "The Matrix" that are best accessorized with mirror shades. *5175 Westheimer, Galleria/Post Oak, 713/993–0697.*

10 *a-1*

NORTH BEACH LEATHER

In many parts of America, wearing leather says nouveau riche. In Houston, it merely says, "Hah! I've got the body for this." Even those a few pounds past the ideal body for vivid yellow steerskin halters, shiny red, fringed jackets, and pastel suede suits shop here. And, of course, it's the prefect source for black leather pants. *5015 Westheimer, Galleria, Galleria/Post Oak, 713/629–5880.*

lingerie

2 *d-3*

FREDERICK'S OF HOLLYWOOD

You can't beat the old standards. Frederick's has been pushing things up and squishing things in and featuring "cutouts" since TV was in black-and-white, so it's hard to say if you're being progressive or retro when you buy a naughty nightie from this boutique. *12300 North Fwy., Greenspoint Mall, North, 281/873–4518.*

14 *c-1*

HOSIERY OUTLETS

As the name suggests, this store carries bins and bins of discounted Evan Picone, Dior, and other top-drawer stockings. The orderly outlet stores also have Jantzen and better swimsuits, and a rich variety of lingerie at astounding prices. *2420 Bissonnet, Rice University Village, 713/522–0748.*

`15` *a-5*

2511 W. Holcombe Blvd., Astrodome/Old Spanish Trail, 713/668–5147.

`4` *b-2*

SHEER FANTASY

If none of the many sizes and styles of foundation garments is a perfect fit, alterations are offered. The store specializes in bras: bridal, prosthetic, and simply fabulous. *1996 FM 1960 W, FM 1960 area, 281/444–4200.*

`7` *b-8*

TOP DRAWER LINGERIE

Both locations not only carry bras, panties, and negligees, but also specialize in prosthetics. *3920 Westheimer, River Oaks, 713/993–9931.*

`6` *f-7*

1343 S. Voss, Galleria/Post Oak, 713/784–8707.

`9` *e-4*

VICTORIA'S SECRET

Men don't seem to enjoy the stores anywhere nearly as much as they do the catalogues, although women find it's much easier to buy T-backs and push-up bras in person. Some Victoria's Secret designs are available only in stores. *750 Bellaire, Sharpstown Shopping Center, Sharpstown, 713/541–3656.*

`10` *a-1*

5058 Westheimer, Galleria/Post Oak, 713/622–8007.

`10` *e-3*

2414 University Blvd., Rice University Village, 713/526–1054.

`6` *c-5*

1000 Katy Fwy., Memorial City Mall, Memorial/Spring Branch, 713/468–0901.

`4` *e-4*

800 W. Sam Houston Pkwy., Memorial/Spring Branch, 713/827–7414.

`7` *b-8*

3942 Westheimer, River Oaks, 713/629–5623.

maternity

`6` *a-5*

MIMI MATERNITY

Mimi concentrates on functional, stylish clothing for the working mother-to-be. *800 W. Sam Houston Pkwy. N, Town &*

Country Mall, Memorial/Spring Branch, 713/932–1125.

`3` *b-7*

MOTHERHOOD MATERNITY

It's possible that women who are not pregnant will envy you when you show up in discreet dresses from Motherhood. *16535 Southwest Fwy., First Colony Mall, Sugar Land/Fort Bend, 281/277–1800.*

`2` *g-8*

19010 Gulf Fwy., Baybrook Mall, Clear Lake/Bay Area, 281/486–7778.

`2` *c-3*

7920 FM 1960 W, Willowbrook Mall, FM 1960 area, 281/890–0837.

`2` *d-1*

1201 Lake Woodlands Dr., Woodlands Mall, The Woodlands, 281/364–8544.

`4` *b-5*

2600 Hwy. 6, West Oaks Mall, Southwest, 281/496–0037.

`2` *f-3*

20131 Hwy. 59 N, Deerbrook Mall, North, 281/540–1955.

`14` *c-3*

A PEA IN THE POD

You may not be feeling particularly athletic, but if there is such a thing as maternity sportswear, A Pea in the Pod has it. *2367 Rice Blvd., Rice University Village, 713/522–3400.*

`10` *a-1*

5075 Westheimer, Galleria, Galleria/Post Oak, 713/961–0604.

`14` *c-3*

WOMEN'S WORK

Breast-feeding mothers will find bras, Medela pumps (sale or rental), and a thoughtful staff who will educate first-time moms. In their aim to be a full-service pre- and postpartum shop, Women's Work sells what can be called dress-for-success ensembles for pregnant and nursing mothers. *2401 Rice Blvd., Astrodome/Old Spanish Trail, 713/664–8155.*

shoes

For cowboy boots, *see* Western Wear *in* Clothing for Men/Specialty Stores.

`10` *a-1*

BALLY OF SWITZERLAND
Oooh, they're like butter. Generations have reveled in the glove-soft leather of Bally loafers, but even if you are only coming in for your second pair, the staff is likely to remember you. Bally also has high heels, dress shoes, belts, wallets, and other accessories. *5015 Westheimer, Galleria/Post Oak, 713/629–4180.*

`7` *a-8*

BRUCALS SHOES
Be kind to your feet with Easy Spirit, Trotters, Soft Spots, and other brands in wide and large sizes. *2027 Post Oak Blvd., Galleria/Post Oak, 713/621–2991.*

`2` *f-7*

BRUCETTES
The name and advertising touting sizes 2 to 14 in every width in the alphabet gives the wrong impression. These well-stocked stores should be known for carrying Bruno Magli, Stuart Weitzman, and other designer shoes. There are limits to what size foot can fit in strappy city sandals, but Magli and Ferragamo make some larger sizes, and Brucettes shelves these alongside good-looking large-size shoes that don't feature great labels. *11510 Gulf Fwy., Almeda Mall, South Houston/Hobby Airport, 713/941–1170.*

`10` *a-1*

4920 San Felipe, Galleria/Post Oak, 713/993–0022.

`7` *b-8*

COLE HAAN
You can find enough loafers and casual shoes in Cole Haan's signature dark tan for every day of the week, possibly enough for every day of the month. *4005 Westheimer, River Oaks, 713/877–1173.*

`9` *e-1*

DSW SHOE WAREHOUSE
What looks like an acre of shoes is carefully arranged in self-serve racks of running shoes, casual clogs, sandals, dress pumps, and decadent spike heels with spaghetti straps. Kenneth Cole makes frequent appearances on the clearance rack. *8383 Westheimer, Richmond Strip, 713/977–8691.*

`1` *a-1*

4849 FM 1960 W, FM 1960 area, 281/537–6061.

`7` *b-8*

E.G. GELLER SHOES
Foot-friendly shoes aren't always ugly or, as it turns out, inexpensive. E.G. Gellers has high-end former hippie shoes such as Mephisto, Anywear Clogs, Beautifeel, Wolky, and more. *4038 Westheimer, River Oaks, 713/993–0488.*

`6` *a-5*

ENZO ANGIOLINI
Feminism has done nothing to diminish the appeal of well-made, delicate Italian shoes. Demand an extra bonus, then spend a hefty chunk on Enzos. *12850 Memorial, Memorial/Spring Branch, 713/722–0552.*

`6` *c-5*

JARMAN
Walk for miles, and in style, with Fila, thick-soled leather Dr. Martens, Skechers, Rockport, and Timberland shoes. *1000 Katy Fwy., Memorial City Mall, Memorial/Spring Branch, 713/984–2395.*

`9` *e-4*

7500 Bellaire Blvd., Sharpstown Shopping Center, Sharpstown, 713/981–6742.

`7` *a-3*

9930 Hempstead, Memorial/Spring Branch, 713/682–2717.

`10` *a-1*

NATURALIZER SHOE SHOPS
Women hoping to make the workday just that much easier depend on plain, completely comfortable dress pumps from Naturalizer. *5075 Westheimer, Galleria/Post Oak, 713/961–0195.*

`2` *d-3*

12000 North Fwy., Greenspoint Mall, North, 281/875–8636.

`2` *g-8*

19010 Gulf Fwy., Baybrook Mall, Clear Lake/Bay Area, 281/486–9813.

`7` *a-3*

9800 Hempstead, Northwest Mall, Memorial/Spring Branch, 713/683–9398.

`10` *a-1*

THE WILD PAIR
They've got the funk, they've always had the funk, and this club-wear chain will be

going strong as long as people dress up and go out dancing. *5075 Westheimer, Galleria, Galleria/Post Oak, 713/961–3484.*

2 *d-3*

12000 North Fwy., Greenspoint Mall, North, 281/875–3550.

swimsuits

3 *a-2*

A-GLEAM SWIMWEAR

This Houston store carries sleek and sturdy suits for competitive swimmers, including team suits and accessories. Plus-size swimwear is also a specialty. *5228 Hwy. 6 N, Katy/Bear Creek, 281/859–0425.*

4 *e-4*

JUST ADD WATER

Even in February, the month when even Houstonians don't swim outdoors, the shops in this chain are stocked with the very latest in stylish swimwear, beachwear accessories, and cover-ups. *780 W. Sam Houston Pkwy. N, Memorial/Spring Branch, 713/461–2672.*

1 *a-1*

2503 Amherst, Rice University Village, 713/526–1385.

10 *a-1*

5085 Westheimer, Galleria, Galleria/Post Oak, 713/961–3891.

western wear

See Western Wear *in* Clothing for Men/Specialty Stores.

CLOTHING FOR MEN/ GENERAL STORES

classic & casual

2 *d-1*

ABERCROMBIE & FITCH

Wholesome and urbanely rugged (lots of plaid, woolly sweaters, flannel shirts), this chain tweaks its apple-pie image by finding excuses to show semi-nude young men in its print ads. *1201 Lake Woodlands Dr., The Woodlands, 281/363–4664.*

10 *a-1*

5085 Westheimer, Galleria, Galleria/Post Oak, 713/629–6221.

10 *a-1*

BENETTON

It's a world of knits, and you'll find a few gabardines, too. *5075 Westheimer, Galleria/Post Oak, 713/850–9211.*

13 *b-3*

BROOKS BROTHERS

Brooks Brothers is not just a store, it's an adjective because the company's almost 200-year tradition of shirts, blazers, and dress pants has created in spades what modern marketing mavens like to call "branding." *1200 McKinney, The Park Shops, Downtown/Theater District, 713/659–4000.*

10 *a-1*

5085 Westheimer, Galleria, Galleria/Post Oak, 713/627–2057.

14 *c-3*

EDDIE BAUER

You need not have been within 300 miles of a trout stream to effect the sporty-casual look popularized by Eddie Bauer. Count on this store for sweaters, shirts, slacks, jeans, boxers, and golf clothes. *2400 University Blvd., Rice University Village, 713/520–9890.*

10 *a-1*

5075 Westheimer, Galleria, Galleria/Post Oak, 713/840–0060.

2 *c-3*

7925 FM 1960 W, FM 1960 area, 281/955–5591.

14 *c-3*

THE GAP

This is the store that made casual Friday possible, and guys are still stopping by for jeans, khakis, supersoft Ts, cotton shirts, and belts. *6225 Kirby, Rice University Village, 713/942–7061.*

6 *c-5*

900 Gessner, Memorial/Spring Branch, 713/932–7000.

7 *b-8*

4030 Westheimer, River Oaks, 713/877–1271.

6 *f-7*

1675 S. Voss, Galleria/Post Oak, 713/783–0931.

12 *f-6*

1000 Westheimer, Montrose, 713/626–8191.

2 c-3

7925 FM 1960 W, FM 1960 area, 281/
890–0493.

4 e-4

600 W. Sam Houston Pkwy. N, Memo-
rial/Spring Branch, 713/932–0600.

2 d-3

12000 North Fwy., Greenspoint Mall,
North, 281/875–1900.

10 a-1

5085 Westheimer, Galleria, Galleria/Post
Oak, 713/626–8191.

7 e-3

HAROLD'S IN THE HEIGHTS

Harold's is like the Brooks Brothers of
the Inner Loop. Generations have relied
on this family-owned Heights shop for
dress shirts, conservative ties, and reasonably priced suits. 350 W. 19th St.,
Heights, 713/864–2647.

10 a-1

J. CREW

Here you'll find the same casual clothes
offered in the catalogue, and, as a plus,
you can return or exchange mail-order
purchases here. 5015 Westheimer, Galle-
ria/Post Oak, 713/626–2739.

12 d-4

JOS. A. BANK CLOTHIERS

Although they don't offer custom-made
tailoring, any of the quality Jos. A. Bank
shirts, suits, casual slacks, and coats
can be expertly altered. 2030 W. Gray,
River Oaks, 713/523–7077.

2 c-3

7608 FM 1960, Commons at Willowbrook, FM 1960 area, 281/955–8100.

10 a-5

4700 Beechnut, Meyerland Plaza, Meyerland, 713/218–6800.

9 c-1

9696 Westheimer, Richmond Strip, 713/
785–0466.

2 d-3

OLD NAVY

Stock up on inexpensive shirts,
sweaters, sweats, and casual wear, but
don't expect the trendy goods to show
signs of wear even as they go out of
style. 4605 FM 1960, FM 1960 area, 281/
587–2093.

10 a-1

5000 Westheimer, Galleria/Post Oak, 713/
917–0469.

10 a-5

4700 Beechnut, Meyerland Plaza, Meyerland, 713/349–9122.

4 b-6

6867 Hwy. 6 N, Katy/Bear Creek, 281/
345–1570.

7 a-3

STRUCTURE

Like its feminine counterpart, The Limited, Structure is always first with new
colors and fabrics. Whenever something
like burnt orange or crushed velvet
comes back on the fashion radar, it will
be at Structure first. 9930 Hempstead,
Memorial/Spring Branch, 713/682–5091.

6 f-7

1635 S. Voss, Galleria/Post Oak, 713/783–
0993.

10 a-1

5075 Westheimer, Galleria, Galleria/Post
Oak, 713/622–5465.

9 e-4

7500 Bellaire, Sharpstown, 713/270–1060.

6 c-5

900 Gessner, Memorial/Spring Branch,
713/467–3886.

4 e-4

800 W. Sam Houston Pkwy. N, Memo-
rial/Spring Branch, 713/464–1599.

14 c-3

2415 University Blvd., Rice University Village, 713/520–6377.

contemporary

13 b-4

A. TAGHI

Women who shop here for men can pick
up a few things for themselves in the
women's department. The long and elite
line of names represented here includes
Stefano Ricci, Versace Classic, Brioni,
and Bruno Magli. 1300 Lamar, Down-
town/Theater District, 713/650–8006.

10 a-1

5116 Westheimer, Galleria/Post Oak, 713/
963–0884.

10 *a-1*

GIANNI VERSACE

Sometimes the extreme looks here appear to be a premonition of what we'll wear after the apocalypse, but for men who want an edge there is no better designer. *5015 Westheimer, Galleria/Post Oak, 713/623–8220.*

12 *b-7*

M. PENNER

This family-owned boutique has earned national attention for an exquisite collection of fine menswear. If the gorgeous window displays aren't enough to lure you inside, then consider this partial list of M. Penner designers: Loro Piana, Canali, Donna Karan, Ferragamo, Hugo Boss, Kiton, Vestimenta, and Ermenegildo Zegna. *2950 Kirby, Upper Kirby District, 713/527–8200.*

discount & off-price

2 *f-6*

MEN'S WEARHOUSE

Founder and CEO of this national warehouse, George Zimmer is as familiar as a neighborhood tailor, thanks to constant commercials. His stores provide everything you need to dress for success, including tie-tying instruction and business-casual and formal clothes. Ask about the VIP program. *1072 Federal Rd., Pasadena/Southeast, 713/453–0423.*

11 *h-6*

8452 Gulf Fwy., South Houston/Hobby Airport, 713/649–4974.

12 *d-4*

1947 W. Gray, River Oaks, 713/529–6191.

6 *c-5*

9311 Katy Fwy., Memorial/Spring Branch, 713/932–6296.

10 *a-1*

6100 Westheimer, Galleria/Post Oak, 713/784–1185.

2 *d-2*

344 FM 1960 W, FM 1960 area, 281/587–8591.

2 *c-3*

7696 FM 1960 W, FM 1960 area, 281/890–8474.

4 *c-5*

12520 Westheimer, Southwest, 281/870–9134.

3 *a-1*

8500 Hwy. 6 N, Cy-Fair, 281/550–8101.

10 *a-5*

4946 Beechnut, Meyerland, 713/592–9892.

9 *f-3*

5810 Hillcroft, Sharpstown, 713/974–3402.

9 *g-2*

5803 Glenmont Dr., Sharpstown, 713/529–7200.

10 *a-1*

6100 Westheimer, Galleria/Post Oak, 713/784–1185.

6 *g-5*

NAL MENSWEAR SUPERCENTER

Both locations offer cut rates and a reasonable selection. The Rice Village location is only open Friday, Saturday, and Sunday. *9447 Old Katy Rd., Memorial/Spring Branch, 281/589–7337.*

9 *e-3*

7130 Harwin, Sharpstown, 713/974–1001.

9 *d-1*

STEINMART

The men's section of this discount department store has a wide selection of dress shirts, sharp shirts for after five, and excellent sportswear. *2640 Fondren, Richmond Strip, 713/266–9742.*

2 *c-3*

5319 FM 1960 W, FM 1960 area, 281/893–5484.

10 *a-5*

4700 Beechnut, Meyerland Plaza, Meyerland, 713/665–6000.

resale, vintage, surplus

3 *f-2*

ARMY SURPLUS STORE

Genuine surplus gear has two advantages: it's inexpensive and durable. *6914 North Fwy., North, 713/695–9517.*

6 *f-3*

COMMAND POST

This store sells another kind of khaki, along with fatigues, T-shirts, boots, and more in a somewhat limited color scheme. *8653 Longpoint, Heights, 713/827–7301.*

unusual sizes

3 f-2

BUCK'S THE BIG MAN STORE

Sizes run up to 6XT and 8XB, and you should be able to find shirts, jackets, and slacks to suit your personal style. *5900 North Fwy., North, 713/691–6113.*

6 c-5

CASUAL MALE BIG & TALL

This friendly chain welcomes gentlemen who are living large. Your comfort is the first consideration. *10321 Katy Fwy., Memorial/Spring Branch, 713/464–0640.*

2 f-5

10913 East Fwy., Pasadena/Southeast, 713/673–7565.

2 d-3

153 Greens Rd., North, 281/873–8532.

2 c-3

4608 FM 1960 W, FM 1960 area, 281/ 583–5121.

9 e-4

6898 Southwest Fwy., Sharpstown, 713/ 784–8542.

4 b-5

2346 Hwy. 6 S, Southwest, 281/752–5560.

11 g-1

GORDON'S MAN'S STORE/BIG AND TALL

This store carries active wear, outerwear, and both leisure and business attire for a select group. *518 Broadway, East End, 713/926–5018.*

CLOTHING FOR MEN/SPECIALTY STORES

formalwear

4 d-3

AL'S TUXEDO OUTLET

Don't let the name make you think of rows of blue velvet–ruffle shirt tuxes from 1978. It's simply a nice place to get a good sale or rental deal. *11290 Northwest Fwy., Memorial/Spring Branch, 713/ 682–2538.*

10 a-1

GINGISS

Standard penguin suits and some more-austere numbers by Perry Ellis, Calvin

Klein, Fumgalli, and Bill Blass are for sale and rent. *5075 Westheimer, Galleria/Post Oak, 713/626–3318.*

2 f-7

11510 Gulf Fwy., Almeda Mall, South Houston/Hobby Airport, 713/943–3721.

2 g-8

19010 Katy Fwy., Baybrook Mall, Clear Lake/Bay Area, 281/488–9096.

2 d-3

12000 North Fwy., Greenspoint Mall, North, 713/875–1730.

4 e-4

800 W. Sam Houston Pkwy. N, Town & Country Mall, Memorial/Spring Branch, 713/464–6020.

3 b-7

16535 Southwest Fwy., First Colony Mall, Sugar Land/Fort Bend, 281/313–0011.

2 c-3

7920 FM 1960 W, Willowbrook Mall, FM 1960 area, 281/890–2727.

4 b-5

2500 Hwy 6, West Oaks Mall, Southwest, 281/493–1966.

2 f-3

20131 Hwy. 59, Deerbrook Mall, North, 281/446–2100.

shirts

10 a-1

ALFRED DUNHILL OF LONDON

Dunhill is the gold standard for quality tailoring. Here, broadcloth shirts with French cuffs are the norm, rather than a specialty item. *5015 Westheimer, Galleria/Post Oak, 713/961–4661.*

9 f-3

BOND CLOTHIER

The best-dressed in Southwest Houston have their shirts custom-tailored here. Skilled tailors stitch collars to fit any neck, sleeves for freedom of movement, and darts for a trim-looking fit on any physique. *5645 Hillcroft, Sharpstown, 713/ 784–7121.*

10 a-1

CUSTOM SHOP

It's always wise to keep a couple of spare shirts in a desk drawer, and you get to decide whether those shirts are in generic plastic wrap, or properly boxed hand-tailored shirts. *5085 Westheimer, Downtown/Theater District, 713/621–2445.*

9 *g-1*
HAMILTON SHIRT CO.
All the little details—cuffs, collar style, cloth weight—are your choice, although the tailors will certainly offer advice. *5700 Richmond, Galleria/Post Oak, 713/780–8222.*

shoes
For cowboy boots, *see* Western Wear, *below.*

10 *a-1*
CHURCH'S ENGLISH SHOES
A classic pair of Church's oxblood wing tips will set you back several hundred dollars, and that's a bargain. These shoes are so well made, a pair you buy in middle age might outlast you. *5075 Westheimer, Galleria/Post Oak, 713/960–9363.*

14 *c-3*
EUROPEAN WALKING STORE
Kick your casual look up a notch with expensive, unusual styles in loafers, oxfords, and clogs. Like all luxury items, these shoes pamper you. *2416 Rice Blvd., Rice University Village, 713/528–4335.*

2 *d-3*
FLORSHEIM
The shoes that launched a thousand sales trips are still worn by salesmen and also by sales reps, modern men, accountants, and other men in gray flannel suits. *12300 North Fwy., Greenspoint Mall, Memorial/Spring Branch, 281/875–2929.*

9 *e-4*
7500 Bellaire Blvd., Sharpstown Shopping Center, Sharpstown, 713/774–1414.

10 *a-1*
5015 Westheimer, Galleria/Post Oak, 713/621–1440.

7 *b-8*
MEPHISTO SHOES
Mephisto's carefully engineered walking shoes are not the most attractive things on earth, but the look has a certain authority. *4038 Westheimer, River Oaks, 713/993–0488.*

9 *h-4*
RED WING SHOE STORE
Doc Martens and Wolverine boots enjoy a vogue from time to time. Men who know work boots stick with steel-toe Red Wings. Along with pole-climbers and safety shoes, Red Wing sells men's and women's work shoes. *5510-C Bellaire, Sharpstown, 713/666–8311.*

6 *c-5*
1007 Gessner, Memorial/Spring Branch, 713/932–0430.

2 *f-5*
13421 East Fwy., Pasadena/Southeast, 713/451–2008.

7 *c-1*
4232 Ella Blvd., North, 713/680–3101.

2 *d-3*
2139 FM 1960 W, FM 1960 area, 281/580–1737.

10 *a-7*
10880 W. Belfort, Southwest, 281/568–2413.

2 *c-3*
17776 Tomball Pkwy., North, 281/807–4720.

12 *c-7*
WHOLE EARTH PROVISION CO.
At this point in history, the boxy, cork-soled, allegedly orthopedic sandals have to be considered a classic. The line includes closed shoes, too. *2934 Shepherd, Montrose, 713/526–5226.*

ties

12 *b-8*
HOLSEY CUSTOM CLOTHES
Perhaps you don't really want a new tie; perhaps you're simply heartbroken because your luckiest Calvin Klein power tie is hopelessly stained, or the shape of your favorite Pierre Cardin is grossly out of date, or your chick-magnet Emilio Pucci is threadbare on the edges. If that's the case, you'll be glad to know that Holsey has an arrangement with Tiecrafters. Instead of spending a couple of hundred bucks, break a twenty and have your tie rejuvenated. *2613 Richmond Ave., Montrose, 713/524–3303.*

7 *b-8*
NORTON DITTO
Many focus on this clothier's large selection of both conservative blue-blazer,

Lacoste-type looks and leading European designer clothing, which is all well and good, but overlook the rich variety of neckties. And, if you've ever considered going the ascot route, a Norton Ditto salesperson can help you make a choice and teach you how to tie it. *4060 Westheimer, River Oaks, 713/688–9800.*

western wear

Everybody and their dog dons big hats and boots for the rodeo, and an awful lot of folks consider polished boots and vivid yoke-style snap-button shirts clubbing attire. No cowgirl would hit the dance floor in anything but Rockies. Department stores don't carry much, if any, cowpoke clothing, but men will find Wahmaker prairie-cut shirts, women will find Nikki peasant blouses, and everyone will find head-to-toe Justin fashions at these Western wear stores. Stop in for the full fashion experience, or just for Cruel Girl and Cinch jeans to augment your Wrangler wardrobe.

14 c-8
BOOT TOWN

The convenient locations may not carry the most exotic reptile-skin boots, and few of the boots on the rack will set you back $1,000. Survey color-coordinated Justin Ropers and belt sets in just about every color you can imagine. Prairie boots and even a few styles of work boots are snatched up almost as soon as they can be stocked. There's also a large clothing department. *8701 Kirby, Astrodome/Old Spanish Trail, 713/799–8001.*

9 d-5
8090 S Gessner Dr., Sharpstown, 713/981–4453.

2 f-5
12032 East Fwy., Pasadena/Southeast, 713/455–1844.

3 d-2
CAVENDER'S BOOT CITY

Country-dancing clubs could not exist without Cavender's. High-end Western-wear shoppers hit Stelzig, low-end Western-wear shoppers find bargains at Marshall's, everybody else tops dance duds with hats from Cavender's. *14045 Northwest Fwy, North, 713/462–1122.*

2 f-5
13580 East Fwy, Pasadena/Southeast, 713/450–3434.

10 d-6
2505 South Loop W, Astrodome/Old Spanish Trail, 713/664–8999.

9 d-1
9525 Westheimer, Richmond Strip, 713/952–7102.

2 g-6
5970 Fairmont, at Beltway Exit 8, Clear Lake/Bay Area, 281/998–2668.

2 f-3
2345 FM 1960 W, FM 1960 area, 281/444–4588.

7 a-3
12141 Katy Fwy., Memorial/Spring Branch, 281/597–1110.

2 g-8
20835 Gulf Fwy., Clear Lake/Bay Area, 281/338–4040.

2 f-3
20155 Hwy. 59 N, North, 281/548–3755.

6 c-5
DON'S WESTERN WEAR

Brands here, such as Justin, Rockies, and Cinch, are available at the chain stores, but some folks prefer Don's because they don't cotton to the idea of buying a big white hat from a franchise. Rodeo fans who need once-a-year getups suit up here. *10901 Katy Fwy., Memorial/Spring Branch, 713/673–6530.*

13 c-3
PALACE BOOT SHOP

Members of the Xydis family have run this small Downtown boot shop since the teens of the 20th century, and over the decades the rich and famous have come here for custom-made boots and brand names like Tony Lamas and the coveted Lucchese. A pope, presidents, and more bona fide cattlewomen then you can shake a stick at have all bought Palace boots. The atmosphere here is one-of-a-kind. *1212 Prairie, Downtown/Theater District, 713/224–1411.*

7 h-6
SHUDDE BROS. HATTERS

Western movies were not in vogue when the Shuddes started blocking hats—heck, most people hadn't seen a moving picture show when this shop opened. Cowboy hats are a specialty, but durable, well-made hats of all styles are offered.

Roy Rogers, Gene Autrey, and Rip Torn have all been fitted here. If you can't part with it, you can have your old ten-gallon beaver reblocked here. *905 Trinity, Heights, 713/223–2191.*

10 *a-1*
STELZIG OF TEXAS
If there is such a thing as couture cowboy clothing, then Stelzig has it. The look is more Lyle Lovett than Travis Tritt, and if you're just a working cowpoke, then you might have to hock a couple of silver belt buckles and a trophy saddle before shopping here. Not a few of the boots and suits are four figures. *3123 Post Oak Blvd., Galleria/Post Oak, 713/629–7779.*

3 *c-2*
TURNER SADDLERY
Nothing says "we love rodeo" like a toddler's hobby buckin' bull. For grown cowboys, the popular shop stocks gloves, ropes, flashy shirts, boot socks, and even cowboy briefs. *6125 W. Sam Houston Pkwy. N, North, 713/466–0781.*

COINS

9 *e-2*
COLLECTORS COIN SHOP
The shop has an old-fashioned attitude although it's in a modern warehouse center. Eager to bring a new generation into the mania, the shop gives kids free coins, hoping that they'll be back to spend their allowance on proof sets and mint sets. *8950 Westpark, Suite 116, Sharpstown, 713/952–2657.*

9 *e-4*
GULF COAST COINS & STAMPS
It's easy to trick family members into a trip to the mall, and then into Gulf Coast where you can browse for coins, coin books, attractive (and protective) display folios, and cigars. (Light the stogie to celebrate a terrific find). *7500 Bellaire Blvd., Sharpstown Shopping Center, Sharpstown, 713/981–6949.*

14 *c-3*
HOUSTON NUMISMATIC EXCHANGE INC.
Make an appointment to peruse a rich collection of U.S. currency (including paper money), doubloons, cobs, and ancient coins. The store also handles

jewelry, silver, and sports cards and memorabilia. *2486 Times Blvd., Rice University Village, 713/528–2135.*

6 *g-5*
US COINS & JEWELRY
Serious collectors and those who have come into coins, bullion, and jewelry can count on this multicertified buyer for appraisals. *8435 Katy Fwy., Memorial/Spring Branch, 713/464–6868.*

COMPUTERS & SOFTWARE

10 *c-2*
COMPUSA
The folks behind this chain were among the first to realize that computer stores should be more like hang-out music stores and less like an electronic parts warehouse. Be careful about getting too comfortable, though. Going crazy in a computer store puts extra digits, not extra dollars, on your credit card statement. *3908 Bissonnet, Rice University Village, 713/665–8520.*

4 *d-5*
12230 Westheimer, Southwest, 281/589–9300.

10 *a-1*
5000 Westheimer, Galleria/Post Oak, 713/629–4333.

4 *b-3*
330 FM 1960 W, FM 1960 area, 281/444–3899.

4 *e-5*
COMPUTER EXPO
This superstore sells Toshiba and Compaq computers, rents and leases desktop and laptop computers, and offers training. *11312 Westheimer, Southwest, 281/531–0990.*

6 *g-5*
COMPUTIZE
Computize is an Apple specialist and authorized Hewlett Packard reseller. *1008 Wirt, Memorial/Spring Branch, 713/957–1000.*

6 *e-5*
CONSUMERS COMPUTER EXCHANGE
This new and used, buy and sell, parts and service computer store is to the PC as a shade-tree mechanic is to a car.

They do good work, but slowly. *9055 Gaylord, Memorial/Spring Branch, 713/ 932–6123.*

COSTUMES & COSTUME RENTAL

14 *g-1*

FRANKEL'S COSTUME CO., INC.

Grand costumes like sequined mermaid suits and regalia reminiscent of Hollywood's most recent historic picture can be hired for a couple hundred bucks. Less ambitious looks are less pricey. If you want to make a major holiday impression, then bear in mind that by midsummer some of Frankel's nearly 60,000 costumes have already been booked for Halloween. *4815 Fannin, Downtown/Theater District, 713/528–6036.*

7 *f-5*

PARTY BOY

Party Boy is ready all year, with all manner of holiday, historic, and horror costumes. They carry Ben Nye makeup and other clown supplies. *1515 Studemont, Heights, 713/861–9080.*

9 *c-1*

PARTY CITY

When Halloween or just a weird mood comes around, head to Party City to buy the famed "alien fetus in a jar." Other gory novelties include various body parts in a jar and severed heads. The chain also carries licensed costumes for children and adults. Pokémon characters, the Scream ghoul, Powerpuff girls, and your garden-variety monsters are all available. You can also get party invitations, decorations, and helium balloons for any kind of party. *9525 Westheimer, Richmond Strip, 713/977–3177.*

2 *c-3*

6476 FM 1960 W, FM 1960 area, 281/ 893–5889.

4 *b-6*

6819 Hwy. 6 N, Katy/Bear Creek, 281/ 345–1400.

4 *b-5*

2525 Hwy. 6 S, Southwest, 281/752–9595.

10 *c-1*

3225 Southwest Fwy., Greenway Plaza, 713/667–5811.

3 *g-2*

7840 W. Tidwell Rd., North, 713/462–0200.

12 *h-8*

SOUTHERN IMPORTERS

Everybody who wants to be somebody else can find manufactured costumes, sewn-in-the-store costumes, or make a custom disguise with Southern Importers theatrical supplies. *4825 San Jacinto, Medical Center, 713/524–8236.*

CRAFTS

12 *d-4*

CIRCA NOW GALLERY

Pure pop for now people is the theme. The gallery deals in hand-painted, high-gloss tableware, clocks, and household accessories. *1983 W. Gray, River Oaks, 713/529–8234.*

6 *a-5*

HANSON GALLERY

Here you'll find delicate hand-carved wooden boxes, remarkable clocks, and a variety of accessories crafted with colored and stained glass. *800 W. Sam Houston Pkwy. N, Town & Country Mall, Memorial/Spring Branch, 713/984–1242.*

2 *c-3*

URBAN ARTIFACTS

Regional and local painters and artisans are represented. Shopping for others is easy with Urban Artifacts gift certificates. *5507 FM 1960 W, FM 1960 area, 888/842–3417.*

DISCOUNT

9 *e-4*

BURLINGTON COAT FACTORY

Why spend a lot of money on winter clothes when we live in this climate? This outlet store also carries clothing and sometimes even swimwear for the other 11 months of the year. *7555 Bellaire, Sharpstown, 713/776–2628.*

7 *f-3*

INSURANCE CLAIMS FIRE SALE

Although some of the merchandise is, frankly, junk, there are amazing bargains to be found. Seriously. Like a whole row of Anne Klein dresses for almost no money. Sure, all the dresses are the same color and size, but you only need one. 222 W. 19th St., Heights, 713/880–0827.

12 g-8
4125 Main, Downtown/Theater District, 713/526–2511.

13 c-4
1515 LaBranch, Downtown/Theater District, 713/659–8640.

7 g-3
2023 N. Main, Heights, 713/225–0618.

5 h-5
6708 Harrisburg, East End, 713/926–7120.

ELECTRONICS & AUDIO

6 c-5
ALL-STAR AUDIO VIDEO
Here you'll find unique gadgets such as GPS tracking devices and two-way and marine radios, along with major merchandise such as home theater systems, satellite dishes, and Direct TV. Brands carried included Philips/Magnavox, Pioneer, Sony, and SharpVision LCD projection systems. 10615 Katy Fwy., Memorial/Spring Branch, 713/464–0014.

10 e-1
ARCHITECTURAL ENTERTAINMENT
You're way past stacking stereo components on cinder blocks, so invite this crew in for built-in installation. 2200 Southwest Fwy., Montrose, 713/528–6783.

2 c-3
BEST BUY
Take advantage of their on-site installation, and put a Rockford Fosgate CD changer in your SUV, or purchase the tiniest Walkman. 7318 FM 1960 W, FM 1960 area, 281/444–5768.

9 e-3
EAST WEST INTERNATIONAL
All the major brands are crowded into this southwest Houston store. 5810 Hillcroft, Sharpstown, 713/789–6611.

12 c-6
RADIO SHACK
If you want, you can buy the parts here and build your own cell phone, but you could also just buy a phone, an answer-

ing machine, or any electronic device excluding TVs. 2415 Westheimer, Montrose, 713/523–3847.

10 d-1
5804 Kirby, Rice University Village, 713/661–7378.

7 e-5
915 N. Shepherd, Heights, 713/861–3795.

13 b-3
1200 McKinney, The Park Shops, Downtown/Theater District, 713/652–9070.

8 e-8
140 S. Wayside Dr., East End, 713/926–6601.

2 f-5
1002 Federal Rd., Pasadena/Southeast, 713/453–2022.

2 f-5
440 Uvalde, Pasadena/Southeast, 713/453–8140.

11 h-6
8458 Gulf Fwy., South Houston/Hobby Airport, 713/643–1017.

7 c-2
1232 W. 43rd St., North, 713/682–7713.

15 f-5
4502 Griggs Rd., Astrodome/Old Spanish Trail, 713/748–8317.

7 g-1
4500 North Fwy., Northline Mall, North, 713/697–7914.

6 c-5
900 Gessner, Memorial/Spring Branch, 713/464–6165.

10 c-6
9307 Stella Link, Astrodome/Old Spanish Trail, 713/665–5219.

14 g-4
2240 W. Holcombe, Astrodome/Old Spanish Trail, 713/665–7491.

9 e-4
7500 Bellaire, Sharpstown, 713/771–1204.

9 c-4
5858 Gessner, Sharpstown, 713/772–4842.

ETHNIC ITEMS

3 e-2
CACTUS KING
Outside, this feeder-road succulent store has a half-acre of cactus, discount cow

skulls, and plain junk. Inside, the low-ceilinged shop carries imports from Africa, Mexico, and Central America. The Zapotec figures and other artifacts are dear. *7800 I–45 N, North, 281/591–8833.*

2 *g-8*
EAGLE DANCER GALLERY
The crafts and art on display include both works by Native Americans and pieces celebrating indigenous cultures. *159 Gulf Fwy., League City, 281/332–6028.*

9 *e-3*
SARI SANSAR
American women who are uncomfortable wearing someone else's traditional style can enjoy these glorious fabrics as wall hangings. *6830 Harwin, Sharpstown, 713/266–1551.*

1 *a-1*
YUBOS
See Home Furnishings, *below.*

EYEWEAR

12 *e-7*
EYES ARE PRECIOUS
Dr. Sue Moss dispenses traditional eye care, nutritional advice, alternative therapy, and every make of contacts, including "Wild Eyes" costume lenses. She stocks designer frames up to Cartier, but will order standard black-frame Hank Hill glasses if that's what you want. *1428 Alabama, Montrose, 713/524–2525.*

2 *c-3*
EYEWEAR FASHIONS
No one in the family can read past the third line of the eye chart? Come in for glasses to suit every age. *10864 FM 1960 W, FM 1960 area, 281/469–7113.*

6 *g-8*
EYEWEAR UNLIMITED
This family-owned and -operated shop keeps up with the trends and offers reasonable glasses and upscale frames from Armani, Luxottica, and more. *6520 San Felipe, Galleria/Post Oak, 713/781–1050.*

10 *a-1*
LUX OPTICS
Whether you had an eye examination here or came in with a prescription, you can choose from thousands of in-stock frames. Designers represented include Matsuda, JOOP!, and Martine Sitbon. *5874 Westheimer, Galleria/Post Oak, 713/782–7776.*

3 *a-6*
VISION CORNER
If you're not ready for laser surgery or other permanent solutions, then the Vision Corner people will fit you with lens or glasses. If style is as important as correction, then choose frames from Dior, Fendi, Calvin Klein, and more. *14621 Beechnut, Southwest, 281/498–1381.*

10 *a-1*
5000 Westheimer, at Post Oak, Galleria/Post Oak, 713/623–2000.

FABRICS

6 *c-5*
CALICO CORNERS
Many of the decorative, bedding, and slipcover fabrics carried here are offered at discount prices. *9198 Old Katy Rd., Memorial/Spring Branch, 713/464–8653.*

2 *c-3*
17395 Tomball Pkwy. Suite 3C, FM 1960 area, 281/477–0047.

9 *e-4*
FABRIC MART
This established store not only carries fine upholstery fabrics but also can order custom goods and do custom work. *7433 Southwest Fwy., Sharpstown, 713/772–4666.*

2 *g-7*
FABRICS ETCETERA
The "etcetera" at this fabric store is a rich selection of classes, designer fabrics, Stretch & Sew Products, and Pfaff sewing machines. *571 W. Bay Area Blvd., Clear Lake/Bay Area, 281/338–1904.*

9 *c-6*
GOLDEN NEEDLE FINE FABRICS
A store for the serious seamstress, Golden Needle has supplies that are compatible with state-of-the-art machines and appliances. *8800 Bissonnet, Sharpstown, 713/774–5865.*

10 c-6

HANCOCK FABRICS

At this chain you'll find a wealth of fabrics, sewing accessories such as rolling cutters, and banks of massive pattern books. *8700 Stella Link, Astrodome/Old Spanish Trail, 713/665–7036.*

2 f-5

5611 Uvalde, Pasadena/Southeast, 281/458–7901.

2 g-7

16701 El Camino Real, Clear Lake/Bay Area, 281/488–5102.

2 c-3

10896 FM 1960 W, FM 1960 area, 281/469–6881.

2 f-7

9960 Kleckley Dr., South Houston/Hobby Airport, 713/946–7621.

4 e-5

12568 Westheimer, FM 1960 area, 281/497–6378.

9 c-1

2553 Gessner, Memorial/Spring Branch, 713/462–8639.

2 d-3

2208 FM 1960 W, FM 1960 area, 281/440–5255.

12 h-6

HIGH FASHION FABRICS

The staffers are ready and waiting for brides, but can also handle less dramatic needs. You'll walk out with the cloth you want and perhaps a dressmaker's number. *3101 Louisiana, Downtown/Theater District, 713/528–7299.*

9 c-1

IT'S A STITCH

Catering to the quilter, this store sells fabrics, patterns, and notions. The store also offers classes and sells Bernina sewing machines. *9389 Richmond, Richmond Strip, 713/785–0097.*

4 b-6

JO ANN FABRIC & CRAFTS

Children can amuse themselves in the ribbon and crafts aisles while parents shop for more serious goods. *9944 Kleckley Dr., South Houston/Hobby Airport, 713/944–6383.*

2 g-8

229 W. Main, League City, Clear Lake/Bay Area, 281/332–4803.

4 d-5

12121 Westheimer, Southwest, 281/597–8686.

13 e-4

LEGGETT FABRICS

Towering rolls of straight-from-the-mill upholstery fabrics line the aisles of this out-of-the-way resource. This is possibly the most efficient place to buy decorative fabrics, bedding, window treatment supplies, and upholstery. *2600 Capitol, Downtown/Theater District, 713/222–2471.*

2 g-8

SEW CONTEMPO FABRIC SHOP

Whether your use your needles and thread for clothing and pillows or quilts, you'll be welcome at this store. A variety of classes is offered, and the store is an authorized Bernina dealer. *18203 Egret Bay Blvd., Clear Lake/Bay Area, 281/333–5322.*

FLOWERS & PLANTS

7 e-4

ANOTHER PLACE IN TIME

Live the life of a Victorian at this gentle shop. The only goods are ferns and used books. *421 W. 11th St., Heights, 713/864–9717.*

14 e-4

BREEN'S BRAESWOOD FLORIST

For more than 50 years, this full-service florist has been sending out flowers, plants, teddy bear bouquets, and wine baskets. *2303 Holcombe, Astrodome/Old Spanish Trail, 713/668–2376.*

7 e-4

BUCHANAN'S NATIVE PLANTS

The informed, articulate staff will help you choose from the selection of local flora and the bug treatments and books to help nurture them. *611 E. 11th St., Heights, 713/861–5702.*

6 f-8

CORNELIUS NURSERIES

This old-guard nursery is best suited for the experienced gardener or the novice with aspirations. *2233 Voss, Galleria/Post Oak, 713/782–8640.*

14 h-5
FLOWER CORNERS
Medical Center and Downtown delivery is free. You'll pay a small fee to send fresh flowers, silk flowers, plants, goody baskets, or a single, perfect rose to another area. *2501 Holcombe, Astrodome/Old Spanish Trail, 713/660–0666.*

14 e-6
7301 Fannin, Astrodome/Old Spanish Trail, 713/796–9494.

10 c-1
GREENWAY PLAZA FLORIST
It seems unlikely that some of the most elegant arrangements would be found underground, yet this professional shop in the Greenway Plaza underground constructs some of the most elaborate arrangements available. *3929 Richmond, Greenway Plaza, 713/871–1313.*

7 e-3
HEIGHTS FLORAL SHOP
Although conveniently located across from Heights Hospital, this family-owned flower store delivers throughout the city. *401 W. 20th St., Heights, 713/862–8811.*

9 e-4
ORCHIDS AND FERNS
The delicate specialty plants are sold for those who grow them or to anyone who will give them a temporary home in a vase. *7802 Bellaire, Sharpstown, 713/774–0949.*

12 a-6
RIVER OAKS PLANT HOUSE
The huge faux topiary figures in the esplanade represent the most garish offerings at this nursery and florist. The store also stocks holiday garlands and arrangements. *3401 Westheimer, River Oaks, 713/622–5350.*

10 b-3
TEA'S NURSERY
This venerable nursery will meet your ambition, whether you want to landscape a few acres with tall trees, flowering plants, and a lily pond, or simply need a pick-me-up bouquet. If you can't make it in to browse the seemingly endless rows of outdoor plants and hot-house specialties, then take the mail-order option. *4400 Bellaire, Bellaire, 713/664–4400.*

FOOD & DRINK

9 h-5
BELDEN'S
This full-size, full-service grocery store is 100% kosher. *5300 N. Braeswood, Braeswood Square, Meyerland, 713/723–5670.*

4 d-3
LEIBMAN'S WINE & FINE FOODS
Although hardly the place to stock up for a week's worth of family meals, this shop provides culinary inspiration with caper berries, imported oddities, and lovely oils. *14010-A Memorial Dr., Memorial/Spring Branch, 281/493–3663.*

breads & pastries

12 a-5
ANDRE'S SWISS CANDIES & PASTRY
Ladies who lunch depend on the quaint shop for a genteel prix-fixe lunch, and leave discreetly with an almost-too-sweet napoleon or other goody from the bakery take-out counter. *2515 River Oaks Blvd., River Oaks, 713/524–3863.*

2 f-6
ARANDAS BAKERY
Pan de leche (milk bread), besos (pastry kisses), and sugar horns are among the Mexican treats sold here. *9267 Gulf Fwy., South Houston/Hobby Airport, 713/941–0100.*

9 d-5
8331 Beechnut, Sharpstown, 713/771–3616.

14 c-3
BAGEL MANUFACTORY
A glass wall exposes this vast bagel manufacturer's manufacturing process. It's a bit Willy Wonka, and frankly, the

---

FANNIN FLORIST CORRIDOR

Between Downtown and the medical center, there is a corridor of flowers— flowers, plants, faux topiary figures, and bouquets. A dozen shops, many open 24 hours, sell decorative plants and fresh-cut flowers at discount rates. The original idea may have been to take advantage of those visiting sick friends, but that's hardly the only customer base now.

sight of that much dough could have a negative effect on your appetite. Concentrate instead on the scent of fresh, hot bagels. *2438 Rice Blvd., Rice University Village, 713/520–7655.*

9 *g-4*

DROUBI'S BAKERY & IMPORTS

Finally, get your fill of sticky-sweet Middle Eastern pastries, crunchy with phyllo dough and nuts, and spiced with cinnamon and citrus. *7333 Hillcroft, Sharpstown, 713/988–5897.*

14 *b-1*

EINSTEIN BROTHERS BAGELS

This chain puts together some rather elaborate, yet light, sandwiches along with bagels and flavored spreads too numerous to mention. But stick with a straight cup of joe—the establishment hasn't quite sorted out coffee drinks yet. The house-brand roasts stand on their own merit. *5300 Kirby, Rice University Village, 713/528–1992.*

10 *a-7*

10273 Post Oak Blvd., Meyerland, 713/726–8550.

3 *c-2*

15745 FM 529, Cy-Fair, 281/861–0088.

9 *f-1*

6383 Westheimer, Galleria/Post Oak, 713/974–6391.

12 *f-6*

3407 Montrose, Montrose, 713/521–3842.

2 *g-7*

923 Bay Area Blvd., Clear Lake/Bay Area, 281/461–3200.

12 *c-4*

2801 Shepherd, Montrose, 713/526–7440.

7 *f-1*

FLYING SAUCER PIE CO.

Many folks only eat Flying Saucer fruit pies at the Livestock Show in February, but you don't have to wait at the booth in the Astro Hall. You can get these thick-crust pies year-round. *436 W. Crosstimbers, North Houston, 713/694–1141.*

4 *d-3*

FRENCH GOURMET BAKERY

Whether you're looking for a breakfast pastry, a fresh sandwich box lunch, or an elaborate gourmet cake, this French shop

can fill your order. *12504 Memorial Dr., Memorial/Spring Branch, 713/973–6900.*

12 *c-6*

2250 Westheimer, Montrose, 713/524–3744.

12 *c-6*

HOT BAGEL SHOP

This tiny storefront is hopping during morning rush hour. On the weekends, the busy time is from dawn until mid-afternoon, and you can enjoy your bagels, coffee, and juice at sidewalk tables. *2009 Shepherd, Montrose, 713/520–0340.*

13 *b-3*

KOLACHE FACTORY

From dawn until just after lunch, folks queue up for more than standard pigs-in-blankets. Sticky pastries and a variety of meat and cheese and breakfast kolaches also come out of the ovens. *777 Walker, Downtown/Theater District, 713/222–2253.*

13 *b-4*

1001 Fannin, Downtown/Theater District, 713/651–1075.

13 *b-3*

817 Milam, Esperson Tunnel, Downtown/Theater District, 713/222–0597.

14 *b-2*

5810 Kirby, Rice University Village, 713/664–2253.

7 *g-8*

2045 Westheimer, Montrose, 713/523–5567.

9 *h-1*

2715 Chimney Rock, Galleria/Post Oak, 713/622–2112.

10 *b-1*

3813 Southwest Fwy., Greenway Plaza, 713/629–9626.

6 *h-8*

5763 San Felipe, Galleria/Post Oak, 713/952–6656.

10 *c-1*

3945 Richmond, Greenway Plaza, 713/626–4580.

10 *b-3*

MOELLER'S BAKERY

In the mid-'90s, gentrification drove the bakery out of Rice Village, but loyal customers followed without question. All of Moeller's cakes, pies, and goodies are top of the line, and the bakery's carrot cake may be the best on earth. *4201 Bellaire Blvd., Astrodome/Old Spanish Trail, 713/667–0983.*

6 *f-5*
SHIPLEY DONUTS
Over the years, as breakfast choices have increased to include gourmet bagels and ritzier pastries, Shipley has remained the same. Shipley's dough is light and cakey, and although the doughnuts are fried in a vat of grease as proper doughnuts should be, they don't absorb too much. The treats are sweet and fatty, but not too much. And, unlike a lot of breakfast stops, they're open for late snacking after the clubs close. *1829 Bingle, Sugar Land/Fort Bend, 713/468–1223.*

cake decorating equipment & supplies

3 *b-7*
CAKE TALK
Sometimes boxed mix in a round pan just won't do. When it's time to roll up your sleeves and put your personal, creative stamp on a richly decorated sheet cake or a towering layered concoction, find the tools you need at Cake Talk. *12240-L Murphy Rd., Memorial/Spring Branch, 281/495–2253.*

7 *g-1*
THE HOBBY HUT
If you have ambition and a sweet tooth, stock up on basic Wilton supplies, unique molds, and a variety of ornaments. *636 E. Crosstimbers, North, 713/694–8692.*

9 *g-4*
MAKE-A-CAKE
Martha Stewart's got nothing on you. Craft pastries with seasonal-shaped pans, gum paste, and other ingredients for handmade decorations, and then deliver your creations in festive boxes. *6218 Evergreen, Sharpstown, 713/777–1871.*

coffee & tea

12 *c-4*
CAFÉ MAISON
A true Mecca for tea-lovers, this boutique has more than the usual variety of coffee beans and cups. Plenty of shelf space is devoted to tea leaves, teapots, tea infusers, tea cozies, and more. *2089 Westheimer, Montrose, 713/528–6750.*

2 *h-7*
DIEDRICH COFFEE
Although most customers stop in for a hot mug and biscotti, you can also buy wonderful roasts to go. *1008 Bay Area Blvd., Clear Lake/Bay Area, 281/461–1325.*

12 *f-7*
4005 Montrose, Montrose, 713/526–1319.

12 *d-6*
1901 Westheimer, Montrose, 713/522–8801.

10 *d-3*
3171 Holcombe, Astrodome/Old Spanish Trail, 713/669–9449.

14 *c-3*
HOUSE OF COFFEE BEANS
You can buy in bulk from bin after bin of flavored coffee, or keep it simple with strong African or Hawaiian beans. *2520 Rice Blvd., Astrodome/Old Spanish Trail, 713/524–0057.*

chocolate & other candy

4 *b-5*
CANDY HEAVEN
The confections range from Jelly Belly jelly beans to handmade truffles. Buy a big bag to take home or order gift baskets for any occasion. *2600 Hwy. 6, West Oaks Mall, Southwest, 281/496–4515.*

3 *b-7*
16535 Southwest Fwy., First Colony Mall, Sugar Land/Fort Bend, 281/565–3700.

7 *e-3*
CHOCLET HOUSE
Although this store specializes in sugar-free chocolates and candy for diabetics, you can also find regular treats. *1900 Yale, Heights, 713/426–6521 or 800/246–2538.*

10 *a-1*
CHOCOLATE DESIGNS
Unfussy gifts such as cans of caramel corn for every one of your sales staff are easy to get here. You can also pick up hand-dipped truffles and fudge for the harder-to-please. *5000 Westheimer, Galleria/Post Oak, 713/622–5990.*

14 *c-3*

CHOCOLATES ETC.
You can set yourself up for a wonderful binge in this all-purpose candy store. Fill your sack with jelly beans, hard candies, imported candies, standard American convenience store candies, fresh chocolates, fudge, and more. Yes, more. *2529 Amherst, Rice University Village, 713/522–7488.*

3 *b-8*

CHOCOLATES & MORE
Why stop off at the Circle K when you can step into this store and choose fine chocolates at reasonable prices? *3520 Hwy. 6 S, Sugar Land/Fort Bend, 281/ 565–5656.*

1 *a-1*

CREOLE CREATIONS PRALINE CANDY
Show your Texas pride by sending praline bouquets all over the country, and order a few for yourself to eat at home. This enterprise also has candied apples and a discount club. There's no storefront, so order by phone or through the Web site. *www.creolecreations.com, 713/772–0072.*

10 *a-5*

FOOD FOR THOUGHT
At this boutique, you can craft gift baskets with divinity fudge, caramels, taffy, Cavendish & Harvey hard candies, and a selection of chocolates. Or you can go for cookies, including High Cotton Inn cookies baked in Bellville. Or show you care with a pasta basket, a kosher basket, a wine basket, a Texas basket, or many other styles. *4534 Beechnut, Meyerland, 713/668–7877.*

10 *a-1*

GODIVA CHOCOLATIER
You can impress someone with merely the sight of a gold Godiva box. You can also keep these silky truffles to yourself. *5075 Westheimer, Galleria/Post Oak, 713/ 623–4707.*

2 *g-8*

19010 Gulf Fwy., Baybrook Mall, Clear Lake/Bay Area, 281/280–0798.

2 *c-3*

7920 FM 1960 W, Willowbrook Mall, FM 1960 area, 281/897–8046.

10 *a-5*

KEGG'S CANDIES
For generations, this confectioner has offered handmade candies for any occasion, including one of those days when you really deserve it. *4844 Beechnut, Meyerland, 713/664–4593.*

15 *a-5*

SEE'S CANDIES
People in other states (including certain well-known advice columnist twins) rely on kind friends to ship them boxes of chocolates each month. The rest of us "accidentally" pick up a few dozen candies when we've stopped in Rice for a bottle of milk (all See's Candies locations are inside a Rice Epicurean). *2617 Holcombe (inside Rice Epicurean), Astrodome/Old Spanish Trail, 713/664–8649.*

7 *b-8*

3745 Westheimer, River Oaks, 713/ 623–4626.

6 *g-8*

2020 Fountain View, Galleria/Post Oak, 713/783–8203.

9 *h-3*

5333 Gulfton, Sharpstown, 713/662–7700.

12 *b-7*

3102 Kirby, Upper Kirby District, 713/526–8961.

14 *c-3*

2500 Rice Blvd., Rice University Village, 713/529–9162.

ethnic foods

4 *d-7*

HALAL MEAT MARKET & GROCERY
Much if not all of the meat sold here comes from the company's Islamic slaughterhouse, and the in-house butchers can be observed cutting and trimming and wielding hefty cleavers with finesse. You'll also find a rich selection of dry and canned groceries and baked goods. Occasionally, the bread rack features spongy Ethiopian flat bread. *11913 Bissonnet, Sharpstown, 281/879–7989.*

13 *a-6*

HOA BINH SUPERMARKET
Find an electric rice cooker at this Chinatown supply house, and pick up some noodles and fish sauce for the night when you opt for something more

adventurous than rice. *2800 Travis, Montrose, 713/520–9558.*

`9` *c-3*

HONG KONG SUPERMARKET

Sea urchins, fresh or frozen, are not a surprise in this warehouse-size supermarket, because this is officially an Asian market. What is surprising is that one section is stocked with odd items like the Thigh Master and Torso Tiger that TV ads assure us are "not sold in stores." The dry goods and produce aisles are packed with foodstuffs favored by a variety of Mediterranean, African, and Caribbean cultures. *5708 Gessner, Sharpstown, 713/995–1393.*

`2` *d-8*

13400 Veterans Memorial Dr., FM 1960 area, 281/537–5280.

`2` *g-8*

10923 Scarsdale, South Houston/Hobby Airport, 281/484–6100.

`4` *e-6*

INTERNATIONAL DISCOUNT FOOD MARKET

Why buy packaged jerk sauce and island-curry mix when this grocer can work up recipes from scratch and perhaps give you a few cooking tips? *6123 Wilcrest, Sharpstown, 281/568–9514.*

`9` *f-2*

KOREA SUPERMARKET

Serving not only Korean, but other Asian shopping lists, this market has spices, noodles, fish, and bags of rice as big as bed pillows. The market also carries aromatic coffee and fresh, crunchy baguettes to fill out a multi-culti meal. *7501 Harwin, Sharpstown, 713/789–4959.*

`9` *f-2*

PATEL BROTHERS

Stock up with 5-pound bags of sweet jasmine and basmati rices, fine jugs of coconut oil (which may have saturated fats, but no harmful trans-fats!), and packets of fresh, pungent spices. Then, make a trip down the drugstore aisle for hair-care products and tooth powders you can't find in conventional stores. *5815 Hillcroft, Sharpstown, 713/784–8332.*

`9` *f-2*

SUPER VANAK INTERNATIONAL FOOD MARKET

There are people in this world who don't have curry at least once a week. You won't find them here, despite the great prices on spices, organic yogurt, and imported beverages that make a great alternative to soft drinks. *5692 Hillcroft, Sharpstown, 713/952–7676.*

fish & seafood

CRAWFISH OF LOUISIANA

This crawfish farm in Louisiana can ship you a burlap bag of mudbugs for your next big boil. The best quality and cheapest crawfish are available in spring. Give 'em a call—they'll include your order on their regular restaurant delivery trips. *800/272–9347.*

`14` *b-5*

J&R SEAFOOD

If you ask nicely, the merchants may be able to get you fresh oyster shells for your oysters Rockefeller. *7277 Bromptom, Astrodome/Old Spanish Trail, 713/664–6630.*

health food

`12` *c-7*

A MOVEABLE FEAST

Excluding the café, fully half of the store is devoted to supplements and vitamins. This very traditional store carries Hain products. *2202 Alabama, Montrose, 713/528–3585.*

`6` *c-5*

9341 Katy Fwy., Echo Lane Shopping Center, Memorial/Spring Branch, 713/365–0368.

`14` *c-3*

AYURVEDIC CONCEPTS

To some they're just snake oil, but others find Stress Care, Mind Care, Immuno Care, and Vigor Care (a natural Viagra) supplements keep them fit and happy. Order Ayurvedic Concepts products direct or find them at area health-food stores. *2411 Times Blvd., Downtown/Theater District, 713/522–5597.*

2 *c-3*

BETSY'S HEALTH FOOD
Along with the standard foodstuff and supplements, Betsy's sells sports and homeopathic products. *5730 FM 1960 W, FM 1960 area, 281/440–9081.*

12 *h-7*

CONNIE'S HEALTH FOOD STORE
Oddly enough, this dark little Downtown store has long been a source of healthful foods and supplements for Houstonians. *3704 Main, Downtown/Theater District, 713/522–9588.*

3 *b-1*

NATURE'S MARKET
Although not a cornucopia of produce, Nature's Market does carry fresh, organic fruits and vegetables. More plentiful is the selection of canned organic foods. *10924 FM 1960 W, FM 1960 area, 281/469–7665.*

4 *c-3*

RANCH CREEK NATURAL FOOD
Visit the juice bar and bakery for a quick pick-me-up or fill a cart with organics for a healthful home kitchen. *13211 Memorial, Memorial/Spring Branch, 713/467–8900.*

6 *d-4*

THE SEEKERS
Echinacea, kava, ginseng, and other plant products, with varieties from everywhere they are grown, are sold here. *9336 Westview, Astrodome/Old Spanish Trail, 713/461–0857.*

4 *d-3*

12171 Katy Fwy., Memorial/Spring Branch, 281/870–9999.

4 *d-5*

WHOLE FOODS
It's not clear when Pepperidge Farm cookies became health food, but you'll find them shelved alongside treats crafted without wheat, without sugar, without cocoa, and without fats. The produce, meat and seafood, and beer and wine sections might also raise the eyebrows of purists. However, this is a great resource for quality fresh foods. *11145 Westheimer, Memorial/Spring Branch, 713/784–7776.*

12 *b-7*

2955 Kirby, Upper Kirby District, 713/520–1937.

6 *g-7*

6401 Woodway, Galleria/Post Oak, 713/789–4477.

herbs & spices

9 *e-4*

INDIA GROCERS
This is one of many local stores distributing India's Spice'N Flavor spices. *6606 Southwest Fwy., Sharpstown, 713/266–7717.*

meats & poultry

4 *c-3*

THE BUTCHER SHOPPE
You don't have to go to an expensive restaurant for ostrich, alligator, or other exotics—they're all carried at this shop. For less adventurous meals, stop in for aged corn-fed Kansas beef, veal, buffalo, or the white meats, pork and poultry. At lunchtime, you can order hamburgers and sandwiches. *13194 Memorial, Memorial/Spring Branch, 713/464–9203.*

12 *b-7*

COOKE'S GOURMET
Alongside the long, well-stocked meat, poultry, seafood, and sausage counter are shelves of "emergency" groceries. Cooke's carries the best in traditional meats and offers a variety of fresh game and exotics, all expertly trimmed to suit you. The deli stocks a to-die-for vichyssoise and a daily selection of casseroles, pâtés and potted meats, and one-dish meals. *2800 Kirby, Upper Kirby District, 713/529–3355.*

7 *d-6*

MATAMOROS MEAT CO.
Here's where you'll find prime cuts of beef, chorizo that may be too hot for an ordinary man to handle, heads and trotters, and other old-fashioned selections. *5526 Washington, Heights, 713/862–7792.*

9 *g-1*

PETE'S FINE MEATS
Stringers of sausages, rump roasts the size of Texas, and lamb loin chops as sweet as spring are among the succulent meats served at this all-purpose

shop. *5509 Richmond, Galleria/Post Oak, 713/782–3470.*

nuts & seeds

9 *f-2*

FREDLYN NUT COMPANY

A terrible pun fits: Fredlyn is nuts about nuts, and if you're not careful, you'll hear more than you wanted to about the history and nutritional value of nuts. While you learn, pick up a gift tin of Macadamias for someone with a nut allergy, raw pecans for pie, big ol' Brazil nuts for snacking, and pumpkin seeds and pignolias for salads. *9350 Westpark, Richmond Strip, 713/781–2710.*

9 *g-7*

HOUSTON PECAN COMPANY

This company really swings into gear during the holidays, when tins of nuts and dried fruit are in demand. *7313 Ashcroft, Sharpstown, 713/772–6216.*

2 *b-7*

LEBLANC'S PECAN AND FEED COMPANY

The company is located in genuine pecan country, but the baskets and tins packaged here are shipped worldwide. *2032 Hwy. 90 E, Sugar Land/Fort Bend, 281/342–2101.*

produce

2 *c-3*

CY-CREEK FARMERS MARKET

Although it's been an awfully long time since the Cypress Creek area was agri-cultural, you can still buy farm-fresh pro-duce here. *9814 Grant, FM 1960 area, 281/469–5200.*

7 *g-2*

FARMERS MARKET

Be careful or you'll go home with several bushels of green beans or a peck of pickling cucumbers or way too many apples for one shopping trip. *2520 Air-line, Heights, 713/862–8866.*

wines & spirits

9 *g-1*

BERT WHEELERS

Bert Wheeler is a moniker befitting a dapper fellow, and, God rest his soul,

the real Wheeler was no slouch. The stores he left have a brisk, cheery, Nor-man Rockwell ambience that, after you've experienced it, doesn't seem at all at odds with the booze business. *6518 Westheimer, Galleria/Post Oak, 713/780–3373.*

9 *e-4*

8306 Southwest Fwy., Sharpstown, 713/777–0187.

10 *a-3*

5212 Bellaire, Bellaire, 713/666–0311.

6 *c-5*

12901 Queensbury, Town & Country Mall, Memorial/Spring Branch, 713/467–5515.

9 *c-1*

A BEVERAGE BARN

For good or ill, a drive-through liquor store is a traditional part of the Lone Star landscape. This barn has party kegs, margarita machines, and drive-through service. *9204 Richmond, Rich-mond Strip, 713/789–5347.*

7 *a-1*

INTERNATIONAL SPIRITS

Nothing says party like a margarita machine. Rent one here or just stock a cooler with six-packs. *3319 Mangum, Memorial/Spring Branch, 713/683–0711.*

10 *b-1*

MANDOLA'S WAREHOUSE LIQUORS

Bar supplies, bar snacks, and, naturally, all the proper liquors for a well-stocked bar can be had here. *4310 Richmond, Greenway Plaza, 713/621–5314.*

9 *c-1*

RICHARD'S LIQUORS AND FINE WINES

No one at this store cares if you have a climate-controlled cellar or if you store vino in the kitchen cabinet, so feel free to ask questions about the vintages on display. *2411 Gessner, Richmond Strip, 713/780–9750.*

14 *c-3*

2514 Rice Blvd., Rice University Village, 713/522–3881.

`10` *c-3*

4000 Bissonnet, Rice University Village, 713/661–8770.

`12` *c-5*

2124 Shepherd, Montrose, 713/529–4849.

`12` *b-6*

2565 Kirby, Upper Kirby District, 713/523–7405.

`12` *d-6*

1701 Brun St., River Oaks, 713/529–6266.

`6` *g-8*

6532 San Felipe, Galleria/Post Oak, 713/781–0022.

`9` *h-1*

5630 Richmond, Galleria/Post Oak, 713/783–3344.

`6` *f-7*

5750 Woodway, Galleria/Post Oak, 713/975–6859.

`2` *c-3*

5050 FM 1960 W, FM 1960 area, 281/893–5080.

`13` *a-5*

SPEC'S LIQUOR WAREHOUSE

Everything fermented on this earth is available at Spec's, from jug wine to Chevalier Montrachet, from Lone Star to Billie's Pooch English Cider, from Hiram Walker apricot brandy to Remy Martin Louis XIII cognac. The highly trained professional staff will help you select what you want at your price. *2410 Smith St., Downtown/Theater District, 713/526–8787.*

`6` *d-5*

963 Bunker Hill Rd., Memorial/Spring Branch, 713/464–2216.

`10` *c-6*

8714 Stella Link, Astrodome/Old Spanish Trail, 713/667–7277.

`14` *g-4*

2314 Holcombe, Astrodome/Old Spanish Trail, 713/669–1722.

`6` *c-5*

UNION BEVERAGE CORP

Front aisles in this brightly lighted, white warehouse are devoted to gifts and novelties. Well-organized wine and spirits stretch to the back of the store. *11777 Katy Fwy., Memorial/Spring Branch, 281/497–1010.*

`12` *c-6*

WINES OF AMERICA

Regular Friday tastings have helped this store build a loyal, and informed, clientele. *2055 Westheimer, Montrose, 713/524–3397.*

FRAMING

`3` *b-7*

DECK THE WALLS

Thousands of prints are in stock, in case you don't currently own anything suitable for matting and framing. *16535 Southwest Fwy., First Colony Mall, Sugar Land/Fort Bend, 281/265–3090.*

`2` *c-3*

7920 FM 1960 W, Willowbrook Mall, FM 1960 area, 281/890–9411.

`2` *f-3*

20131 Hwy. 59 N, Deerbrook Mall, North, 281/540–3013.

`10` *b-1*

FINE ART & FRAMING GALLERY

You may choose to let the artists select a matting scheme for you. *4703 Richmond, Greenway Plaza, 713/960–1270.*

`14` *c-2*

KIRBY GALLERY

Frame art you own, prints by Texas artists represented by the gallery, or prints and photos you thought were beyond salvage. The shop also does restoration. *2418 Sunset Blvd., Rice University Village, 713/520–5422.*

`1` *a-1*

MICHAEL'S

See Art Supplies, *above.*

`9` *e-2*

WAREHOUSE FRAMES & GALLERY

Decorators and professional accounts make up the bulk of the business, but this frame shop is open to the public. *3815 Fondren, Richmond Strip, 713/974–6000.*

GIFTS & SOUVENIRS

`9` *e-2*

ALL UNIQUE

Whether you're searching for funky, freaky, or absolutely fabulous gifts to delight, alarm, or bring about an epiphany, this eclectic shop has got something that fits the bill. *2727 Fondren, Richmond Strip, 713/266–3338.*

10 *a-1*
BUILD-A-BEAR WORKSHOP
You don't have to be an elf or even a Santa affiliate to build cuddly plush toys in this workshop. Why settle for brand-name snugglers when you can give a truly unique keepsake gift? Even if you're all thumbs, the tools on hand and workshop staff will make sure your bear is one-of-a-kind because of your creativity, not because of defects. It's as easy as making a Mr. Potato Head. *5075 Westheimer, Galleria/Post Oak, 713/355–3388.*

9 *h-3*
JEANE'S ROCK & JEWELRY
Forget antiques, the fossils in this store are many millions of years old, and a museum budget isn't necessary. For less than a C-note, paleo fans can find a few 60 million-year-old fish or a few fine trilobites. Please a rock hound with the gift of uncut geodes, or choose unique jewelry for more conventional friends. When you stop by, don't forget to say howdy to Joshua, the store cat. *5420 Bissonnet, Bellaire, 713/664–2988.*

12 *d-7*
LATITUDES SOUTH
Instead of baskets, blankets, and painted wooden toys, this shop offers fine arts, lush carpets, and handmade furniture from exotic countries such as Ecuador, Peru, Thailand, Myanmar, and more. *1837 Alabama, Montrose, 713/520–1233.*

2 *d-2*
MICHELLE'S GIFTS
Amid the potpourri, wind chimes, and garden decorations are every brand-name bear, including Boyds. *219 Gentry, Suite C, Spring, 281/288–8786.*

14 *g-1*
MUSEUM OF FINE ARTS GIFT STORE
Books, games, jewelry, and objects related to the current marquee exhibition take center stage, but you'll always find Masterson jewelry, intriguing puzzles, and fine art coffee table books with price tags almost as hefty as the tomes. *1001 Bissonnet, Rice University Village, 713/639–7300.*

7 *e-3*
OCTOBER GALLERY
Spend a little, like five bucks, for a swell '50s ashtray or a lot, like a couple thousand, for a one-of-a-kind, work-of-art piece of functional furniture. *224 W.19th St., Heights, 713/861–7475.*

7 *f-4*
OLD FASHIONED THINGS
Old-time two-wheelers like the bike depicted on the sign outside this quaint shop aren't guaranteed to be in stock. You will find quaint gifts, however, from estate antiques to contemporary jewelry crafted by local artists. *811 Yale St., Heights, 713/880–8393.*

1 *d-2*
OLD TOWN SPRING
All year long, more than 150 quaint shops are open in the historic village. Christmas is the high season. *123 E. Midway, Memorial/Spring Branch, 281/353–9310.*

10 *a-1*
THE SHARPER IMAGE
Whenever Hollywood has a hit creature feature, the Sharper Image stocks 6- to 8-ft-tall foam rubber replicas of the creature. Other toys in stock are gadgets that owe their market value to decades of James Bond movies. *5075 Westheimer, Galleria/Post Oak, 713/961–0123.*

13 *b-8*
1200 McKinney, The Park Shops, Downtown/Theater District, 713/652–2507.

2 *c-3*
Y'ALLS TEXAS STORE
Here you'll find all things jalapeño and booted, from cookbooks to quilts. *7920 W. FM 1960 W, Willowbrook Mall, FM 1960 area, 281/955–0100.*

2 *d-1*
1201 Lake Woodlands Dr., Woodlands Mall, The Woodlands, 281/364–1560.

10 *a-1*
5085 Westheimer, Galleria, Galleria/Post Oak, 713/572–9271.

6 *c-5*
1000 Katy Fwy., Memorial City Mall, Memorial/Spring Branch, 713/465–5410.

HOME FURNISHINGS

14 c-3
ALYSON JON
Sadly, few of us have a globetrotting Auntie Mame to leave us a houseful of eclectic antiques. Fortunately, by furnishing with sofas, settees, and sideboards from this designer store, you can give the impression of coming from a long line of wealthy eccentrics. *2444 Bolsover, Rice University Village, 713/524–3171.*

9 c-1
CANTONI
Guests may be reluctant to sit on the exquisite and unusual furnishings ordered through this shop. Instead of ordinary chairs, the wares look like museum pieces. *9889 Westheimer, Memorial/Spring Branch, 713/787–9494.*

10 a-1
CRATE & BARREL
Crate & Barrel is careful to be just a step behind the curve. This chain caters to people who need time to get used to a trend before adopting it. Samantha's furniture in the current Sex and the City season will show up at Crate & Barrel in about 18 months. Crate & Barrel is a terrific source of stemware and kitchen gadgets. *5175 Westheimer, Galleria, Galleria/Post Oak, 713/621–7765.*

6 c-5
COST PLUS WORLD MARKET
Almost everything graduates need for their first apartment is stacked in this ethnic-look store. Furniture, throw pillows, and textiles are always styled to suit the current cultural vogue. *10519 Katy Fwy., Memorial/Spring Branch, 713/827–8611.*

2 c-3
7885 FM 1960 W, FM 1960 area, 281/469–6446.

10 a-1
5125 Richmond, Galleria/Post Oak, 713/963–8833.

DAVID S. TOOMBS & CO.
Bird's-eye maple isn't easy to come by, and authentic African mahogany is rarer still. However, the designers at David S. Toombs will search the world for the necessary materials and then build amazing items for you. Start the process with a free in-home estimate. Call to set up an appointment. *281/835–0782.*

3 b-7
THE DESIGN FIRM
The size of this showroom rivals Gallery Furniture, and they offer higher-end furnishings in cutting-edge styles. *13013 Southwest Fwy., Sugar Land/Fort Bend County, 281/494–4433.*

3 f-2
GALLERY FURNITURE
The difference between native and naturalized Houstonians and everybody else: Houstonians have at least one piece from Gallery founder and owner Jim "Mattress Mac" McIngvale in their home. Schoolchildren who cannot name a single American president can recite Gallery Furniture slogans at the drop of a hat. *6006 North Fwy., North, 713/694–5570.*

4 e-4
HOME AMBIANCE
Let the classic styles and tasteful accessories function as Henry Higgins to your Eliza Doolittle. The finishes, fabrics, and finely turned legs will make you elegant. *770 W. Sam Houston Pkwy., Memorial/Spring Branch, 713/464–0888.*

6 g-5
IKEA
The best deals are downstairs by the checkout in the clearance bins. Some of the cute, slightly small-scale Swedish furniture from the showroom ends up, with little wear and tear, near the exit at half-price or less. *7810 Katy Fwy., Memorial/Spring Branch, 713/688–7867.*

2 h-6
ORIGINALS IN WOOD
La Madeleine's French Country look was crafted by Alain and Ann Virlouvet, and the couple will craft original furnishings and architectural details for you, too. Although Alain is French, his designs include Shaker and Mission influences. *423 S. 8th St., Clear Lake/Bay Area, 888/470–8666.*

7 b-8

POTTERY BARN

What will Pottery Barn do if brocades and baroque styles come back? The institution is associated with earthy colors and fabrics and finishes, dressed up with the occasional vaguely ethnic beadwork. Wood and wicker and leather in browns and grays and plums are going strong, but what will the chain do if trends go away from the whole crafty antique look? *4001 Westheimer, Highland Village, Galleria/Post Oak, 713/627–8901.*

6 c-5

12850 Memorial Dr., Town & Country Mall, Memorial/Spring Branch, 713/722–0307.

7 f-4

YUBOS

In this Heights workshop you'll find custom-made furniture with a Southwestern flair. Occasionally, the craftspeople add imported and antique furniture to their stock. If your timing is right, you may be able to pick up pieces from Guatemala, Honduras, and Mexico. *1012 Yale St., Heights, 713/862–3239.*

7 f-4

ZOCALO

Tables and table settings with a south-of-the-border accent are imported along with kitchenware and outdoor furniture. *933 Studewood, Heights, 713/869–1501.*

architectural artifacts

14 g-1

ADKINS ARCHITECTURAL ANTIQUES

Although Houston is a "new" city, it has considerable access to columns, gas lamps, and Tiffany windows that are from, or evoke, the past. *3515 Fannin, Medical Center, 713/522–6547.*

12 e-6

THE EMPORIUM

Need a 40-ft black maple bar face? No? Well, you'd be surprised how appealing massive period structures can be. People in the aisles can be observed mentally remodeling their homes to accommodate impressive finds like 12-ft stained-glass doors. Safely vent your urge to buy something right now with a few feet of reproduction Victorian gingerbread or a few hundred dollars' worth of art deco bathroom fixtures.

1800 Westheimer, Montrose, 713/528–3808.

6 f-8

2303 S. Voss, Galleria/Post Oak, 713/782–2223.

12 d-7

SETTLERS HARDWARE

If you are not lucky enough to need drawer pulls and Howard's finishing supplies for a terrific garage sale find, perhaps you can use these elegant finishings to dress up the kitchen cabinets. *1901 W. Alabama, Montrose, 713/524–2417.*

carpets & rugs

13 e-7

CARPET GIANT

The monstrous figure of the "Carpet Giant" (a towering roll of Astroturf with big eyes and a smile) and years of late-night commercials on UHF channels give the impression that this warehouse deals in end lots of cheap industrial carpet. You can, in fact, get end lots of cheap industrial carpet, and take it home on a roll and not worry about padding or stretching or anything, and for remarkably low prices. You can also, however, get very nice carpets, and have them installed the next day, still for good prices. *3407 Hwy. 45, East End, 713/224–2213.*

12 b-7

PARVIZZIAN

Proudly going out of business throughout the '90s—at least the regular appearance of sale signs made it seem that way—this mirrored, two-story showplace has stacks of rugs from China, the Middle East, and all points in between. *3303 Kirby, Upper Kirby District, 713/520—0611.*

ceramic tiles

3 c-2

MARASZZI TILE

Contractors and decorators depend on Maraszzi for ceramics, stone, and hand-painted tiles for every possible home use. However, both stores are open to the independent homeowner. *13130 Hempstead Hwy., North, 713/939–9500.*

5 b-4

3461 Alabama, River Oaks, 713/627–8453.

11 *e-3*

MISSION TILE DISCOUNT WAREHOUSE

This warehouse is stocked to the rafters with imported tiles and all the latest trendy domestic floorings, all at budget prices. *5722 Gulf Fwy., East End, 713/928–2100.*

china, glassware, porcelain, pottery, silver

BERING'S
See Housewares & Hardware, *below.*

14 *c-3*

BRITISH ISLES
Discover brilliant Scottish crystal amid the floral-pattern Aynsley, Beleek, and Spode tableware and tea services. *2366 Rice Blvd., Rice University Village, 713/522–6868.*

10 *a-1*

CHRISTOFLE
Brides who know their friends and family will come through, register here, and then sit back and wait for the Limoges and Baccarat to roll in. *5075 Westheimer, Galleria/Post Oak, 713/572–2557.*

14 *c-3*

EKLEKTIC SILVER
Many of the pieces here are purely decorative, but just as many are delightful home accessories. *2401 Times Blvd., Rice University Village, 713/526–7899.*

furniture & accessories

4 *e-4*

BO CONCEPT
The store walls are lined with wall systems in every possible wood. If your books and CDs won't fill the shelves sold here, then pick up some Concept accessories and other knickknacks. *770 W. Sam Houston Pkwy., Memorial/Spring Branch, 713/465–3312.*

4 *c-2*

EURWAY FURNITURE
Sleek, sexy, ultramodern home furnishings at surprisingly low prices are the main draw. Whimsical accessories will bring you back. *2411 S. Eldgridge Pkwy., Katy/Bear Creek, 281/920–0909.*

12 *c-8*

FRONTERA FURNITURE
Certainly, the faux pioneer household goods are well constructed and durable and can be blended into any decor or assembled for a true Texas mood. But what's most important is that these pieces are fun. *2110 Richmond, Montrose, 713/527–8196.*

9 *e-1*

LEATHER FURNITURE SHOPS
Leather furniture has a place other than the boardroom or bachelor pad, and the lovely pieces here prove that. *2670 Fondren, Richmond Strip, 713/785–6011.*

9 *f-1*

LIFESTYLE FUTONS
Buy a futon, a chair, and other furniture with matching upholstery for a grown-up living room. The discount warehouse is in River Oaks. *6441 Westheimer, Galleria/Post Oak, 713/789–9883.*

12 *f-4*

2620 W. Dallas, River Oaks, 713/528–6444.

12 *e-6*

LOFT & HOME ESSENTIALS
Unusual candleholders and painted tableware are popular items here. You'll also find wall hangings and picture frames. *1009 Missouri, Montrose, 713/522–5638.*

12 *c-8*

MERCADO MEXICO
Choose a gaily colored pot to use as a birdbath, or select a hand-painted sink for your home. *2210 Richmond, Montrose, 713/528–6101.*

10 *a-3*

MING CLASSICS
The bargain-minded don't seem to mind that many of the accessories, carpets, vases, and furnishings in this sprawling warehouse are not quite museum quality. *6108 S. Rice, Bellaire, 713/839–7881.*

12 *e-5*

ODEON ART DECO GALLERY I & II
Don't be fooled by the less than striking exterior. Inside you'll find well-cared for (or properly restored) art deco, art nouveau, Mission, Arts and Crafts, studio,

and Bauhaus furnishings. *2117 Dunlavy, Montrose, 713/521–1111.*

6 *c-8*

PIER 1

Patchouli's popularity comes and goes. When it's the fragrance of the moment, Pier 1 returns to its '60s roots. When it's not, the chain fills display space with splashy contemporary accessories. *1016 Gessner, Memorial/Spring Branch, 713/465–1132.*

7 *a-8*

2411 Post Oak Blvd., Galleria/Post Oak, 713/933–0432.

9 *c-1*

9524 Westheimer, Richmond Strip, 713/977–1153.

2 *c-3*

5650 FM 1960 W, FM 1960 area, 281/440–7351.

4 *b-5*

2703 Hwy. 6 S, Southwest, 281/531–9937.

2 *b-5*

6815 Hwy. 6 N, Katy/Bear Creek, 281/345–7662.

14 *c-3*

2501 Rice Blvd., Rice University Village, 713/529–8820.

12 *d-4*

1927 W. Gray, River Oaks, 713/524–3092.

12 *d-6*

QUATRINE WASHABLE FURNITURE

Yep, you can just ball these couches up and toss 'em in the washer. No, it's not quite that easy. The real deal is that the supersoft, overstuffed furniture here is designed with easily removable, completely washable slipcovers. *1911 Westheimer, Montrose, 713/521–1915.*

12 *d-4*

URBAN OUTFITTERS

Following the Pier 1 formula, this hipster spot for youthful fashion stocks both mod and exotic home accessories, like nightlamps (and lava lamps), bed covers, and throw pillows. *2501 University Blvd., Rice University Village, 713/529–3023.*

7 *b-8*

VERANDA HOME & GARDEN ACCESSORIES

Houston heat will always mar the illusion, but the indoor and outdoor benches and decorative items at this Highland Village store will go a long way toward making you feel like you're living in the English countryside. *3838 Westheimer, River Oaks, 713/840–1717.*

12 *c-7*

XIPANGO

Inventory rages from the ethereal (essential oils) to sturdy armoires crafted by woodworkers in the Far East and from south of the border. *3113 Shepherd, Upper Kirby District, 713/524–5800.*

lamps & lighting

2 *c-3*

CHAMPIONS LIGHTING

A huge selection of lamps, light fixtures, and chandeliers are in stock, but if you'd prefer to have an heirloom made right again, repair and restoration service is offered. *5211 FM 1960 W, FM 1960 area, 281/440–5339.*

12 *f-6*

LIGHT BULBS UNLIMITED

Browse the tiny shop for decorative celebration lights, artful desk lamps, and black lights. Ask at the counter for a pencil-sized replacement bulb to fit your office halogen light. *1203 Westheimer, Montrose, 713/521–0330.*

12 *d-7*

NICOLETTI'S HOUSE OF FINE LAMPS AND SHADES

Many furniture stores would be dwarfed by this gracious two-story superstore. The staff asks that, when shopping for shades, you bring the lamp in for proper sizing. *2032 Alabama, Montrose, 713/526–1525.*

paint & wallpaper

7 *e-4*

PREMIUM PAINTS OF HOUSTON

High-end brands such as Graham, Schreuder, and Waverly are always in stock. *1218 Durham, Heights, 713/862–8012.*

14 *c-3*

WALLPAPERS TO GO

A seemingly endless supply of wallpaper is in stock at every location, ready for you to take home, or to order as part of an installation deal. *6121 Kirby, Rice University Village, 713/526–4475.*

6 *d-5*
9651 Katy Fwy., Memorial/Spring Branch, 713/932–1466.

2 *g-8*
1203 Bay Area Blvd., Clear Lake/Bay Area, 281/338–1194.

3 *b-7*
15263 Southwest Fwy., Sugar Land/Fort Bend, 281/565–4444.

2 *f-1*
20022 Hwy. 59 N, North, 281/319–5507.

stone

3 *c-3*
YELLOW STONE MARBLE AND GRANITE
Imagine having a bathtub as big as a king-size bed and all in soft-polished pink granite. If you have other ideas about how to use fine quarried stone in your home, this store can fix you up. *4069 Hollister, Memorial/Spring Branch, 713/462–4207.*

HOUSEWARES & HARDWARE

5 *a-1*
BBQ PITS BY KLOSE
Pick up a folksy drum-style grill or go to town and spend six figures on something that can smoke a herd of brisket. Klose will weld you a whimsical pit with the look of a longneck, longhorn, or anything else you desire. *2214-½ W. 34th St., North, 713/686–8720.*

10 *a-5*
BED, BATH & BEYOND
Well-priced goods for cleaning, organizing, and redecorating the bedroom and bath are sold, along with kitchen items such as table linens, appliances, cookware, place settings, and cookery gadgets. *4700 Beechnut, Meyerland, 713/666–9926.*

6 *c-5*
10515 Katy Fwy., Memorial/Spring Branch, 713/461–6509.

2 *c-3*
7736 FM 1960 W, FM 1960 area, 281/890–9781.

4 *b-5*
2306 Hwy. 6 S, Southwest, 281/497–4636.

9 *g-1*
BERING'S
Need to pick up some plumbing fixtures, Baccarat crystal, and a belt sander? Bering's mix of boutique housewares, nuts and bolts, tools, and home and garden hardware covers a broad territory. *6102 Westheimer, Galleria/Post Oak, 713/785–6400.*

10 *a-1*
THE CONTAINER STORE
Early in its history, perhaps, this fetish central for obsessive types may have dealt in things to put things in, but now along with under-bed storage boxes, laundry room storage systems, and college dorm storage accessories, the chain carries cunning accessories and not-insignificant furnishings. *2511 Post Oak Blvd., Galleria/Post Oak, 713/960–1722.*

10 *a-2*
HOME DEPOT
The West Loop store is open 24 hours, and all locations sell everything for the home, except possibly a quart of milk. Pick up a flat of pansies, a new Jacuzzi, or the granddaddy of all table saws. *5445 West Loop S, Sharpstown, 713/662–3950.*

7 *f-2*
999 North Loop W, Heights, 713/802–9725.

2 *g-6*
13400 Market St., Pasadena/Southeast, 713/451–9600.

2 *g-8*
12336 Gulf Fwy., South Houston/Hobby Airport, 713/941–0960.

9 *e-3*
7110 Bellerive, Sharpstown, 713/953–1443.

3 *c-3*
1100 Lumpkin Rd., North, 713/461–9898.

2 *c-3*
18355 Tomball Pkwy., FM 1960 area, 281/894–0634.

4 *b-6*
2828 Hwy. 6 S, Southwest, 281/870–9369.

9 *h-1*
11500 Chimney Rock, Southwest, 713/723–1400.

9 *b-4*

6800 W. Sam Houston Pkwy. N, North, 281/498–6445.

2 *f-4*

KING HARDWARE

The hard-core handyman will find parts for name-brand appliances like Maytag, Whirlpool, General Electric, and more. Come by during the holidays for a freshly flocked tree. *8006 C.E. King Pkwy., North, 281/458–4581.*

cutlery & gadgetry

7 *g-1*

ALLIED-KENCO SALES

Once you've concocted the perfect deep-fried turkey marinade, use a 16-inch injector to get the spices deep into the bird. *26 Lyerly St., North, 713/691–2935.*

12 *d-4*

ARCHWAY GALLERY

You'll find inventive versions of ordinary objects such as spoon holders, switch plates, pet food bowls, and more, plus purely decorative pretties. *2013 W. Gray, River Oaks, 713/522–2409.*

9 *f-5*

INTERNATIONAL STAINLESS

Use the goods here to slice, dice, and heat evenly, in the oven and on top of the stove. *6618 Imogene, Sharpstown, 713/777–6021.*

4 *c-3*

WILLIAMS-SONOMA

An ambitious cook may become a little overexcited at the sight of so much gleaming kitchenware. *12850 Memorial, Memorial/Spring Branch, 713/465–4775.*

7 *b-8*

4076 Westheimer, River Oaks, 713/622–4161.

JEWELRY

9 *g-1*

ABE KATZ

The current vogue for platinum has really caught on in this pricey institution. If the sort of Twinkie jewelry advertised in Sunday supplements and weekend arts section ads strikes you as a horrible waste of perfectly good gemstones, then Abe Katz is the store for

you. They have better things to do with a marquise-cut emerald than flank it with diamond baguettes. *6222 Richmond, Galleria/Post Oak, 713/783–3399.*

9 *g-1*

ANSLEY'S FINE JEWELRY

This traditional store offers jewelry and loose gemstones. Tennis bracelets, simple gold bands, and six-prong solitaires fill the cases. *6222 Richmond, Galleria/Post Oak, 713/787–6568.*

4 *b-6*

DESIGNS IN GOLD

Gold charms are not a thing of the past. A wide rage of delicate charms, bracelets, chains, and classic jewelry are in this store's inventory. *2610 Hwy. 6 S, Southwest, 281/493–4653.*

9 *d-1*

HOUSTON JEWELRY

When we're not wildcatting or staging avant-garde opera, we Texans are a traditional lot, and our brides like the sort of plain gold bands and great big ol' solitaires Houston Jewelry showcases. *9521 Westheimer, Richmond Strip, 713/784–1000.*

10 *c-3*

I. W. MARKS

The slightly awkward figure of I. W. himself is often seen on television, and his name is very often seen on the benefactor list of art programs. Funds for fine arts are provided by steady trade at his seemingly ordinary strip-center shop. Big, crude "gold nugget" styles are still popular here, as well as goods such as fine watches and clocks, pens, and Judith Leiber bags. *3841 Bellaire Blvd., Astrodome/Old Spanish Trail, 713/668–5000.*

antiques & collectible items

9 *h-1*

BULLOCK'S

You'll find estate jewelry, preowned jewelry, loose gems, watches (and bezels), clocks, and other heirlooms at this well-established dealer. *5901 Westheimer, Galleria/Post Oak, 713/783–8150.*

3 *c-3*

GUIDRY'S FINE JEWELRY
Well-set cubic zirconia has prominent placement in the displays, which means the estate pieces sold here are reasonably priced. *2121 W. Sam Houston Pkwy. N, Trade Mart, North, 713/467–2506.*

6 *c-5*

JAMES AVERY CRAFTSMAN
Even today, it's not easy for a girl to get through middle school without a couple of sterling silver pretties from the James Avery catalogue. If you frequently travel out of state, buy the Texas signet ring and wear it with pride. *900 Gessner, Memorial/Spring Branch, 713/932–1434.*

12 *a-6*

3960 Westheimer, River Oaks, 713/621–0135.

2 *c-3*

5315 FM 1960 W, FM 1960 area, 281/440–5167.

12 *f-6*

SILVERLUST
If you envy the scarabs of mummies or the complex necklaces worn by Byzantines depicted in frescos, then you'll finally be satisfied by the contemporary, imported, and antique body art at Silverlust. *1338 Westheimer, Montrose, 713/520–5440.*

contemporary pieces

B. WHEELER DESIGNS
Birdie Wheeler uses primitive tools, such as teeth, claws, and stones, and modern methods to craft unique gold jewelry and designer eyewear. Call for an appointment. *River Oaks, 713/439–1183.*

14 *c-3*

J. SILVER
Bangles, bracelets, chokers, collars, keyhole necklaces, and other neo-Victorian baubles dripping with beads and crystal spheres are central to the collection. Sterling jewelry and gifts are also available. *2412 Rice Blvd., Rice University Village, 713/807–1644.*

12 *c-5*

MASTERSON DESIGN
Visit Marquita Masterson's studio and see the handmade glass and silver pieces in their natural habitat. *2138 Welch, Montrose, 713/522–6774.*

LEATHER GOODS & LUGGAGE

10 *a-1*

BAG-N-BAGGAGE
Although the casual name seems fitting to backpacks and lunch coolers (which are available), this store trades in Halliburton, Hartmann, Samsonite, and other fine travel goods. *5015 Westheimer, Galleria/Post Oak, 713/629–8380.*

13 *b-3*

3900 Polk, The Park Shops, Downtown/Theater District, 713/223–2181.

6 *c-5*

1000 Katy Fwy., Memorial City Mall, Memorial/Spring Branch, 713/468–8258.

10 *a-1*

FENDI
See Handbags & Gloves *in* Clothing for Women/Specialty Stores, *above.*

10 *a-1*

GUCCI
Snap up a little bitty zippered coin purse, pack for a weekend with a chic city bag, or spend several thousand dollars on handbags to match every pair of shoes you might ever own. *5085 Westheimer, Galleria/Post Oak, 713/961–0778.*

10 *a-1*

LOUIS VUITTON
One so rarely has the chance for a top-notch ocean voyage that it's fortunate you can show off your signature LV logo vanity case on even a group ski trip. *5075 Westheimer, Galleria/Post Oak, 713/961–3441.*

9 *c-3*

LUGGAGE AND LEATHER
There's no practical way to roll a matching seven-piece set with wheels down the concourse by yourself, but a skycap can help you heavy packers. The skycaps will thank you. *9880 Harwin, Sharpstown, 713/266–0237.*

2 *c-3*

6540 FM 1960 W, FM 1960 area, 281/444–8552.

2 *g-8*

1185 W. NASA Rd. 1, Clear Lake/Bay Area, 281/332–0115.

3 *c-3*

1055 W. Sam Houston Pkwy. N, North, 713/468–7977.

7 *b-8*

MAX LANG

Lang's first fashion enterprise was selling show halters from a trailer, with colorful skins and Arabian tack a specialty. For a couple of decades, however, the trade has been custom belts and buckles and a small jewelry line. *4020 Westheimer, River Oaks, 713/960–8845.*

LINENS

12 *b-8*

THE LINEN HOUSE

Indulge your fabric fetish with this boutique's Spanish brocades, Oriental silks, jacquards, and satins. Textiles at the Linen House range from pure, perfect white table napkins to baroque bed canopies, and you can custom order pieces or rent table linens for a big event. (Psst, this little side street is a hidden enclave of designer stores.) *2405 Norfolk, Upper Kirby District, 713/522–1711.*

4 *c-3*

LINENS 'N THINGS

The titular "'n things" are sachets, baskets of scented soaps, arty nail brushes, and other items fit for a boudoir. *12850 Memorial, Memorial/Spring Branch, 713/464–7994.*

7 *a-7*

1751 Post Oak Blvd., Galleria/Post Oak, 713/963–9699.

12 *d-4*

LINENS UNLIMITED OF HOUSTON

You may be surprised to learn that this "unlimited" shop is a tasteful boutique instead of a semidiscount volume vendor. *1988 W. Gray, River Oaks 713/529–4446.*

quilts & duvets

BED, BATH & BEYOND

The bed region of these spacious stores carries a wide variety of quilts, duvets, and even featherbeds all year round. *See* Housewares & Hardware, *above.*

4 *d-3*

GREAT EXPECTATIONS QUILTS

The name is somewhat of a misnomer—the fine quilts here are not just for the nursery. When it's not possible to travel out of town for true country quilts, this strip-mall store offers colorful, patterned quilts with big-city prices and a down-home look. *14090 Memorial Dr., Memorial/Spring Branch, 281/496–0033.*

MAPS

12 *f-7*

KEY MAPS INC

The detailed, easy-to-use street-finder "Key Map" books are only the beginning. The inside of this ugly little store holds maps of pretty much all the world and the heavens, too, along with all manner of globes (including one designed to store Scotch), puzzles and games, educational toys, and a rich selection of geography-themed gifts. *1411 W. Alabama, Montrose, 713/522–7949.*

3 *b-7*

TRAVEL EXPO

From tickets to battery-operated timepieces, you'll find all your travel needs at the superstore. The book department has practical guides, fantasy travelogues, and maps. *12690 Fountain Lake Circle, Sugar Land/Fort Bend, 281/242–1500.*

MEMORABILIA

3 *c-2*

COLLECTIBLE TREASURES

Practicing figurine tolerance, this treasure chest places Tom Clark gnomes and Harmony Kingdom religious statues side by side. *6850 Oakwood Trace Ct., North, 800/484–2856, enter 9110 at prompt.*

MINIATURES

7 *a-7*

IMPERIAL MINIATURE ARMORY

Battle big tensions by pitting a couple of little armies against each other. *10547 S. Post Oak Rd., Galleria/Post Oak, 713/729–8428.*

1 *a-1*

SMALLER THAN A BREADBOX

Houston artist Helen David has earned a national reputation with her dollhouse miniature floral arrangements. David gives classes and workshops and sells her wee creations. For more information, shoot an E-mail to "Helen's Helper," richard@smallerthanbreadbox.com.

MISCELLANY

7 *f-6*

ARNE'S WAREHOUSE

Both stories of this ugly, old warehouse are packed with housewares (from a 52-piece Wilton cake-decorating kit to a barbecue set), party goods, and, for whatever reason, pet supplies. If you're shopping for a holiday or festive occasion, Arne's can hook you up with colored tablecloths, giant plastic punch bowls (or crystal), and plastic stemware and punch cups (or crystal). Wrapping paper, ribbons, and bridal shower and wedding decorations are also available. For any occasion, Arne's has terrific prices on candles. You can get a gross of 12-inch white, dripless tapers for a few bucks. *2830 Hicks St., Heights, 713/869–8321.*

14 *c-3*

VARIETY 5 & 10

Annual feature stories about this genuine old-fashioned notions store are anticipated much like the holidays. Everyone loves this anachronism, even if they only have clove gum part of the time. Stop in often, and when they do have clove gum, buy the whole lot. The factory makes it according to demand. The next time you're on your way to an office supply store, a drugstore, or a toy store, come to Variety 5 & 10 instead. You'll find what you're looking for and have a great time. *2415 Rice Blvd., Rice University Village, 713/522–0561.*

MUSIC

cds, tapes, & vinyl

12 *c-5*

CACTUS MUSIC AND VIDEO

Let's see. In-store performances and disc signings, large and well-organized inventory, nice mix of the newest releases and classic cuts, listen-before-you-buy policy,

and an informed and friendly staff. What more could you want? *2930 Shepherd, Montrose, 713/526–9272.*

10 *a-5*

CD WAREHOUSE

Low prices on the latest releases and excellent prices on used music, DVDs, and games make this chain a popular place to find popular music. *4782 Beechnut, Meyerland, 713/218–0553.*

6 *h-8*

5884 San Felipe, Galleria/Post Oak, 713/781–1900.

12 *d-7*

2620 Shepherd, Montrose, 713/521–7275.

3 *h-2*

RECORD CITY

Needles? Yes, so you won't scratch classic gospel and blues recordings with worn-out stereo equipment. Tapes, CDs, and dance tunes are also carried. *8513 Mesa Dr., North, 713/633–8311.*

12 *d-7*

RECORD RACK

Anybody who has a mix-tape made before most people have even heard the new tunes knows about this very in-the-moment specialty store. *3109 Shepherd, Montrose, 713/524–3602.*

2 *c-3*

VINYL EDGE

Purists flock to this odd, out-of-the-way, and totally obsessive record store. *13171 Veterans Memorial Dr., FM 1960 area, 281/537–2575.*

musical instruments

9 *f-1*

EVANS MUSIC CITY

For more than a half century, musicians, would-be musicians, and kids with garage bands have relied on Evans for equipment (sales and rental) and all the latest accessories. Factory service and composer software are also offered. *6240 Westheimer, Galleria/Post Oak, 713/781–2100.*

12 *b-7*

FORSHEY PIANO COMPANY

After stepping into this impressive building—it looks like Tara, minus the plantation—it's hard to resist a full-sized Steinway grand. The walls are decorated with photos of pianos past. *2920 Kirby, Upper Kirby District, 713/524–2900.*

2 *h-7*

3311 Preston, Clear Lake/Bay Area, 281/ 487–3127.

9 *h-3*

H&H MUSIC COMPANY
Band members and their burdened parents depend on H&H for instruments, sheet music, and lessons. When kids move on to other interests, H&H will buy the used instruments. Rentals are available. *5510 Weslayan, Rice University Village, 713/666–2090.*

13 *b-4*

1211 Caroline, Downtown/Theater District, 713/652–0857.

12 *d-8*

ROCKIN' ROBIN GUITARS & MUSIC
This friendly little shop will do an awful lot to make a musician out of you. You can order a new Taylor acoustic made of African ovangkol or check out a vintage 1956 Gibson Les Paul solid-body electric. Rockin' Robin also offers guitar and drum lessons. *3619 Shepherd, Montrose, 713/529–5442.*

sheet music

12 *h-7*

WADLER-KAPLAN MUSIC SHOP
Any type of tune that can be notated is archived in this inventory. Whether you play something standard, like a keyboard, or would rather have early church vocal music or a ditty for your dulcimer, this is your resource. *3907 S. Main, Downtown/Theater District, 713/529–2676.*

NEEDLEWORK & KNITTING

2 *c-3*

IDLE HANDS, INC.
The name is a warning, not a description of the clientele. Naturally, instead of doing the devil's work, patrons put their time to good works in knitting and stitching. *13718 Schroeder, FM 1960 area, 281/469–5484.*

NEWSPAPERS & MAGAZINES

2 *a-4*

SUPERSTAND
Those who fear that the Internet will be the death of print media have not been to a Superstand. Each store is as big as the average drugstore and stocked with what looks like thousands of magazines and newspapers from around the country and overseas. *553 S. Mason Rd., North, 713/599–8188.*

12 *c-6*

2077 S. Shepherd, River Oaks, 713/521– 2288.

10 *a-1*

5348 Westheimer, Galleria/Post Oak, 713/ 626–4888.

OCCULT

12 *d-1*

BOTANICA EL HIJO DE CHANGO
Hopeful and amused Houstonians stop in to pick up lurid potions with labels like "Love potion and floor cleaner" and "Make money hand lotion." It's all fun, and maybe lucky. *4416 Washington Ave., Heights, 713/861–4957.*

8 *d-5*

STANLEY DRUG CO.
Shopping for decor or more, Houstonians have stopped in for candles, herbs, oils, soaps, and statuettes since 1938. The shop frequently provides readings, consultations, and books for those who prefer do-it-yourself psychic experiments. *2718 Lyons, Fifth Ward, 713/222–0800.*

PETS & PET SUPPLIES

7 *f-6*

ARNE'S WAREHOUSE
You can multitask in this warehouse by grabbing supplies for your pet while you shop mainly for party supplies. *2830 Hicks St., Heights, 713/869–8321.*

3 *d-3*

PETCO
Birds and fish and pet supplies are advertised, but most locations have cat and dog adoptions on weekends, too. Various shelters bring in homeless ani-

mals and hope kindly folk will take them home. Petco offers training classes, grooming, food, and treats. Ask for a keycard for discounts. Every type of premium pet food is carried, and the stores often have pots of kitty grass in stock. *12015 Northwest Fwy., Memorial/Spring Branch, 713/957–4341.*

12 *c-6*
2110 Shepherd, Montrose, 713/521–1005.

10 *c-3*
5450 Weslayan, Rice University Village, 713/665–4150.

9 *e-1*
7510 Westheimer, Richmond Strip, 713/781–9010.

2 *g-5*
13341–13345 Hwy. 10 E, Pasadena/Southeast, 713/455–8900.

2 *g-6*
3680 Spencer Hwy., Pasadena/Southeast, 713/944–1777.

4 *b-4*
2350 S. Hwy. 6, Southwest, 281/493–0199.

2 *c-3*
4431 FM 1960, FM 1960 area, 281/580–3335.

4 *b-6*
6883 Hwy. 6 N, Katy/Bear Creek, 281/345–1215.

4 *c-5*
PETSMART
Many of Petsmart's products are house brand. The food aisles feature all the premium brands, but in the beds and brushes and other accessories, there's not quite so much variety. *10500 Old Katy Rd., North, 713/973–7642.*

4 *c-5*
12533 Westheimer, Southwest, 281/496–9884.

10 *a-2*
5415 West Loop S, Sharpstown, 713/661–5585.

2 *d-2*
140 FM 1960, Pasadena/Southeast, 281/821–4355.

2 *a-5*
19945 Katy Fwy., Katy/Bear Creek, 281/599–1125.

POSTERS

12 *c-8*
ARNOLD MOVIE POSTER CO.
Looking for a poster from movies starring Arnold Schwarzenegger or directed by John Arnold? You'll probably find them here, along with glossy three-sheets from other contemporary films, the history of sci-fi in poster form, and rare early film posters. *2315 Southwest Fwy., Montrose, 713/524–9000.*

12 *d-7*
RETRO GALLERY
Although only a modest shop on a two-lane street, this gallery is an internationally respected dealer of vintage advertising posters. All items are original. *1839 W. Alabama, Montrose, 713/784–5778.*

SPORTING GOODS & CLOTHING

2 *f-5*
ACADEMY
Authentic in spades, this family-friendly, budget-minded chain hawks everything for the playing field, the hunting field, and just about anything else you might do outdoors. *565 Uvalde Rd., Pasadena/Southeast, 713/453–8366.*

6 *d-5*
8723 Katy Fwy., Memorial/Spring Branch, 713/465–9565.

12 *c-8*
2404 Southwest Fwy., Montrose, 713/520–1795.

2 *f-7*
9990 Kleckley Dr., South Houston/Hobby Airport, 713/944–7511.

3 *h-6*
6039 Telephone Rd., South Houston/Hobby Airport, 713/649–3215.

9 *d-5*
8236 Gessner, Sharpstown, 713/271–1679.

2 *f-3*
OSHMAN'S
All-American athletics are represented, by duds and gear, and thanks to this Houston-based company's officer, Marilyn Oshman, the chain has special programs for women and girls. Find out whether your girls' team can get one of

the grants for girls. *20416 Hwy. 59 N, North, 281/446–7519.*

7 *a-8*
2131 Post Oak Blvd., Galleria/Post Oak, 713/622–4940.

6 *c-5*
975 Gessner, Memorial/Spring Branch, 713/467–1155.

2 *g-8*
19801 Gulf Fwy., Clear Lake/Bay Area, 281/332–6818.

2 *c-3*
8625 FM 1960 W, FM 1960 area, 281/807–9020.

3 *b-7*
12730 Fountain Lake Circle, Sugar Land/Fort Bend, 281/240–3388.

6 *h-5*
REI
The climbing wall might be your first clue that this place is, at heart, devoted to the serious outdoors person. *7951 Katy Fwy., Memorial/Spring Branch, 713/688–3500.*

12 *d-4*
WILDERNESS EQUIPMENT
Need Serengeti sunglasses with rose-colored photochromic lenses to defeat glare while scaling 18,500-ft peaks in Peru (or do you just want to look cool at the wheel of your SUV)?. Either way, this very high-end outdoor and environmental education store will serve your purpose. This store stocks climate-control clothes fit for active days on the water, hill-country hiking, and Arctic peaks, along with travel books and an impressive gift and education toy selection. *1977 W. Gray, River Oaks, 713/522–4453.*

6 *f-7*
WHOLE EARTH PROVISION CO.
Cynical shoppers may come to believe that Whole Earth is selling the look rather than the sweaty, muscle-pulling lifestyle. Why quibble when the sturdy natural-fiber clothes are cute, and the selection of walking, hiking, and climbing shoes is top drawer. *6560 Woodway Dr., Galleria/Post Oak, 713/467–0234.*

12 *c-7*
2934 Shepherd, Montrose, 713/526–5226.

billiards

9 *d-1*
ANNIE O'S PRO SHOP
WPBA veteran Anne Mayes has dropped trick shots with sticks by Black, McDermott, and Meucci, and she prefers her own custom-crafted cues. Have her build you one. In some ways, a custom cue is more personal than a tattoo. *9208 Rasmus, Katy/Bear Creek, 832/251–0055.*

boating

12 *f-4*
GIBB'S BOATS & MOTORS
Commuters passing the Grady-White, Dargel, and Javelin boats on display at this boat store, oddly located on the northwest corner of a busy intersection, are often happily distracted. *1110 W. Gray, River Oaks, 713/526–4349.*

2 *d-3*
PIER 45 MARINE
Cobia, Kenner, Wellcraft, Maxum, Voyager, and other names you know and lust after are on display in the main store showroom, and offered at other locations. *9930 Hwy. 45 N, North, 281/999–5666.*

2 *h-7*
2551 South Shore Blvd., Pier 14, Clear Lake/Bay Area, 281/334–7898.

2 *h-7*
4949 NASA Rd. 1 (Parkside Marina), Clear Lake/Bay Area, 281/362–2948.

1 *c-1*
14510 Hwy. 105 W (Papa's on the Lake), Montgomery, 409/447–4646.

2 *d-4*
RINKER'S BOAT WORLD
Not one to be Gulf-centric, Rinker's World sells and repairs JC Pontoons for people who boat on lakes. Not that Rinker's is without 34-ft powerboats for offshore action. *2500 W. Mount Houston Rd., North, 281/847–0064.*

bowling

9 *f-3*
STRIKE ZONE PRO SHOP
People are bowling all day, all over Houston. Get yourself a Day-Glo ball (for extreme bowling at midnight) and join the fun. *6121 Tarnef (Dynamic Lanes), Sharpstown, 713/773–9663.*

camping

REI
See Sporting Goods & Clothing, *above*.

2 c-3
SUN & SKI SPORTS
Here you'll find super lightweight tents and Poly Coat for when you forget what the clerk told you (which is that you'll strip that tent of waterproofing by washing it with detergents. Poly Coat re-waterproofs tents made of delicate, ultralight synthetic fibers). *5503 FM 1960 W, FM 1960 area, 281/537–0928.*

4 d-3
12526 Memorial, Memorial/Spring Branch, 713/464–2639.

10 a-1
6100 Westheimer, Galleria/Post Oak, 713/783–8180.

fishing tackle & supplies

7 a-7
ANGLER'S EDGE
Test your wrist at the casting park, and then step inside the store to study Rosario custom flies and top-of-the-line ultralight gear. *1141–05 Uptown Park Blvd., Galleria/Post Oak, 713/993–9981.*

2 a-5
BASS PRO SHOPS OUTDOOR WORLD
It's not fishing. It's a way of life, and this chain from Springfield, Missouri, understands that. *5000 Katy Mills Circle, Katy Mills, Katy/Bear Creek, 281/644–2200.*

golf

2 d-3
GOLFSMITH GOLF CENTER
Lynx, Titleist, Adams, TaylorMade, and others are always in stock, and Golfsmith always has the latest drivers and woods. You can also improve your game with on-site swing analysis. *16747 N. Hwy. 45, FM 1960 area, 281/537–0101.*

9 c-1
JOE'S GOLF HOUSE
Every location offers full-service sales and a huge inventory, with all major brands represented in each location. *9633 Westheimer, Richmond Strip, 713/339–4566.*

6 c-5
10901 Katy Fwy., Memorial/Spring Branch, 713/464–1661.

7 a-8
2121 West Loop S, Galleria/Post Oak, 713/871–0010.

3 d-2
13474 Northwest Fwy., North, 713/462–8000.

10 a-1
6508 Westheimer, Galleria/Post Oak, 713/974–7575.

3 c-8
NEVADA BOB
Thinking of Nevada Bob's as the Wal-Mart of golf might not be too far off the mark. Callaway and liquid-metal drivers are featured, but the budget-minded duffer can also get slick deals on new and used clubs. *11922 Murphy Rd., Southwest, 281/495–5511.*

10 a-1
6516 Westheimer, Galleria/Post Oak, 713/783–6224.

riding & saddlery

CHARLOTTE'S SADDLERY
Houstonians who want a horse, have a horse, or ever had a horse know Charlotte's. Western riders, dressage and hunter-jumper, and even fans of the gaited horse count on Charlotte's for the big buys, like saddles (they can help you order a Hermes, or fit you with a Passier or Kieffer dressage saddle), boots (field boots for the ring and rubber muck boots for the barn), and silver-and-gold Quarter Horse show halters. Equestrians stop in regularly for the little things, like hoof picks, liniment, and gossip. If you want a used saddle, a new trainer, or an honest horse, come down to Charlotte's and use the grapevine. *11623-A Katy Fwy, Memorial/Spring Branch, 281/596–8225.*

3 b-1
DOUBLE R TRADING CO.
Each weekend, folks from Double R come in from Madisonville to a booth at Trader's Village. Urban cowboys can find baby saddles, rifle boots, and well-priced Western tack. *7979 N. Eldridge Pkwy., Traders Village, North, 281/955–1715.*

10 *a-1*

STELZIG OF TEXAS

Silver and snakeskin show halters gleam from the tack side of the store. In the larger clothing area, satin and silver conchos shine. *3123 Post Oak Blvd., Galleria/Post Oak, 713/629–7779.*

3 *c-2*

TURNER SADDLERY

Nothing says we love rodeo like a toddler's hobby buckin' bull. For grown cowboys, the popular shop stocks gloves, ropes, and flashy shirts. *6125 W. Sam Houston Pkwy. N, North, 713/466–0781.*

running

9 *c-6*

ATHLETE'S FOOT

New Balance, Puma, and good ol' Converse are among the top brands sold here. You'll also find Timberland and other hiking boots, and outerwear. *9600 Bissonnet, Westwood Mall, Sharpstown, 713/771–4150.*

9 *e-4*

7500 Bellaire Blvd., Sharpstown Shopping Center, Sharpstown, 713/777–3314.

10 *a-1*

5015 Westheimer, Galleria, Galleria/Post Oak, 713/965–9843.

4 *b-5*

2600 Hwy. 6, West Oaks Mall, Southwest, 281/493–9092.

13 *b-3*

FOOT LOCKER

Way back when Adidas were a big deal, Foot Locker was ready with running shoes for America in the grip of a fad. These days, the store carries a wide selection and can fit the serious runner, other athletes, and people who like to wear comfortable shoes. *815 Main, Downtown/Theater District, 713/237–0220.*

14 *c-3*

2548 University Blvd., Rice University Village, 713/942–7576.

7 *g-1*

4500 North Fwy., Northline Mall, North, 713/699–4472.

7 *g-1*

36 E. Crosstimbers, North, 713/699–8322.

6 *c-5*

900 Gessner, Memorial/Spring Branch, 713/465–8738.

2 *c-3*

7920 FM 1960 W, Willowbrook Mall, FM 1960 area, 281/890–2414.

4 *b-5*

2600 Hwy. 6, West Oaks Mall, Southwest, 281/493–5066.

11 *f-4*

7000 Gulf Fwy., Gulfgate Mall, South Houston/Hobby Airport, 713/643–4408.

10 *c-1*

12000 North Fwy., Greenspoint Mall, North, 281/874–9700.

7 *a-3*

9930 Hempstead Rd., Memorial/Spring Branch, 713/682–3413.

2 *f-7*

11510 Gulf Fwy., Almeda Mall, South Houston/Hobby Airport, 713/943–3801.

9 *c-6*

9500 Bissonnet, Sharpstown, 713/772–3896.

10 *a-1*

5085 Westheimer, Galleria, Galleria/Post Oak, 713/621–7238.

9 *e-4*

7500 Bellaire Blvd., Sharpstown, 713/771–0658.

12 *c-8*

RUNSPORT

From whole track teams needing to suit up, to ordinary suburbanites looking like Albert Brooks in "The Lonely Guy," anyone who jogs, runs, or sprints is served by this specialty store. *2137 Richmond, Montrose, 713/524–6662.*

scuba

2 *c-3*

SEA SPORTS SCUBA

Certify the city. That's the goal of this dive shop. Lessons, equipment rental and sale, travel arrangements, and diver-to-diver networking are all put in service of the cause. *9564 FM 1960 W, FM 1960 area, 281/580–4853.*

9 *c-6*

9301 Bissonnet, Sharpstown, 713/777–3483.

9 e-1

7543 Westheimer, Richmond Strip, 713/977–0028.

2 d-3

16300 Kuykendahl, FM 1960 area, 281/580–7777.

skating

9 e-3

ICEPROSHOP.COM

Take the next Tara Lipinski in to have her fitted for Klingbeil custom boots or pick up ready-made skating sets with plenty of spangles. 7300 Bellerive, Sharpstown, 888/770–2008.

12 g-4

MONTROSE SKATE & CYCLE

In-line skaters flock to this funky shop. 1406 Stanford, River Oaks, 713/528–6102.

2 c-3

SKATE TEXAS

All the boots are pretty similar, but the means of locomotion differ. Pick from roller skates, in-line, figure, hockey, and more. 17776 Hwy. 249, North, 281/970–1015.

STATIONERY & OFFICE SUPPLIES

office supplies

14 c-3

DROMGOOLE'S TYPEWRITER SHOP

If you still have a typewriter, this is one place where the staff will respectfully suggest repairs instead of an upgrade. Pick up a Visconti, Aurora, or other fine pen to deal with correspondence while your machine is out of commission. 2515 Rice Blvd., Rice University Village, 713/526–4651.

2 g-8

OFFICE MAX

Whatever your attitude toward the spokes-stick figure, you can't argue with the chain's wide selection and bulk discounts. 11546 Gulf Fwy., South Houston/Hobby Airport, 713/946–1669.

12 e-4

1576 W. Gray, River Oaks, 713/523–1399.

9 d-5

8100 Gessner, Sharpstown, 713/772–1110.

2 d-3

11314 Hwy. 45 N, North, 281/931–0010.

4 d-5

10250 Westheimer, Memorial/Spring Branch, 713/974–8059.

6 c-5

10516 Old Katy Rd., North, 713/465–2555.

2 c-3

7640 FM 1960 W, FM 1960 area, 281/894–8111.

pens & pencils

9 c-1

JEFFREY STONE LTD.

Not in the mood for a new Mont Blanc or Cartier available at any high-end luxury goods store? Look over Jeffrey Stone's selection of antique pens. All the finest styles, from all the finest penmakers (including Mont Blanc and Cartier) are found here, fully refitted and in working order. 9694 Westheimer, Richmond Strip, 713/783–3555.

10 a-1

5000 Westheimer, Galleria/Post Oak, 713/621–2812.

10 a-1

MASSIN'S OFFICE SUPPLY

Select reliable, steady Cross pens when you need a dozen graduation gifts, then choose Sensa or Lamy for a Phi Beta Kappa. 5757 Westheimer, Galleria/Post Oak, 713/782–4540.

TEXAS ART SUPPLY
See Art Supplies, above.

stationery

9 g-1

BERING'S

Soft and staid kid stationery, baroque marbleized note cards and envelopes, and colorful paper-by-the-pound sheets and envelopes have their own tidy section between the lighting fixtures and household appliances. 6102 Westheimer, Galleria/Post Oak, 713/785–6400.

14 *c-3*

ICONOGRAPHY

Velvety-soft Crane stationery and other dainty writing papers are lovingly stocked in this genteel shop. *2552 University Blvd., Rice University Village, 713/529–2630.*

12 *c-6*

MORE THAN PAPER

Much of the paper here is along the lines of disposable tablecloths printed "Oh lordy, look who's 40," but along with party supplies and wrappings you'll find kid stationery and card stock for more powerful sentiments. *2055 Westheimer, Montrose, 713/526–0824.*

7 *a-8*

2035 Post Oak Blvd., Galleria/Post Oak, 713/961–1163.

TOBACCONISTS

14 *c-3*

BRIAR SHOP

Houston has a few walk-in humidors but no other is home to 400 cigars. Don't let the overwhelming choices drive you to the corner store and Swisher Sweets. Just make a habit of coming in to try a few cigars each week until you settle on what you like. *2412 Times Blvd., Rice University Village, 713/529–6347.*

12 *a-7*

HOLLYWOOD FOOD STORE

This fourth-tier convenience store chain is an Inner Looper's best source for fresh imported cigarettes. *3641 Alabama, Upper Kirby District, 713/963–0054.*

8 *c-3*

3145 Crane St., Third Ward, 713/674–3762.

12 *c-7*

2003 Alabama, Montrose, 713/942–8688.

12 *e-6*

1660 Westheimer, Montrose, 713/528–3234.

9 *c-1*

JEFFREY STONE LTD.

In addition to fine pens, Jeffrey Stone Ltd. also sells fine cigars and attendant accessories. *9694 Westheimer, Richmond Strip, 713/783–3555.*

10 *a-1*

5000 Westheimer, Galleria/Post Oak, 713/621–2812.

13 *b-4*

MCCOY'S FINE CIGARS & TOBACCOS

Cigar crawlers can often be found here, stocking up for the next event, which might well start with lunch and conclude way past bedtime after stops at bars, clubs, and fine restaurants all over the city. You can check McCoy's counters for flyers advertising upcoming crawls. *1201 Louisiana, Downtown/Theater District, 713/222–1700.*

9 *e-2*

RICHMOND AVENUE CIGAR

Pipes and lighters are the only merchandise lacking a deep, rich aroma. Pipe tobacco, imported cigarettes, and cigars give the place a distinct, woodsy-sweet scent. *3301 Fondren, at Richmond, Richmond Strip, 713/975–9057.*

TOYS & GAMES

collectibles

13 *a-4*

VINTAGE LIONEL TRAIN XCHANGE

Trainiacs Bill, Madeline, Carole, and Chris are crazy about trains. Hook up with them to buy antiques, maybe even find the make and model of your first Lionel, or, if your ex was foolish enough to leave boxcars, engines, and their original boxes in the garage, haul 'em in for an appraisal or just sell 'em outright. *1600 Smith St., Suite 4230, Downtown/Theater District, 713/951–0230.*

new

4 *d-3*

CHILD'S PLAY

Here's a spot for swanky Santas focusing on teddy bears by Gund, dolls from Madame Alexander, Brio trains, and Breyer horses. *12506 Memorial, Memorial/Spring Branch, 713/465–4664.*

10 a-1

F.A.O. SCHWARZ

Everything shiny and new, and a spotlight on strong sellers, including endless merchandise in the Barbie room (check out the giant fountain of Barbie shoes), is the focus of this classic toy store. The grand toy chest has been celebrated on the big screen, but the formal atmosphere may be off-putting to younger children. You'll be amazed at what you'll find, and you'll probably spend too much. *5000 Westheimer, Galleria/Post Oak, 713/623–8292.*

14 a-5

IMAGINATION TOYS

Like many alternative toy stores, Imagination has Brio and Madame Alexander dolls. Although dolls and chic stuffed animals are offered more as collectors' items than playthings, Lincoln Logs and science fun kits are clearly intended to be played with, gotten dirty, and eventually, gloriously maimed and broken. *3849 Bellaire Blvd., Rice University Village, 713/662–9898.*

4 d-3

THE TOY MAKER

Pokémon isn't exactly the enemy. It's just that some folks believe classic and creative toys are best. Colorful blocks and simple wooden toys are emphasized in the toddler section. For older kids, there are classic parlor games, like Boggle, and—better than a Game Boy—even electronic travel chess sets in which kids can play against a chess machine. *12859 Memorial Dr., Memorial/Spring Branch, 713/461–7830.*

14 c-3

2368 Rice Blvd., Rice University Village, 713/521–2251.

7 b-8

4022 Westheimer, River Oaks, 713/888–0206.

6 c-5

TOYS R US

Toys are them, indeed. These warehouse stores are crowded floor to ceiling with popular plush toys, kits, board games, dolls, and everything that's part of a licensing deal. *9655 Katy Fwy., Memorial/Spring Branch, 713/465–0087.*

2 d-3

11210 North Fwy., North, 281/999–9914.

10 e-4

1212 Old Spanish Trail, Astrodome/Old Spanish Trail, 713/796–8697.

9 f-1

6145 Westheimer, Galleria/Post Oak, 713/785–8697.

9 e-4

7887 Southwest Fwy., Sharpstown, 713/270–9630.

2 b-4

10220 Almeda Genoa Rd., South Houston/Hobby Airport, 713/941–1920.

7 a-1

6433 W. 43rd St., Memorial/Spring Branch, 713/686–3100.

3 d-2

9649 W. Wingfoot Rd., North, 713/462–0615.

role-playing & pub

9 b-1

RICK'S DARTS & GAMES

Being grown up doesn't mean giving up wholesome games, and Rick's is at the ready with traditional board games, sets for classic games like mahjong and cribbage, every card game known to man, and, if you want to play outside, disc golf gear and kites. *10236 Westheimer, Memorial/Spring Branch, 713/952–5900.*

VIDEO

12 e-4

AUDIO VIDEO PLUS

Unlike large chains, AV Plus doesn't change inventory, they only add to it. You can find almost anything among tens of thousands of titles for rent in VHS and Beta. The sales selection of tape, laserdisc, and DVD is designed for the connoisseur. *1225 Waugh Dr., River Oaks, 713/526–9065.*

9 g-1

5909 Richmond, Galleria/Post Oak, 713/782–8346.

12 d-4

BLOCKBUSTER VIDEO

You're not going to find Slavic experimental films at any Blockbuster location, but you'll find fair deals on new and recent releases and popular games. Drive for 10 minutes in almost any direction and you'll spot Blockbuster's familiar blue and yellow sign. There are more than 100 locations in Houston. *1917 W. Gray, River Oaks, 713/520–0301.*

12 *f-6*
HOLLYWOOD VIDEO
Hollywood gives you five full days with new releases and discounts for early returns. The Montrose flagship store is housed in a former movie palace, the Tower Theater. Call information to find out which of the few dozen Hollywood stores is nearest to you. *1201 Westheimer, Montrose, 713/520–1883.*

WATCHES & CLOCKS

antique

12 *c-5*
LITTLE WATCH SHOP
Quaint as all get out, this Montrose institution sells and repairs antique and contemporary clocks and watches. *1919 Shepherd, Montrose, 713/524–2648.*

contemporary

10 *a-1*
ELDO ROSSI
Don't be intimidated by the selection of Rolex and other luxury watches. Before opening this intimate business, Rossi spent many years with Sweeny Jewelers. *5433 Westheimer, Bank of America Bldg., Galleria/Post Oak, 713/621–2032.*

7 *a-7*
WAZEL
This authorized Patek Philippe and Rolex sales and service dealer has an extra advantage: some of the stock is preowned and priced accordingly. *1114–02 Uptown Park Blvd., Uptown Park, Galleria/Post Oak, 713/627–7497.*

chapter 3

PARKS, GARDENS & SPORTS

Except for August and February (the hottest and coldest months), Houston weather allows for outdoor activity all year round, and Houstonians take advantage of it. In North Houston, you'll find rugby teams of Compaq employees and Huntsville prison guards taking on Texas A&M Aggies, the Houston Harpies women's hockey team tearing up the ice at rinks throughout the city and in surrounding areas, and Inner Loop night owls shooting hoops at Spotts Park way after dark. Not all the activity is organized, or even serious. Miniature golf courses, batting cages, and go-cart race tracks at Mountasia Family Fun Center let adults play like, or with, kids. Find pickup games in area parks, or enjoy nature in solitude.

It may appear that Houstonians built the current sprawl of strip centers and planned communities on an acrid mud flat. However, we are actually at the center of several rich ecosystems, and volunteers at area nature centers provide education and delightful insights about the diversity of life here where freshwater, saltwater, forest, and prairie habitats collide. Wear comfortable shoes, lather up with bug spray, and you'll have a truly wonderful time exploring natural Houston.

parks

park information
For general information on city parks near you, call 713/845–1000. For information about park activities, call the events line, 713/845–1111.

4 *c-6*
ALIEF COMMUNITY PARK/QUILLIAN CENTER
Four tennis courts, baseball fields, and lap lanes in the pools provide the proper parameters for structured sporting contests and practice space for serious athletes, while a playground for kids and plenty of green space create a free play area for everyone else. *11903 Bellaire Blvd., Southwest, 281/564–8130.*

4 *c-1*
BEAR CREEK PARK
Except on the glossy green golf course, the flora and fauna has the dusty, sun-baked charm of west Texas. Miles of roads and trails wind through the woodsy areas surrounding Bear Creek and Langham Bayou. Two-lane roads and paved parking make it easy for families to enjoy the elaborate playground, fields for soccer, football, and rugby, ball fields, covered picnic and play areas, open-pit grills, and grassy spaces designed for croquet, volleyball, and the like. A children's zoo is across the road from the baseball and softball fields, and a designated wildlife sanctuary is a light hike west of the main activity area. *3535 War Memorial Dr., off N. Eldridge Pkwy. or Clay Rd., Katy/Bear Creek, 281/496–2166.*

12 *f-8*
BELL PARK
Area residents flock to this small park after work, and on weekend afternoons wedding parties are likely to take over. For some couples, the attractive aspects of the park overcome the sound of traffic on Montrose. Dogs play in the pond on summer afternoons, and locals find a bench or rock to plant themselves on while taking in the fresh air. *Montrose at Banks, Montrose.*

9 *f-4*
BURNETT BAYLAND PARK
Along with the usual open spaces and playground equipment, this neighborhood park has a serious league ballpark. *5500 Gulfton, Sharpstown.*

14 *g-3*
HERMANN PARK
Houston's 400-acre backyard has a zoo, a duck pond, a Japanese garden, jogging and bridle trails, a children's choo-choo train, and so many picnic tables that it sometimes seems every single Houstonian is celebrating a birthday party or family barbecue here. Recent renovations include adding larger and improved restrooms to Miller Outdoor Theatre, more parking for the zoo, and a general tidying-up upgrade of the 18-hole golf course and driving range. The park, including golf course and zoo, is bordered by North and South MacGregor (Golf Course Drive, the route to clubhouse and zoo parking is off North MacGregor), Ben Taub Loop, Fannin,

and Hermann Drive. Golf Course Drive winds through the park, and the other route in begins at the statue of Sam Houston, between the park and the Museum of Natural Science, where Fannin crosses Herman Drive. *6001 Fannin, Medical Center, 713/845–1000.*

7 *b-6*

MEMORIAL PARK
Between Shepherd and the Loop, Memorial sees two concurrent rush hours: commuters inching down the street while runners sprint on the wide dirt track adjacent to it. Memorial Drive has three lanes, while walkers, joggers, and runners can travel six-abreast. The park also has trails for mountain bikers (which are often closed for maintenance), tennis courts, a top-flight golf course, picnic areas, and some of the tallest trees in Houston. Although some parts border on being too well manicured, this is still very much a family park. Inside Memorial Park, the Houston Arboretum, thanks to the diligence of Arboretum staff who close and open trails and ponds to prevent damage from overuse, is a great example of what this region looks like without conventional groundskeepers. *6000 Memorial Dr., Memorial/Spring Branch.*

7 *h-6*

SAM HOUSTON PARK
Although downtown revitalization, a program big on paving and short on landscaping, gets all the hype, this park provides a welcome expanse of lawn and tall, healthy trees to break up the man-made monotony. Sam Houston Park also showcases fine and historic homes from Houston's past. A cabin that predates the Republic was moved here from the wetlands now known as Clear Lake. Other structures are of slightly more recent vintage. Heritage Society docents lead regular tours of the homes, especially during the beloved Christmas Candlelight Tours. Fairs and special events, including Houston's famous International Festival, crowd the park on spring weekends. *1100 Bagby, Downtown, 713/655–1912.*

7 *f-6*

SPOTTS PARK
Great hoops and a great view of the downtown skyline keep this spot hopping. Powerful lights enable night games. *Allen Pkwy. at Montrose, Montrose.*

other green spaces

BOTANICAL GARDENS

1 *f-4*

ARMAND BAYOU NATURE CENTER
Volunteers can help you learn more about the plants and wildlife or teach you about the turn-of-the-century lifestyle illustrated by the Martyn Farm. On foot or by paddle craft, you can explore 2,500 acres featuring pristine Gulf Coast prairie, woodlands, and estuarine bayou. Group activities, tours, and boat trips are frequent events. *8500 Bay Area Blvd., Pasadena/Southeast, 281/474–2551. Open Tues.–Sat. 9–5, Sun. noon–5.*

1 *c-6*

BRAZOS BEND STATE PARK
Truly a gem, this park features prairie, hardwood forest, and swamp. Well-maintained trails such as 40-Acre Lake Trail, Hoots Hollow Trail, Elm Lake Loop Trail, and others make it easy for hikers and bikers to get around. Brazos also features the country's first fully accessible nature trail. It's paved for wheelchairs, with slight curbs to mark the edge, and punctuated with signs giving information in Braille and raised letters. Depending on the time of year, you can see a past-season eagle nest in the nature center, or nesting bald eagles. Park naturalists host regular programs, overnight camping is allowed, and this park is home to the George Observatory. *21901 FM 762, Sugar Land/Fort Bend, 409/553–5101.*

1 *a-1*

EDITH L. MOORE NATURE SANCTUARY
This sanctuary, home to Audubon Society Headquarters, offers less-serious bird-watchers a view of wildlife along Rummel Creek. The 18-acre tract is home to many species year-round. Birders can count on seeing rails, and gallinules and coots are likely. Grassland birds such as weavers, vireos, and warblers are also common. There have been concerns about Rummel Creek, so please, don't abuse the banks in wet weather. *440 Wilchester Blvd., Memorial*

Spring Branch, 713/464–4900. Park open daily 8:30–6; building daily 9–5.

7 *b-7*

HOUSTON ARBORETUM

This 155-acre preserve is inside the Loop and so convenient that Downtown, Galleria, Greenway, and I–10 area workers can enjoy the outdoors during their lunch breaks. You can look for birds and other critters while strolling through the arboretum's wide, half-mile loop or wandering any of dozens of side paths. Tall pines, spreading oaks, and fragrant southern wax-myrtle shade the park, and flowering trees like parsley hawthorn, Eastern redbud, and snowdrop trees are each attractions in their season. The Memorial Park location makes it easy for families with different interests to share a weekend. The jocks can take advantage of Memorial Park amenities while nature lovers explore the arboretum. Paths pass several ponds, and Buffalo Bayou runs past the south end of the arboretum. The arboretum has a Nature Center with gift shop and classrooms and a Discovery Center, which is open 10–6, Tuesday through Sunday.

PLAYGROUNDS

Houston's got plenty of space for play.

Alief Park (11903 Bellaire)
Beverly Hills Park (10201 Kingspoint)
Blueridge Park (5600 Court Rd.)
Carnegie Elementary SPARK park (10401 Scott St.)
Crestmont Park (5100 Selinsky Rd.)
De Chaumes Elementary SPARK park (155 Cooper Rd.)
F. M. Law Park (6100 Vassar)
Gregory-Lincoln Education Center SPARK park (1101 Taft St.)
Kashmere Gardens Elementary SPARK park (4901 Lockwood Dr.)
Poe Elementary SPARK park (5100 Hazard St.)
Swiney Park (2812 Cline)
Terrell Alternative School (4610 East Crosstimbers)
Travis Elementary SPARK park (3311 Beauchamp Houston)
Home of the triceratops!
Sharpstown Middle School SPARK park (8330 Triola La.)
Willow (10400 Cliftwood)
Woodland Acres SPARK park (12936 Sarahs La.)
Featuring a kid's castle.

School groups, scouting groups, church groups, and others can attend programs at the center. *4501 Woodway, Memorial/Spring Branch, 713/681–8433.*

2 *f-3*

JESSE H. JONES PARK AND NATURE CENTER

Some come to this 225-acre preserve for the nature and pioneer day programs. You might see costumed reenactors cooking, blacksmithing, making candles, or practicing Native American crafts. Programs always feature Wilma, the pig. When there is no entertainment planned, families come to hike the 5 mi of wooded trails, bike, and canoe or fish in Spring Creek. Even on rainy or cold weekends, you can get the kids out of the house for a session inside the nature center. *20634 Kenswick Dr., Tomball/Spring, 281/446–8588.*

2 *f-3*

MERCER ARBORETUM AND BOTANIC GARDENS

A rich selection of native plants is lovingly tended in this 253-acre garden. Highlights include succulents, lilies, and intriguing display gardens of swamp flora. Classes and programs are held on weekends. *22306 Aldine Westfield Rd., North, 281/443–8731. Open daily 8–5.*

10 *b-5*

NATURE DISCOVERY CENTER

The live animals displayed here are not to be petted or poked, but almost all the rest of the collection is designed for hands-on learning. Standing Texas wildlife exhibits are augmented by educational programs, story times, adult programs, guided walks and tours, and temporary exhibits relating to flora and fauna around the world. *7112 Newcastle, Bellaire, 713/667–6550. Open Tues.–Fri. and Sun. noon–5:30, Sat. 10–5:30.*

PLAYGROUNDS

In Hermann Park, it's sometimes hard to tell the playground equipment from the public art, and most kids don't bother to distinguish—they just climb. Thanks to the SPARK School Park program, many kids have access to updated local parks, a safe place to play, and in some cases, public art from artists such as Barnabas Strickland and Paul Kittleson. SPARK parks are designed to use school money, federal grant money, and corporate sponsorship money to create a community park (usually on a school playground). Under the rules, the school must provide pedestrian access to the park. Underage kids are not allowed during school hours, but after school hours, summer, and holidays, the jogging trails and playground equipment are open to the public. FUNDay in the park Sunday programs are also held in SPARK parks throughout the year. *See* the box on Playgrounds for listings.

zoos, aquariums & animal preserves

2 f-8
BAYOU WILDLIFE PARK
Texas has a surprising number of zebra, nyala, axis deer, and other nonnative quadrupeds. Wildlife officials have a continuing concern that the huge population of African and Asian hoofed mammals at game ranches, private ranches, and tourist parks like Bayou Wildlife Park are properly contained. Even if the fences failed, the critters here would probably stick around, enjoying good grazing, protection from predators, and the occasional tasty handout. Four hundred different animal species have free range of this park's 86 acres (although Bonnie and Shorty, the rhino residents, are housed up front). You can tour the animals' home via a safe tram ride. Before or after viewing the wildlife, little kids can have a pony ride or totter through the petting zoo. *Alvin, 5050 FM 517, Brazoria County, 281/337–6376.*

1 e-7
BRAZORIA NATIONAL WILDLIFE REFUGE
More than 5 mi of graded gravel-road make getting in and out of this otherwise rugged wild bird refuge accessible. The 40,000 acres of salty marsh, while not overtly appealing to our species, is prime habitat for Gulf Coast creatures from fiddler crabs the size of a quarter to sandhill cranes standing 5 ft tall. The park is open daily fall, winter, and spring. During summer months, the park is open the first complete weekend of each month. Call for information on other tour dates and activities. Fishing is allowed, and there are several dedi-

cated hunting days. The refuge is a popular and fruitful spot during the Audubon Society's annual Christmas Bird Count. From the intersection of FM 523 and Hwy. *2004 intersection, take FM 523 another 5½ mi to County Rd. 227. Turn left. The refuge is 1.7 mi. 409/849–6062.*

14 g-3
HOUSTON ZOOLOGICAL GARDENS
Our modest zoo has been quietly participating in the species survival program from early on. When the American Zoo and Aquarium Association (AZA) developed the Species Survival Plan in 1981, the Houston Zoo was already breeding animals. Endangered snow leopards breed like rabbits in their cages here, and the zoo is actively involved in conservation efforts for several species. Siberian tigers, cheetahs, Asian elephants, maned wolves, Micronesian kingfishers, great hornbill, and Chinese alligators all seem content to reproduce in their Houston Zoo homes. (The alligator pair has produced 41 offspring). More than 100 endangered, threatened, and vulnerable species are represented, along with traditional favorites like lions, giraffes, and hippos. During the '90s, the zoo remodeled to make the site more comfortable for humans, and new displays, signs, and a bigger shop have given it a more modern look. Ongoing programs in the Brown Education Center and regular "Meet the Keeper" and guest lecture appearances provide a more complete view of big-eyed mammals, sleek reptiles, and other fascinating creatures we're more likely to anthropomorphize than understand. Mindful of Houston's diversity, the zoo maintains a full Spanish Web site (www.houstonzoo.org). *1513 N. MacGregor Dr., Museum District, 713/523–5888.*

1 d-7
SEA CENTER TEXAS
Dow Chemical and the Texas Parks Department joined forces to build this red drum and spotted sea trout hatchery and educational center. The hatchery is about as interesting to look at as a sorghum field; basically, it's a plainly man-made rectangular tank. It is also as productive as a farmer's field, and below the water, a crop of fingerlings is growing. Inside the Sea Center building, however, aquarium display tanks feature informative simulations of local marine environments. Colorful fish, along with

Houston Zoological Gardens

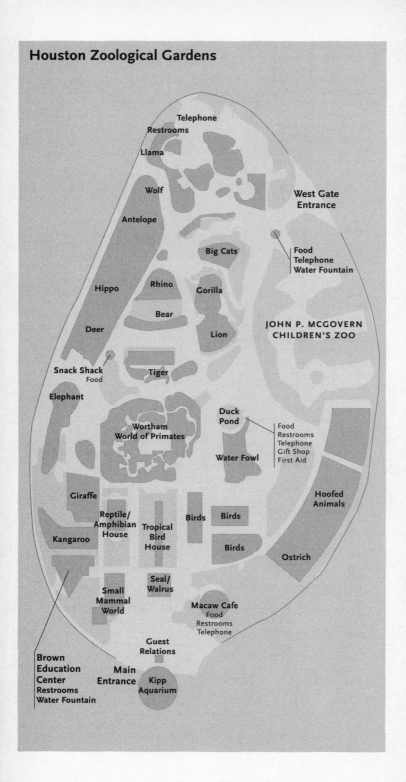

Telephone
Restrooms
Llama
Wolf
Antelope
Big Cats
Hippo
Rhino
Gorilla
Bear
Deer
Lion

West Gate
Entrance

Food
Telephone
Water Fountain

JOHN P. MCGOVERN
CHILDREN'S ZOO

Snack Shack
Food
Tiger
Elephant

Wortham
World of Primates

Duck
Pond
Food
Restrooms
Telephone
Gift Shop
First Aid

Water Fowl

Giraffe

Reptile/
Amphibian
House
Tropical
Bird
House
Birds
Birds
Birds

Hoofed
Animals

Kangaroo

Ostrich

Seal/
Walrus

Small
Mammal
World

Macaw Cafe
Food
Restrooms
Telephone

Guest
Relations

Brown
Education
Center
Restrooms
Water Fountain

Main
Entrance

Kipp
Aquarium

regularly caught species like redfish and snapper fill the tanks, but the most popular is Gordon the grouper. Gordon is actually more than one fish. Temperamental and aggressive 200-pound-plus groupers alternate time in the tank with black-tipped sharks, and this is to protect the sharks. After too much time in the tank, a grouper will harass the sharks. *300 Medical Dr., Clear Lake/Bay Area, 409/292–0100. Open Tues.–Fri. 9–4, Sat. 10–5, Sun. 1–4.*

stadiums

10 *c-1*

COMPAQ CENTER
Home of the three-time WNBA Champion Comets and a men's basketball team that has won a couple of NBA Championships, this 16,666-seat facility is also home to the IHL Aeros, ThunderBears Arena Football team, championship bull riding, annual Ringling Brothers appearances, stadium concerts, and any number of "on-ice" extravaganzas. Good parking in nearby garages, a good food court, and pretty good freeway access make this a convenient place to see sports or a show. *10 E. Greenway Plaza, Greenway Plaza, 713/627–9470.*

13 *d-3*

ENRON FIELD
The Astros played their first ball game on this new field in spring 2000. Our dear old Astrodome (the first-ever domed stadium) had the advantage of allowing fans to get out and root, root, root in any kind of weather—but no one ever went home with a beer buzz aggravated by a stadium sunburn. The 42,000 fans (that's about 12,000 fewer fans than the Dome held) at Enron can enjoy old-fashioned open-air baseball, but if the open air takes on the feel of a sauna, the glass roof can be closed. In 12 to 20 minutes, you'll be enjoying a big cup of flat beer in the indoor, air-conditioned comfort Houstonians know and love. *Texas at Crawford, Downtown/Theater District, 713/355–2164.*

sports & outdoor activities

Upside: with the possible exception of February, Houston has a Southern climate. Downside: "Southern climate" can mean 100+ temperatures in the summer, and humidity off the scale. We make the best of both worlds, though. Houston parks and green spaces are rife with casual games and organized leagues, with folks going out for everything from Hacky Sack to lacrosse, and when the mercury rises we dive into pools or head for one of the city's many ice-skating rinks. For information on activities in city parks near you, call 713/845–1190 for adult athletics and 713/845–1083 for youth sports.

BASEBALL & SOFTBALL

teams to watch

13 *d-3*

HOUSTON ASTROS
Perhaps support would be stronger had the Astro's continued with the old name, the Colt 45s. Being named after a malt liquor could liven up a team's fan base. However, in 1964 the team went Space Age, and through ups, like trips to the playoffs or Larry Dierker's no-hitter season, and downs, like David Letterman's relentless sniping about Buddy Biancalana's miserable hitting, fans have had a consistently lukewarm reaction. Pitcher Nolan Ryan has an expressway named after him, which may be a tribute to his money-making (he was the first baseball millionaire) rather than his pitching. But other greats don't get so much as a sandwich. Alan Ashby, Cesar Cedeno, and Rusty Straub are hardly celebrated. Side note: The Astros' early '70s uniform, with the "Ronald McDonald" look, was much mocked when introduced. But today, skin-tight trousers are the norm, baggy flannels have been banished, and fans, a certain type of fan, are grateful for the change. *Enron Field, Texas at Crawford, Downtown/Theater District, 713/355–2164.*

Compaq Center

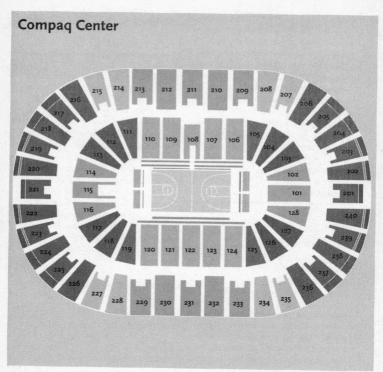

Enron Field

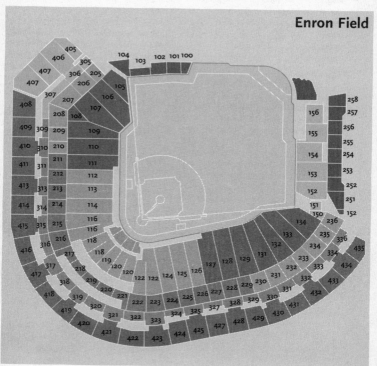

where to play

Perhaps the reason Houstonians don't turn out to support pro teams is that they're off starring in their own games. Surely the Astros' attendance suffers because the city has so many baseball and softball teams, slow pitch and otherwise. Boys and girls can start out with Little League play in a club like Sharpstown Little League (713/779–7755). Aging athletes join the senior section of Houston Men's Adult Baseball League (713/866–6586, www.hmabl.com), a roster for adults. Even the 40 and up teams play real baseball: hardball with metal cleats.

For milder athletic competition, men, women, and youth turn to the more gentle pastime of softball. Slo-pitch, fast-pitch, modified fast-pitch and all the other incarnations of the sandlot game are available. To join a softball game, call the Houston Amateur Softball Association (281/391–0500).

Alcoholic beverages are not allowed in public parks and ball fields, and clubs abide by this rule without missing out on any fun. The number for reserving a field is 713/845–1206. If you join a team, your league will have taken care of scheduling. If you are just looking for a game with friends, you'll just have to hope the local field isn't booked. The following parks, although popular with leagues, have enough room for informal games:

Burnett Bayland Park (6400 Bissonnet, Sharpstown, 713/496–2177)

Bear Creek Park (3535 War Memorial Dr., off N. Eldridge Pkwy., Katy/Bear Creek, 281/496–2177)

Diez Street Park (4700 Diez, East End, 713/845–1000)

J. T. Trotter Park (7809 E Little York, North Houston, 713/845–1000)

Rasmus Park (Blossom Heights) (3700 Fondren, Sharpstown, 713/845–1000).

BASKETBALL

teams to watch

10 *c-1*

HOUSTON COMETS

At the end of the 20th century, the Houston Comets had not only won every possible championship in their three-year-old league, they were the only WNBA team to have a championship. Twenty-first-century fans can look to the Comets and the WNBA for the revival of the old-fashioned skill game. *Compaq Center, 10 E. Greenway Plaza, Southwest, 713/627–9470.*

10 *C-1*

HOUSTON ROCKETS

The Rockets, two-time world champions and perennial contenders, get no respect on the national news—"Knicks lose!" is how the team's '94 championship was broadcast—but they do draw a crowd, and sports bars always fill up for away games. *Compaq Center, 10 E. Greenway Plaza, Southwest, 713/627–9470.*

where to play

Playing at middle and high school courts on the weekends is not exactly kosher—schools being HISD property and all—but we have noticed that an awful lot eschew the city's 174 public courts for school backboards.

10 *a-3*

BELLAIRE RECREATION CENTER

A City of Bellaire Recreation Card is required to use the courts here. It costs $5 for residents, $10 for nonresidents. *5125 Laurel St., Bellaire, 713/662–8280.*

13 *a-3*

FONDE RECREATION CENTER

Possibly the city's best use of municipal funds, the court at this parks and recreation facility sees action from high-caliber players all over the city, and not a few from the NBA, WNBA, and even the occasional European pro. But that doesn't mean you can't call next. *110 Sabine, Heights, 713/226–4466.*

7 *f-6*

SPOTTS PARK

Great hoops and a great view of the downtown skyline keep this spot hopping. Powerful lights enable night games. *Allen Pkwy. at Montrose, Montrose.*

BICYCLING

Our most obvious bikeways are long-standing paved trails along the Braes and Buffalo bayous. Then there's the famed Ho Chi Minh trail in Memorial Park and the trail on top of Barker Dam. Groups of cyclists, including casual riders, always show up for the Moonlight Bicycle Ramble in October. Athletic riders wear their training duds to the Thursday night festivities at Party on the Plaza downtown, and show up at regular festivals such as the International Festival or the Greek Festival or Fourth of July festivities along Buffalo Bayou. When you stop to add it up, Houston's a pretty serious bike town. If you don't want to ride alone, join a club or the Houston Area Tandem Society (281/531–7750).

HOUSTON AREA BICYCLIST ALLIANCE

This long-standing and earnest club participates in the Houston Bicycle Advisory Committee, which works with the city and the Texas Department of Transportation to make life (if not the hopeless road conditions) better for cyclists. Bike rodeos and safety programs for kids are always on the calendar. To learn more, call 713/729–9333.

HOUSTON BICYCLE CLUB

This large and cheery club has loosely organized rides throughout the area. Early risers cruise residential streets and then seek out sweet pastries and coffee. Serious trainers head for the hills of Sealy on the weekends. For more information, talk to the president, 281/395–6220.

GREATER HOUSTON OFF-ROAD BIKING ASSOCIATION

In fall 1999, the rough riders of the Houston Area Mountain Bike Riders Association and the Memorial Park Mountain Bike Association merged. The alliance works to gain access to trails. To get in touch with the membership committee, call 281/544–3855.

MS 150

Occasionally a brave soul will skate the MS 150, a two-day rolling tour to Austin, to raise money for the National Multiple Sclerosis Society. Most folks, however, do their bit for the cause by bike. It takes place in September. For more information, call 800/745–4148.

MOONLIGHT BICYCLE RAMBLE IN OCTOBER

The Houston Area Bicycle Alliance and fellow pro-bike groups hold an annual 2 AM tour under the silvery light of the moon (and Houston's forest of powerful streetlights). Monies raised are used to help promote HABA's agenda: more bike lanes, and more education for cyclists and motorists alike. The recreation event is all about fun, and not particularly about athletics. Riders cruise a mellow route of up to 20 mi. For more information about this tradition, begun in 1972, visit www.bikehouston.org or call 713/729–9333.

BILLIARDS

1 c-3
CLICKS BILLIARDS
This upscale spot has not only elite Gold Crown pool tables, but also upscale Foosball. *13380 Northwest Fwy., North, 713/895–9992.*

11 h-6
SLICK WILLIE'S FAMILY POOL HALL
This chain may not be as "family" as AstroWorld, but the billiards are good for a casual night out. *8503 Gulf Fwy., South Houston/Hobby Airport, 713/943–2917.*

12 f-6
1200 Westheimer, Montrose, 713/522–2525.

1 e-3
12138 East Fwy., Pasadena/Southeast, 713/451–0406.

3 c-6
11852 Wilcrest, Southwest, 281/564–3323.

12 f-5
WAUGH DRIVE POOL HALL
Although deep in the Loop, this lazy little pool hall has a small town ambience, which means bonuses like inexpensive drinks and a laid-back attitude. One minus is that this very casual attitude includes a nonchalance about conventions like regular hours. Those arriving in the evening, or late on a slow night, may find Waugh Drive closed. *2202 Waugh, Montrose, 713/526–8611.*

BIRD-WATCHING

Whistling ducks, black-bellied ducks, and fulvous ducks can be found splashing around with mottled ducks, cinnamon teal, canvas-back, and other ducks in area waters. Shores are home to dramatic roseate spoonbills and Louisiana heron, and you'll spot little blue herons fishing in city bayous. Suburbanites watch hummers determinedly seeking out nourishment, and Gulf Coast boaters may spot a magnificent frigate bird (Fregata magnificent). Spring migration brings birders from around the world, and the fall migration is beginning to generate a national buzz. Birds like it here. In fact, a Dow Chemical parking lot has become a nesting ground for skimmers, by the birds' choice, and local birders welcome new watchers. The Dow skimmer sanctuary is a fenced 4 acres at the Freeport operations plant (2301 N. Brazosport Blvd.). For information on summer open houses, call 409/238–2323. If you spot a rare bird, please report your sighting to the databanks of the Texas Rare Bird Alert (281/992–2757).

6 *a-6*

HOUSTON AUDUBON CHAPTER

This chapter typically has the nation's largest Christmas Bird Count, which is not a surprise when you consider the vast number of migratory species traveling through Texas and this society's membership—one of North America's largest. Throughout the year, the group has birding and naturalist field trips. *440 Wilchester Blvd., Memorial/Spring Branch, 713/932–1639.*

9 *f-5*

HOUSTON ORNITHOLOGY GROUP

Members share knowledge and wet, muddy mornings during the best watching days of the migratory season. Most months, the group meets the first Monday at 6:30 PM at the Bayland Community Center. *6400 Bissonnet, Sharpstown. Houston Ornithology Group, 713/541–9951.*

1 *f-4*

ARMAND BAYOU NATURE CENTER

White-tailed hawk may be spotted here, along with Cooper's and sharp-shinned hawks. Kestrel have also been spotted.

Birders also go for a selection of coastal birds such as egrets, herons, and ibis. *8500 Bay Area Blvd., Pasadena/Southeast, 281/474–3074.*

4 *c-1*

BEAR CREEK PARK

During the cooler months, careful watchers have spotted a full set of owls—barn, barred, great horned, screech, and short-eared. *3535 War Memorial Dr., off N. Eldridge Pkwy., Katy/Bear Creek, 281/496–2177.*

1 *c-6*

BRAZOS BEND STATE PARK

This is a good spot for amateurs because the steady traffic has acclimated the birds to people peeping at them. The bald eagles don't exactly appear on cue, but a beginner can easily see a nice set of species. *21901 FM 762, Sugar Land/Fort Bend, 409/553–5101.*

2 *f-3*

JESSE H. JONES PARK

Traditional birds like the red-headed woodpecker, along with travelers like the eastern kingbird, orioles, and Mississippi kites, flit in the tall trees here. *20634 Kenswick Dr., North, 713/446–8588.*

7 *b-7*

HOUSTON ARBORETUM

Only 160 types of bird live in or migrate through the 155-acre arboretum, a number that would be considered a draw in most areas. Because the species here represent only a portion of the birds to be seen in the Houston area, the arboretum's advantage is how easily the birds, and flora, can been seen. *4501 Woodway Dr., Memorial/Spring Branch, 713/681–8433.*

BOATING

1 *f-2*

TERRAMARE LAKES

Water-skiers, bare-footers, wake-boarders, and knee-boarders find this watersports complex the perfect spot for training or competition. TerraMare has two 2,300-ft-long lakes served by well water when the weather won't cooperate. The jumps course and slick water are 25 minutes from George Bush Intercontinental Airport/Houston. *Off FM*

2100, at Redland Rd. and Miller Wilson Rd., North, 281/441–4220.

BOWLING

Bowling is big in Houston. From early in the morning until way past bedtime, the lanes are full. Trivia: the first 300 game recorded by league-sanctioned automatic pin-setting equipment was bowled by Houstonian Bill Phillips in 1953.

6 d-5
AMF BUNKER HILL
Bowling lessons aren't just for Marge Simpson; you, too, can learn from a pro. The Palladium Pro shop at AMC Bunker Hill offers all levels of instruction. Or, you can teach yourself in open play. 925 Bunker Hill Rd., Memorial/Spring Branch, 713/461–1207.

GAY AND LESBIAN SPORTS

Houston's gay and lesbian community (and their friends) enjoy a host of organized sports, with both teams and groups dedicated to, for instance, the glory of roller skating.

Greater Houston Pocket Billiards League (713/863–8482)
Houston Metropolitan Billiards League (HMBL) (713/299–8969)
Independent Billiard League (IBL) (713/524–9261 or 713/524–4190)
Houston Wednesday Night Mixers Bowling (713/522–9612)
Inner Loop Sunday Bowling (713/522–9612)
Monday Night Women's Bowling (713/437–6218 or 713/862–3630)
Montrose Monday Night Men's Bowling (713/641–5424)
Rainbow Fishing Club (713/523–6381)
Houston Women's Flag Football League (713/981–6753)
Houston Outdoor Group (713/526–7688)
Texas Gay Rodeo Association (281/873–0641)
Lambda Rollerskating Club (713/523–9620)
Houston Women's Softball League (713/688–9468)
Montrose Softball League (713/867–3913)
Houston Tennis Club (713/864–8468)
Lone Star Volleyball Association (713/878–4629)

---

3 a-2
COPPERFIELD BOWL
Where do people get the time? This alley, like so many others, has league play every single day. It's also set up for private parties and bumper bowling for kids. 15615 Glen Chase Dr., Cy-Fair, 281/550–8710.

9 f-3
DYNAMIC LANES
Former Hall of Famer Lucy Bonneau helped institute the rich and complex league structure at this accurately named alley. 6121 Tarnef Dr., Sharpstown, 713/772–1063.

10 b-3
PALACE LANES
Don't go just for the cheeseburgers and onion rings, although they are memorable. The venerable Palace Lanes also boasts 44 lanes and "suggestion" screens; the scoreboard display illustrates the best strategies for picking up a spare. 4191 Bellaire Blvd., Astrodome/Old Spanish Trail, 713/667–6554.

CROQUET

Houston and San Francisco, of all places, are the only U.S. cities with public courts. Houston has two in Memorial Park (take Memorial Loop Drive into the park, the courts are behind the golf course first green), and every Wednesday afternoon the Houston Croquet Association (713/263–9904, www.houstoncroquet.com) offers free, introductory lessons to its six-wicket game style.

DOG ACTIVITIES & TRAINING

In Houston, man's best friend is active, too. Agility, flyball, Frisbee, tracking, and obedience clubs spend evenings and weekends working with their dogs, preparing for, or attending, regional dog shows. Some are in it for slobbery fun, others reach serious levels of competition or public service.

agility
In contrast to the beauty pageants of the breed ring, and the military rigors of obedience, agility offers a sort of obstacle course fun-run for dogs. Border col-

lies clearly have an edge over other dogs, but all breeds and mixes race around a course overcoming colorful obstacles like a teeter-totter ramp, a tunnel, jumps, and a cloth tunnel. Dogs compete in size-based classes. For information on local agility groups, call 972/231–9700 or PAWSitive Impact Agility (281/692–9053, www.pawsitiveimpact.com).

flyball

Dogs tend to take to this sport—pups race down a straight line of hurdles, poke a lever with a paw to pop a tennis ball in the air, catch that ball, and then race back down the line. Owner of dogs who were thought to have behavior problems find that a couple afternoons of flyball practice each week and regular tournaments make their mutts calm and peaceful members of the household. Bouncing terriers and hard-headed herding dog types rule the sport, but long-eared, low-slung basset hounds on the track always draw an "awww" from the audience. Contact the Houston Flyball Association (281/787–6806; www.flyball.com) or Lone Star Flyball Team (www.home.inreach.com/stouthrt/wizzaw.html) for more information.

FENCING

2 g-7
CLEAR LAKE FENCERS CLUB
Feint and parry with the enthusiastic fencers of this nonprofit club. Coaches Michael Mergens and Jerry Dunaway can help you prepare for USFA tournaments. Find more information at www.flash.net/~clfc. *16706 Fernwood Way, Clear Lake/Bay Area, 281/ 486–0724.*

14 g-8
SALLE MAURO
The Bayou City salle, Salle Mauro, offers the art of foil, epee, and saber, and the instructors are able to see the potential grace in anyone. The organization is a member of the USFA and hosts USFA events. Locate their homepage at www.ruf.rice.edu/~mauro. *7969 Almeda, Astrodome/Old Spanish Trail, 713/668–1990 or 713/666–1662.*

FISHING

Believe it or not, there is fishing inside the Loop. Catch-and-release anglers hit bayous and ponds for a quick afternoon's fishing. Outside the city, there are lakes to the north, creeks and rivers to the west, and bays and the Gulf to the east and south. Pack an ice chest and head to the Texas City Dike for a night's fishing, take the family to Lake Conroe for a lazy afternoon, or book a six-pack game fish charter out of Galveston. You have plenty of options, but you will need a license for any activity. There's even a bag limit for mullet. The licensing rules raise a lot of questions: What happens if you accidentally catch a freshwater trout without a stamp? Is it legal to gig flounder with a Type 220 temporary resident sport fishing license? Is it possible to give a Type 111 "Super Combo" as a gift? Call 800/895–4248 for information before visiting any of thousands of license sales locations. The CCA (an organization that began in Texas as the Gulf Coast Conservation Association) is both active in management and well aware of where the best fishing is. To join or find out more, log on at www.ccatexas.org or call 713/626–4234.

To join the obsessed anglers of the Houston Big Bass Club, you must first attend a meeting. Except in December and January, they meet at the Williams (formerly Transco) Tower Central Plant Conference Room (2800 S. Post Oak) the first Thursday of each month at 6:30 PM.

north

Kids can fish Lake Houston, the Sheldon Reservoir, and other public water for crappie and sunfish. More advanced anglers can collect a fish fry's worth of bass, carp, and catfish. Waters in Bear Creek Park are stocked with rainbow trout. Lake Conroe, like Lake Houston, is stocked with striped–white bass hybrids. While you're at the water's edge, keep an eye out for salamanders, but don't use them for bait.

south

Redfish, trout, and flounder can be found inshore throughout the bay area. Offshore, using light fly or traditional tackle, anglers go for red snapper, snook, tarpon, king mackerel, amberjack, bonito, and the occasional shark or barracuda for kicks.

west

The Colorado River has a number of public access points, as do Lake Texana and Coleto Creek. Area anglers have favorite spots along the Brazos and Colorado rivers, and if you ask just right they might share their knowledge.

FLYING

SOARING CLUB OF HOUSTON

Fly in silence. Fly, not fall. Soaring Club enthusiasts promote glider flying. No previous pilot training is required. Try it. It's said to be addictive. *713/953–1335.*

2 *d-2*

SOUTHWEST FLYING CLUB

Maybelle Fletcher founded this club in the early '60s. Membership is limited to 45, but those members enjoy active, safe, and insured flying opportunities. *David Wayne Hooks Airport, 20803 Stuebner Airline Rd., Tomball/Spring, 281/376–5436.*

FOOTBAG & HACKY SACK

You don't need to drive all the way to Galveston to kick around a Hacky Sack. Some folks freestyle, that is, stand in a circle and pass the bag from player to player, with each demonstrating a few tricks before sending the footbag on. In other games, players pass the footbag over a net. Depending on the league or event sponsors, players might use any old footbag, or they may be limited to trademarked Hacky Sack bags. Area parks see frequent games. For starters, you might try hooking up with the Houston Skyliners Footbag Club (281/242–8696 or garrhow@aol.com). They play Sunday afternoons in Memorial Park (take East Memorial Drive into the park, and look for the games going on across from the Diving Range).

FOOTBALL

Where to watch? Not L.A., that's for sure. Houston beat the West Coast bid for the 32nd NFL franchise deal. Bob McNair will be bringing us a new team for the 2002 season. There was little weeping and wailing when the Oilers and Bud Adams, unpopular Oilers franchise owner since 1960 and AFL founding father, departed in 1996. Two years later, despite the well-publicized nostalgia of former Oiler running back Earl Campbell and other stars, Adam's team was renamed "Tennessee Titans." Bob McNair, who paid a record-breaking $700 million for his franchise, hopes that his new team's 2002 debut will generate loyalty to rival the obsession of Packers fans. Who is this team? Future fans can buy logo gear with the proud, albeit vague slogan "Houston Football." "Stallions," "Apollos," and "Texans" are all possible names, but the final choice won't be announced until late in 2000.

where to watch

10 *c-1*

HOUSTON THUNDERBEARS

We also have Arena Football, which is just like NFL football only more compact and faster. The Houston Thunder-Bears play in Compaq Center. For group tickets, call 713/627–7277. For single-game tickets, call 713/629–3700. Seats sell for as little as $8.75. *10 E. Greenway Plaza, Greenway Plaza, 713/627–9470.*

14 *d-2*

RICE UNIVERSITY OWLS

The Rice Owls play in Rice Stadium. For tickets, call 713/522–6957 or Ticketmaster, 713/629–3700. *Stadium: 6100 S. Main.*

15 *c-1*

TEXAS SOUTHERN UNIVERSITY TIGERS

The Texas Southern University Tigers, who received a sweet equipment donation from former Tiger and now NFL All-Pro Michael Strahan in 1999, can always be counted on for a lively game. For tickets, call 713/313–7271. *Stadium: 3100 Cleburne Ave., East End.*

15 *f-1*

UNIVERSITY OF HOUSTON COUGARS

The Cougars inaugurated O'Quinn Field at Robertson Stadium in September 1999. For tickets, call 713/743–9444. *Stadium: Scott at Wheeler, East End.*

where to play

The Oilers up and left, but flag, touch, tackle, and beer-fueled football games can still be found in larger parks, and on broad lawns along Buffalo and Braes bayous.

GOLF

1 *b-3*
GOLF CLUB AT CINCO RANCH
A whole lot of water is your main difficulty on this tightly laid out course. Greens fees are around $50, with carts included. The 18-hole course has a par level of 72. *23030 Cinco Ranch Blvd., Katy/Bear Creek, 713/395–4653.*

5 *g-4*
GUS WORTHAM PARK GOLF COURSE
This pleasant 18-hole public course has a men's par of 72 and ladies' of 71, and you can play for less than $20, and less than $10 if you don't hire a cart. *7000 Capitol, East End, 713/921–3227.*

2 *d-1*
HOUSTON GOLF ASSOCIATION
The HGA sponsors charity events, brings top-level tournaments to the area, and supports youth golf with training programs, certification clinics, and scholarships. *1830 South Millbend Dr., The Woodlands, 281/367–7999.*

2 *f-7*
HUMBLE OIL PATCH GOLF CENTER
No golf carts whir on this peaceful public course, and whether you wish to play a round or just whack the little white pills on the driving range, you'll find the fees easy to handle. The nine-hole course has all 100-yard holes, 3-par each. *2107 N. Houston Ave., North, 713/548–7273.*

2 *b-7*
OLD ORCHARD
Make reservations at least a week in advance. This high-level Southwest course will probably not welcome you if one day, out of the blue, you manage to clear your desk by noon and want to hit the links at 3. All three nine-hole courses—Stables, Barn, and Range, have a par of 36 for both sexes. *13134 FM 1464, Richmond, Sugar Land/Fort Bend, 713/277–3300.*

2 *h-8*
SOUTH SHORE HARBOR
Winds off Clear Lake make play complex, but the course layout allows players at any level to pick a tee that suits their skills. The 18-hole course is par 71. *4300 South Shore Blvd., Clear Lake/Bay Area, 281/334–0521.*

2 *g-2*
TOUR 18
The quaint notion here is that each of the 18 holes represents a famed course. The unforgiving par-72 course is not cheap, and reservations are required at least seven days in advance. *3102 FM 1960 E, North, 281/540–1818.*

2 *d-1*
TOURNAMENT PLAYERS COURSE
This elite 18-hole course was designed by Von Hagge-Devlin and hosts the Shell Houston Open each year. Houston as a whole is pretty flat, but this complex, par-72 course has elevated greens. *1830 S. Millbend Dr., The Woodlands, 281/367–7285.*

GREYHOUND RACING

1 *f-5*
GULF GREYHOUND PARK
Dogs race every day of the week, all year round. Pari-mutuel betting is encouraged. If you're only interested in the running, local UHF stations run broadcasts of the day's races during the wee hours. *LaMarque, Exit 15 off the Gulf Fwy., Clear Lake/Bay Area, 800/275–2946.*

HANDBALL

Better health clubs and many area Y's have handball courts. Check with facilities in your area.

HIKING

Houston hikers, well supplied with water, take to many of the same trails cyclists use (*see Bicycling, above*). Rigorous walks can be taken in Brazos Bend and Bear Creek parks, or the Brazoria Natural Wildlife Refuge. You might also join the Houston Chapter of the Sierra Club (713/895–9309) for local or more extensive excursions. Other options include Lone Star Hiking Trail Club (281/837–8114), and the Sugar Land–based West Texas Trail Walkers (281/265–3772). Volkssport walks tend to conclude at restaurants or outdoor festivals. All ages participate in this low-effort sport, and some walkers tow toddlers and babies in wagons. Sightseeing and camaraderie are also crucial elements of the exercise. Generally, the point of a walk, such as a tour of the Museum District, is to get a good look at something. To learn about groups and events in your area, call the American Volkssport Association hot line (800/830–9255).

HOCKEY

teams to watch

10 *c-1*

HOUSTON AEROS

Houston's IHL team plays in the Compaq Center. Because American hockey leagues have some weird rules, you will see NHL players who are doing double duty. Between players having multiple responsibilities, and trading right up to the playoffs, it's hard to know who you will see on the ice. Of course, the caliber of the players may not matter so much if you're the type of fan who enjoys mascot Chilly Dog, sumo wrestlers, and other antics. For tickets, call 713/974–7825. *Compaq Center, 10 E. Greenway Plaza, Greenway Plaza, 713/627–9470.*

where to play

Northern transplants are pleasantly surprised to find that Houston has a thriving hockey community. But why wouldn't we? The rough and tumble attitude of hockey is very cowboy, and air-conditioning is a local art form. The Houston Harpies, a women's team, is open to all comers. Can't skate? Not a problem. Worried about your health? The Harpies boast a player who's had open-heart surgery. Wonder if hockey's for you? Come out and skate with the Harpies for free, no pressure. To contact a Harpie, e-mail widget@wobbet.com. *See also* Ice Skating, *below.*

2 *c-7*

SUGAR LAND AERODROME

Like its sister complex in Willowbrook, this skate facility offers a variety of disciplines and hockey. Youth and adult hockey lessons and leagues are active year-round. There are also special clinics and camps. *16225 Lexington Blvd., Sugar Land/Fort Bend, 281/265–7565.*

2 *c-3*

WILLOWBROOK AERODROME

Along with Houston Aeros–affiliated hockey leagues, the rink hosts figure skating, broomball, and more. *8220 Willow Place Dr., FM 1960 area, 281/897–9772.*

HORSEBACK RIDING

To get into the horsy set, you can contact the Houston Dressage Society (281/550–3968), or meet up with the Greater Houston Horse Council (713/995–8432). Meetings are held third Mondays of the month, 7:30 PM at the Golden Corral restaurant at the intersection of Highway 290 and Hollister.

Hundreds of real and weekend ranchers join up each February for the Houston Livestock Show and Rodeo trail ride (713/791–9000). The congregation that moseys through Houston on parade day is actually a jamboree of dozens and dozens of area trail rides. Some groups come in from as far away as Louisiana. On the trail, riders enjoy catered meals, dancing to live music, and waking up early to pull out at 8 AM for 20 or more miles of riding.

3 *a-5*

ALBE FARM

Horsey girls from master-planned communities in Richmond and Sugar Land study dressage and jumping in Albe's huge indoor and outdoor rings. *9611 Gaines Rd., Sugar Land/Fort Bend, 281/561–0607.*

14 *h-2*

HERMANN PARK STABLES

This is the only stable that those who live in the city proper can reach without a lengthy drive. Park rides are another draw for students. Throughout the week, the barn offers Western and English (flat and jumping) classes. Weekends, holidays, and during the summer, kids enjoy pony parties and camps. There are also hippotherapy programs. Prices are reasonable, the horses are reliable, and everyone hopes that this whiff of the original gentry remains a fixture in Hermann Park no matter how far contemporary town-house gentrification goes. *5716 Almeda Rd., Medical Center, 713/942–7669.*

3 *b-7*

SOUTHERN BREEZE EQUESTRIAN CENTER

Horse owners can take advantage of boarding and training, the horseless can take English lessons—and keep an eye on the horses for sale and lease, just in case a bargain shows up. *Fresno, 3800 FM 521 (Almeda Rd.), Sugar Land/Fort Bend, 281/431–4868.*

2 *b-5*

GREAT SOUTHWEST EQUESTRIAN CENTER

Pin Oak Stables was bulldozed long ago to make way for some superstores, but the show goes on at Great Southwest, which is sort of a horsey superstore. The facility's 80 acres include several round pens and outdoor rings, an indoor ring, a grand prix arena (which seats 4,000), a polo field, and access to trails. There are boarding stalls for 600 horses, some of which house school horses. A number of instructors offer lessons in most disciplines. The center hosts horse shows and rodeos most weekends, and the large banquet center is available for events and concerts. *2501 South Mason Rd., Katy/Bear Creek, 281/578–7669.*

3 *b-2*

KENDELWOOD FARMS

This Western barn offers limited rentals and lessons with an emphasis on the needs of very young riders. *14003 FM 529, North, 281/855–1942.*

HORSE RACING

1 *a-1*

SAM HOUSTON RACE PARK

Thoroughbred racing runs from October through April. The track has other types of racing, such as quarter horse, on the dirt and turf tracks, and live simulcasts of national races in the clubhouse. Feel free to wager on any. *7575 N. Sam Houston Pkwy. W, North, 281/807–8700.*

ICE SKATING

9 *e-3*

ALPINE SKATE

Sign up for basic skills classes or haul out your skates and stick and join a hockey league. *7115 Clarewood, Sharpstown, 713/981–6667.*

10 *a-1*

GALLERIA

An Olympic-size rink is smack-dab in the middle of the mall. Hoards of once-in-a-while skaters wobble around the edge of the ice while figure skaters practice competitive moves in the middle. *5015 Westheimer, Galleria/Post Oak, 713/621–1500.*

2 *g-7*

TEXAS ICE STADIUM

The Figure Skating Club of Texas is headquartered here, but if you prefer something more exciting, there's hockey. If you'd rather not do anything organized, there is plenty of free-skate time on the schedule. *18150 Gulf Fwy., Clear Lake/Bay Area, 281/486–7979.*

IN-LINE & ROLLER SKATING

Of all places, Downtown is one of the favorite skate spots, although the skaters show up after rush hour, when most of the cars have cleared the streets. Houston has several street-skating clubs, such as the Bad Blades (281/498–8185). Skate Trash has a rough motto, "Skate or Die," but the members are friendly enough to offer skating instruction. Groups meet at several Downtown and Heights locations for informal group skates. For information, drop by Montrose Skate Shop (1406 Stanford, 713/528–6102) The Clear Lake Space Rollers (281/867–0823) shoot through the smooth suburban streets south of Houston.

In-line skates have by no means wiped out traditional skates or quads. The following rinks rent rollers: Dairy Ashford Roller Rink (1820 S. Dairy Ashford, Southwest, 713/493–5651); Trade Winds Roller Rink (5006 W. 34th St., Memorial/Spring Branch, 713/682–5312).

7 c-6

MEMORIAL PARK

The park's paved Picnic Loop (on the south side of Memorial Drive) is a haven for skaters. *6000 Memorial Dr., Memorial/Spring Branch.*

JET SKI

2 h-7

PARASAIL CLEAR LAKE

Rent personal watercraft, Jet Skis, or Wave Runners, or sign up for parasailing at this waterfront party spot. Group watercraft more your speed? Hire a party boat. *3000 NASA Rd. 1, Clear Lake/Bay Area, 281/333–2816.*

LACROSSE

In some neighborhoods, the Gulf Coast looks a bit like the East Coast, and if you see players on Rice University campus, don't assume they're students. The school occasionally hosts games. The Houston Metropolitan Lacrosse Club (713/997–8377) and the South Texas Storm Lacrosse Club (713/750–8369) are always looking for a few good players. The Gulf Coast Lacrosse Association (281/997–8377) shepherds area competition.

MARTIAL ARTS

3 a-2

AMERICAN BLACK BELT ACADEMY

Although teaching rigid discipline, this institute isn't rigid about the disciplines taught. Currently the school offers karate, tae kwon do, "kardio kickboxing," and other martial arts. *4978 Hwy. 6, Katy/Bear Creek, 281/859–9566.*

13 c-4

1615 Clay, Downtown/Theater District, 713/652–0586.

2 a-5

20235 Katy Fwy., Katy/Bear Creek, 281/ 647–0680.

9 c-1

HOUSTON INSTITUTE OF CHINESE MARTIAL ARTS AND MEDICINE

Tai chi classes here include movement workshops and sword work. *9603 West-heimer (behind the Westchase United Methodist Church), Southwest, 713/ 781–4483.*

9 h-2

HOUSTON KICKBOXING GYMS

As John Cusack playing underdog Lloyd Dobler asserted in Say Anything, "Kickboxing, sport of the future." Although his true love's father was unimpressed, thousands listened. This workout space emphasizes aerobic benefits, women's self-defense, and the lower back and ab power kickboxing is known for. Children's classes, grappling, and other martial arts are also offered. *5610 Southwest Fwy., Galleria/Post Oak, 713/ 780–2345.*

6 g-1

KIM SOO KARATE

Tenth Dan Grandmaster Kim Soo first brought kung fu fighting to Houston in the Summer of Love and he's been teaching at Rice (where students honor him as professor summa cum laude), the University of Houston, and his own studios ever since. Soo's ChaYon-Ryu training may include karate, kung fu, tae kwon do, hapkido/aikido, jujitsu, stick forms, and weapons training. There is no full-contact fighting. Instead, Soo's schools emphasize health, strength, and discipline. Free class-review consultation sessions are offered. *1740 Jacquelyn, Memorial/Spring Branch, 713/681–9261.*

MINIATURE GOLF

2 c-3

MOUNTASIA FAMILY FUN CENTER

Freaky blue-green water tumbles down the "mountain" at this vivid amusement center. If whacking balls through the obstacle courses doesn't strike your fancy, head indoors for video games. *17190 Tomball Pkwy., FMI 960 Area, 281/ 894–9791.*

9 e-5

PUTT-PUTT GOLF COURSES AND BATTING CENTER

The daytime all-you-can-play deal Monday, and Thursday evenings both offer hours on the complex putting course for a mere $4. The well-designed course features intricate challenges instead of cartoon figures. *7914 Fondren, Sharp-stown, 713/995–5161.*

MOTOR SPORTS

1 *f-4*

HOUSTON RACEWAY PARK

Weekend to weekend, the style of racing changes but the speed remains the same. Drag racing, SGP, NHRA, stock racing, Harley events, truck shows, and other automania events are regularly on the schedule. Top events include the NHRA Pennzoil Nationals, NHRA Matco Tools SuperNationals, and the NHRA Slick 50 Nationals. There are also bracket racing events and chances for ordinary motorists to take out their road rage on the tracks. *Baytown, 2525 FM 565, Baytown 281/383–2666.*

ROCK CLIMBING

2 *c-3*

EXPOSURE INDOOR ROCK CLIMBING GYM

Serious climbers practice holds across the 7,000 ft of walls, but novices are also welcome. All climbers must take a safety class before heading up the walls. Equipment rental is available. *6970 FM 1960 W, FM 1960 area, 281/397–9446.*

6 *d-5*

TEXAS ROCK GYM

Both of Monty Queener's facilities are set up for group events and parties. Go ahead. Invite 50 folks to a climbing party. The gym can handle it. Solo climbers and students also find room on the faux rocks. *9716 Old Katy Rd., Memorial/Spring Branch, 713/973–7625.*

2 *g-8*

201 Hobbs Rd., League City, Clear Lake/Bay Area, 281/338–7625.

RODEO

The annual Houston Livestock Show and Rodeo is the granddaddy of area cowboy action, but between small rodeos out off Highway 288, championship bull riding in the Compaq Center, and smaller rodeo games at the Great Southwest Equestrian Center, you can find rodeo most of spring and summer. For information about Cy-Fair Rodeo Association events, call 281/955–8558.

14 *d-8*

HOUSTON LIVESTOCK SHOW AND RODEO

From mid-February to mid-March, the Dome, Astroarena and Astro Hall go Texan. One million eight hundred thousand spectators, give or take a kid or two, attend the event to see the top rodeo athletes compete for nearly a million dollars in prize money—and to see area teens compete in the calf scramble. This popular event pits youths weighing around 100 pounds against calves weighing 600 to 800 pounds. Calves are loose, kids have a rope halter, and the goal is to grab a calf, halter it, and drag it into the center of the ring. It's quality entertainment. Conventional entertainment and concerts starring country, Tejano, and major radio stars close the show every night. All day, and long after the rodeo ends, there's a genuine country fair and carnival in the Astro Hall, Astroarena, and Dome parking lot. More than 30,000 specimens of prime livestock, if you count blue-ribbon bunnies as "livestock," are on display. Although the show is crowded, you're never more than 40 ft from a food booth. While the primped and preened beef are judged, herds of carnival goers clog the midway. Tickets are available at Foley's, Fiesta, and Kroger stores, and at the Astrodome box office. *Astrodome, 8400 Kirby, Astrodome/Old Spanish Trail, 800/726–1313.*

RACQUETBALL

Many area health clubs have courts.

Chancellors Racquet & Fitness Center (6535 Dumfries, Meyerland, 713/772–9955).
Downtown YMCA (1600 Louisiana, Downtown, 713/659–5566).
Jewish Community Center (5601 S. Braeswood, Meyerland, 713/551–7211).
Memorial Athletic Club (14690 Memorial Dr., Memorial/Spring Branch, 281/497–7570).
Northwest Fitness and Sports Club (5304 Hollister, North, 713/ 895–688).
Post Oak YMCA YMCA (1331 Augusta, Galleria/Post Oak, 713/781–1061).
Westside Tennis Club (1200 Wilcrest Dr., Memorial/Spring Branch, 713/783–1620).

ROWING

2 *h-7*

BAY AREA ROWING CLUB

Self-described as "the best little oar-house in Texas," this club puts in shells at Mud Lake near Clear Lake. If you can't already scull, club classes will give you the skills. *5086 NASA Rd. 1, at Mud Lake, Clear Lake/Bay Area, 281/326–5098*

RUGBY

Sometimes it seems every muddy grass patch in Houston is a pitch for groups like the Texas Invitational Touring Side (a group which goes by the acronym), the Bay Area Rugby Football Club, the Galveston RFC, Houston Athletic Rugby Club, Houston Old Boys RFC, Houston Strikers, Woodlands RFC, and the Houston Hurricanes (a women's club). You can find these teams on the Texas Rugby Club Web site, www.io.com/texasrugby, or at certain pubs like the Richmond Arms or Gingerman. There are 121 city parks with rugby-football-soccer fields.

4 *c-1*

BEAR CREEK PARK

This multipurpose park has four dedicated rugby fields. *3535 War Memorial Dr., off N. Eldridge Pkwy., Katy/Bear Creek, 281/496–2166.*

2 *d-1*

FALCONWING PARK

Bedroom communities see action, too; the Woodlands Rugby Club plays its home games here on Saturday. *5610 Falconwing Dr., The Woodlands, 936/273–4990*

RUNNING & WALKING

Despite the 100+ heat and humidity that can make it seem as though you're wrapped in a wet wool blanket, Houston runners are all over the roads and trails. Memorial Park's loop, the bayou trails, and thousands of suburban streets are all filled with runners morning and evening. For formal training, you can join Houston Fit's Urine Nation (713/752–1813), a Houston Marathon work-shop with major emphasis on hydration. This group preps for the marathon in

Memorial Park. The Houston Area Road Runners Association (713/797–8602) is a well-organized umbrella group. Some coaching and training groups have membership fees and some are more casual. Oh, and there is a hash in Houston. The Houston Hash House Harriers (713/968–9053), proudly proclaiming, "20 years, 1 million beers," is open to irreverent runners.

Memorial Park has a 3-mi loop. The tree-lined Marvin Taylor exercise loop is only 2 mi, but the route's people-watching possibilities keep extra laps from being dull. The track around Rice University is longer, 3 mi, but some parts are on sidewalk, and uneven sidewalk, so the run is almost as much agility training as jogging.

AIDS WALK

Houston has a number of incorporated cities, bedroom communities, and one-time outlying small towns that are now all but swallowed up, and many of these places—the Bay Area, Galveston, and Richmond—have their own AIDS Walk in March. To register or volunteer, call AIDS Foundation Houston (713/623–6796 or 888/524–2437).

CONOCO 10K RODEO RUN

No one is foolish enough to run in cow-boy boots, although there is a definite Go Texan mood for this February event. Entrants walk, run, and wheelchair from Downtown to the Dome to benefit the Rodeo Educational Fund. The hot line number is 281/293–2447.

HOUSTON MARATHON

The name has changed more than a few times, but this 26-mi race in January is still the "big one" for local runners, and more sedentary types enjoy watching from various points along the course. More than 5,000 runners start in front of the George R. Brown Convention Center, and a good number of them make the full loop to finish in front of it again. The course wends through Downtown, Hermann Park, Rice Village, the Galleria area, Tanglewood, and Memorial Park. To register or volunteer, call 713/957–3453.

SUSAN G. KOMEN RACE FOR THE CURE

Though only a 5K, this October race is a very big deal. Proceeds from the Komen Race for the Cure benefit breast cancer research, and Houston has one of the largest runs in the nation. Seventy-five percent of the funds raised in Houston are allocated to Houston. To register or volunteer, call 713/783–9188.

SAILING

Houston sailors have access to lakes and bays, and the only trick is remembering that without proper boat maintenance, switching back and forth between fresh and saltwater can cause expensive problems. If you are not all that interested in the work of sailing, charters are available. In Kemah, Gateway Charters (281/334–4606) offers sailing lessons, day trips, and weekend charters. Houston-area sailors can learn to trim and tack with the American Red Cross (713/526–8300). Class locations are determined by instructor availability and student interest. At the Helm (281/334–4101), a Galveston school, has a two-day class. You spend classroom time in their bayside offices, and then set sail in 25-ft boats. At the Helm's second-level classes cover docking and more-advanced maneuvers in Galveston Bay. In the Galveston area, you can put in at Morgan's Point, Eagle Point, Redfish Bar, Pier 21, Bolivar Roads, and the Flagstaff Pier on the Gulf side. For information on Galveston conditions, call 713/673–1860 (from Galveston 409/766–1031).

SCUBA DIVING

Despite the silty murk in many area waterways, diving is popular. You can learn more about local diving at the international SEASPACE convention each May, or by hooking up with a club. The Houston Underwater Club (713/467–6675) is a great place to start. Flower Gardens, a protected area about 100 mi south of the Sabine River mouth, is popular with charters. Visibility can be better than 100 ft, and divers regularly see manta rays, vast whale sharks, and of course, the small colorful fish who live in the thriving coral reef. Rig trips are available from Matagorda Harbor in Bay City. Game fish like snapper, amber-

jack, and bluefish are popular spearfish trophies on these dives. Galveston has a number of rig charters—and from a marine-life standpoint, rigs might as well be wrecks. As soon as a platform is set, the pilings develop a coat of barnacles, attract marine flora, and may be covered with ivory coral. Small creatures hide in these new habitats, and schools of spade fish and colorful angelfish circle the rig. A bit farther out, rays, barracuda, and big ugly groupers swim. Divers also see dolphins and sharks.

SKYDIVING

Some Houstonians can list many reasons for jumping out of a perfectly good airplane. You'll find such adrenaline junkies at Skydive USA (281/561–5867) in Wharton (a little better than an hour from Downtown), and Skydive Houston (800/586–7688) in Waller.

SOCCER

Soccer moms don't necessarily just drive. The Houston Women's Soccer Association (713/267–1517) gets grown girls (and coed teams) on fields all over town for fall, spring, and summer seasons. Men and women over 18 can find league play in the Texas State Soccer Association (281/479–8221). The spawn of soccer moms can be found on teams throughout the Houston Youth Soccer Association (281/980–7553).

SWIMMING

Red Cross chapters can teach you to swim in any of the area's public pools, lakes, bays, and beaches. For more information on which public pool you will be diving into at 7 AM, call 713/526–8300. Once you've learned to swim, the City of Houston Parks and Recreation (see Sports & Outdoor Activities, above) has information on the 44 municipal pools and family programs such as water babies and junior lifeguard. For information on city pools, call 713/845–1009. City of Houston and most other public pools are open Memorial Day through Labor Day, and closed for maintenance on Monday.

Popular swimming pools include Downtown YMCA (1600 Louisiana St., Downtown, 713/659–5566); Grady city pool (1700 Yorktown, Galleria/Post Oak, 713/

964–9919); Houstonian (111 N. Post Oak La., Galleria/Post Oak, 713/ 680–2626); Lansdale city pool (8201 Roos, Southwest, 713/272–3687); Oak Forest city pool (1400 Dubarry, Memorial/Spring Branch, 713/684–1819); Post Oak YMCA (1331 Augusta, Galleria/Post Oak, 713/781–1061.).

4 c-6

ALIEF COMMUNITY PARK/QUILLIAN CENTER
Lap lanes in the pools are dedicated to structured sporting contests and practice space for serious swimmers. *11903 Bellaire Blvd., Southwest, 281/564–8130.*

9 c-4

HOUSTON SWIM CLUB
Former Olympic coach Phill Hansel founded his club at the now-demolished Shamrock Hotel, but for 30 years, competitive, amateur, and just-splashing-around swimmers have learned strokes and practiced at this Southwest Houston pool center. Now owned by former manager Bonnie Howe, the club is known for a dedicated master program and a great atmosphere for inexperienced or awkward swimmers. *8307 Augustine St., Sharpstown, 713/774–7946.*

3 g-7

THE REEF
The proprietors call this a "water-based family park." It is, in fact, a 20-acre man-made lake (Texas has no natural ones) filled with clear, blue water that makes for brilliant swimming, diving (a few "wrecks" have been sunk at 40 ft for training purposes), fishing, and light boating. There are rest rooms, a snack bar, and some equipment rental on site. This may be the only Houston body of water fit for swimming. *4800 Schurmier Rd., South Houston/Hobby Airport, 713/991–3483.*

TABLE TENNIS

Some people take the game more seriously than the average den or TV-room player. Join enthusiasts at the Houston Table Tennis Center (4997 W. Bellfort, Southwest, 713/721–7529) for league play.

TENNIS

Houston's many public courts and private clubs see plenty of action even though, as Mitch Hedberg says, tennis is a game in which the average person can lose to a wall. The annual River Oaks Tennis Tournament is a major spectator event each April. Area clubs and USTA tournaments give citizens a chance to compete. Adults and juniors test their skills at the Houston Coca-Cola Open (713/973–7636) held at Lee LeClear and other Houston courts in April.

The city's active junior team tennis program gives kids 10 to 16 a chance at organized play (713/803–1112). With or without organized instruction, youth and adult players can work up a game at 81 neighborhood courts in city parks. Houston also has three civic tennis centers: Memorial Park (on Memorial Loop Drive, entrances on Memorial Drive and Wescott, 713/867–0440); Homer Ford (5225 Calhoun, East End, 713/842–3460); and Lee LeClear (*see below*). The centers take reservations, and courts fees are $3 to $5.50, depending on when you want to play. The city's neighborhood courts are free.

4 c-1

BEAR CREEK PARK
The wide, dry, windy stretches of the Bear Creek area seem more suited for tumbleweeds and wagon trains than kids in K-Swiss shoes, but the kids ignore the dusty scenery to concentrate on the ball. *4503 Hickory Downs Dr., Katy/Bear Creek 281/859–2200.*

9 e-2

FONDREN TENNIS CENTER
The indoor courts are air-conditioned and heated, but the heat is rarely used. The club offers a partner-matching program. *3035 Crossview, Memorial/Spring Branch, 713/784–4010.*

9 d-6

LEE LECLEAR TENNIS CENTER
A compliment to the facility's quality, tournament organizers regularly choose the courts here to host their events. Reservations are strongly suggested, but bear in mind that you should arrive early on weekends. Courts fees are $5 for all-day play, and a surprising number of people have the stamina to literally play all day. *9506 Gessner, Sharpstown, 713/272–3697.*

10 *a-1*

UNIVERSITY CLUB

On the roof of the Galleria, this club offers 10 indoor courts, a running track, and the usual weights and aerobic classes. *5051 Westheimer, Galleria/Post Oak, 713/621–4811.*

3 *c-5*

WESTSIDE TENNIS CLUB

Take a tour of playing surfaces—including French red clay—at this large and well-equipped sports center. There are 46 tennis courts, racquetball courts for faster action, and a pool for cooling off in. *1200 Wilcrest Dr., Memorial/Spring Branch, 713/783–1620.*

2 *b-2*

WIMBLEDON RACQUET CLUB

Lessons at all levels are offered on the 29 lighted courts here. *16400 Sir William Dr., Tomball/Spring, 281/370–5801.*

VOLLEYBALL

Memorial Park has some sand volleyball courts on Picnic Lane (south of Memorial Drive), and Cullen Park (19008 Saums Rd., Katy/Bear Creek, 281/ 496–2177) has five sand courts that are lighted at night. It is also possible to catch casual pickup games in Galveston.

12 *a-1*

BUBBA'S BEACH CLUB

The outdoor volleyball court and indoor bar complement each other nicely. *6225 Washington Ave., Heights, 713/861–7161.*

13 *b-4*

DOWNTOWN YMCA

Competitive league play and open play are both available on the Y's wood-floored basketball/volleyball courts. *1600 Louisiana, Downtown/Theater District, 713/659–8501.*

2 *g-6*

SALVATION ARMY RECREATION CENTER

Hard-core indoor volleyball players eschew the Y's and city rec centers for Thursday night games here. *2732 Cherrybrook La., Pasadena, 713/378–0020.*

WATERSKIING

From shortly after Valentine's Day through Halloween, the weather is warm enough for behind-the-boat sports. *See also* Boating and Fishing, *above*, for locations.

2 *h-5*

MIKE MUNN'S INTERNATIONAL WATER SKI SCHOOL

Basically, there are two ways to learn: on your own while friends hoot derisively from the boat, or by taking lessons from a pro. Mike Munn offers classes throughout the year. *2010 Grace La., Highlands, 713/515–6494.*

WINDSURFING

Particularly enthusiastic windsurfers and kite surfers hit the waters in and around Galveston Bay. The following covers the top spots: Texas City Levee, Texas City Dike, Bacliff Spillway, Houston Yacht Club, Mud Lake, and El Jardin. Galveston is considered a terrific spot for advanced windsurfers. Mud Lake is a great place for beginners, and those who don't like beginning alone can get in touch with Windsurfing Sports (281/ 291–9199) for lessons.

WRESTLING

Several area clubs, affiliated with USA Wrestling (719/598–8181), grapple on mats in strictly supervised contests. Folkstyle and freestyle/Greco are coached. To find a nearby amateur group, call the USA office.

YOGA

14 *e-2*

BOUSTANY STUDIOS

Serious students and casual stretchers take advantage of a drop-in class policy at Robert Boustany's studio. The short, fat-free, and seemingly boneless yogi also teaches Houstonian Club members. *1728 Bolsover, Rice University Village, 713/523–8932.*

7 *a-6*

111 N. Post Oak, Houstonian Hotel, Galleria Post Oak, 713/680–2626.

6 *e-3*

CENTER POINT PROJECT
Yoga, meditation, past-life regression, and other New Age and Far East health and healing techniques are offered at this center. *1920 Hollister, Memorial/ Spring Branch, 713/932–7224.*

5 *b-4*

HOUSTON IYENGAR YOGA STUDIO
Stretch and tone in this homey, inner-city studio. *3712 Alabama, Montrose, 713/ 850–8812.*

14 *c-1*

YOGA CENTER OF HOUSTON
John Coon offers classes in Hatha/Raja, Pranayam, Dyana, Ayurveda, and therapeutic yoga. The studio is somewhat strict, as these things go. *2438 South Blvd., Rice University Village, 713/524–4572.*

fitness centers, health clubs & spa services

CLUBS

You could rise early to jog around the neighborhood, but isn't it better to work out under the perky guidance of a frighteningly fit aerobics instructor and then shower with unlimited hot water and towels someone else will have to launder? Sure it is. Most of the clubs listed below offer weight rooms, various machines and classes, and rivers of hot water.

6 *e-4*

24 HOUR FITNESS
If you need treadmills, lap pools, or a Stairmaster at God-thirty in the morning, a 24-hour fitness location will be waiting for you, fluorescent lights aglow. Fees start at around $24 per month for an individual membership. *1000 Campbell Rd., Memorial/Spring Branch, 713/ 984–0606.*

10 *a-1*

5080 Richmond, Galleria/Post Oak, 713/ 963–9644.

2 *d-3*

4950 FM 1960 W, FM 1960 area, 281/ 583–9333.

9 *g-1*

5800 Richmond, Richmond Strip, 713/ 783–8448.

9 *a-1*

11320 Westheimer, Southwest, 281/870– 8600.

4 *d-5*

12400 Westheimer, Southwest, 281/493– 1874.

9 *a-5*

6801 Baneway Dr., Southwest, 281/495– 2605.

2 *f-7*

12260 Gulf Fwy., South Houston/Hobby Airport, 713/943–2220.

2 *d-3*

BALLY TOTAL FITNESS
The colorful spandex this club is known for isn't all the chain has to offer. Many locations have child care and pools. Various packages are offered, so what you pay depends on what area the club is in, how often you plan to go, and so on. Average monthly fees are $35. Most clubs add extra fees for "Fitness Plus" classes such as tai chi, salsa dancing, and spinning. *5215 FM 1960 W, FM 1960 area, 281/440–9835.*

4 *a-3*

15415 Katy Fwy., Katy/Bear Creek, 281/ 578–9191.

14 *b-2*

2500 Dunstan, Rice University Village, 713/521–3113.

7 *e-1*

3936 N. Shepherd, North, 713/695–5824.

6 *c-5*

9825 Katy Fwy., Memorial/Spring Branch, 713/467–8181.

10 *c-3*

3905 Bellaire, Astrodome/Old Spanish Trail, 713/666–0141.

3 *c-2*

13350 Northwest Fwy., North, 713/460– 2620.

9 f-6

BODY MASTER FITNESS STUDIO

Baylor Sports Medicine Institute—certified personal trainers can rehabilitate the injured, firm up the flabby, or give you a therapeutic massage after a long, grueling workout. Sessions with a trainer have varying rates, depending on the length of the session and the complexity of the workout. However, you can count on discounted rates if you book multiple sessions. *9500 Fondren, Southwest, 713/773–0077.*

13 b-4

DOWNTOWN YMCA

The constant renovations almost keep pace with the wear and tear on this proud old club. It's a bit difficult to find your way around at first. Over time, you'll be able to navigate several stories, a couple of weight rooms, activity rooms, racquetball, handball, basketball, and volleyball courts—and even find the fabulous juice bar and cafeteria. Downtown membership comes with a $125 joining fee, and monthly payments of $42. The rate for a whole family is about a $10 bump, depending on the package you chose. *1600 Louisiana, Downtown/Theater District, 713/659–8501.*

6 g-8

POST OAK YMCA

An eight-lane pool 35-yards long, wide-open ball fields, and plenty of kiddie programs make this the perfect family Y. Indoor attractions include a well air-conditioned weight room, racquetball courts, aerobics, and a swell cafeteria. To join, an individual makes a $78 "down payment" and pays $48 dollars per month. *1331 Augusta, Galleria/Post Oak, 713/781–1061.*

12 e-6

THIRD COAST FITNESS

This is a quiet place to practice the Pilates method, which lengthens and strengthens muscles, particularly in the abdominal area. Third Coast does the East Coast or "hard style." Rates are $40 per hour for semiprivate or duo sessions. *1415 Harold, Montrose, 713/529–1533.*

DAY SPAS

14 c-3

BEAUTIQUE DAY SPA & SALON

Women who were born after Beautique opened are now going in for fine-line plumping facials and all-over exfoliation. *2507 Times Blvd., Rice University Village, 713/526–1126.*

6 d-7

BETTER LIVING HEALTH AND DAY SPA

Although the staff treats your vanity and angst with conventional spa luxuries and provides medical physical therapy and other treatments, your insurance company is unlikely to pick up the spa part of your tab. *12526 Memorial Dr., Memorial/Spring Branch, 713/468–5495.*

10 a-1

CLARINS INSTITUT

Blond wood and gold-flecked tiles make the South Texas site of this European spa seem far more expensive than it is. The massages, facials, manicures, pedicures, wraps, and make-up consultations with Clarins' own products bolster that impression. *5075 Westheimer, in Saks in the Galleria, Galleria/Post Oak, 713/623–4893.*

4 f-4

D' ELEGANCE SALON & DAY SPA

A $60 bath is well worth the price—when the water is infused with an energizing blend of eucalyptus, juniper, pine, sage, and rosemary oils. Tubs can also be filled with a detoxifying blend of oils and seaweed, or marine extracts. Soaking is not the spa's only solution. Massage, skin treatments, and makeovers are also available. *10001 Westheimer, Carillon Shopping Center, Memorial/Spring Branch, 713/784–0050.*

2 g-8

FACES AND FIGURES

Sports, deep tissue, and reflexology massages are offered here. If you don't have time for that, then settle for a chair massage. The spa also offers skin treatments and facials. *906 W. Main St., League City, Clear Lake/Bay Area, 281/554–3223.*

12 *b-6*

THE GREENHOUSE

Yes, you'll be wrapped in herbs and soothed with plant-based lotions, but the Greenhouse has been in business since 1965 and they don't mess around. Laser peels, laser hair removal, and anything else the medical community can come up with are every bit as popular as the Eastern ways of healing. *2535 Kirby, River Oaks, 713/529–2444.*

7 *a-7*

THE HOUSTONIAN HOTEL SPA

Shiatsu, sports, and Swedish are all included on the massage menu. Mud and minerals are also used to relax and rejuvenate your body. And, hair removal ranges from arching an eyebrow to making men beach-ready with a back waxing. *111 N. Post Oak, Memorial/Spring Branch, 713/680–0626.*

10 *a-1*

NATURE'S WAY DAY SPA & SALON

For $45 they'll give you tickle-ready toes. Manicure prices are slightly less. Or, select mix-and-match packages with all-Aveda product hair styling, facials, massage, and sugaring (less painful than waxing). *5000 Westheimer, Suite 160, Galleria/Post Oak, 713/629–9995.*

MASSAGES

6 *a-3*

ABSOLUTE MASSAGE

Jimena Callejas has a padded table and will travel. Execs in Downtown office towers and office parks along the energy corridor have an easy, confident air not because they're masters of the universe, but because Callejas shows up weekly for 20-minute sessions with top management. We've heard of young companies holding off on coffee and office supply orders when money was tight, but Callejas's sessions are considered a vital operating expense. She also offers

Swedish relaxation and some deep tissue massage from her home office. *10300 Mayfield, Memorial/Spring Branch, 281/221–9343.*

3 *b-7*

BODY & SOUL

Therapeutic and reflexology massages are practiced in this large salon with an emphasis on feet. Foot reflexology is billed as an aid to many minor ailments including cramps and arthritis. Soothed and kink-free feet are worth the price. *11333 Fountain Lake Dr., Stafford, Sugar Land/Fort Bend, 281/340–2219.*

10 *a-1*

GREGG HILL'S JAPANESE MASSAGE AND REFLEXOLOGY INSTITUTE

The titular practitioner is an accomplished public speaker and yoga teacher and former military instructor. His specialty is reflexology on the hands, ears, and feet. *6300 Richmond, Galleria/Post Oak, 713/858–9925.*

14 *c-3*

LOVENA'S THERAPEUTIC MASSAGE

Gym time not doing the job? Lovena Hayle offers cellulite treatments, along with old-fashioned Swedish massage and an accent to match. *2520 Times Blvd., Rice University Village, 713/942–2233.*

9 *g-1*

MASSAGE THERAPY SERVICES

Instead of a red door like Elizabeth Arden, this healing place has a pink building. Inside, you'll be subject to neuromuscular massage therapy, Reiki therapy, and Swedish massage. Aromatherapy is frequently combined with massage and heated stone therapy (hot rocks right on your pressure points). Many services are offered off-site, too. *2620 Fountainview, Galleria/Post Oak, 713/784–9400.*

chapter 4

PLACES TO EXPLORE

galleries, museums & more

Houston doesn't really have any obvious, dramatic sights—no River Walk, no French Quarter, no Amish people driving carriages around town. What this city does have is a lively and diverse population. At Latin dance clubs in the Heights, Elvis is still the King—that is, Elvis Crespo—and stylish couples spin every night; Vietnamese clubs on the periphery of the Richmond Strip play ballroom music while all ages take the floor for a foxtrot or Viennese waltz; and tots and tottering old folk alike two-step at Eddie's Country Ballroom in Manvel. The city is full of idiosyncratic and unique places like the Kaldi Café's alley patio, the Downtown tunnels, the Orange Show, the Museum of Printing History, the American Funeral Service Museum, the Williams Tower water wall (a nearby duck pond, which is usually entertaining some fly fishermen and a lab), the kugel ball outside the Cockrell Butterfly Center, the goofy train that still choo-choos around Hermann Park, the Frisbee Disc Golf course along Buffalo Bayou, and hundreds of started-on-a-shoestring ethnic restaurants.

Although there are 12 museums within walking distance of each other in the Museum District, you might just find some places in which to while away a few hours in your own neighborhood. See what kinds of interesting shops are tucked into the local strip malls, spend some time in the neighborhood parks, visit the little clubs and struggling art galleries on your way home. When you have explored the unique aspects of your community, revisit the tried and true—Six Flags AstroWorld, the Museum of Fine Arts, the George Observatory. Once you get to know Houston, you'll find you don't have time to do all the things you want to do.

where to go

AMUSEMENT PARKS

10 *e-6*

SIX FLAGS ASTROWORLD

When it opened in the '60s, this sprawling amusement park was named AstroWorld in keeping with the Astrodome and general Space-race frenzy. Eventually, however, it became part of the Six Flags chain and part of the Looney Tunes empire, complete with a Marvin the Martian ride and high school students employed as Bugs and Daffy characters, who make merry throughout the park in felt costumes with giant cartoon character heads. Even during the mid-winter holiday season, the park is packed. During crowded summer days, air-conditioned rides like the Mayan Mindbender, shoot-the-chutes water voyages like the Tidal Wave, Thunder River, and the venerable Bamboo Chutes (soaking park-goers since the early '70s) keep thrill-seekers cool, and parents and kids can bump around on minor rides like the Runaway Rickshaws, the Wagon Wheel, the carousel or the Antique Taxi miniature cars. The taxis are "antique" not only because the minis are modeled after Tin Lizzies, but because this ride has been around since the park opened. But who cares about baby rides? The real deal is monster coasters like the Texas Cyclone, a wooden roller coaster built like the Coney Island Cyclone, but with very modern speeds of 65 mph, and the Ultra Twister, with a nine-story drop and 360-degree loops. The Serial Thriller, a 102-ft-high corkscrew, hits 55 mph. If the intensity overwhelms, the sister park, WaterWorld (*see below*) is right through the gate, with zillions of gallons of clear, chlorinated water and inner tube rentals. Their Web site, www.sixflags.com, is the best way to keep track of the seasonal hours. *9001 Kirby, Astrodome/Old Spanish Trail, 713/ 799–1234. Mid-Aug.–mid-May, the park is open weekends and select holidays only. Late May–mid-Aug., daily 11–10. Adults $37.99, 2-day pass $39.99, season pass $74.99. Children under 48" tall $19 (if disabled $18), children under 2 are free. Over 55 years old and disabled adults $24.99. Family passes are available.*

10 *e-6*

WATERWORLD

This slip-and-slide adjunct to AstroWorld (*see above*) contains almost as much water as a Houston rainstorm will dump in your yard. A 30,000-sq-ft pool, a water slide almost 90 ft high, a slew of smaller ponds like Lil' Buccaneer Bay and attractions keep Houstonians from drying up in the scorching summer (and spring and fall) heat. By the way, all Lil' Buccaneers must be strapped into park-approved waterproof diapers and older babes are warned not to wear provocative swimwear. *9001 Kirby, Astrodome/Old Spanish Trail, 713/799–1234. Mid-May–Labor day, 10–6. Adults and children above 48" tall: $19.99, under 48" tall: $14.99.*

ARCHITECTURE

14 *g-1*

1 WAVERLY COURT

(Glassman Shoemake Maldonado, 1999.) Easily seen from Bissonnet, this wild, zinc-and-aluminum fantasy home may not be the average dream home, but the three chunks visible (a skewed metal-sided tower, a clean brick center tower, and windowed balconies over the garage) are a nice complement to the nearby Contemporary Arts Museum. *1 Waverly Ct., Museum District.*

6 *c-6*

12020 TALL OAKS ROAD

(Frank Lloyd Wright, 1954.) Houston's only Frank Lloyd Wright house is not one of his best efforts (elaborate considerations for the main gathering room compromised the livability of the non-master bedrooms), and over the years much has been changed. The master bedroom, however, and certain exterior details remain. *12020 Tall Oaks Rd., Memorial/Spring Branch.*

7 *c-8*

3811 DEL MONTE

(Howard Barnstone, 1969; additions Eugene E. Aubry, '70s, and William F. Stern, 1998.) River Oaks is not all Georgian with matte-red library walls. This wonderfully weathered cypress compound moves the neighborhood into modern times. *3811 Del Monte, River Oaks.*

7 *a-5*

5135 BAYOU TIMBER LANE

(Howard Barnstone & Eugene Aubry, 1969.) A slight anomaly among the sprawling ranch houses and upright Georgians popular in Houston's old guard neighborhoods, this clapboard home was designed to complement the original owner's early American furniture. It's easy to imagine that beneath the cold, puritanical steep gables, the family breakfasts on scrapple and maple syrup. Satisfaction with this home influenced Aubry's subsequent career. *5135 Bayou Timber La., Memorial/Spring Branch.*

13 *e-2*

550 PRAIRIE

(Morris/Aubry Architects, 1987.) The dramatic futuro-Gothic exterior and Fish Plaza have been featured in a number of movies, most notably Robocop. However, the real interest is inside. The Cullen and Brown theaters seat 2,225 and 1,102, respectively. Acoustics are brilliant, everyone has a clear view, and even an evening of Wagner can be enjoyed without stiffness or cramps. The Grand Foyer, featuring Albert Paley art, is unfortunately marred by the ugliness of an entirely necessary escalator carrying patrons up, up, up to the main lobby. Tours are available, and anyone can visit the lobby for a free brown-bag performance on certain Wednesdays at noon. *550 Prairie, Downtown/Theater District.*

13 *b-3*

BANK OF AMERICA CENTER

(Johnson/Burgee Architects and Kendall/Heaton Associates, 1983.) The city is unreasonably proud of its all-new style, which sometimes comes at the cost of genuinely significant buildings. On the other hand, this engaging neo-classical, staggered tower, rife with elaborate neo-Gothic details, at least reminds us a 56-story building can still have a sense of fun. The 125-ft lobby, with skylights and striking iron-look accents, is easy to appreciate. It leads to a well-trafficked tunnel area with delis, a newsstand, and a frozen yogurt shop. *700 Louisiana, Downtown/Theater District.*

13 *b-3*

BAYOU PLACE

(Caudill Rowlett Scott, 1967; Gensler & Associates, 1998.) A face-lift for the former Albert Thomas Convention center was slow in coming, but after years of back-and-forth, a viable project began. The institutional look of the old hall vanished behind a lively, colorful facade, which includes an inviting overhang sheltering a plaza and balcony areas. Instead of a square hall, the interior now comprises a movie theater, restaurants, a pool hall, and the multiuse Aerial Theater, suitable for anything from rock-'n'roll road shows to dance performances. Situated across from Jones Plaza, Bayou Place sees extra traffic on Party on the Plaza evenings. *500 Texas Ave., Downtown/Theater District, 713/221–8883.*

2 f-7
BEST PRODUCTS
(SITE, 1975.) There's a name for this particular store in the Best chain, Indeterminate Façade, and the image of a seemingly bombed white brick box against a blue sky was celebrated during the '70s. Such extremes are not so popular now, but the store continues to have a busy trade. *10765 Kingspoint Rd., South Houston/Hobby Airport.*

9 a-4
BROWN & ROOT
(S.I. Morris Associates, 1980.) It's nice to imagine that the seven service and circulation cylinders are styled to look like the grain silos that once rose from the flatlands that became Southwest Houston. The cylinders are stacked along a "bow-tie," and that shape marks an otherwise unremarkable stack of stone and window rows. *10200 Bellaire, Southwest, 281/575–3000.*

12 f-7
CHAPEL OF ST. BASIL
(Philip Johnson, 1966.) Even this graceful, solemn Catholic chapel is not immune to Texas bragging. Much is made about the chapel having the "largest gilded dome in Texas." Such swaggering is not unreasonable, not for the dome and not for the building as a place of worship. The structure is a soothing blend of mission proportions and modern minimalist lines, and the dazzling 23½-karat cap makes the whole thing uniquely Texan. Like a number of significant Houston buildings, the chapel was designed by Philip Johnson. *3800 Montrose Blvd., Montrose, 713/522–7911 or 800/460–8878.*

4 e-5
ENSERCH TOWER
(Lloyd Jones Brewer & Associates, 1982.) Perhaps the first proof that yet another "downtown" was emerging, this 21-story tower was one of the first to be built this far out on Richmond. Now, the building's gray glass and stainless stripes share a landscape with dozens of office towers. Parts of the upper floors are contrived to have the look of an accordion fold, which makes this building stand out even as new Beltway construction encroaches. *10375 Richmond, Memorial/Spring Branch.*

9 h-1
FUDDRUCKERS
(Clovis Heimsath Associates, 1980.) All over town, restaurants make an effort to look like small-town icehouses, or dockside shacks, or border-town bars, and yet it seems only this chain outlet got it right. From the billowing yellow awning out front to the beer garden in back, the burger joint is the spitting image of any Hill Country tin-roof joint. (The building was originally another restaurant.) *3100 Chimney Rock, Galleria/Post Oak, 713/ 780–7080.*

13 c-3
HARRIS COUNTY CIVIL COURTS BUILDING
(Lang & Witchell, 1910.) Having a courthouse on this plot was part of the Allen brothers' original plan for Houston, and, indeed, with allowances for scale, the shape and style of this domed courthouse would seem at home in many small-town Texas squares. *301 Fannin St., Downtown/Theater District, 713/755–5552.*

13 b-3
HOUSTON CITY HALL
(Joseph Finger, 1939; renovations, Ray Bailey Architects.) The original Texas Cordova shell limestone may have seemed a bit dowdy during the boom years, but now that the dust has settled, this stoic old building offers a safe and friendly note in the midst of revitalized Downtown. Like a maiden aunt at a family reunion, City Hall's central tower and long, narrow reflecting pool are always a steady, reassuring presence during Downtown festivals. Except in the worst weather, Downtown workers show their appreciation for this unrepentantly all-American building by enjoying lunch on the plaza or alongside the reflecting

pool. A scheme to "dress up" the structure with colored lights at night was not well received by the public, but continues. *901 Bagby, Downtown/Theater District, 713/247–1000 or 713/457–5200.*

13 *c-2*

HOUSTON COTTON EXCHANGE AND BOARD OF TRADE BUILDING

(Eugene T. Heiner, 1884.) A rare intact Victorian, this vivid redbrick retains seemingly all of its original dazzling trim and limestone detailing. Luck and a loving 1971 restoration by Graham B. Luhn are responsible for the Cotton Exchange's condition. It's currently an office building, and the roof no longer features a zinc cotton bale sculpture or brass flagpole. *202 Travis, Downtown/Theater District.*

13 *b-4*

HOUSTON HOUSE

(Charles M. Goodman Associates and Irving R. Klein & Associates, 1966.) The first abortive attempt at revitalizing Downtown still stands. And although adrift in a sea of parking lots, the 33-story, 400-unit apartment complex is not wanting for tenants. The view from the outside is not unlike a stack of shoeboxes with bold white trim. Inside and from their balconies, tenants enjoy spectacular views of the city. *1617 Fannin, Downtown/Theater District., 713/659–4781.*

13 *c-4*

HOUSTON LIGHTING AND POWER CO. ENERGY CONTROL CENTER

(Caudill Rowlett Scott and Robert O. Biering, 1972.) A cantilever reaches an eye-popping 45 ft, jutting almost over Crawford. The striking feature, along with the name, evoke quite a sci-fi feel. This building's poured-in-place, sandblasted concrete and the white finish of the squatting Alley Theatre are both tailor-made for futuristic movie roles. *1313 LaBranch, Downtown/Theater District.*

6 *f-6*

HOUSTON RACQUET CLUB

(MacKie & Kamrath, 1969.) Although erected at the end of the decade, this building screams '60s. White bricks and low sloping roofs seem to slide into the superwide driveway and parking lot. You can practically see the muscle cars pulling into their parking places. *10709*

Memorial Dr., Memorial/Spring Branch, 713/464–4811.

13 *c-2*

MAGNOLIA CAFÉ

(Cooke & Co., 1911.) Although no longer associated with a brewery, the pristine Edwardian café rooms of this distinctive blossom-yellow structure are occasionally rented out for festivities. The somewhat French and somewhat Spanish influences seen in the cornice and parapet make the building quite Southern. *719 Franklin Ave., Downtown/Theater District, 713/223–8508.*

13 *b-3*

NIELS ESPERSON BUILDING

(John Eberson, 1927.) After so many years, the memorial atop the building is still lighted every evening. Mellie Esperson's original, richly detailed Italian Renaissance styling is still largely present, in some cases even in the tunnels below. The only downside is that the elevators in this quaint relic are hardly modern. *808 Travis, Downtown/Theater District, 713/224–1663.*

13 *b-3*

ONE SHELL PLAZA

(Skidmore, Owings & Merrill and Wilson, Morris, Crane & Anderson, 1971.) Although the 50-story office building doesn't look like much now against the extreme and inventive buildings that followed, this simple travertine tower was Gerald D. Hines's first Downtown project, the beginning of what would come to be known as the "Oz skyline." Shell's decision to headquarter in Houston gave this city a buzz as an energy capital. Those who are concerned with the innards of architecture should note that this makes an early, and vanguard, use of engineer Fazlur R. Khan's framed-tube concept. (Two Shell Plaza, catty-corner, was built in 1972). *910 Louisiana, Downtown/Theater District.*

3 *b-7*

ONE SUGAR LAND PARK

(Johnson/Burgee Architects and Richard Fitzgerald & Partners, 1982.) Perhaps because of its way-outside-the-Loop location, the efficient humor of this office park (a stripped-down take on Alamo themes popular in the '30s and Western movies) has not received much critical attention. *1250 Shoreline Dr., Sugar Land/Fort Bend.*

15 *h-1*

THE ORANGE SHOW (A FOLK ART ENVIRONMENT)
(Jefferson Davis McKissack, 1979.) Postal worker Jefferson Davis McKissack had an obsession with oranges (and, like many outsider artists, an obsession with steam power), a certain amount of spare time, and lots of concrete. He turned his home into a monument to his favorite fruit, opening the folk art environment to the public in 1979. The Orange Show foundation has turned the late Mr. McKissack's creation into an art and performance space, with art and summer lunch programs for children, and a vast folk art library. Funding The Orange Show is the raison d'être for Houston's beloved Art Car Weekend (*see* Arts Events, *below*). *2402 Munger, East End, 713/926–6368. Weekends and holidays noon–5. Adults $1, children free.*

13 *b-3*

PENNZOIL PLACE
(Johnson/Burgess Architects and S. I. Morris Associates, 1976.) This is actually two buildings with an astonishingly narrow 10-ft sliver between each 36-story tower. The exterior of deep brown glass is perhaps meant to suggest oil. In any case, the look is both appealing in its own right and a notable contrast to the profusion of blue- and green-glass "ice-cube" buildings throughout the city. During rainstorms, the sight of water sheeting down the raked base is mesmerizing. A lucky few have seen a stormy sky through the glass walls and triangular roof of the penthouse. *711 Louisiana, Downtown/Theater District, 713/224–5930.*

7 *a-8*

POST OAK CENTRAL
(Johnson/Burgee Architects, 1973.) The three dark charcoal and silver towers, with their red accents, look a bit like replicas of the building in Edward Hopper's "Nighthawks." Instead of a diner, the lower floor contains delis and Federal Express offices. However, the buildings do have an unusual importance. The first building was the legendary Philip Johnson's first project for Gerald D. Hines. *1980–2000 Post Oak Blvd., Galleria/Post Oak, 713/840–1170.*

13 *c-3*

RICE HOTEL
(Mauran, Russell & Crowell, 1913; remodeled Page Southerland Page, 1998.) A grand old landmark, the Rice came perilously close to rotting, standing derelict for almost 20 years. In 1996, developer Randal Davis and the city formed a partnership to prove there was life in the ol' gal yet. The lower floor is now home to restaurants and shops, whereas the former guest rooms are the ne plus ultra in loft living. (Hungry for a taste of Rice history? The original red leather bar furniture lives at McElroy's in Shepherd Square.) *909 Texas, Downtown/Theater District, 713/228–7423.*

2 *g-5*

SAN JACINTO MONUMENT
(Alfred C. Finn, Architect, and Robert J. Cummins, 1936.) Obelisk-style monuments are a dime a dozen, but being in Texas, the San Jacinto monument is, natch, the world's tallest. And it has a lone star on top. All 570 ft are to commemorate the 1836 battle that won Texas's independence from Mexico. Grounds are open free 9–6 daily. There are fees and different hours for the observation deck (9–5:50) and the Jacinto Museum (9–6). Admission to the deck and museum is $6 for adults. *3523 Hwy. 134, Clear Lake/Bay Area, 281/479–2431.*

7 *b-5*

SOCIETY FOR THE PREVENTION OF CRUELTY TO ANIMALS
(Jackson & Ryan, 1993.) The old SPCA, residences, and green space along the Buffalo Bayou nearby were bulldozed to make room for yet another bald apartment complex. The long, low-hipped roof allows the new SPCA facility to sit solemnly in an otherwise unattractive industrial area, and the pink brick and taut blue trim add interest without being unfaithful to the nature of the institution. The building welcomes prospective pet owners each weekend. *900 Portway, Memorial/Spring Branch, 713/869–7722.*

12 *e-3*

STAR ENGRAVING CO. BUILDING
(R.D. Steel, 1930.) Ah, a sign of Spanish influence! The tile roof and towers have a definite mission look, and the storybook grace suits the building's new use as an arts center. *3201 Allen Pkwy., River Oaks, 281/931–5808.*

`13` *c-3*

SWEENEY, COOMBS & FREDERICKS BUILDING

(George Dickey, 1889; refurbished by Welton Becket and Associates, 1968.) Sitting brightly on a Downtown corner, this quaint, white, three-story, turreted Victorian is a startling reminder that there was a Houston before 1968. *310 Main, Downtown/Theater District.*

`13` *a-3*

TEXACO HERITAGE PLAZA

(M. Nasr & Partners, 1987.) This eye-catching, deep green skyscraper is a key feature in the Oz skyline. Granite details at the base and the funky granite pyramid on top are said to be homage to ancient architecture of the Yucatan. *1111 Bagby, Downtown/Theater District, 713/666–8000.*

`13` *c-3*

TEXAS COMMERCE TOWER (NOW OFFICIALLY CHASE TOWER)

(I. M. Pei & Partners, 1981.) The one-time "tallest west of the Mississippi" tower makes quite a show, but perhaps the most intriguing detail is below street level. A granite water garden offers a slice of park space suitable for lunch-hour picnics. *600 Travis, Downtown/Theater District.*

`10` *a-1*

TRANSCO TOWER (NOW WILLIAMS TOWER)

(Johnson/Burgee Architects and Morris/Aubry Architects, 1983.) An impromptu survey of locals might lead you to believe that this is the tallest building in Houston. After all, the beacon can be seen from Galveston. Actually, the 901-ft glass deco tower is only number three. Citizens are proud of the gleaming green building. It's second only to the Astrodome in name recognition, but occasionally commuters headed home on the Loop are less than happy to see the sun glinting off the glass. *2800 Post Oak Blvd., Galleria/Post Oak, 713/621–8000.*

`12` *e-7*

WILSHIRE VILLAGE APARTMENTS

(Eugene Werlin, 1940.) The spreading magnolia and fig trees on the grounds grow stronger every year, while the thoughtfully and artfully designed apartments slowly fall to pieces. The ideal of outdoor spaces and plenty of light will probably vanish with the inevitable wrecking ball, leaving Houston with block after block of unpleasant, unimaginative apartments whose single windows overlook parking lots. For now, a few residents in the habitable buildings enjoy the blond wood and glass brick interiors and the grassy spaces outside, and the burden of doing all their own home repairs even though they rent. *1715 W. Alabama, Montrose, 713/528–6765.*

ART EVENTS

year-round

`12` *b-8*

COLQUITT GALLERY WALKS

Barbara Davis and her gallery are at the center of regular group openings. Parking is awful, but mavens enjoy strolling the tree-shaded sidewalk of the block, stopping in at MD Modern, New Gallery, and the rest. *Colquitt at Kirby, Upper Kirby District, 713/520-2627.*

march–april

`13` *e-2*

FOTOFEST

Galleries, museums, and alternative spaces throughout Houston devote exhibition space to this citywide photography showcase in even-numbered years. Photography from local artists, archive treasures, and nationally and internationally known works are displayed. *1113 Vine St., Suite 101, Downtown/Theater District, 713/223–5522.*

april

`13` *b-3*

BAYOU CITY ART FESTIVAL

There can be a little bit of confusion about what is and what isn't the Westheimer Arts Festival. Long story short: once upon a time, a couple decades back, there was one arts festival on Westheimer. Festival organizers didn't always have the same goals or get along so now there are a number of arts festivals inside the Loop that have made claims to being the "original." Instead of trying to sort out the details of this event's history, head Downtown in both April and October to survey the fine arts from some of the better area artists and artists who tour the festival circuit.

Booths manned by respected restaurants provide high-level snackage. Instead of something on a stick, have a to-go cup of Kim Son spring rolls. *Hermann Square and Tranquility Park, Downtown/Theater District, 713/521–0133.*

13 *b-3*

ART CAR WEEKEND

Celebrating the artist in everyone, or at least creativity aided by Super Glue, the Art Car Weekend showcases rolling folk art creations. Vehicles range from decorated trikes to flatbed trucks bearing astounding architectural works. At the Art Car Ball, held in a parking garage a couple of days before the parade, a mix including school groups who have decorated cars and Harley riders gather for music, food, and intriguing, original performance art. Several thousand people attend this annual fundraiser for the Orange Show (*see* Architecture, *above*). The following Saturday, the art cars and other creations roll through Downtown in the world-famous Art Car Parade. Usually it rains during part of the parade, but no one minds. This unique family event is a perfect example of the whimsical, idiosyncratic spirit of the average Houstonian, and you really need to experience it, at least once. *Downtown/Theater District, 713/926–2277.*

july–august

12 *g-8*

LAWNDALE ART CENTER, "THE BIG SHOW"

Works by artists who live and work within a 100-mi radius of Houston are selected for this annual show. Artists chosen receive cash awards, and patrons get to see a rich selection of local work. *4912 Main, Museum District, 713/528–5858.*

ART GALLERIES

fine art

6 *d-5*

ALTERMAN & MORRIS GALLERIES

Oilmen looking for standard Western art such as Remington and Russell turn to this gallery. Other 19th- and 20th-century artists are represented and dealt, and the scope of Western art includes Native American works and paintings and sculptures inspired by Native American traditions. *952 Echo La., Memorial/Spring Branch, 713/461–6006.*

12 *f-4*

ART LEAGUE OF HOUSTON

The busy members of the league create a space for a variety of American contemporary works. *1953 Montrose, Montrose, 713/523–9530.*

12 *b-8*

BARBARA DAVIS GALLERY

Works by popular sculptor James Surls and other well-known local artists are shown here, but the most exciting personality may be Barbara herself. The same feisty, ever-curious attitude that marks her collector's eye makes her a fine conversationalist. *2627 Colquitt, Upper Kirby District, 713/520–9200.*

15 *f-1*

BLAFFER GALLERY

Although certainly a resource for University of Houston art students, the gallery is perhaps more important as a public exhibition place. Since the doors opened in 1973, the staff has provided an enlightening spectrum of art with exhibits ranging from works by Lubbock-based country singer and artist Terry Allen to an exhibition of Frank Stella's works, and drawing and sketchbooks. (The Stella show was presented in conjunction with his mural project for the university's Moore's School of Music.) *University of Houston (entrance #16 off Cullen Blvd.), East End, 713/743–9530.*

13 *a-7*

COMMUNITY ARTISTS COLLECTIVE

This valuable art space is a showcase for the art of African-American women. Exhibitions and programs are often designed to involve kids. *1501 Elgin, Medical Center, 713/523–1616.*

12 *d-2*

DEVIN BORDEN HIRAM BUTLER GALLERY

This low-profile, side-street gallery is one of the most significant in Houston. Important contemporary and modern artists are represented, such as Vernon Fisher, James Terrell, and Robert Rauschenberg. Local artists, such as James Surls, Paul Kittleson, and Kathy Packlick (owner of West End Gallery), have also had their sculptures and paintings handled by the gallery. The gallery is often involved in public art projects and is not exactly shy about hosting political events. *4520 Blossom, Montrose, 713/863–7097.*

12 *d-6*
THE FIREHOUSE
What was once a modest home is now the pleasant showcase for works chosen by the Houston Women's Caucus for Art. Contemporary work, usually with themes related to or directly addressing women's issues, is displayed in this alternative space. *1413 Westheimer, Montrose, 713/520–7840.*

14 *d-2*
GREMILLION & CO.
Something about the crisp exterior and sleek entryway make this fine art gallery seem a wee bit like a set from Woody Allen's Sleepers. However, the gallery is serious about abstracts and other modern and contemporary works. *2501 Sunset Blvd., Rice University Village, 713/522–2701.*

12 *b-8*
HOOKS-EPSTEIN
Thanks to long experience, this cagey gallery has a knack for ferreting out new talent and being the first to show Tex-patriots, like Rick Lewis, who have gone on to success in larger markets. *2631 Colquitt, Montrose, 713/522–0718.*

14 *f-1*
INMAN GALLERY
Again we see the advantage of lax zoning restrictions. Fans of sharper abstracts and contemporary work with verve can view such works at their leisure in this homey neighborhood dwelling-cum-gallery. *1114 Barkdull, Montrose, 713/529–9676.*

12 *d-2*
LAS MANOS MAGICAS
Throughout the '90s, this gallery was a rich source of Mexican folk art and jewelry. At the end of the decade, the gallery expanded in size and scope. They now also carry Russian and Romanian icons, and Central American folk art and crafts. *4819 Blossom, Montrose, 713/802–2530.*

12 *g-8*
LAWNDALE ART CENTER
This funkier aspect of the Museum District offers thoughtful exhibitions and beloved annual events such as the "Big

Show" for Houston artists and the Day of the Dead celebration in the fall. *4912 Main, Downtown/Theater District, 713/528–5858.*

PROJECT ROW HOUSES
See Historic Streets and Structures.

12 *b-7*
ROBERT MCCLAIN & CO.
Big dogs such as Cy Twombly and Willem de Kooning and comers such as Dan Havel and Tierney Malone are among the prominent artists represented. *2818 Kirby, Upper Kirby District, 713/520–9988.*

12 *b-1*
RUDOLPH POISSANT GALLERY
Look no further for proof that serious art can be loads of fun. This gallery showcases an excellent selection of regional and national works (you may be surprised by their New York connections), and when it comes time for an opening, they aren't stingy with the beverages. *5102 Center St., Heights, 713/802–1886.*

12 *g-8*
SALLY SPROUT GALLERY
Long before she acquired her own gallery, Sally Sprout was a key figure in the Houston arts scene. Her gallery is a fine place to learn about Houston art, either by examining works by Michael Kennaugh, Darra Keeton, Carla Poindexter, and the often-underrated Elizabeth McBride, or by chatting with Sprout. *706 Chelsea, Montrose, 713/526–6461.*

12 *b-7*
SICARDI-SANDERS GALLERY
The force and power of both traditional and contemporary Latin American art is revealed here. If you are considering collecting Latin art, this gallery is a good place to begin. *2623 Kipling, Montrose, 713/529–1313.*

12 *d-4*
TEXAS GALLERY
Fredericka Hunter and Ian Glennie have a grave, important, and very successful gallery located behind the River Oaks Shopping Center. Artists represented range from local nobodies to William Wegman. *2012 Peden, River Oaks, 713/524–1593.*

15 *d-1*

TEXAS SOUTHERN UNIVERSITY

Another of TSU's art treasures, this gallery holds an impressive collection of African tribal artifacts and works of art. *3100 Cleburne, Robert J. Terry Building, East End, 713/313–7101.*

12 *c-7*

THOMAS V. ROBINSON GALLERIES

This staid and steady gallery sells well-known 20th-century works to high-paying, although perhaps not adventurous, clients. *2307 W. Alabama, Upper Kirby District, 713/521–2215.*

12 *b-2*

WEST END GALLERY

Kathy Packlick's small, quaint gallery is a wonderful venue for local artists. For added spice, Packlick often curates unique shows such as the notorious "Anonymous Show," a sort of emperor's new art show in which art is hung with no information about the artist. Mavens are forced to voice opinions formed solely on the merits of the work. Packlick's own work has been seen in various galleries and at the Museum of Fine Arts, Houston. *5425 Blossom, Heights, 713/861–9544.*

crafts

2 *e-3*

URBAN ARTIFACTS GALLERY

The unique works in this gallery have made it one of Houston's favorite gift spots. Pottery, fiber-art, metal works, glass, and more are represented in the ever-changing collection. *5507 FM 1960 W, FM 1960 area, 281/537–7331.*

photography, prints, posters

12 *b-8*

JOHN CLEARY GALLERY

The many styles and attitudes of 20th-century (and now 21st-century) photography are represented here. The gallery also deals in coffee-table books, specializing in out-of-print and hard-to-find books. *2635 Colquitt, Upper Kirby District, 713/524–5070.*

14 *b-3*

FINE TOON ANIMATION ART

Original animation cels for recent and early 20th-century cartoons are brokered here, along with original art from strip comics, and merchandising gewgaws. The staff will be glad to teach you how to care for cels and strips. (Like all film and paper antiques, they are quite delicate.) *6125 Kirby, Rice University Village, 713/522–6499.*

12 *d-4*

GERHARD WURZER GALLERY

Woodcuts, etchings, lithographs, and other tried and true media can be a good entry into collecting. Wurzer himself is generous with his knowledge and can help you find what you need in his inventory. *1217 Shepherd, Montrose, 713/523–4300.*

12 *f-7*

HOUSTON CENTER FOR PHOTOGRAPHY

The ultimate goal of most HCP students is to make a show, and that does happen. Most of the time, though, the back rooms are for education and the front gallery is reserved for important photographic, film, and even video works. *1441 Alabama, Montrose, 713/529–4755.*

ART MUSEUMS

12 *f-7*

BYZANTINE FRESCO CHAPEL MUSEUM

Architect Francois de Menil designed the chapel especially for the 13th-century frescos from Cyprus. The gleaming wood, polished glass, and contemporary stone of this somber building are a fitting home for the religious artifacts. Visitors with an interest in art often discover that the chapel building is awesome in the original, decidedly nonsecular sense. Menil staff is overly defensive about the acquisition of the frescos. Like many ancient works of art, they've been conquered and stolen and almost lost. The rich turquoise- and gold-colored images were restored and installed with the approval of the Church of Cyprus. Note the sluice fountain on the side of the building, one of the few mobile elements in the entire Menil complex. *4011 Yupon, Museum District, 713/521-3990. Free. Sun.–Wed. 11–6.*

14 g-1

CONTEMPORARY ARTS MUSEUM HOUSTON

Sitting catty-corner from the Museum of Fine Arts, Houston, the triangular, silver-sided CAM looks like a giant wedge of Laughing Cow cheese. Sometimes with whimsy, and sometimes with religious seriousness, the floor and basement levels showcase contemporary works of every stripe. Recent installations have included a bubbling Robert Rauschenberg mud tub and a Kara Walker silhouette. *5216 Montrose, Museum District, 713/284–8250.*

14 g-1

MUSEUM OF FINE ARTS, HOUSTON

An exhibition of Egyptian antiquities from the Pelizaeus Museum, the Jewels of the Romanovs, and Picasso's work shown along with his notebooks and drawings all drew attention, but those past glories pale next to MFA's major opening of the 21st century: the Audrey Jones Beck Building, inaugurated March 2000. This 192,477-sq-ft addition was designed by Spanish architect Rafael Moneo as a space for rarely and never seen pieces from the MFA collections and for traveling exhibits. European art (up through 1920) and impressionist and postimpressionist paintings by artists such as Monet, Renoir, and Seurat now have a showcase. Pieces from the museum's collection of works on paper, prints, and drawings are also displayed in the Beck.

Meanwhile, in the Caroline Wiess Law Building, Sunday programs such as drop-in family days (the second Sunday of each month), storytime (weekly, reservations requested), and creation station (ongoing afternoons) and self-guided tours continue. Although the Law building is home to Western art starting from and including Greek and Roman antiquities, also on display are African gold and art from sub-Saharan Africa and Asian, Oceanic, Native American, and Pre-Columbian art and artifacts.

Random Audio Guides (with eight hours of narrative on the permanent collection), museum bookstore resources, and regular educational programs make the works displayed accessible to all.

The MFAH film program is the museum's only curatorial department required to run in the black. The Brown Auditorium, which is also used for a variety of lectures and talks, features several repertory film programs each year, featuring everything from 19th-century silents to cutting-edge experimental films.

Thursday is free admission day, and between 5 PM and 9 PM special exhibitions are half-price. On Saturday and Sunday, visitors under 18 with a Houston Public Library Powercard are admitted free. Membership starts at $40 per person per year. The Bayou Bend collection and gardens, Renzi (formerly the home of Harris Masterson III), the Lilly and Roy Hugh Cullen Sculpture Garden, and the Glassell School are operated under the auspices of the MFAH. *1001 Bissonnet, Museum District, 713/639–7300.*

12 f-7

MENIL COLLECTION

Dominique Schlumberger de Menil left the city of Houston a stunning legacy. During the '80s she worked to build a public home for her personal collection of medieval and modern art and African, Oceanic, and Byzantine art and antiquities. The Menil Collection, a simple, elegant building with gray cedar sides and a serpentine of light baffles arching from the roof, has displayed Menil art and special exhibitions since 1987. Dramatic modern art by Rene Magritte are beloved by regular visitors, as are Byzantine and medieval works, which provide a fascinating contrast to the Spanish Catholic Christ image predominate in Texas. Within easy walking distance are the other public Menil galleries: the Rothko Chapel, the Cy Twombly Gallery (designed by the artist, architect Renzo Piano, and de Menil herself), the Byzantine Fresco Chapel Museum, and Richmond Hall. *1515 Sul Ross, Museum District, 713/525–9400. Free. Sun.–Wed. 11–7.*

12 f-4

MUSEUM OF PRINTING HISTORY

This odd little museum may be one of the best-kept secrets in Houston. A regular series of exhibitions, such as "original" images of Santa Claus from Thomas Nast's 1860 illustrations, provide variety, whereas treasures such as the 764 Dharani Scroll, one of the oldest printed works, and a first edition of the first newspaper published by William Randolph Hearst are on permanent display. *1324 W. Clay, Montrose, 713/522–4652. $2 adults, $1 children & senior citizens. Tues.–Sun. 10–5.*

135

14 *g-1*

THE LILLIE AND HUGH ROY CULLEN SCULPTURE GARDEN

Sculptor Isamu Noguchi designed this garden as a showcase for significant works by Caro, Giacometti, Rodin, Frank Stella, and other 19th- and 20th-century works in the MFAH collection. The art, as it turns out, is something of a bonus. The greenery, tranquility, and graceful marble curves of the garden make this a spot well worth stopping into. *1001 Bissonnet, Museum District, 713/639–7300. Free. Daily 9 AM–10 PM.*

12 *f-7*

RICHMOND HALL

Possibly a case of a found art space, Richmond Hall was originally a grocery store. The narrow building, which is not visible from the walkway surrounding the Menil Collection, is now used as an exhibition gallery for the Menil. Since 1998, the hall houses a large light installation by Dan Flavin. *9275 Richmond, Museum District, 713/334–9088. Free. Sun.–Wed. 11–6.*

BRIDGES

13 *d-2*

MCKEE STREET BRIDGE

(James Gordon McKenzie, 1932; decorative improvements in 1985.) The graceful girders and the piers beneath are a true cause for civic pride: A city engineer designed this bridge. *700 McKee, at Buffalo Bayou, Downtown/Theater District.*

CHILDREN'S MUSEUMS

14 *h-2*

CHILDREN'S MUSEUM HOUSTON

East Coast architects Robert Venturi and Denise Scott-Brown are respected professionals, perhaps because of the cleverness that enables them to create a building that looks like a child's drawing yet is thoroughly suited to its purpose. The garish yellow structure is unflaggingly cheery on even the grayest days of February, and within kids can fiddle with "how does it work" exhibits, play in the Bubble Lab, visit "Yalagag, a Mountain Village in Mexico," and enjoy regular performances and workshops. Almost every weekend sees Spotlight

Performances and craft classes, such as the annual holiday series that has segments on Kwanzaa, Hanukkah, Christmas, and more. The permanent exhibits are complemented by a schedule of traveling entertainment in the Kaleidoscope Gallery and Kids' Hall. Free family night is Thursday 5–8. *1500 Binz, Museum District, 713/522–1138. $5 adults & children over 2, $4 senior citizens, $3 per person from 3–5. Sun. noon–5, Tues.–Sat. 9–5.*

CHURCHES & SYNAGOGUES

Houston has more than 1,000 places of worship, and almost every faith that is practiced on earth is observed in Houston. Although the city has a handful of grand old steepled churches, most are post–World War II and were built during the era of planned communities. Recent arrivals may meet in community halls and other spaces until funds can be raised.

7 *f-4*

ALL SAINTS CATHOLIC CHURCH

Among the postwar churches of Houston, San Antonio architect Frederick B. Gaenslen's dramatic French Romanesque building, with a stark tower and crisp detail, is unique. *215 E. 10th St., Heights, 713/864–2653.*

9 *g-1*

APOSTOLIC CATHOLIC ORTHODOX CHURCH

The Most Reverend Diana C. Dale leads this progressive Southwest Houston congregation. *2650 Fountainview, Galleria/Post Oak, 713/977–2855.*

12 *a-6*

BETHANY CHRISTIAN CHURCH

Interestingly, this dark-stone Gothic church, which would fit more easily into a Brönte novel than the suburban sprawl of Houston, is the home of the Houston Tidelanders Barbershop Quartet. *3223 Westheimer, Upper Kirby District, 713/523–1609.*

14 *f-2*

CONGREGATION EMANUEL TEMPLE

This progressive reform synagogue has an architecturally significant temple. The MacKie & Kamrath and Lenard Gabert structure provides a modern take on historic standards. *1500 Sunset Blvd., Museum District, 713/529–5771.*

9 *d-6*

EPISCOPAL CHURCH OF THE EPIPHANY

The funky waved roof serves a purpose: the structure was designed to hold a round stained-glass window so that light streams through it onto the pulpit during the Eucharist. *9600 S. Gessner, Sharpstown, 713/774–9619.*

14 *e-2*

FIRST CHRISTIAN CHURCH

The bright blue mosaic nave has been an eye-catching face on the building since it first went up in 1958. The image is still striking, as is the equally attractive landscaping. *1601 Sunset Blvd., Rice University Village, 713/526–2561.*

14 *g-1*

FIRST UNITARIAN UNIVERSALIST CHURCH

The modern facility looks a bit more like a nursing home than a church, and although most of what goes on is conventional worship and child care, the church does serve brunch. *5200 Fannin, Museum District, 713/526–5200.*

6 *g-5*

MENNONITE CHURCH

This is one of Houston's best sources for crafts. Each November, Texas Mennonite churches have a quilt auction and craft sale. The fundraiser for the church's relief and development fund features crafts from 33 countries and a variety of folk art items—and it's just in time for early holiday shopping. *1231 Wirt Rd., Memorial/Spring Branch, 713/464–4865.*

12 *h-2*

METROPOLITAN COMMUNITY CHURCH OF THE RESURRECTION

This gay- and lesbian-friendly church also has an annual blessing of the animals. It doesn't get more accepting than that. *1919 Decatur, Montrose, 713/861–9149.*

12 *f-7*

ROTHKO CHAPEL

Mark Rothko designed this world-famous ecumenical chapel as a meditative environment, which means that it's supposed to provide the soul-soothing benefits of a religious sanctuary without the baggage. It works. Art and architecture students, and harried people from all walks of life enjoy the quiet of Rothko, and many weddings have been held here. *Office: 1409 Sul Ross (adjacent to the Menil Collection); chapel: 3900 Yupon, Montrose, 713/524–9839. Daily 10–6.*

13 *b-5*

SACRED HEART CHURCH (SACRED HEART CO-CATHEDRAL)

The Houston–Galveston diocese is based in this very traditional church building. *1111 Pierce Ave., Downtown/Theater District, 713/659–1561.*

7 *a-6*

SECOND BAPTIST CHURCH

The "Fellowship of Excitement" was founded in 1927 and grew slowly and steadily until the arrival of its fifth pastor, Dr. Ed Young. The unceasing evangelism of Young, seen on TV almost as often as Houston's Mattress Mac, has done nothing but good for the church. The main building of the Woodway campus went up in the mid-'80s, but growth continues with new amenities. The church claims the largest single adult ministry in the United States and a total membership of more than 20,000. Naturally, the entire congregation cannot all meet in the 6,000-seat sanctuary at the same time. The church has several services, and a second location was added in the fall of 1999. Following the naming conventions of modern corporations, Second Baptist has the Woodway Campus and the West Campus. *6400 Woodway, Galleria/Post Oak, 713/465–3408.*

12 *a-5*

ST. JOHN THE DIVINE EPISCOPAL CHURCH

The staid, yet slightly contemporary church was crowned in 1999 by the addition of an athletic facility for St. John's school, but the narrow bell tower still stands out. *2450 River Oaks Blvd., River Oaks, 713/622–3600.*

6 *e-3*

ST. PETER UNITED CHURCH OF CHRIST

Naturally, the original 1864 structure has been improved and repaired. However, modern improvements haven't diminished the white-board charms of this southern "country" church. *9022 Long*

Point Rd., Memorial/Spring Branch, 713/
465–1424.

3 e-7

WINDSOR VILLAGE UNITED METHODIST CHURCH

Pastor Kirbyjohn Caldwell is on television less often than some other leaders,
but he is arguably the most important
minister in the area. His thriving congregation shares in services, Bible study,
and classes ranging from piano lessons
to Christian Mother in Action parenting
sessions. Caldwell is also the face and
voice for Corinthian Point, a 108-acre
subdivision to be built by a community-
based organization. "God's kingdom
builders in action" is how the congregation describes the project. 6000 Heather-
brook Dr., Southwest, 713/723–8187.

3 d-7

YOUNG ISRAEL OF HOUSTON

Rabbi Yehoshua Wender has a lively,
although profoundly observant, philosophy. The Young Israel community is also
active in community initiatives, such as
scheduling boys only and girls only
swim days at the community pool. 7823
Ludington, Southwest, 713/729–0719.

2 c-3

ZION CHINESE BAPTIST CHURCH

Reverend Victor Wong leads this north
Houston congregation. Services are in
Mandarin. 19911 Hwy. 249, FM 1960
area, 281/469–3389.

GRAVEYARDS & CEMETERIES

Houston's long history of razing and
rebuilding means that even some large
early burial grounds are gone. Children
in newly planned communities sometimes find a few headstones while
exploring, such as a final resting place
off I–10 at Maxey Road, which is now
cluttered with debris. Even a onetime
major city cemetery lies under what's
left of the Jefferson Davis Hospital.
However, on those rare days when
Houstonians look to the past, venerable
grounds such as Olivewood Cemetery
(an African-American cemetery sometimes known as Hollywood) have been
preserved. If you have an interest, you
may wish to join Save Texas Cemeteries
(512/257–7283).

12 d-4

COLLEGE PARK CEMETERY

From time to time, there is an effort to
rally preservation efforts for this 19th-
century African-American cemetery.
Many who use Dallas as a corridor to
Downtown, however, may see only a tan-
gled lot. There are 4,400 graves on College Park's 5 acres, including John Henry
"Jack" Yates and many members of his
prosperous family. Although the Yates
house in Sam Houston Park is surely
safe, development on the south side of
Buffalo Bayou threatens the graveyard.
3500 W. Dallas at Gross, River Oaks.

11 c-1

FOREST PARK LAWNDALE

Among the nationally famous persons
buried along with more than 100,000
Houstonians are Larry Blyden, longtime
host of "What's My Line" and Tony-
award winner for a Broadway role in "A
Funny Thing Happened on the Way to
the Forum," and blues artists Sam
"Lightnin'" Hopkins and Katie Webster.
6900 Lawndale, Heights.

12 h-3

FOUNDERS MEMORIAL PARK

Naturally, those who first named this
cemetery didn't have the hubris to name
it "Founders." What was once City
Cemetery was eventually renamed to
honor the Texas (and in many cases
Republic of Texas) leaders buried here.
John Austin Wharton, after whom the
county is named, is here. Both of the
Allen brothers, and many victims of a
mid-19th-century yellow fever epi-
demic—some in graves that may never
have been marked—are also among the
close to a thousand Houstonians resting in this 2-acre site. 1217 Dallas, at
Valentine, Downtown/Theater District.

12 h-1

GLENWOOD CEMETERY

The pretty cemetery just outside of
Downtown is best known for being the
final resting place of Howard Hughes.
Many area political figures, including
last president of the Republic Anson
Jones, governors Ross Sterling and
William P. Hobby, George H. Hermann,
wildcatter Glenn McCarthy, Astrodome
auteur Roy Hofheinz, and Post pub-
lisher Oveta Culp Hobby are here. Gene
Tierney also lies in peace here. 2525
Washington Ave., Heights, 713/864–7886.

`12` f-4

MAGNOLIA CEMETERY

Many residents consider this late-19th-century cemetery a pleasant spot for an evening jog. Go a little slower and you will find a number of mid-20th-century Hispanic plots and markers. Brightly colored tiles are a hallmark, with stars and colorful crosses marking many of the headstones. *2510 Dallas, Montrose.*

`7` f-5

OLIVEWOOD CEMETERY

The cemetery was established in the 1870s, although it seems many of the towering trees were standing tall even then. Although there has not been sustained maintenance in the last half of the 20th century, occasional private and county efforts have been made, and many of the grand tombstones, family plots, and statuary are intact. In fact, some still feature shells, a common decoration in early African-American gravesites. Some evidence suggests the cemetery was also known as Hollywood and there are gravesites that date to nearly a century before Olivewood was founded. It is kept locked, but a key is available from Houston Parks and Recreation. *Whichman at E. 2nd St., Heights.*

HAUNTED PLACES

`12` b-7

ALE HOUSE

Rumors of an Ale House ghost are widespread, but so varied, ranging from a tragic barmaid to a homesick sailor, that it's difficult to put any stock in them. *2425 W. Alabama, Upper Kirby District.*

`13` b-3

HOUSTON PUBLIC LIBRARY, CENTRAL BRANCH, IDESON BUILDING

Not all the history in the Texas Room is on the shelves. A now-departed janitor named Cramer is said to make occasional visits. His dog, which worked alongside him, has not been seen or heard from. Cramer lived and worked in the original library until his death in 1936, and librarians sometimes report hearing violin music from the basement rooms that were his quarters. The building's namesake, librarian Julia Ideson, died in 1945 and has not been heard from since, except in her legacy. *500 McKinney, Downtown/Theater District, 713/236–1313.*

`2` b-2

WUNSCHE BROTHERS AND SALOON

Contemporary waitresses at this institution sometimes report that Old Man Wunsche, a Spring patriarch, is still keeping tabs on the café staff. *103 Midway, Tomball/Spring.*

HISTORIC STRUCTURES & STREETS

`14` d-8

ASTRODOME USA

Poor old Dome. Despite being big, ugly, and unabashedly commercial, it was without a doubt the only Houston building ever to have serious national attention. Before its 1965 completion, popular press quoted engineers and architects who said the structure could not be built (in fact, some contracts were difficult to secure because vendors doubted the viability of the project). After Roy Hofheinz debuted his "Eighth Wonder of the World," there was a rush to build domed stadiums everywhere else and Astroturf became a standard sports surface. At this point, the 642-ft clear span roof, 218 ft at its highest point, arches mostly over monster trucks, motor-cross, and daredevil entertainment. Baseball has moved to the Downtown Enron stadium (which showcases the current stadium vogue, a retractable roof), the rodeo would like a new home, and when our NFL team comes, they will not play here, and the Dome may end up, like so many other structures, a parking lot. Until then, regular Astrodome tours discuss the size, structure, and seating capacity, and offer historical tidbits. *8400 Kirby, Astrodome/Old Spanish Trail, 713/799–9834.*

`13` c-3

LA CARAFE

Most evidence suggests that this 1847 Nathaniel Kellum structure is the oldest public two-story frame building in Houston. Kellum was a significant figure in early Houston building. La Carafe was first the Kennedy family general store and bakery. (Some like to spread an urban legend that two stuffed pigeons displayed in a shadow box are the last pair of passenger pigeons.) *813 Congress, Downtown/Theater District, 713/229–9399.*

13 c-3
MAJESTIC METRO

A neon marquee still heralds this 1926 movie palace. By the '70s, the features were mostly cheap exploitation films, but the theater rebounded, refurbishing the plush interior and adding modern sound and light systems to make it suitable for concerts, events, and weddings. *911 Preston, Downtown/Theater District, 713/224–7226.*

13 c-3
MARKET SQUARE

City founders designed this square as a true city center. Houston now spreads farther than they could have imagined, and has "centers" in the Medical Center, Galleria, Greenspoint, and more, and the grassy square sees lunch-hour picnics and spring festivals. Photos from Houston's early days are on display beside a sunken walkway, and a James Surls sculpture stands at the center of this pleasant park. Two sides of the square still have vestiges of the original buildings. The other two sides have parking lots. *Bounded by Preston, Milam, and Travis, Downtown/Theater District.*

5 g-4
PORT OF HOUSTON

Completed in 1914, the Houston Ship Channel is, year in and year out, one of America's busiest ports of call. The 50-mi channel funnels at least 5,000 ships and 40,000 barges between the docks here and the Gulf of Mexico each year. There are boat tours and an official observation deck. The best bet may be to watch the tugs and massive barges from Shanghai Reds, a surf and turf restaurant with a full bar. Patrons can watch the ship channel from a patio or the dining room. *7300 Clinton Dr., Gate 8, East End, 713/670–2416.*

15 d-1
PROJECT ROW HOUSES

Local artist Rick Lowe organized volunteers and funds for the restoration of 22 shotgun-style houses. The goal, which has been fully realized, was to celebrate Houston's African-American history (this neighborhood dates back to the Civil War), serve the community, and develop and nurture African-American art. Ten of the houses serve as galleries for visual arts projects, with new installations every six months or so. Another house hosts performing arts projects. The rest of the houses are devoted to service projects such as the Young Mothers Residential Program. There is always something interesting going on, and there are usually opportunities to contribute to keeping the houses and their grounds up, and assisting with children's projects. *250 Holman, Third Ward, 713/526–7662.*

13 b-3
SAM HOUSTON PARK

The buildings here have been moved to the site, but perhaps that can be forgiven considering the care taken to preserve the homes and educate the public. After a stop at the Heritage Society's museum center, you can view or tour a variety of structures. An Austin colonist's log cabin, the 1950 Nichols-Rice-Cherry house, and a Lutheran church built in 1891 are on a plot that was dedicated as city park in 1899. *1100 Bagby, Downtown, 713/655–1912.*

HISTORY MUSEUMS

2 d-2
AMERICAN FUNERAL SERVICE MUSEUM

Thousands have gone for the kitsch or creepy aspects and found themselves fascinated with the breadth and depth of this rarely discussed aspect of society. *415 Barren Springs Dr., FM 1960 area, 281/876–3063.*

2 g-5
BATTLESHIP TEXAS

A veteran of both world wars, the U.S.S. Texas is a popular tourist stop for both young and old alike. *3527 Battleground Rd., Clear Lake/Bay Area, 281/479–2411.*

12 b-3
BAYOU BEND COLLECTION AND GARDENS

Miss Ima Hogg, never Ms., left many wonderful gifts to the city of Houston, including her 14-acre estate. Her rich and varied collection of 5,000 pieces of early American furniture, household goods, art, and gardens and woodlands can be visited on guided tours. The audio and docent tours are spiced with stories of East Coast collectors gnashing their teeth when Hogg bested them at auctions. After touring you may decide to paint your dining room gold with a cherry blossom motif, or add wrought iron balconies all around. *1 Westcott St., Heights, 713/639–7750.*

2 *h-5*

BAYTOWN HISTORICAL MUSEUM

One thing about the South: we care about the past. As this museum proves, anytime you have any sort of community, a historical society will form and present artifacts for public view. *220 W. De Fee St., Pasadena/Southeast, 281/427–8768.*

2 *h-6*

BRAZORIA COUNTY MUSEUM

With the History Channel seal of approval, this small regional museum features exhibits on the Austin colony and Reconstruction. Staff will help the curious and scholars explore the photo and documents archives. *100 Cedar St., Brazoria County, 409/864–1208.*

2 *a-7*

CONFEDERATE MUSEUM

Weapons of the Civil War and some antique furnishings make up the bulk of the exhibits. Other displays relate to Civil War veterans. There are also paintings of the war and war heroes, and reprints of various stately memoirs. *2925 Westland, Sugar Land/Fort Bend, 713/622–1936.*

2 *a-5*

FORBIDDEN GARDENS

Unless someone opens a "History of the Moon" museum, the miniatures here represent the most far-off culture celebrated in Houston. You'll see the Forbidden City in Beijing (in one-third scale), and the emperor Qin's army (6,000 replica terra-cotta soldiers). The soldiers are based on 3rd-century BC models unearthed in 1974. This 40-acre "dollhouse" effectively conveys Chinese culture—all the clay men were painstakingly crafted to honor the art and memory of Qin's era, and are displayed in earnest. The gardens are outside, so check the weather before planning a visit. *23500 Franz Rd., Katy/Bear Creek, 281/347–8000.*

1 *d-1*

HERITAGE MUSEUM OF MONTGOMERY COUNTY

Mostly docent and volunteer-run, this sweet little museum has a nice assortment of artifacts and displays covering the development of the surrounding area. Hefty, rough-hewn farming tools and needles, wool combs, spinning wheels, and other household tools are featured. *1506 Hwy. 45 N, Montgomery County, 409/539–6873.*

14 *g-1*

HOLOCAUST MUSEUM

A dramatic exterior (evoking the image of gas chambers) holds standing exhibits, traveling shows, and educational programs. Contemporary art might be on display, but all exhibits focus on the Holocaust. *5401 Caroline, Museum District, 713/942–8000.*

13 *a-5*

HOUSTON FIRE MUSEUM

Station No. 7 is still working for fire prevention, and providing a few thrills. Since 1982, the building has been a museum with photographs (some quite intense) and memorabilia from Houston's firefighting past, along with helmets and tools from fire-fighting history. *2403 Milam, Downtown/Theater District, 713/524–2526.*

13 *f-8*

HOUSTON SPORTS MUSEUM

Initial appearances notwithstanding, this is a charming and well-located museum. The home plate in the floor is a genuine relic of the Houston Buffs Texas League. Great players, teams, and moments in Houston sports are revisited with photographs and memorabilia. *4001 Gulf Fwy., in Finger's Furniture, East Side, 713/221–4441.*

2 *g-6*

PASADENA HISTORICAL MUSEUM

Although this town, a satellite of Houston, did not begin until late in the 19th century, the docents and volunteers feel there is a story to tell. That story, by the way, is not all chemical refining. Strawberries and other agriculture are celebrated in the little museum. *201 Vince St., Pasadena/Southeast, 713/477–7237.*

5 *h-1*

RAILROAD MUSEUM OF THE GULF COAST

The National Railway Historical Society is alive and well, and chapters such as the Gulf Coast group are eager to share the joy of trains. Here you'll enjoy antique railway cars, railroad models, and more history than you can possibly absorb in one trip. *7390 Mesa Dr., North, 713/631–6612.*

LIBRARIES

13 *b-3*

HOUSTON PUBLIC LIBRARY, CENTRAL BRANCH

Although the business reference room upstairs in the main building is probably the busiest area, make a point of visiting the Texas Room in the old building, where a helpful staff has compiled an archive of Houston. (Note: some of Houston's finer families seem to have "misplaced" the awkward newspaper clippings filed in their folders.) Weekends see students, recent immigrants, and others busy at all the tables, trying to get ahead. *500 McKinney, Downtown/Theater District, 713/236–1313. Sun. 2–6, weekdays 9–9, Sat. 9–6.*

14 *g-1*

CLAYTON LIBRARY CENTER

Tens of thousands of annual visitors use the genealogy resources here. The library also has a wealth of important historic papers. *5300 Caroline, Medical Center, 713/284–1999. Mon–Wed. 9–9, Thurs.–Sat. 9–5.*

14 *g-1*

HIRSCH LIBRARY AT THE MUSEUM OF FINE ARTS, HOUSTON

Visitors can review books, periodicals, artist files, and other sources during the library's public hours. This is not a circulation library. *1001 Bissonnet, Museum District, 713/639–7300. Tues.–Wed. and Fri. 10–4:45, Thurs. 10–8:45, Sat. noon–4:45.*

14 *e-3*

HOUSTON ACADEMY OF MEDICINE—TEXAS MEDICAL CENTRAL LIBRARY

Think the Internet has put all medical knowledge at your fingertips? Think again. The library also has medical history collections and the Atomic Bomb Casualty Commission Collection. *1133 M. D. Anderson Blvd., Medical Center, 713/795–4200. Sun. 1–10, Mon.–Thurs. 7–midnight, Fri. 7–9, Sat. 9–5.*

15 *g-1*

O'QUINN LAW LIBRARY (UNIVERSITY OF HOUSTON)

Nobody really trusts a lawyer, right? That's why this is such a terrific

resource. Stop in to research the issues you're dealing with before you talk to a lawyer. *3800 Calhoun, Entrance No. 19, East End, 713/743–2300. Sun. 9 AM–11 PM, weekdays 7:30–midnight, Sat. 9–7.*

SCHOOLS

9 *e-4*

HOUSTON BAPTISTS UNIVERSITY

The college opened in 1963, and has been a full four-year institution since 1966. Graduate studies were introduced in 1977. Business, education, and science programs complement theology and humanities programs. There is also a nursing school. *7502 Fondren, Sharpstown, 281/649–3000.*

13 *a-7*

HOUSTON COMMUNITY COLLEGE SYSTEM

Five campuses and some distance-learning options have allowed many Houstonians to get a leg up. Some students come for certification programs or extra career and computer training. Others go for full degrees and MA programs at convenient system campuses. Many students headed for the University of Houston and other schools take their 101 classes here to save money. It's also worth noting that several respected Houston chefs learned their culinary skills with HCCS. *1300 Holman, Montrose, 713/718–6000.*

14 *f-2*

RICE UNIVERSITY

William Marsh Rice left an endowment for the boys and girls of Texas, something many Houstonians have learned at local-theater performances of "The Trust." At this point, the university is second only to Princeton in private research institution endowment. A relatively small school, Rice enjoys a five-to-one student-teacher ratio. The George R. Brown School of Engineering is perhaps the strongest program, and Rice is also respected for the Shepherd School of Music, its architecture program, and studies in the sciences. *6100 Main, Museum District, 713/348–0000.*

15 *d-1*

TEXAS SOUTHERN UNIVERSITY

Established in 1947, TSU serves more than 8,000 mostly African-American students on a 145-acre campus. Barbara Jordan, Mickey Leland, and Craig Washington are all alumni. The Thurgood Marshall School of Law is still producing politicians, and the university has an impressive collection of art, both in galleries and in public spaces. *3100 Cleburne, Medical Center, 713/313–7011.*

15 *g-2*

UNIVERSITY OF HOUSTON SYSTEM

The 550-acre central campus alone might as well be a city. On an average day, an estimated 30,000 students show up for class. Students, many of whom are many years past high school graduation, can choose between 103 bachelors programs, 119 masters programs, and 53 doctoral programs. The central campus has 10,000 computer workstations and many athletic and arts events. Those who don't have time for the drive can take classes at UH-Downtown, UH-Clear Lake, UH-Fort Bend, and UH-Victoria campuses. *4800 Calhoun, East End (Central Campus), 713/743–9621.*

12 *f-7*

UNIVERSITY OF ST. THOMAS

The contemporary graduate programs such as the Cameron School of Business might surprise the Basilian fathers who founded this university in 1947. Nonstudents benefit from gallery shows, music school performances, and the recent addition of a gold-domed Chapel of St. Basil. Architect Philip Johnson's nonsecular creation is genuinely awe-inspiring. *3800 Montrose Blvd., Montrose, 713/522–7911 or 800/460–8878.*

SCIENCE MUSEUMS

3 *h-8*

BRAZOSPORT MUSEUM OF NATURAL SCIENCE

Beachcombers can get a shell fix on rained-out or winter days. Local shells like Mitchell's wentletrap has its own case. Other exhibits cover whelks worldwide. There's also a dash of dinosaurs on display and touch cases for bones, fur, and other natural artifacts. *400 College Dr., Brazoria County, 409/265–7831. Free. Sun. 2–5, Tues.–Sat. 10–5.*

2 *b-8*

GEORGE OBSERVATORY

For a small fee, the public can watch the skies through a 36-inch telescope. Smaller scopes are free. On public event nights, members of local astronomy clubs set up their own scopes and give informal lessons. There are free Saturday night star parties all year long. *21901 FM 762, in Brazos State Park, Sugar Land/Fort Bend, 409/553–4300.*

14 *g-1*

HOUSTON MUSEUM OF NATURAL SCIENCE

Curious adults and parents looking for educational and entertaining diversions for their kids take advantage of the museum proper, the Burke Baker Planetarium, Cockrell Butterfly Center, and museum-sponsored classes and trips. The Wiess Energy Hall is devoted to a branch of science near and dear to the Houston heart, the petrochemical industry. At this point in history, not every school kid has a dad or uncle from the oil patch, so it can be enlightening. Like most natural science museums, this one has dinosaur bones. Models and murals that depict alarming paleo facial expressions add context to the Precambrian, Mesozoic, and Cenozoic fossils. There's also a giant armadillo, dug from the banks of Brays Bayou in1955. Common local sea shells, and rare shells such as an Adanson's slit shell, a mollusk thought to be extinct until recently, are displayed in the Strake Hall of Malacology. Gems and minerals, a safari's worth of stuffed African and Texas animals, and a few NASA artifacts are also displayed. For live wildlife, wander amongst 2,000 flitting butterflies in the Cockrell Butterfly Center.

As for admission options, you can buy tickets for the museum only, butterfly center only, planetarium only, IMAX only, IMAX double feature, or IMAX plus one, two, or three additional venues. When the museum hosts a touring exhibition, the show is considered an additional venue. It's best to purchase IMAX tickets in advance to avoid disappointment at sold-out shows. It's also wise to register as early as possible for summer camp sessions. The marine biology session fills up fast. *One Hermann Circle Dr., Museum District, 713/639–4600. Museum: $5 adults, $3 children and seniors, members and children under 3 are free, free after 2 PM Tues. Mon.–Sat., 9–6, Sun. 11–6.*

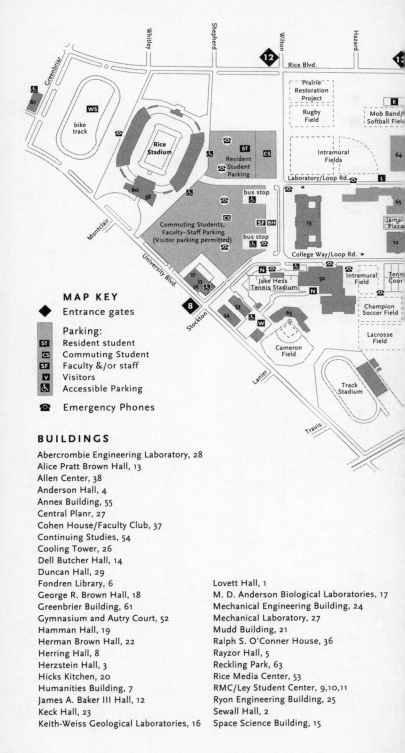

MAP KEY

◆ Entrance gates

Parking:
- **ST** Resident student
- **CS** Commuting Student
- **SF** Faculty &/or staff
- **V** Visitors
- ♿ Accessible Parking

☎ Emergency Phones

BUILDINGS

Abercrombie Engineering Laboratory, 28
Alice Pratt Brown Hall, 13
Allen Center, 38
Anderson Hall, 4
Annex Building, 55
Central Planr, 27
Cohen House/Faculty Club, 37
Continuing Studies, 54
Cooling Tower, 26
Dell Butcher Hall, 14
Duncan Hall, 29
Fondren Library, 6
George R. Brown Hall, 18
Greenbrier Building, 61
Gymnasium and Autry Court, 52
Hamman Hall, 19
Herman Brown Hall, 22
Herring Hall, 8
Herzstein Hall, 3
Hicks Kitchen, 20
Humanities Building, 7
James A. Baker III Hall, 12
Keck Hall, 23
Keith-Weiss Geological Laboratories, 16

Lovett Hall, 1
M. D. Anderson Biological Laboratories, 17
Mechanical Engineering Building, 24
Mechanical Laboratory, 27
Mudd Building, 21
Ralph S. O'Conner House, 36
Rayzor Hall, 5
Reckling Park, 63
Rice Media Center, 53
RMC/Ley Student Center, 9,10,11
Ryon Engineering Building, 25
Sewall Hall, 2
Space Science Building, 15

Rice University

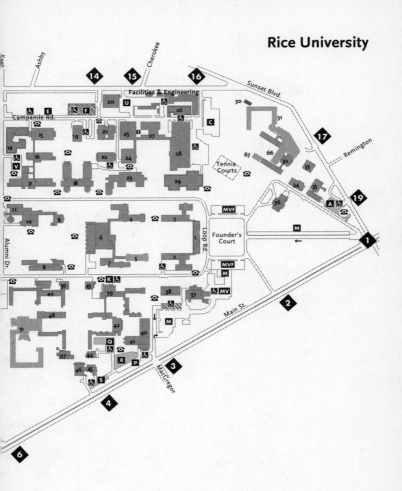

Facilities & Engineering

Campanile Rd.

Sunset Blvd.

Remington

Tennis Courts

Founder's Court

Loop Rd.

Alumni Dr.

Main St.

MacGregor

RESIDENTIAL COLLEGES

Mary Gibbs Jones College, 32
Margaret Root Brown College, 34 & 35
Edgar Odell Lovett College, 40 & 41
James A. Baker College, 39
Sid Richardson College, 45 & 46
Will Rice College, 42 & 44
Henry C. Hanszen College, 47 & 48

Parking

Parking

Elgin St.

Parking

Baseball
Field

Rebecca and
John J. Moores
School of Music

Athletics/
Alumni Facility

University
oh Houston
Science Ctr.

Wortham
Theater
Complex

Garrison
Gymnasium

Hofheinz
Pavilion

Science &
Research
Bldg. 2

Graduate
School of
Social Wo

Hoffman St.

Parking

Science &
Research
Bldg. 1

Agnes Arne
Auditoriur

Parking

Parking

Arnold
Hall

Fleming
Bldg.

Sciences Bldg.

Parking

Robertson
Stadium

Charles F.
McElhinney
Hall

Farish
Hall

Fred J. Heyne
Bldg.

Roy G. Culle
Bldg.

Parking

A.D. Bruc
Religion C

Parking

Housing

Bates
(Residence)
Hall

Ta
(Resi
H

Oberholzer
(Residence)
Hall

Wheeler

Se
(Res

Cameron
Bldg.

Parking

Housing

Housing

South
Office
Annex

Parking

Clinical
Research
Services

146

University of Houston

147

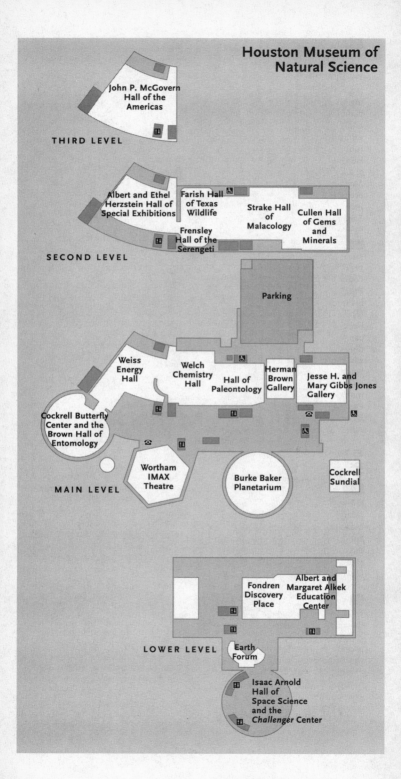

Houston Museum of Natural Science

THIRD LEVEL

John P. McGovern Hall of the Americas

SECOND LEVEL

Albert and Ethel Herzstein Hall of Special Exhibitions

Farish Hall of Texas Wildlife

Frensley Hall of the Serengeti

Strake Hall of Malacology

Cullen Hall of Gems and Minerals

MAIN LEVEL

Parking

Weiss Energy Hall

Welch Chemistry Hall

Hall of Paleontology

Herman Brown Gallery

Jesse H. and Mary Gibbs Jones Gallery

Cockrell Butterfly Center and the Brown Hall of Entomology

Wortham IMAX Theatre

Burke Baker Planetarium

Cockrell Sundial

LOWER LEVEL

Fondren Discovery Place

Albert and Margaret Alkek Education Center

Earth Forum

Isaac Arnold Hall of Space Science and the *Challenger* Center

148

14 g-2

MUSEUM OF HEALTH AND MEDICAL SCIENCE

The Visible Man model concept is writ large here. Other aspects of the Amazing Body Pavilion include a 10-ft brain suitable for touring, interactive exhibits, and a varied program of events and exhibitions. The gift shop sells gross rubber toys any child will love. Bring the kids on family night, Thursday from 4 to 7; it's a free visit. *1515 Hermann Dr., Medical Center, 713/521–1515. $4 adults over 12, $3 senior citizens & children, members and children under 3 are free. Sun. noon–5, Tues.–Sat. 9–5, Thurs. 9–7.*

2 g-5

PROCTOR MUSEUM OF NATURAL SCIENCE

Founder, proprietor, and docent T. W. Proctor may not have air-conditioning in his museum, but he's got everything else from, oh, a million years more and back. By appointment, you and yours can wander through the collections of dinosaur, mammal, fish, and plant fossils, minerals, and preserved insects. You can learn a lot about natural science and, not incidentally, about collecting mania from Proctor. *630 Uvalde, Pasadena/Southeast, 713/453–8363. Free. By appointment only.*

STATUES, MURALS & MONUMENTS

13 b-3

BALLET DANCER

(Marcello Mascherini, 1950.) Marcello Mascherini's realistic bronze is a pleasant companion for those who lunch on the picnic tables arranged on Jones Hall's plaza. *615 Louisiana (Jones Hall), Downtown/Theater District.*

7 d-6

BEER CAN HOUSE

(John Milkovisch, 1974.) In the groovy '70s, many were content merely to make pop-top chains. A one-time railway worker, however, took it upon himself to drape his house in tab chains and nail flattened beer cans onto almost every exterior surface of his home. The place has been a beloved landmark ever since. *222 Malone Ave., Memorial/Spring Branch.*

7 g-4

DINOSAUR

(Paul Kittelson, 1992.) Travis Elementary playground is a popular SPARK park with a faux triceratops fossil to play on and under. The concrete bones are part of a larger dino theme. Although Kittelson is the artist, local children had a say in the original design. *3311 Beauchamp, Travis Elementary, Heights, 713/802–4790.*

13 b-3

FEDERAL OFFICE BUILDING AND U. S. COURTHOUSE

Both of the murals here are a refreshing change from the justice themes common in court buildings. Both were commissioned in 1941, and Texas painters Alexandre Hogue and Jerry Bywaters elected to depict life along Buffalo Bayou. *515 Rusk, Downtown/Theater District.*

13 b-3

FIRST SUBSCRIPTION COMMITTEE

(1935.) This Ruth Pershing Uhler mural is one of several extant WPA projects in the original library building and around town. Pershing's work is best seen climbing the stairs from the first to second floor. In the mural, women's reading clubs and other associations that worked to develop Houston's library are honored in ladylike pastel tones. *500 McKinney, Houston Public Library, Downtown/Theater District, 713/247–2222.*

13 b-3

GEOMETRIC MOUSE X

(Claus Oldenburg, 1975.) When the building opened on January 18, 1976, Oldenburg's red stop sign abstract was outside, ready. Since then, thousands of kids and festival goers have banged on it, pulled on its chains, and thanked the anonymous donor who bequeathed the frankly cute sculpture to the city. *500 McKinney, Houston Public Library, Downtown/Theater District, 713/247–2222.*

12 f-3

LARGE SPINDLE PIECE

(Henry Moore, 1975.) This massive Henry Moore bronze shows signs of loving and wear along the edges where hands have polished the metal to a high sheen. Joggers and bikers using the nearby trails admire the abstract, and it's a restful sight for commuters funneling into downtown. There are several other artworks along the trails, and the disc-golf equipment also has an intriguing look. *Allen Pkwy., Montrose.*

15 *g-2*

MOORES SCHOOL OF MUSIC, UNIVERSITY OF HOUSTON

(Frank Stella, 1997.) Although it was mostly created in studio, Frank Stella's 5,000-square-ft abstract mural now adorns the ceiling of the music school. *3800 Cullen, Entrance No. 16, East End, 713/743-3009.*

13 *d-7*

NEGRO WOMAN IN AMERICAN LIFE AND EDUCATION

(John Biggars, 1953.) Fortunately for contemporary Houstonians, John Biggars's significant contribution, a bold mural, has not been painted over, remodeled out of existence, or otherwise destroyed. *Blue Triangle Community Center, 3005 McGowen Ave., Medical Center.*

13 *c-3*

PERSONAGE AND BIRDS

(Joan Miró, 1970.) Joan Miró's more than 50 ft of vivid color adds a festive note to the gray plaza in front of the Texas Commerce Tower. The abstract statue is always an arresting sight and a gathering spot for lunchtime brown-baggers in clement weather. *600 Travis, Downtown/Theater District.*

14 *g-2*

SAM HOUSTON STATUE

(Enrico Cerraccio, 1916.) Somewhat of an anomaly among the many modern and contemporary pieces scattered throughout Houston, this figure of the general on his horse is classic war hero statuary. Houston points east, toward San Jacinto, where a decisive battle gained Texas's independence from Mexico. Politically, anyway. *South of the border culture still holds sway here. Hermann Dr. at Fannin (entrance to Hermann Park), Museum District, 713/526-0077.*

15 *d-1*

WEB OF LIFE

(John Biggars, 1978.) Inspiration from a mid-'50s trip to Africa led Biggars to produce a book of drawings, which was published by Texas Southern University Press in 1972, and then to create this mural, which employs Biggars' use of hallmark spiritual symbols, geometric abstractions, and human forms, to celebrate the Africans he observed on his journey. This energetic John Biggars mural is not alone at TSU. The university is also home to three murals by Carroll Simms. *3100 Cleburne, TSU, Samuel M. Nabrit Science Center, East End, 713/313-7011.*

VIEWPOINTS

13 *b-4*

HOUSTON HOUSE APARTMENTS

It's impossible to see the deck from the ground, but the mezzanine floor of this building has a large patio surrounding a good-size pool. There are no nearby buildings, and you're high enough to be above billboard, freeway, and streetlights. You can float on your back for an unobstructed view of the stars, or look out over Houston to the north, south, and west. If you're standing on the diving board, the Maxwell House neon coffee cup is north-northwest. Residents and their lucky friends enjoy the view. If you're desperate for a peep, perhaps the desk clerk will give you a nod if you explain, earnestly, that you want to see the very pool where Ninja Bachelor Party was filmed. *1617 Fannin, Downtown/Theater District, 713/659-4781.*

14 *f-1*

NORTH AND SOUTH BOULEVARD

On mild mornings, sunny afternoons, and especially foggy evenings, the wide boulevards are as gracious and scenic as any antebellum neighborhood in New Orleans or Savannah. In most cases, there are no sidewalks in front of the gracious homes. You'll walk on a brick path in the center of the esplanade. The street, path, and most of the homes are sheltered under ancient oaks. *1600 and 1700 blocks, Museum District.*

14 *g-1*

PARK PLAZA WARWICK

The ballroom, which may well be full of festive sights, such as well-dressed people primed for romance and sparkling beverages, has a fine westward vista. The tall trees of Hermann Park and Rice, and the lights of the Medical Center offer a varied view. *5701 Main, Museum District, 713/526-1991.*

`13` *c-3*

TEXAS COMMERCE TOWER SKY LOBBY

Elevators facing the main entrance ferry visitors to the 60th floor. The vista: a good chunk of Downtown's ongoing revitalization and spreading Southwest Houston. *600 Travis, Downtown/Theater District.*

`10` *a-1*

TRANSCO TOWER (NOW WILLIAMS TOWER)

Stunning stonework is the first sight. The elevators to the observation deck are works of art. The altitude affords nice views of the city, although some of the closer landmarks such as the legendary congestion at the intersection of the Loop and Highway 59 are hardly storybook. Afraid of heights? See, and feel, the ground-level cooling system. A grassy park at the base of the tower is home to a waterwall, a striking sculpture whose cascading streams are part of the physical plant. *2800 Post Oak Blvd., Galleria/Post Oak, 713/621–8000.*

guided tours

BUS TOURS

GRAY LINE/KERRVILLE BUS AND TOUR COMPANY COACH USA

The company offers local sightseeing tours and casino trips, and can be chartered for local group travel. *713/671–0991.*

SPECIAL-INTEREST TOURS

CARRIAGE RIDES

Typically, romantics can find horse-drawn carriages in the Theater District, Downtown, and at large festivals. For preplanning, your best bet is to get a card from a driver and then make arrangements with that driver. You might also try phoning Southwest Carriage Livery. *713/789–3737.*

CORPORATE AND CONVENTION SERVICES

Designed for the tag–along tourist, these half- and full-day excursions are for spouses and families traveling along on business trips. *713/880–3287 or 713/880–3200.*

TOURWORKS OF HOUSTON

Package trips include tours of Space Center Houston, San Jacinto Monument, Old Town Spring, the George Ranch, and a grand tour of Houston. Custom tours can be arranged. Pickups are Downtown, Galleria Area, Medical Center, and from Astrodome hotels. *888/868–7839.*

WALKING TOURS

DISCOVER HOUSTON TOURS

Sandra Lord, who calls herself "The Tunnel Lady," leads regular treks through the miles of air-conditioned underground passages below Downtown. The nation's oldest and longest set of tunnels is effectively an old-fashioned town square, complete with shoe stores and ice cream shops. *713/222–9255.*

events

JANUARY

DANCE MONTH AT THE KAPLAN

See Dance *in* Chapter 5.

HOUSTON MARATHON

See Running & Walking *in* Chapter 3.

MARTIN LUTHER KING DAY

Festivities in Hermann Park and other spots around town follow a Downtown parade.

FEBRUARY

BLACK HISTORY MONTH

Observances and festivities vary from year to year, but the public libraries, Shrine of the Black Madonna, Kuumba House, and Main Street Books are usually focal points.

CONOCO RODEO RUN

See Running & Walking in Chapter 3.

HOUSTON LIVESTOCK SHOW AND RODEO

First the trail riders, thousands of them, ride into town from points all over Texas. Nightly news shows do a feature on the cowboy campout in Memorial Park, and the next day traffic is a nightmare as horses and wagons walk on over to the Dome. The rodeo itself is a smaller part of the extravaganza (unless you're a contestant looking at prize money in the six figures). Nightly concerts featuring country and western superstars and a few token popular musicians conclude each rodeo (which begins with indoor fireworks and a horseback drill show), and the carnival and fat stock show run from mid-morning until way past midnight for the three weeks. Horse shows, mule shows, bunny shows, and pig races are among the attractions. There is also a carnival and more than enough concessions, from the on-a-stick variety to serious beef. 713/791–9000.

MARCH

AZALEA TRAIL

Each year, the River Oaks Garden Club hosts this tour devoted to one of the more elite members of the rhododendron family. 713/523–2483.

TEXAS BREWERS FESTIVAL

Fittingly, this craft-beer event is held Downtown at Market Square, which was originally only a few blocks from Houston's brewery row. Those old breweries are all gone, but the new local microbreweries are all represented at the festival. Food and live music are also featured. Contact the Visitors Bureau (800/4-HOUSTON) for information.

AIDS WALK HOUSTON

See Running & Walking in Chapter 3.

PIN OAK CHARITY HORSE SHOW

Some attendees never leave the swank, silent auction in the clubhouse. Others get dusty watching grand prix jumping, hunter jumper classes, and gaited horses. The show features crafts, concessions, and jewelry sales. *Great Southwest Equestrian Center, 2501 S. Mason Rd., Katy/Bear Creek, 713/621–6290.*

APRIL

FOTOFEST

See Arts Events, *above.*

HOUSTON INTERNATIONAL FESTIVAL

Our own vast wang-dang-doodle was the brainchild of a philosophy major, and it's far more than a couple of food booths and a drumming group. Blocks of Downtown are taken over by merchant stalls, food vendors, and several performance stages. School groups perform at the festival, and before each year's festival, school kids are sent study kits designed to teach them about the honored country. Art Car Weekend (*see* Arts Events, *above*) is part of the fête. 713/654–8808.

MS 150

See Bicycling in Chapter 3.

HOUSTON COCA-COLA OPEN

See Tennis in Chapter 3.

BAYOU CITY ART FESTIVAL

See Arts Events, *above.*

MAY

BUFFALO BAYOU REGATTA

Anything that floats is a water-borne answer to the Art Car Parade. Crafts of every design drift down a 14½-mi course on Buffalo Bayou. Watch from the banks or build your own boat and enter. *713/752–0314.*

HISTORIC HEIGHTS HOME TOUR

Six homes are chosen for the tour each year with the criteria being variety and architectural interest. It's always held the second weekend in April. *713/861–4002.*

SHELL HOUSTON OPEN

Millions, as in three or four, go to this world-class PGA golf tournament. The Tournament Players Course in The Woodlands hosts the show, and attendant parties and receptions are part of the fun. *281/367–7999.*

JUNE

JUNETEENTH

This celebration of emancipation is a state holiday (June 19th), celebrated with family gatherings and public events. Area parks, including the George Ranch, host festivities. The Juneteenth Gospel Festival (at Miller Outdoor Theatre in Hermann Park and Sam Houston Park) takes place the Sunday and Monday before Juneteenth. *713/284–8352.*

JULY

JEWISH THEATER FESTIVAL

See Theater *in* Chapter 5.

FOURTH OF JULY CONCERT

Huge crowds come to enjoy a corny holiday band concert with glitter, Sousa marches, and a fireworks show that can be seen from all over. Arrive well before sundown. Parking is tough and it's tougher to get a good spot on the hillside. For details, call Miller Outdoor Theatre, 713/284–8356. There are also festivities at Sam Houston Park, along Buffalo Bayou, and AstroWorld and Cynthia Woods Mitchell Pavilion.

LAWNDALE ART CENTER, "THE BIG SHOW"

See Arts Events, *above.*

AUGUST

HOUSTON INTERNATIONAL JAZZ FESTIVAL

Several Downtown locations, and some venues outside the Loop, book local and nationally known artists. The mayor's jazz breakfast is the traditional kick-off. *713/839–7000.*

BALLUNAR LIFTOFF FESTIVAL

Ironically enough, Space Center Houston's Rocket Park is ground zero for a celebration of this early form of flight. The just after sunset "balloon glow" is a not-to-be-missed sight, with dozens of hot-air balloons taking flight, lighted by their propane jets. *281/488–7676.*

HOUSTON SHAKESPEARE FESTIVAL

See Theaters *in* Chapter 5.

SEPTEMBER

TEXAS RENAISSANCE FESTIVAL

Thousands of Houstonians load up each weekend for ye olde fun in Plantersville. The festival begins just as the weather becomes bearable, in late September, and continues through the first serious chill, mid-November. For some, it's a craft-shopping trip. For others, it's just all about the performances (from Shakespeare to puppets), and for still others, it's just a big party in the country. *FM 1774 between Hwy. 105 in Plantersville and FM 1488, Magnolia, 800/458–3435.*

OCTOBER

WINGS OVER HOUSTON

Ellington Field's air show is a dramatic and popular annual event. Army, Navy, Air Force, and Marine fighter jets execute dazzling acrobatics, and vintage planes do barn show stunts. Ask about ticket discounts and special deals. *11903 Galveston Rd., Clear Lake/Bay Area, 713/266–4492.*

SUSAN G. KOMEN RACE FOR THE CURE

See Running & Walking *in Chapter 3.*

BAYOU CITY ART FESTIVAL

See Arts Events, *above.*

NOVEMBER

AUTORAMA

Going above and beyond the average car show, this expo held at the Astro Hall and Astroarena shows off new models, fantasy cars, and classics. Celebrities appear, even such unlikely superstars as Homer and Bart Simpson. *713/799–9500.*

INTERNATIONAL QUILT FESTIVAL

This is not a bad spot for early holiday shopping. The show has the very best in contemporary and antique quilts on display, along with craft sales, classes and workshops, and a chance for area quilters to show off their stuff. This is one of the largest shows in the country, and peak times find the George R. Brown Convention Center crowded. *George R. Brown Convention Center, 1001 Avenida De Las Americas, 713/853–8000.*

DECEMBER

DYNEGY ICE PLAZA

Gung-ho Christmas enthusiasts manage to get hot chocolate down, even though temperatures are often in the 70s. Still, it isn't often that we get a chance to ice skate outside and enjoy storybook scenes, so make the most of it. Rental skates are available, or you can bring your own. *Texas Ave. between Bayou Pl. and the Wortham Theatre Center, 713/250–3670.*

CHRISTMAS CANDLELIGHT TOURS

Sam Houston Park's historic homes are carefully lighted, and carolers provide a soundtrack to the docent's discussion of celebrations past. *713/655–1912.*

LIGHTS IN THE HEIGHTS

Traditionally the first weekend in December, this beloved celebration takes place on two streets (Bayland is always one of the streets). Carolers, chamber music groups, and Elvis impersonators entertain from porches, an astonishing number of residents offer open-house treats, and traffic moves along at about 2 mph. Park nearby and then walk. Bring a thermos of cocoa, or something stronger. This event is as close as you can come to a "white Christmas" mood. *713/861–4002.*

day trips out of town

BRENHAM

There's more to this Washington County town than Blue Bell ice cream and bluebonnets during wildflower season, not that those aren't reason enough to make the trip. Bluebonnet trails are most traveled from March through June, but some flowers bloom well into fall. The well-known "little creamery in Brenham," Blue Bell Creamery (FM 577 between Main and Tom Green, 800/327–8135, www.bluebell.com) offers 40-minute tours ($2.50) on weekdays throughout the year. Make reservations before arriving.

Whether or not your trip includes wildflowers, you may want to stop in at the Antique Rose Emporium (9300 Lueckemeyer Rd., 800/441–0002). Court a loved one with two-gallon roses (look for a well-developed root ball), or simply tour the grounds to enjoy the beauty and fragrance of tea roses and climbing roses. These early roses are hardier and more fragrant than many modern varieties. Native plants and herbs are also grown on the grounds, and tours of the gardens and 19th-century buildings are free.

Other mellow options are browsing the antiques stores of downtown Brenham and the nearby Chapel Hill district and poking into historic museums like the Burton Cotton Gin & Museum (near the intersection of FM 2502 and FM 2780, 979/289–3378). For rowdier action, visit the working Neuces Canyon Ranch (9501 Hwy. 290 W, 800/925–5058). Neuces Canyon offers cowboy demos, cutting horse shows most weekends, and miles of trails for hiking or riding. You can also stay at the ranch's bed-and-breakfast or inn. We're not suggesting you get into trouble, but we have heard that people jailed in Brenham for outstanding Houston traffic warrants get a free phone call and dish of ice cream. For more information on the area, call 888/BRENHAM.

EAGLE LAKE

It's well known that Eagle Lake has the best goose hunting in Texas. What's not so well known is that after years of being a sportsman's hideout, Eagle Lake has developed attractions for nonhunters. Most of the lodges and hotels, like the Farris Hotel (201 N. McCarty Ave., 979/234–2546), have luxurious accommodations and gourmet chefs. Downtown features the Prairie Edge Museum (408 E. Main St., 979/234–7442). The Alamo-style strip-center building attempts to educate tourists on the very early history of the area, the time of the Karankawa (also known as Carankawa, mostly known in lore for being giants who ate alligators and wore alligator grease to protect their skin from sun and 'skeeters, and for possibly being cannibals). Early settlers and their adventures in rice growing, and the area's rail-shipping industry, are, albeit less dramatically, described. Convenient to Eagle Lake's downtown, Splashway (on Hwy. 90 in Sheridan, 979/234–7718.) water park has slides and rides to splash around in. Brand-name deals at the Sealy Outlet Center (Exit 721 off Hwy. 90, 979/885–3200) is 15 minutes away.

The Colorado River, and its many tubing outfitters, is nearby, and hard-core nature lovers can visit the Attwater Prairie Chicken National Wildlife Refuge (979/234–2780). This successful refuge covers 8,000 acres near the San Bernard River and was once, for no obvious reason, mentioned by Mike Nesmith on The Monkees. To reach the refugee from

Eagle Lake, head northeast on FM 3013 for 7 mi. To drive direct from Houston, get on Highway 36 at Sealy, take it to FM 3013, and head west for 10 mi. Each April, the three-day Prairie Chicken Festival has serious education events, such as refuge tours, lectures, and open houses in 19th-century Eagle Lake structures, along with traditional festival fun like dances, foods on a stick, and crafts and antiques booths.

Eagle Lake is one hour west of Houston. You can take Highway 59, Interstate 10, or the scenic route, Farm Road 1093 through Simonton, Wallis, and quiet miles of farms and forest. For more information about Eagle Lake, call the chamber of commerce, 979/234–2780.

GALVESTON

Galveston, accessible by Highway 45 from Houston, the bridge at San Luis Pass from Surfside, or free ferry from Bolivar Point, has long been a playground for Houstonians. A veritable fleet of charter boats offers day and overnight deep-sea fishing trips, and despite the crowds, fishing is good at public piers and in the surf near San Luis Pass.

On the island, there are 32 mi of beach to spread out on, and you can enjoy them almost all year round. (By the way, the water isn't dirty. It's silty. Gulf sand is light and easily suspended.) West Beach, along Seawall Boulevard near 13-Mile Road, is a state park with a small per-day per-vehicle charge. Seawall beaches, a 10-mi stretch on the east shore, are public, and those who don't feel like swimming can rent bicycles, skates, and canopied four-wheel pedal carts to roll up and down the promenade. West of Galveston, the beaches are wilder, and you're more likely to find burger and barbecue joints than après surf showers and fine seafood restaurants.

The 16-ft seawall, which is hardly an attractive feature, was built after the Great Storm, a 1900 hurricane that all but destroyed the island's city. You can learn about the Great Storm and the rich history of late-19th-century Galveston at the east end of the island. The Galveston County Historical Museum (2219 Market, 409/766–2340) has original Edison footage taken just after the storm, exhibits on the original inhabitants, the 16th-century Spanish occupants, and the Gilded Age. Other museums, the Tall Ship Elissa, and a number of Victorian homes are open year-round.

Mardi Gras Galveston is a popular annual event, and there's even a Mardi Gras museum (2211 Strand St., 409/763–1133). During the holidays, Galveston makes the most of the Victorian district with Dickens on the Strand, a sort of Mardi Gras in top hats and tails. Basically, it's a chance to drink and sing in the streets. Instead of crewes parading, actors dressed up like Tiny Tim and Scrooge and so on wander about being Christmasy. This God Bless Us, Everyone mood is hard to maintain when the temperature hits 80, but most of the paid performers and a surprising number of partiers manage to carry it off. Wise visitors book hotels and stay overnight. It's tough to drive all the way back to Houston after a full day or long evening of celebrating.

For more information on Galveston, call the convention and visitors bureau, 888/425–4753.

GEORGE RANCH

Part of a working ranch, the visitor areas of the George Ranch comprise a living history museum, and facilities and exhibits are dedicated to three main periods, the 1830s, 1890s, and 1930s. In addition to the displays, the ranch hosts a dozen events throughout the year, like Texian Market Days and Cowboy Christmas. The Jones Stock Farm, representing the 1830s, has a pioneer cabin complete with livestock and frequent demonstrations of daily chores. The Davis House, representing the 1890s, is a lavishly furnished Victorian mansion. A blacksmith shop, which is used for the ranch, is part of the Victorian complex. Contemporary ranch structures are used for the Depression-era exhibits. The ranch house, smokehouse, and other buildings offer a wealth of information about working cattle in the early days, and contain significant oral history contributions from African-American wranglers. Along with all this information about and illustrations of ranch life for the last 150 years, the George Ranch has a terrific, must-see tree house. The ranch is open daily 9–5, except New Year's Eve and Day, Thanksgiving Day, Christmas Eve, and Christmas. *10215 FM 762, Sugar Land/Fort Bend, 281/343–0218. Adults $7.50, children $4, seniors $6.50.*

MCFADDIN AND TEXAS POINT NATIONAL WILDLIFE REFUGES

This rough patch of swamp, too much ooze for one refuge, is not for first-time bird-watchers. Mud, bugs, and even snakes can cause trouble for the unwary. Properly attired (that is, wearing sturdy shoes and several coats of bug spray) and properly cautious visitors have the chance to see bobcats, gray foxes, mink, and river otters. There are also coyotes, and coyote–red wolf crosses, skulking through the brush. If you have a boat, bring it. If you don't, there are a few rental boats available. The refuges are adjacent to one another, about 90 mi east of Houston on Highway 87. The headquarters are on Clam Lake Road, 15 mi south of Port Arthur. *409/971–2909.*

SAN BERNARD WILDLIFE REFUGE

Proximity to Freeport, and all the petrochemical industries of that area, doesn't seem to bother the vast flocks of birds that live in or migrate through this 27,000-acre haven of scrub brush and marsh. Ducks and geese, including fulvous whistling-ducks and lesser snow geese, as well as all the familiar coastal wading birds, are easily found here. Fishing is allowed, and most of the Gulf Coast favorites are caught in the swampy waters of Cedar Lake and Cow Trap Lake. On land, keep an eye out for coyotes, ugly little nutria, and deer. Do be wary: the refuge is home to feral hogs and alligators, and if you are not Crocodile Hunter Steve, you do not want to get mixed up with those beasts. The soft light of dusk and dawn are prime times for wildlife-watching. Park management maintains a 3-mi self-guided tour around Moccasin Pond, and there are other trails and driving routes through the refuge. From the intersection of Highway 36 and FM 2611 in Brazoria County, take FM 2611 south for 4 mi to FM 2918, then drive 1 mi to County Road 306. Turn right and find the headquarters in 1 mi. *979/964–3639.*

SPACE CENTER HOUSTON

The 580-seat IMAX theater is not as big a draw as the archive footage from early training and missions. Skylab, man, it's still the bomb. Kids also rush right past interactive computer displays to ogle the giant Lego astronaut. Inside the main Space Center building, along with the aforementioned IMAX, other films, and computer toys, visitors can climb into the cockpit of a shuttle and touch an actual moon rock. There's also a tram tour of NASA, with occasional stops for trips inside the buildings, and the chance to see a Saturn V rocket. Summer hours are 9–7; winter hours are 10–7. Space Center Houston is closed Christmas day. *1601 NASA Rd. 1, Clear Lake/Bay Area, 281/244–2130. Adults $13.95, children $9.95, seniors $12.95.*

chapter 5

ARTS, ENTERTAINMENT & NIGHTLIFE

Houstonians can be staunch traditionalists, abiding by the teachings of quaint, down-home songs like "The Nightlife Ain't No Good Life, But It's My Life" or "I've Got Friends in Low Places." Space City or no, it's hard to drive more than 20 minutes in any direction without bumping into a real honky-tonk, like Blanco's, or a modern attempt such as Billy Blues BBQ and Grill.

However, if we've got the money, honey, we've just as likely got the time for fine arts. Houston dollars—and that's bucks largely from private citizens and corporations, not tax coffers—have built up our internationally renowned ballet, opera, and symphony. The Alley Theatre has developed shows that have made it to Broadway, and a variety of smaller theaters, like Stages Repertory Theater, enrich Houston's lively theater scene. Funky spots like the Little Room Downstairs complement the more traditional productions presented at Miller Outdoor Theatre and by touring bus and truck companies.

Although we've slowed down a bit since the days when Bill Hicks and Sam Kinison were honing their acts at the Comedy Workshop, Houston has several good comedy clubs, and the Arena Theater has almost monthly headline acts. If you're looking for low-cost entertainment, buckets of garage bands get rowdy at small clubs all over Houston, and ballroom dancers have practice nights in unlikely spots like Café Express.

performing arts

CHORAL AND CHAMBER GROUPS

The Sunday and Monday before June 19th, the Juneteenth Gospel Festival (713/284–8352) takes place at Miller Outdoor Theatre in Hermann Park and Sam Houston Park (*see* Parks *in* Chapter 4).

1 *f-4*

BAY AREA CHORUS

This Clear Lake–area nonprofit organization is a member of the Cultural Arts Council of Houston and Harris County. The all-volunteer chorus has been active since 1965, and eagerly welcomes area school and church chorus members to perform in their concerts. Pop standards, show tunes, and even contemporary easy listening are all in the Bay Area repertoire. 713/684–6030.

1 *c-4*

FORT BEND BOYS CHOIR

International competitions and hometown Christmas concerts at Jones Hall or a large church are always on the annual schedule, although the boys find time to sing in venues such as Westminster Abbey and Kennedy Center for the Performing Arts. Auditions come up twice a year. Boys as young as six can begin at Music Magic level. The Training Choir prepares boys for the Town Choir. Members of the Tour Choir have been through rigorous auditions. Boys whose voices change may join the Cantabile. 281/240–3800.

9 *e-2*

HOUSTON BOYS' CHOIR

Boys whose voices have not yet changed are invited to audition for this prestigious choir. Membership has its privileges, but parents should also note that it comes at a price—voice lessons aren't cheap. Boys 8 to 12 are the choir, and perform hymns, carols, and some light pop and show tunes. 5750 Bintliff, Sharpstown, 713/743–3398.

HOUSTON CHILDREN'S CHORUS

Children from throughout the city rehearse at several sites around town, and perform around the world. Traditional religious and classical choral works are performed, along with a wide variety of contemporary tunes. The choir offers scholarships to children whose families cannot pay the annual tuition. 713/529–8900.

HOUSTON MASTERWORKS CHORUS

Auditions are held throughout the year, but there are only 125 spots. With the help of volunteers (some of whom are hoping to pass an audition soon), generous sponsors, and frequent guest conductors, the singers rear back and belt out two or three oratorios annually; like most choirs, the group is familiar with Mendelssohn. 713/529–8900.

11 b-2

REVELS HOUSTON
Volunteer singers and backstage help organize early in the year to prepare for the annual Christmas concert. Revels is something like a Renaissance fair, except that they vary the period. Past revels have celebrated early American Christmas traditions, gypsy culture, and such diverse rituals as an exploration of Meso-American ways. Typically, the holiday event is held in the Moores Opera House at the University of Houston. 713/668–3303.

PERFORMANCE VENUES

13 b-3

AERIAL THEATER AT BAYOU PLACE
Houston's newest multiuse performance space can be arranged three ways: for general admission concerts, stage shows, and cabaret productions. Large touring shows often stop here on their way through Houston. 520 Texas, Downtown/Theater District, 713/ 230–1666.

10 c-1

COMPAQ CENTER
Big shows that come through town, from the indefatigable AC/DC to the latest boy band, usually play this arena. A full-house configuration, used for sports and a few concerts, has seating for 17,000 screaming fans and their glow sticks. Strong acts, that is, those who can set a higher ticket price, usually play in a proscenium configuration. For this, only seats facing toward the stage are used, and the area behind the stage is simply blocked off. Beloved acts, like Bette Midler, the circus, and skating shows perform in the Compaq Center. Typically, tickets go on sale through brokers like Ticketmaster first, and are available at the Compaq Center box office two or three days later. Compaq Center box office, 713/843–3995; Ticketmaster, 713/629–3700.

14 f-2

EDYTHE BATES OLD RECITAL HALL
Rice Shepard School of Music students and faculty perform throughout the year, and several concerts each year feature renowned organists from around the world. The massive and elegant organ was commissioned especially for this space, and its construction began in 1995. Extensive and detailed work to install and "tune" the organ took more than a year, and the process would fascinate engineers, musicians, and fans of the Discovery Channel. Although hard evidence is impossible to come by, musicologists are confident that this organ can reproduce the music of the 17th-, 18th-, and 19th-century organs. 6100 Main, Rice University Village, 713/348–4047.

14 f-2

HAMMAN HALL
Predating Stude Concert Hall, this intimate 500-seat theater is still used for Rice University student and faculty performances and also hosts other musical productions. 6100 Main, Rice University Village, 713/527–8101.

ARTS FOR KIDS

Looking toward the "audience of the future," many institutions have daytime entertainment for the small fry.

Da Camera
They go to the zoo, literally. There are short musical programs in the open air and what Da Camera calls an instrument petting zoo. Children are allowed to touch and hold violins, violas, and other instruments. See Orchestras & Ensembles.

Houston Ballet
The Nutcracker. Every Christmas they roll out this war horse for little girls in velvet dresses. See Dance.

Houston Grand Opera
Opera To Go performances are trimmed down and tightened up for younger audiences, and presented at schools throughout the city. To find out how to get a performance at your child's school, call 713/546–0231. See Opera.

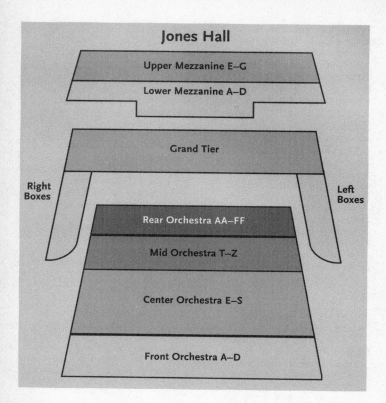

Jones Hall

Upper Mezzanine E–G

Lower Mezzanine A–D

Grand Tier

Right Boxes

Left Boxes

Rear Orchestra AA–FF

Mid Orchestra T–Z

Center Orchestra E–S

Front Orchestra A–D

9 *e-4*

HOUSTON ARENA THEATER
The original theater in the round, which looked something like a cement turtle, has been almost overwhelmed by office towers. Onstage, however, shows continue with Vegas acts like Joan Rivers and Don Rickles, African-American comedy tours, and high-profile concerts like Tom Jones and revered soul acts. *7326 Southwest Fwy., Sharpstown, 713/988–1020.*

13 *b-3*

JONES HALL
Even now, decades after the original construction, Jones Hall's special honeycomb ceiling provides stunning acoustics. Still the home of the Houston Symphony, the grand theater also hosts Society for the Performing Arts events and touring shows of all types. *615 Louisiana, Downtown/Theater District, 713/227–3974.*

14 *g-2*

MILLER OUTDOOR THEATRE
Here's the drill for covered seating: on the day of the performance, free tickets

for the 1,500 covered seats are released at 11:30 AM. On a first-come, first-served basis, people can pick up as many as four free tickets. Any ticket remaining after 1 PM will be offered again starting one hour before the performance. That's for covered seating. Up to 20,000 people can picnic on the hill. The annual Shakespeare Festival, a number of bus and truck shows, holiday celebrations (including Martin Luther King Day, Juneteenth, and Fourth of July concerts), and local musical theater groups like HITS Unicorn Theater and TUTS are all popular offerings. Local professionals, like HGO, the Houston Ebony Opera Guild, and Houston Symphony, also perform. Because of the hillside's strong slope, mud is rarely a problem. People typically tough it out through light rains. *100 Concert Dr., Hermann Park, Museum District, 713/284–8350.*

14 *f-2*

STUDE CONCERT HALL
Both students and faculty from Rice University Shepherd School of Music and visiting professionals perform in this well-appointed 1,000-seat hall. A

smaller theater, the Duncan Recital Hall, is in the same building. *6100 Main, Rice University Village, 713/348–4933.*

13 *b-2*

WORTHAM CENTER

The Brown and Cullen auditoriums comprise the Wortham Center, which is the home of the Houston Ballet, Houston Grand Opera, and Theater Under the Stars. The center itself has appeared as a set piece for cinema Sci Fi fantasies. Most of the performance center's $72 million dollars in construction funding came from individuals and Houston-based enterprises with civic pride. The elegant six-story lobby does not set the scale for the theaters. While the open lobby is designed to be a vast showcase, the plush red seats of the theaters are arranged for audience comfort. Whether in a box or nosebleed seat, patrons have unobstructed views and enjoy sterling acoustics. Tip: Save time between acts by pre-ordering intermission drinks or dinner. *500 Texas Ave., Downtown/Theater District, 713/237–1439.*

15 *g-1*

UNIVERSITY OF HOUSTON'S MOORES SCHOOL OF MUSIC ORGAN RECITAL HALL

Not exclusively reserved for student performances, the facility is also used for professional concerts and faculty recitals. *4800 Calhoun, East End, 713/743–3313.*

CONCERTS IN CHURCHES

14 *d-2*

CHRIST THE KING LUTHERAN CHURCH

The church's "Bach" organ was designed and built by the Noack Organ Company and is said to have the look, feel, and sound of an 18th-century Saxon organ. Each year, the church has a series of Bach vespers. *2353 Rice Blvd., Rice University Village, 713/523–2864.*

DANCE

companies

9 *g-5*

DISCOVERY DANCE GROUP

The millennium ushered in Discovery's 33rd year—a longevity that is quite an

accomplishment for a dance troupe. Pamela Ybarguen-Stockman, a long-time student and colleague of founder Camille Long Hill, has been the director since 1987. Movement and dance classes are offered for tiny tots, children over five, teenagers, and adults. Although offering a strong core of ballet, modern, and jazz-influenced work, the troupe also offers ethnic dance styles. *8434 Pontiac, Bellaire, 713/667–3416.*

13 *b-2*

HOUSTON BALLET

Principal dancer Lauren Anderson began her training at the Houston Ballet Academy when she was seven, joined the company in 1983, and now seems poised for superstardom. She's been a guest artist throughout the world. In 1999, choreographer David Rousseve created a work for her, and in March 2000 she danced the title role in Ben Stevenson's production of Cleopatra. Artistic director Ben Stevenson, an Englishman with a background in both classic storybook-style ballet and musical theater, has developed native-Houstonian Anderson and the ballet with the same sure vision. The Houston Ballet has an international reputation (it was the first American company invited to tour China) built on a foundation of traditional ballets and inventive works such as "Second Before the Ground," choreographed by Stevenson protégé Trey McIntyre. The Wortham Center is the ballet's home, although they sometimes do special performances in other venues. *550 Prairie, Downtown/Theater District, 713/535–3230.*

9 *g-6*

WEAVE DANCE COMPANY

Dance events and festivals in Houston typically provide a showcase for this lively all-female company. The dancers are Texas-bred, and when not performing original works at the Kaplan (*see* Festivals, *below*) or breast cancer benefits, most teach at Houston programs. *713/526–6884.*

festivals

9 *g-6*

DANCE MONTH AT THE KAPLAN

The JCC hosts an impressive selection of national and international companies in March. Many of the choreographers also lead workshops and master classes during their stay. *Jewish Community Center, 5601 S. Braeswood Blvd., Meyerland, 713/551–7255.*

FILM

theaters & programs

`13` *b-2*

ANGELIKA FILM CENTER

A mix of art films and mainstream movies are shown in this eight-screen cinema in Bayou Place. Après-flick cocktails can be had at the Angelika Café. *510 Texas Ave., Downtown/Theater District, 713/225–5232.*

`7` *f-2*

AURORA PICTURE SHOW

Houston's thriving microcinema has twice-monthly evenings for low- and no-budget film and video and renowned experimental films. *800 Aurora, Heights, 713/868–2101.*

`14` *g-1*

BROWN AUDITORIUM (MUSEUM OF FINE ARTS, HOUSTON)

The film program must support itself (it is the only MFAH curatorial program that must stay in the black), but the bottom line never compromises the repertory program. Regional premiers and celebrity events are common. *1001 Bissonnet, Museum District, 713/639–7300.*

`10` *c-1*

LANDMARK GREENWAY 3

Patrons filling the 800 seats in these three underground theaters may not be in the newest or fanciest seats, but the sight lines are terrific, and odds are your local plex isn't featuring the indies and imports on screen. *5 E. Greenway Plaza, Greenway Plaza, 713/626–0402.*

`12` *d-4*

LANDMARK RIVER OAKS 3

Original deco details remain in the main auditorium, but both upper screening rooms (once the balcony) are smaller and more modern. Patrons enjoy independent and foreign films and suitably avant-garde concessions. *2009 W. Gray, River Oaks, 713/524–2175.*

`14` *e-2*

RICE MEDIA CENTER

The media center was founded at the end of the '60s by Jean and Dominique de Menil and continues under the auspices of Rice University. Inventive film programming includes premiers and repertory cinema and appearances by filmmakers. *2100 University Blvd., Museum District, 713/348–4853.*

festivals

`1` *a-1*

BLOWIN' UP A SPOT!

Producer Angela Willamston, also a regional producer for Def Poetry Jam, curates a program of short films by, mostly for, and about women. African-American, other minority, and lesbian voices are emphasized, although the festival does not exclude any female experience. Spoken work artists appear at the festival. For information, call 713/220–9395. The program takes place the first weekend of October at the Angelika Film Center.

`14` *g-1*

HOUSTON PAN-CULTURAL FILM FESTIVAL

Ancestral Films Inc. artistic director Mohammed Kamara brings a couple dozen films, usually from a specific region or culture, to the Museum of Fine Arts in early February. Filmmakers and actors give talks during the festival. In 1998, when the festival was devoted to Latin works of the '70s, '80s, and early '90s, Edward James Olmos was a guest. For more information, call Ancestral Films Inc. (713/527–9548).

HOUSTON GAY AND LESBIAN FILM FESTIVAL

Spanning two weeks and across the city, a rich and diverse selection of short and feature-length films are eagerly attended by gays and lesbians and their friends. Screenings are at both of the Landmark Theatres, the Angelika Film Center, the Museum of Fine Arts, Rice University Media Center, DiverseWorks, and the Aurora Picture Show. Filmmakers appear at many screenings, and others have discussions and panel groups in conjunction with the film. It's held the last week of May and the first week of June. For information, or if you want to volunteer to work on the parade float, e-mail hglff@swamp.org.

OPERA

13 *b-2*

HOUSTON GRAND OPERA

Many cities have opera. Few cities see outdoor bleacher seating packed hours in advance, but that's what happens when an HGO Plazacast broadcasts the opera to an audience on Fish Plaza. Three thousand people see each Plazacast performance from the bleachers, and many more watch from the steps of Bayou Place. Houston audiences aren't the only ones to queue up for HGO. Since its founding in 1955, Houston Grand Opera has had 24 world premieres, such as Nixon in China and Treemonisha. Under the guidance of director David Gockley, HGO continues to bring innovation and build on traditions in opera. Children who can't be expected to sit through even the finest production of Wagner's Tristan and Isolde are delighted by Opera to Go!, a touring program that introduces opera to local students. The season at Wortham Center runs from October through May. *510 Preston, Suite 700, Downtown/Theater District, 713/546–0200.*

7 *f-3*

HOUSTON EBONY OPERA GUILD

The guild has long been a strong and exquisitely trained voice in the African-American community. A handful of performances are offered each year and are keenly anticipated by opera and music fans from all social strata. *713/529–7664.*

3 *e-3*

OPERA IN THE HEIGHTS

Several professional-quality performances are mounted each year. *Lambert Hall, Heights Christian Church, 17th and Heights Blvd., Heights, 713/861–5303.*

ORCHESTRAS & ENSEMBLES

Several area schools and universities have worthwhile concert schedules offering both variety and high-quality performances for a few bucks, or even for free. For schedules and ticket information, contact High School for the Performing and Visual Arts (713/942–1960); Houston Community College System (713/718–6000); St. Thomas University (713/525–3520); Rice University Shepherd School (713/348–4854); University of Houston Moores School of Music (713/743–3009).

performing groups

DA CAMERA

Artistic director Sarah Rothenberg programs lively seasons of chamber music with stimulating themes (such as surrealism) to illustrate and explore the cultural and political attitudes influencing composers. There are also Da Camera programs in collaboration with a who's who of Houston music, including jazz artist and educator Noe Marmolejo. Da Camera shows civic pride with "A Little Day Music," free lunchtime concerts in the Wortham foyer, "Da Camera Goes to the Zoo" Saturday afternoon performances, and educational performances and programs. Da Camera also tours extensively, and Rothenberg works on other projects. (Tip: occasionally, when Da Camera performs in the Menil foyer, it's possible to hear the performance outside, in the scent of magnolias.) *713/524–7601.*

HOUSTON CIVIC SYMPHONY

The Houston Civic Symphony is a largely volunteer-run, community orchestra offering music lovers a lower-cost alternative to the Houston Symphony and providing musicians the opportunity to perfect their skills and perform. During the symphony's more than 30 seasons, they have performed in a variety of auditoriums, always looking for inexpensive and convenient houses. *713/747–0018.*

13 *b-3*

HOUSTON SYMPHONY ORCHESTRA

The Houston Symphony has existed in some form or another since 1913. The first half of the symphony's history saw a number of conductors, but when Leopold Stokowski arrived in 1955, the symphony came into its own. Following his successful tenure was that of Sir John Barbirolli, André Previn, and others who further developed the orchestra—

and Houston's taste for both the classics and modern music. Christoph Eschenbach arrived in 1988, and during his decade the symphony became the institution we know today: a full symphony orchestra and chamber group who record widely, tour, and perform around 200 concerts a year, including pops and holiday concerts. Mondays are the cheap nights, and there are occasional opportunities to attend rehearsals. Jones Hall is the home of the symphony, but throughout the year there are also concerts at Cynthia Woods Mitchell Pavilion and other venues. *713/224–4240.*

music festivals

11 *b-2*
IMMANUEL AND HELEN OLSHAN TEXAS MUSIC FESTIVAL
Each June for the last decade, nascent professional musicians, including UH and A&M students, enjoy a four-week residency program at the UH Moores School of Music. During this program, public concerts featuring residents, faculty, Houston Symphony musicians, and artists brought in to teach master classes are held. For information, call 713/743–3167 or e-mail tmf@uh.edu.

THEATER

13 *e-1*
ATOMIC CAFÉ
Productions here are always energetic and frequently excellent. Both brand spanking new plays (in some cases, not quite finished until the afternoon before opening night) and standards like Little Shop of Horrors have been fully realized in this frisky theater. *1320 Nance, Downtown/Theater District, 713/222–2866.*

13 *d-1*
DIVERSEWORKS
Houston's most ardently alternative performance space provides a venue for touring artists and local talent. The recent Downtown boom has been a boon to this often-overlooked gallery and performance space. *1117 East Fwy., Downtown/Theater District, 713/223–8346.*

companies

14 *b-1*
ACTORS THEATRE OF HOUSTON
After a couple of decades, fans of well-wrought drama are resigned to the rather awkward seating arrangements here. Founder Chris Wilson is said to be the best acting coach in town, and she could, if she chose, cite former students such as Janeane Garofalo. *2506 South Blvd., Rice University Village, 713/348–6606.*

12 *b-7*
A. D. PLAYERS
Each year sees an original play from the pen of the redoubtable Jeanette Clift George, and the seasons are completed with a selection of both family-oriented and frankly religious shows. Shortly before January 2000, the theater expanded its parking lot, making it easy for the company's many fans to park. Some nights, the A. D. hosts improv Christian comedy. *2710 W. Alabama, Upper Kirby District, 713/526–2721.*

13 *b-2*
ALLEY THEATRE
Several large-stage productions, such as Jekyll & Hyde, have gone on to be national touring shows. The annual Christmas show is always popular, and the Alley's reputation and budget attract guest stars such as Ellen Burstyn and various Redgraves. Of course, the real draw is a local star: Houston diva Annalee Jefferies, an Alley resident and veteran of 14 seasons. The only caution for Houston's most professional theater is this: comedies usually don't come off well. *615 Texas, Downtown/Theater District, 713/228–8421.*

3 *d-6*
THE COMPANY ONSTAGE
Another theater that managed to survive after the oil boom ended, this nonprofit rarely strays from standard community theater fare. *536 Westbury Sq., Southwest, 713/726–1219.*

13 *a-6*
ENSEMBLE THEATRE
This black-owned professional theater provides Houstonians with an education in African-American theater history. The Ensemble mounts vital productions of classic and contempo-

rary theater, along with recent works. *3535 Main, Downtown/Theater District, 713/520–0055.*

INFERNAL BRIDEGROOM PRODUCTIONS

Genuinely a gypsy company, the troupe brings a rowdy spirit to its collaborations with well-known directors. Productions have been held in warehouses, abandoned shopping centers, at Stages Theatre, and DiverseWorks. *713/522–8443.*

14 b-1

THE LITTLE ROOM DOWNSTAIRS

Intimate (seating 30, max) and always fun, the Little Room is a delightful addition to the Houston theater scene. A drag take on Mae West's Sex, Clive Barker's Frankenstein in Love, and My Night With Reg have had successful runs here. *2326 Bissonnet, Rice University Village, 713/523–0791.*

14 b-3

MAIN STREET THEATER

When Rebecca Udden founded the company in 1975, it was housed in the Episcopal Diocese's Autry House on Main Street. In 1981, the nonprofit moved to its current home. Each season sees a mix of classics (like Julius Caesar and works of Aphra Behn), contemporary drama and comedy, and, of course, children's theater. *2540 Time Blvd., Rice University Village, 713/524–3622.*

12 g-8

MAIN STREET THEATER— CHELSEA MARKET

To the surprise of many, Main Street Theater artistic director Rebecca Udden's decision to open a second theater in a large, defunct comedy club housed in what may have been Houston's only failing shopping center was a good idea. This is one of Houston's most comfortable venues. *4617 Montrose, Montrose, 713/524–6706.*

12 e-3

STAGES REPERTORY THEATER

Rob Bundy, brought in during the '90s, has done a great deal to revitalize the theater. The offering includes a fine mix of local works, recent off-Broadway hits, and contemporary classics. Subscribers seem more than willing to attend the

more experimental works, and local playwright Rob Nash may owe his career to Stages' support. *3201 Allen Pkwy., River Oaks, 713/527–8243.*

7 g-5

THEATER LAB

Surprisingly good parking makes it easy for suburbanites to enjoy the inventive programming of this small, adventurous inner-city theater. *1706 Alamo, Heights, 713/868–7516.*

2 d-2

THEATRE LENZ & CO.

This suburban community theater will not put on any plays you haven't heard of (in fact, you may well have seen the movie), but the 300-seat auditorium and thrust stage offer the neighborhood a pleasant live-entertainment option. *3337 FM 1960 W, FM 1960 area, 281/397–9067.*

9 e-1

THEATRE SOUTHWEST

Although the 40-year-old community theater devotes most of its season to tried and true Broadway hits of the last 20 years, the annual playwrights' festival offers a showcase for local writers. *8944 Clarkcrest St., Richmond Strip, 713/977–6028.*

7 c-1

THEATRE SUBURBIA

Modest charm and not inconsiderable talent are the hallmarks of this venerable community theater. *1410 W. 43rd St., North, 713/682–3525.*

THEATER UNDER THE STARS (TUTS)

TUTS, although long performing inside under Fresnels instead of the stars, is Houston's source for lively musicals. *800/678–5440.*

festivals

15 g-1

CHILDREN'S THEATER FESTIVAL

This summer festival usually has three one-hour plays, and each play is on stage for close to a month, with weekend and some weekday performances. Traditional tales and original works are presented. *University of Houston, Lyndall*

Finley Wortham Theatre, Entrance 16 off
Cullen Blvd., 713/743–2929.

7 g-5

HOUSTON FRINGE THEATER FESTIVAL

Gerry LaBita and his cohorts at Theater LaB produced the first Houston Fringe Festival in 1997, making Houston one of the cities holding a sister event to the internationally renowned Edinburgh Fringe Festival. Houston's first fringe and subsequent festivals showcased the frisky, aggressive spirit that characterizes Theater LaB productions. Like main-stage productions, the festival shows are almost always Houston or even American premieres. It's held in May and June. *1706 Alamo, Heights, 713/868–7516.*

14 g-2

HOUSTON SHAKESPEARE FESTIVAL

The University of Houston School of Theater stages two plays each August at Miller Outdoor Theatre, and on occasion actors must wear traditional Shakespearian garb. Don't worry though, there are air-conditioning vents in the stage floor, blowing cold air up onto the actors. The audience on the hill keeps cool with hand-held fans and whatever they have in their Igloos. Pets are permitted, glass containers are not. *713/284–8352.*

TICKETS

HOUSTON TICKET CENTER

Many fine arts companies, such as the Houston Ballet, use the Houston Ticket Center. Tickets may be purchased in person at Ticketmaster outlets, but you can only charge by phone through the Houston Ticket Center. Bonus: the hold message is useful with downtown traffic reports, weather, and other updates. *713/227–2787.*

TICKET ATTRACTIONS

Get good seats for sports, concerts, and more from a bonded broker. *800/256–4163.*

TICKETMASTER

All tickets, all the time. Charge by phone from anywhere. Face-to-face transactions are available at many venue box offices and at many Foley's, Randall's, and Fiesta stores. Arts event tickets can be purchased at any Ticketmaster outlet, but can only be charged by phone through Houston Ticket Center. *713/629–3700.*

nightlife

In accordance with marketing tradition, live music venues often advertise showtimes as 7 or 7:30 PM when the reality is that very few bands are onstage before 9 (all the better for the bar to sell more beverages as bandgoers wait patiently). Be aware, too, of bar time. Frequently, if you see a clock on the wall at your watering hole, it has been set 10 minutes fast so last call can be taken care of well before it becomes a legal issue. All drinks off the table means just that, so don't give the waitress a hard time. Most clubs will call a cab for you if you don't have a designated driver and need one. Cover charges range from $2 to $20, depending on the caliber of the band and the night of the week. Advance tickets are available at the more popular live music venues.

BARS AND LOUNGES

If you're not from Texas, you might not be familiar with the bar description of ice house. Back in the "good old days," an ice house once stored ice—and happened to sell beer, thanks to the handy place it had to keep the beverages cold. The house is a low, thick-walled building, usually with long porch eves in front, so that no flicker of sun can get through the door. Most of the beverage service in today's ice houses is in this porch area, and at picnic tables on the property, even though the buildings themselves are no longer full of ice. A real ice house serves, at best, a dozen beers.

12 *e-4*

AQUARIUM LOUNGE

Once upon a time a dive in the shadow of Downtown, this funky old bar now hugs the curb between two large, lot-filling ugly buildings. Continuing gentrification of the neighborhood does not seem to be a threat to the mecca of cheap beer and Elvis memorabilia. *3322 Dallas, River Oaks, 713/528–1592.*

2 *e-3*

AVIATOR'S PUB

Don't worry—despite its proximity to the airport, this is not where pilots come to drink before takeoff. This is where the clock-punchers who run the airport and area businesses go after their shifts. *2738 Greens Rd., North, 281/442–3936.*

10 *a-2*

BUBBA'S TEXAS BURGER SHACK

A crude wooden sign, one of many crude wooden features at Bubba's, proudly, albeit in uneven letters, proclaims that this is an icehouse. Technically, this is not true. The rickety wooden building isn't even properly air-conditioned, let alone designed for cool. In spirit, however, this burger joint may be the finest neighborhood bar in all of Houston. After a tiring trip through the aisles of nearby Home Depot, the well-heeled of Bellaire and West U stop in. And, after a long day of repairing the "home improvements" attempted by homeowners, contract laborers also stop in. All gather on the wooden deck of this feeder-road bar to enjoy the unremarkable view of some warehouses and canned beer. Why? No one knows. We just go. *5230 Westpark Dr.., Galleria Post Oak, 713/661–1622.*

7 *f-5*

CHARLIE'S POOL HALL

Actually, Charlie's Pool Hall is a low-key bar with live music. The term pool hall merely indicates that management makes an effort to keep the felt in good shape and provide unwarped bar cues. *2225 Katy Fwy., Katy/Bear Creek, 281/395–5222.*

9 *g-1*

DAVE & BUSTERS

Basically a Chuck E Cheese for adults, this 24,000-square-ft funplex has a complete restaurant, several full bars, a dance floor, and seemingly acres of video games, Skee ball, and other cheap thrills. *6010 Richmond, Richmond Strip, 713/952–2233.*

12 *c-8*

DAVENPORT

The stock of top-drawer scotches (more than three dozen) and sleek Sinatra-era furniture suggest that this club was supposed to be a theme place. However, it's just a comfortable and popular neighborhood bar. *2115 Richmond, Montrose, 713/520–1140.*

14 *b-1*

KAY'S LOUNGE

People liked Ike when this place opened, and Elvis may very well be hiding in one of the darker corners. Low yellow lights and painted windows provide a 24-hour gloom, and it's possible that the electricity saved on lighting is used to keep the beer coolers working at peak coldness. *2324 Bissonnet, Rice University Village, 713/528–9858.*

12 *c-7*

LITTLE WOODROW'S NEIGHBORHOOD

There is a real Woodrow's, and it is a real icehouse, but this most recent offshoot is merely a friendly saloon with an icehouse attitude. *2301 W. Alabama, Montrose, 713/529–0449.*

12 *f-5*

LOLA'S DEPOT

Not the hipster haven it once was, Lola's nonetheless continues in dim instead of nonexistent lighting and faux finishes instead of grubby graffiti. *2327 Grant, Montrose, 713/528–8342.*

12 *d-4*

MARFRELESS

Notorious for very public displays of affection (what some might term animal urges unbridled), this quiet little hideaway is actually not a bad place for a nice glass of wine with friends. (The blue door under the stairs is unmarked. If you can't find it, ask at the River Oaks box office). *2006 Peden, River Oaks, 713/528–0083.*

12 *f-6*

MAUSOLEUM

When this Goth spot opened, few would have bet on such a long life for the narrow bar. Beating the odds, the club continues, with some nights devoted to the music of Robert Smith, others to open-mike poetry, and always with an open bar and plenty of coffee drinks. Belly dancing is a regular entertainment. *411 Westheimer, Montrose, 713/526–4648.*

7 *a-1*

ROLL-N SALOON

This old-style, smoky, stale-peanuts bar offers a fine history lesson to balance Nick at Nite's sterilized version of the fabulous '50s. In the '50s, people smoked, drank hard liquor, and worried about the horrors of the future. At the Roll-N, they still do. *4200 San Felipe, Galleria/Post Oak, 713/877–0187.*

9 *h-1*

SAM'S BOAT/SAM'S PLACE

For all intents and purposes, this is one bar, and a busy bar at that. With the look

of an icehouse and prices to match, this loud and lively place is often the first stop on Friday and Saturday nights. *5720 Richmond, Richmond Strip, 713/781–2628.*

7 *f-3*

SHILOH CLUB

Possibly, the club part of the name dates back to the days when "dry" neighborhoods could bend the rules with private clubs. In any case, that's certainly the feel at this old-time neighborhood bar. *1321 Studewood, Heights, 713/869–8354.*

12 *c-7*

T K BITTERMAN'S

Mysteriously decorated in contemporary Chicago Cubs with touches of White Sox memorabilia and one large boat paddle, Bitterman's is known as a media-type hangout, the home of a great martini, and a beloved neighborhood bar. To avoid leaving after happy hour, many patrons make a meal of bar pizza and peanuts. *2010 W. Alabama, Montrose, 713/529–8979.*

14 *b-1*

TIMBERWOLF PUB

Pub by name and not by nature, the Timberwolf has a Nanook of the North decor and vast beer selection. The same marketing research team who decked out the bar in early Eskimo was also careful to stock the bar with bellinis or cosmopolitans and whatever else the in-crowd is said to be sipping. *2511 Bissonnet, Rice University Village, 713/526–1705.*

14 *c-1*

VOLCANO

Loud, crowded, and with a fair number of TVs, this bar makes no effort to be anything but ordinary. Patrons drink, watch sports, mingle, and cruise, drawn in by no other theme than "we serve alcohol." The non-formula has enduring success in a neighborhood where other bars are part of a chain or watering holes with contrived concepts. *2349 Bissonnet, Rice University Village, 713/526–5282.*

13 *c-3*

WARREN'S INN

Warren himself is long gone, and this is not the original building (that's now rubble under the parking lot across Market Square), but Warren's is still a drinker's bar. It is not designed for conversation or for meeting people. From the coasters (squares of indoor-outdoor carpet) to the uninspiring beer and wine selection, this place is about the business of liquor. *307 Travis, Downtown/ Theater District, 713/247–9207.*

9 *g-2*

WOODIE'S ICE HOUSE

Despite being in the shadow of the Galleria, this little icehouse is so authentic that reality-based cop shows use it for reenactments. Woodie's has stood in for bars in every town in Texas where a former cheerleader was murdered. Producers figure, why drive out to the sticks and put the crew up in a roach motel when you can shoot realistic bubba footage within walking distance of nice hotels. *2806 Greenridge Dr., Galleria/Post Oak, 713/974–1131.*

9 *h-1*

WOODROW'S

Baskets of burgers and fries and buckets of cold beer put Woodrow's on the map. When you feel the need for longnecks and onion rings, Woodrow's is there for you. *Chimney Rock Rd., Galleria/Post Oak, 713/784–2653.*

BLUES

7 *c-2*

BIG DOGZ ICEHOUSE

Even if there isn't live music when you go, there will be an authentic atmosphere. *2307 Ella Blvd., Heights, 713/880–3765.*

9 *g-1*

BILLY BLUES BBQ & GRILL

Trendoid elements such as a gift shop notwithstanding, this is, in fact, an excellent source of both live blues music and barbecue. *6025 Richmond, Richmond Strip, 713/266–9294.*

7 *f-2*

DAN ELECTRO'S GUITAR BAR

See Pop/Rock, below.

15 *d-3*

ETTA'S LOUNGE

Most bands play the blues and most patrons couldn't be happier. Frankly, few establishments on Earth work harder to

take care of their customers. *5120 Scott St., Medical Center, 713/528–2611.*

4 *d-3*

SHAKESPEARE PUB

More proof that the strip center is Houston's most important type of architecture, this modest club offers quality blues (along with zydeco and country) and a reasonable selection of beers. *14129 Memorial, Memorial/Spring Branch, 281/497–4625.*

BREWPUBS & MICROBREWERIES

14 *d-2*

BANK DRAFT BREWING COMPANY

In a modest and decidedly not snobby way, this establishment is a haven for true beer lovers. Along with the Bank Draft's own brews, the bar offers an extensive menu of bottled and draft beers. The look and feel is small-town café, but if you want to eat, ask the bartender for a take-out menu and order from Antone's or other nearby eateries. *2424 Dunstan, Rice University Village, 713/ 522–6258.*

2 *d-3*

HUEY'S

A big American flag flapping outside and feisty brew names, like Double Eagle Gold and Copperhead Red, inside are just a few examples of the good ol' boy pride rampant at this North Houston watering hole. Brewmasters regularly turn out two or three beers, including a brew that's not only pale but actually "light" in the "lite" sense. Seasonal specials round out the beverage menu. *15335 North Fwy., North, 281/ 875–2260.*

14 *d-3*

TWO ROWS

For mysterious reasons, this brewery set up shop across the street from the Gingerman. For even more mysterious reasons, proximity to one of Houston's most popular beer joints has not been a problem. Tidier, a bit more . . . prissy than your average beer barn, Two Rows has a respectable selection of dark beers and, for the teetotalers, a root beer. *2400 University Blvd., Rice University Village, 713/529–2739.*

CABARET

`12` *b-7*

RADIO MUSIC THEATER
See Comedy, *below.*

CIGAR BARS

`13` *c-3*

THE MERCURY ROOM
A very elegant staircase from slightly before the Jazz Age and extraordinary blond wood accents provide the perfect backdrops for sweet young things showing off. Those enjoying the view can order champagne and caviar (Beluga, Oscetra, or Sevruga), or slip away to the smaller downstairs bar and puff a selection from the well-stocked humidor. *1008 Prairie, Downtown/Theater District, 713/225–6372.*

`10` *b-1*

RINGSIDE AT SULLIVAN'S
Upstairs from the steak house, this intimate club offers live music (usually jazz), a full bar, and fine stogies. *4608 Westheimer, River Oaks, 713/961–0333.*

COMEDY

`2` *f-7*

COMEDY SHOWCASE
Weekend shows feature regional favorites and big names on national tours. *12547 Gulf Fwy., South Houston/Hobby Airport area, 281/481–1188.*

`13` *c-3*

COMEDY SPORTS
All-improv shows pit the comics against each other, and even the audience teams against each other in a fast-paced interactive show. *315 Travis (Treebeards, upstairs), Downtown/Theater District, 713/868–1444.*

`9` *d-2*

JUS' JOKIN'
Many shows see a capacity crowd (500) with a very good time had by all. This African-American comedy club attracts both national acts, like Dolomite, and young hopefuls. Note: shows are not scheduled every week. *9344 Richmond, Sharpstown, 713/975–7262.*

`2` *c-3*

LAFF SPOT COMEDY CAFÉ
Raised booths comprise the back rows of the 300-seat showroom so that everyone has a good view of the stage. On that stage, you'll see classic stars like Rich Hall and Emo Phillips and comers fresh from their first Letterman appearance. *17776 Tomball Pkwy., FM 1960 area, 281/955–9200.*

`12` *d-4*

LAFF STOP
A-list comics like Dave Attell, Mitch Hedberg, and Brian Regan are regular headliners, and the opening acts come from owner Mark Babbitt's stable of local talent. Monday is open mike, Wednesday's late show is often a showcase for locals, like Bryan Hurzie and Joanie Coyote, and the club hosts reviews like Bosco's, the Whiskey Brothers, and Brassy Broads. Occasionally, the club has an after-hours all-blues review. *1952 W. Gray, River Oaks, 713/524–2333.*

`12` *b-7*

RADIO MUSIC THEATER
Steve Farrell and wife Vicki were cofounders of the legendary Comedy Workshop. There they wrote the first of the Fertle Family sketches that are now part of Houston tradition. The Farrells and their costar, Rich Mills, create dozens of characters for each original musical. Shows usually run for two or three months, and reservations are required (weeks in advance for the annual Fertle Family holiday show). *2623 Colquitt, Upper Kirby District, 713/522–7722.*

COUNTRY & WESTERN

`12` *a-7*

BLANCO'S
Novices should not expect to learn new steps on the dance floor, not in the middle of the headliner's set. The dance floor is packed with pros. If you can't keep up, watch from the sidelines. (You can polish your moves early in the evening to recorded music.) *3406 W. Alabama, Upper Kirby District, 713/439–0072.*

2 *f-2*

BLUE ANGEL NITE CLUB
Nothing says country like red, white, and blue patriotism—something this dance hall has in spades. The name is homage to the Navy fliers. *19333 Hwy. 59 N, North, 281/548–2884.*

1 *e-5*

EDDIE'S COUNTRY BALLROOM
All ages enjoy this big ol' barn. Toddlers wobble around the edge of the dance floor, fierce white-haired couples twirl in perfect time at the center, and starry-eyed youth slip off to snuggle in the shadows. *Off FM 1128, Brazoria County, 281/489–8181.*

3 *a-2*

TEXAS HONKY TONK
Tuesday, of all things, is a big dance night here. Perhaps an early and mid-week emphasis on fancy footwork is best, because the weekend shot specials might handicap your style. *5406 Hwy. 6 N, North, 713/463–0820.*

2 *b-3*

TIN HALL
Although run by the same family since 1890, this dance hall has gone through some changes. Originally a giant pole barn for dancing, the entertainment complex now has 4,400 square ft of dance hall space throughout a 24,000-square-ft, two-story party complex. *14800 Huffmeister Rd., Cy-Fair, 713/664–7450.*

DANCE CLUBS

10 *a-1*

CITY STREETS
Instead of cruising from bar to bar, the singles-night theme-park that is City Streets allows you to simply roam from room to room when you want to change bars. The country and western room is often the most popular. *5078 Richmond, Galleria/Post Oak, 713/529–3956.*

12 *h-5*

CLUB SOME
This after-hours club opens at 1 AM Wednesday through Sunday. There are several major rooms representing a variety of subgenres and attitudes so anyone up late can find a stage for their

look. Note to the ladies: this is not the best neighborhood, especially around 4 AM. Have someone walk you to your car. *2700 Albany, Montrose, 713/520–3956.*

12 *b-8*

JAMAICA JAMAICA
Neighboring businesses, including bars and clubs, have done their best to find some sort of ruling or ordinance by which this beloved nightspot can be shut down. So far, no dice, which is good news to the hundreds of high-spirited youth who build their weeks around Jamaica Jamaica. *2631 Richmond, Upper Kirby District, 713/529–8800.*

9 *g-1*

MAX'S 2001 CLUB
Perhaps the modern-day equivalent of a cotillion, this polite singles spot features Top 40 from the '70s, '80s, and '90s, with the '80s best represented. Some nights feature live music, but you will never, ever see a stage dive. Jeans are not allowed, especially on men. Max's has a quiet patio for cocktails. *2630 Augusta, Galleria/Post Oak, 713/781–8838.*

13 *c-3*

METROPOL
Although not the first Houston establishment to use the name Metropol, it seems to be the most successful. This very grownup dance club occasionally sees after-concert parties. *804 Fannin, Downtown/Theater District, 713/237–1505.*

9 *g-1*

POLLY ESTHER'S
On the average weekend, any number of cute women convince their boyfriends and dates that it would be "fun" to shake booty at this '70s and '80s retro club. The music and decor celebrate Sherwood Schwartz sit-coms and disco. *6111 Richmond, Richmond Strip, 713/972–1970.*

13 *a-5*

RICH'S
See Gay & Lesbian Bars & Clubs, *below.*

9 *f-1*

SHOCK
Billed as a radioactive dance factory, Shock offers a variety of lighting effects, TV screens, and DJs who have never really gotten past their Madonna phase.

The dress code does allow jeans, but men need to wear loafers, lace-ups, or boots. Oversized and torn clothing are also verboten. *6367 Richmond, Richmond Strip, 713/978–7673.*

13 c-2
SPY
It's difficult to guess how much money and time went into the vivid, half-retro half-futuristic decor of the club bars and dance floors, and yet the best feature of the club is a large patio overlooking Downtown. The drink of the moment is first poured at Spy. You might also see celebrities. Bill Murray and Michael Jordan, for instance, have been spotted here. *112 Travis, Downtown/Theater District, 713/225–2229.*

13 c-3
TONIC
Hmmm . . . is it a good thing or a bad thing to tuck a disco into the historic Sweeney Coombs building? The dance and lounge areas take up two floors and have been fitted out in the latest luxe finishings. Although there is a dance floor, the club can seem like a boy's club. *310 Main, Downtown/Theater District, 713/228–7978.*

DINING & DANCING

12 d-4
BIRRAPORETTI'S
The restaurant has a large dance floor that sees a lot of use on big band nights. There is also a jazz brunch on Sunday. *1997 W. Gray, River Oaks, 713/529–9191.*

9 g-1
ELVIA'S CANTINA
You can merengue, and do the cha-cha, and, oh, so much more. Professional introductory lessons are offered Wednesday evening. Learn mostly, but not exclusively, Latin moves. *2727 Fondren, Richmond Strip, 713/266–9631.*

ECLECTIC

13 c-3
NOTSUOH
Eclectic is a generous term for this odd Downtown nightspot. Many nights, the only entertainment is moldering board games, conversation, and herb tea. Other nights, there may be dance, film, theater, or enterprising panhandlers to stimulate the intellect. *314 Main, Downtown/Theater District, 713/222–0443.*

FOLK & ACOUSTIC

12 f-5
ANDERSON FAIR
It was alternative country back when alternative country was, elsewhere, called "folk." The club is dark and can be a bit unfriendly to the first-time patron, but the respect for music (which nurtured talents such as Lyle Lovett and Nanci Griffith) is pure. If your friends don't like acoustic, don't take them here. To the nonfan, the small, tile-floor, low-ceilinged showroom looks and feel exactly like an elementary school classroom. *2007 Grant, Montrose, 713/528–8576.*

7 f-5
FITZGERALD'S
Punk, rock, and straight-up country acts have been on the funky wooden stage over the years, but this big-frame building is best known for nights like an all-acoustic show with Joe Ely and Jeff Healy, or rousing polka concerts with Brave Combo. The dance hall is very down home and constantly rumored to be doomed. *2706 White Oak, Heights, 713/862–7580.*

12 c-8
MCGONIGEL'S MUCKY DUCK
The interior is styled as an English club, the food (and there is a full menu) and drink comprise an English pub theme park, and the musical calendar is a mix of folk, country, and Celtic. A dart room off to the side and a rear patio offer quiet places for conversation. *2425 Norfolk, Upper Kirby District, 713/528–5999.*

GAY & LESBIAN BARS & CLUBS

12 g-5
611 HYDE PARK
This friendly spot is for men mostly, but lesbians are more than welcome. Hyde Park is known for outdoor cookouts. *611 Hyde Park, Montrose, 713/526–7070.*

`12` f-7

GALLERY BAR
Cowgirls kick up their heels, especially on Saturday night. *903 Richmond, Montrose, 713/523–4227.*

`12` g-5

JR'S
With something of a Miss Kitty decor, the main club is friendly and has a variety of lounging, dancing, watching, and cruising areas so you can drift around and cater to your mood. The bartenders, by the way, mix a beautiful sea breeze. *808 Pacific, Montrose, 713/521–2519.*

`12` f-6

MARY'S LOUNGE
Small, not fancy, and populated with drab bar stools and pool tables, Mary's is nonetheless an institution. If Archie Bunker were gay, this is the type of bar he'd go to. *1022 Westheimer, Montrose, 713/527–9669.*

`12` g-5

MONTROSE MINING COMPANY
Many Montrose establishments boast of being for gays and lesbians and their friends. This is not one of them. Lesbians and straight people are admitted and even served, but this is at heart a gay man's bar. *805 Pacific, Montrose, 713/529–7488.*

`12` g-5

PACIFIC STREET
A cruisy men's bar with dancers and drink specials and a wild dance floor await you. *710 Pacific St., Montrose, 713/523–0213.*

`13` a-5

RICH'S
Ten years ago, Rich's was the most popular gay dance club in Houston. Times have not changed. Although vogues in fashion, tunes, and drinks come and go, Rich's continues to be the place for pure party people. Those who don't dance hang in the upstairs bar that offers a bird's-eye view of the dance floor, and plenty of places to lounge. Thursday is "straight" night. *2401 San Jacinto, Downtown/Theater District, 713/759–9606.*

HOTEL BARS

`12` g-3

ALLEN PARK INN
Cool air wafting over the pool and gardens makes the secluded outdoor patio one of the city's most peaceful places for a drink. Rules require enjoying the afternoon, sunset, or evening sky with cocktails in plastic cups. *2121 Allen Pkwy., River Oaks, 713/521–9321.*

`13` c-3

THE STATE BAR & LOUNGE
Certainly, it would be unfair to expect the revival of this old Rice Hotel institution to become, again, a genuine smoke-filled room. In its current incarnation, the State is a popular bar with scenesters, and the balcony patio offers pleasant breezes and a lovely view. *909 Texas, Downtown/Theater District, 713/229–8888.*

JAZZ

The Houston International Jazz Festival (713/839–7000) takes place in August. Several downtown locations and some venues outside the Loop book both local and nationally known artists. The mayor's jazz breakfast is the traditional kick-off to the event.

`12` f-6

CATBIRD'S
Although the jazz is almost never live, the mood in this tiny, friendly club suits jazz fans even when the music turns to swing or oldies. *1336 Westheimer, Montrose, 713/523–8000.*

`12` f-7

CÉZANNE
The decor is appropriate for the quality jazz presented here. Minor appetizers are available from the Black Lab downstairs, and there is a full bar. *4100 Montrose, Montrose, 713/522–9621.*

`12` f-4

GRAPINO DENINO
A parking lot is the view from the patio, but no one seems to mind. Inside or out, this Italian spot offers a full bar and a fine selection of wines and more grappa-based drinks than it is healthy for you to know about. The tinkly bar jazz generally performed does not seem subpar to the chatty professionals who

flock here. *2817 W. Dallas, River Oaks, 713/522–5120.*

12 *b-3*
OVATIONS
Joe LoCascio, who does wonderful things with the Houston Community College System jazz department, also has this cabaret as a showcase for his musical taste. The lack of rosy colors (no yellow lights, red, or wood-tone accents) is a bit disturbing at first, but the acoustics in the narrow, high-ceiling gray box will win you over. *2536 Times Blvd., Rice University Village, 713/522–9801.*

13 *c-3*
SAMBUCA JAZZ CAFÉ
Cozy booths and more-public seating provide options for jazz fans. A fine wine list, access to the restaurant's appetizers, and soft lighting make this club easy to enjoy. A fairly steady roster of local musicians is spiced with monthly national-act bookings. Note: if you order coffee, expect it to be flavored with the club's namesake liqueur. *909 Texas, Downtown/Theater District, 713/224–5299.*

12 *f-6*
SCOTT GERTNER'S SKY BAR
Scott's bands are often the entertainment. Dazzling views of Houston from the large patio are always there to be enjoyed. *3400 Montrose (Penthouse), Montrose, 713/520–9688.*

LATIN
Although there are a lot of clubs in the Heights, on your way back to the car in the wee hours of the morning, you may see knife fights or be robbed at gunpoint. At all clubs, the music styles are mixed. There's a lot of Tejano-type music, but you'll also hear current dance music up to and including that Cher tune about believing in love.

9 *f-2*
COCO LOCO
Forget Tai-Bo and spinning. A couple of hours on this dance floor and you'll be more fit than you've ever been. *3700 Hillcroft, Sharpstown, 713/781–5354.*

9 *f-3*
CRYSTAL
Houston's well-heeled Hispanics are the core clientele, but anyone who enjoys an elegant atmosphere and well-produced dance music can have a quality evening out at Crystal (pronounced kris-tal). Hint: go a few times and get on the good side of the staff, then take a date and make an impression as a player. *6680 Southwest Fwy., Sharpstown, 713/784–7743.*

PIANO BARS

9 *g-1*
CAPS PIANO BAR
The Grateful Geezers (a full band) play every Monday night. *2610 Briar Ridge Dr., Galleria/Post Oak, 713/784–0024.*

2 *d-3*
RESA'S PRIME STEAKHOUSE & PIANO BAR
Make like a wildcatter or cattle baron and enjoy a branch water and bourbon with a fine cigar in the masculine luxury of Resa's piano bar. *14641 Gladebrook, FM 1960 area, 281/893–3339.*

12 *f-6*
RUGGLES PIANO BAR
Hopeless parking has never hurt this stylish lounge or Ruggles, the restaurant across the valet parking lane. Back in the day, Liza Minnelli was known to drop in. *903 Westheimer, Montrose, 713/942–7051.*

10 *c-1*
SPIDER'S PIANO BAR
Perfect lighting, enhanced by the fireplace glow, brings a sheen to the cozy room's mahogany accents, gleaming dance floor, and crystal. Although pricey, this room is très romantic. Live music starts at 5 Monday through Saturday, and lasts until way past bedtime. *3755 Richmond (Maxim's), Greenway Plaza, 713/877–8899.*

POP/ROCK

2 *c-3*
CROOKED FERRET
Live music, varying in style and quality, is here as often as five nights a week. Other options are big-screen TV sports

and drinks on the spacious deck. *11835 Jones Rd., FM 1960 area, 281/894–0055.*

7 *f-2*

DAN ELECTRO'S GUITAR BAR

Shrines like this were the model for beasts like the Hard Rock. Dan Electro guitars are displayed throughout the club, and guitar artists who believe in blues, country, folk, and alternative music play here. For a break from the music, step outside and sip inexpensive draft beer under the trees of the courtyard. *1031 E. 24th St., Heights, 713/862–8707.*

12 *h-5*

EMO'S

Early in the evening, former Emo's devotees stop in for an after-work drink. By the time the nightly news is over, the youth of today start rolling in. Now-aging punk legends make their Houston tour stops here, and area hard-core bands play regularly. *2700 Albany, Montrose, 713/523–8503.*

12 *e-1*

FABULOUS SATELLITE LOUNGE

Giant garage doors open onto the street for some extra air, and those who need more fresh air can step out onto the small fenced yard out back. All this oxygen is necessary. Although a small club with poor acoustics, the Satellite is always packed. Free bingo and local bands on Monday, Texas bands through the week, and national acts on the weekends all draw huge crowds. *3616 Washington, Heights, 713/862–2665.*

9 *g-2*

FIREHOUSE SALOON

It's not a gay bar, but the name and the sight of a shiny antique fire truck outside the club have given plenty of people that impression. You might not want to suggest the Firehouse to your new, ultraconservative boss, but it's actually a relaxing alternative to some Richmond area bars. In fact, it's basically a bar with plenty of places to sit, adequate cover bands, and spicy snack foods. *5930 Southwest Fwy., Richmond Strip, 713/977–1962.*

12 *e-8*

INSTANT KARMA

Slowly evolved from a Rice-area wine bar, the boxy, nondescript building that was once Munchies has been dressed up a bit. It's now fronted by a fenced and flowering beer garden. Inside or out, this is a friendly place to see local bands and enjoy better wines and imported beers. *1617 Richmond, Montrose, 713/528–3545.*

10 *d-3*

MONROE'S GALLANT KNIGHT

Hands down, this is one of Houston's finest clubs. There is live music Wednesday through Saturday. You get a nice mix of people and musical styles. Blues and Motown are central to that style, but any dance tune will do. If Foo Fighter Dave Grohl ran a club, it would probably have the Gallant Knight's mix of funk and fun. *2337 W. Holcombe, Medical Center, 713/665–9762.*

12 *g-6*

NUMBERS

Most Saturday nights, Numbers is a concert hall for bands on tour while their first Top 40 hit is still a draw. Other nights, it's a dance club. Thursday is usually Goth night, and on Friday the DJs often cater to aging New Wavers. It's worth noting that Numbers was going strong during New Wave days and continues, without any redesign, to pack 'em in. *300 Westheimer, Montrose, 713/526–8338.*

9 *g-1*

OUTBACK PUB

A nice enough spot for beer and cover bands, the pub's Aussie decor offers a bit of atmosphere. *3100 Fountainview, Richmond Strip, 713/780–2323.*

13 *b-3*

PARTY ON THE PLAZA

This open-air party is held Thursday evenings in spring and summer, when Downtown construction allows. Festivities begin at 5, and the music starts at 6. Beer is cheap, beer lines are short, and there are usually food concessions if you need pizza, barbecue, or to-go Mexican food after a long day at the office. Still-touring monster bands, like Blue Oyster Cult, headline, whereas the opening acts are generally local bands, like Reckless Kelly or Carolyn Wonderland. Heat and, on occasion, mild rain do not daunt the partiers on the plaza. A contingent of weekend bikers rolls up on gleaming hogs, a crew of cyclists roll up on bikes, skaters roll around, and occasionally Houstonians dressed for the opera or ballet linger on the plaza before crossing the street to the Wortham. *Jones Plaza, 601 Louisiana, Downtown/Theater District, 713/ 230–1666.*

12 *f-5*
RUDYARD'S
The shabbiness of this venerable spot has been improved somewhat by the addition of a dressier upstairs area. A multitude of beers and a steady stream of mostly local bands are offered. *2010 Waugh, Montrose, 713/521–0521.*

COCKTAILS IN THE OPEN AIR

In the clement evenings of spring and fall, having a cocktail outside is a wonderful diversion. A selection of places for breezes and booze includes:

Allen Park Inn
Although you can't actually see the sunset, this is the best place to watch the sunset's effects. It's quiet and you can see the colors change in the clouds. See Hotel Bars.

Angelika Café
A full menu and extensive wine list make this a lovely spot for relaxing and watching people. Avoid Thursday; the Party on the Plaza crowd is too loud. See Film.

Black Lab
The pub patio, which may include spillover from Cézanne, has waves from lunch on—late lunchers, the after-work crowd, people gearing up for a night out, or winding down from one. See Pubs.

Bubba's Texas Burger Shack
Enjoy a beer (or champagne brunch) in the shade of the freeway. Sit at a wire-spool table on a patio on a feeder road to reach a Zen state of slack. See Bars & Lounges.

Spy
The très hip Downtown nightclub has a giant outdoor deck. The view and the fresh air are well worth the work of getting in on a busy night. See Dance Clubs.

PUBS & TAVERNS

12 *c-7*
ALE HOUSE
The Englishmen who run this fine old pub actually own the property, so despite rumors and fears and the occasionally minor harassment from area developers, it looks like the Ale House will stand even as the blocks around it become gentrified. The clubby interior has an air-conditioned chill. There's a great jukebox, and upstairs beloved local bands perform (Joe "Guitar" Hughes appears at least once a month). The outdoor patio with wide wooden picnic tables is simply a lovely place to sit and talk over a few pints. *2425 Alabama, Upper Kirby District, 713/521–2333.*

12 *f-7*
BLACK LAB
The crowd, which consists more of hungry professionals than thirsty slackers, and the menu, which is long and expensive, make the Black Lab look a lot like a restaurant. On the flip side, it has authentically horrible English pub furniture, uncomfortable in the extreme, and the bartender draws a steady stream of Bass, Harp, and Samuel Smith, and layers the occasional black and tan. *4100 Montrose, Montrose, 713/529–1199.*

13 *c-2*
BREWERY TAP
Plank tables, rough-hewn beams, and bulging, mildew-stained plaster walls mark this as one of the few places in the city that dates to before color TV. Those in search of a good brew enjoy choosing from the dozens of beers on tap. Although some cowboys and girls feel Guinness looks, smells, and tastes like hoof dressing, the stuff is so popular you can get it at many convenience stores. However, only a few select spots like the Tap have Guinness on tap. *717 Franklin, Downtown/Theater District, 713/ 237–1537.*

12 *g-4*
CECIL'S
Despite almost supermarket-bright lights in the pool table area, Cecil's is a perennial favorite. The game area is lighted publike, and the patio has flattering lighting. *600 W. Gray, Montrose, 713/ 527–9101.*

14 c-3

THE GINGERMAN

The ever-popular Gingerman serves 800 or 900 beers, at least it seems that way, and many of them are on tap. Folks who work in the Medical Center or Downtown and occasional Rice students gather here pretty much all the time. *5607 Morningside, Rice University Village, 713/526–2770.*

12 c-6

KENNEALLY'S

Fine Irish pizza is served along with an endless list of beers, or something from the full bar. Irish pizza? If you think there's no such thing, you tell 'em. *2111 Shepherd, Montrose, 713/630–0486.*

12 b-7

LIZZARD'S PUB

During happy hour, light from the front windows and side sliding door offer patrons a full, clear view of the cheese and wings set out for "snacks." The spawn of River Oaks, wearing real pearls and running a tab with daddy's American Express card, sit and sip alongside Inner Loopers who, because of unfortunate career choices like academia, social work, or forestry, are paying with cash, and counting carefully. *2715 Sackett St., Upper Kirby District, 713/529–4610.*

12 c-8

MCELRY'S PUB

The men behind the bar often have U.K. accents, enhancing the atmosphere. This cozy spot has a beer garden and a lovely selection of scotches, and you can sit back and sip with friends in red leather furniture from the original Rice Hotel bar. *3607 Sandman, Montrose, 713/524–2444.*

SPORTS BARS

12 f-8

ERNIE'S ON BANKS

Local residents who enjoy the quiet charm of this neighborhood do not enjoy finding bar patrons parked in their spots, but management makes on effort to keep sports fans on their best behavior, and the upstairs deck also seems to have a civilizing effect. Inside, both upstairs and down, the TVs show satellite programming of events ranging from bowl games to "strongest man" competitions featuring burly northern Europeans who can pull a truck with their teeth. *1010 Banks, Museum District, 713/526–4566.*

2 g-8

HOOTERS

No matter where you sit, you can get a good, clear look at those great big . . . TVs. Heterosexual male patrons may care that the waitresses wear painted-on T-shirts and short-shorts, but other sports fans only want to talk to the girls when they need extra ranch dressing for their buffalo wings. *20790 Gulf Fwy., Clear Lake/Bay Area, 281/332–9464.*

2 d-2

120 FM 1960 W, FM 1960 area, 281/893–9464.

2 c-3

SRO SPORTS BAR

Both locations look a little bit like gambling rooms in Vegas or Atlantic City. At SRO, however, the bright displays and big-screen TVs are devoted to scores, stats, and games in progress—there is no wagering. Swank seating in "VIP lounges" and upscale coffee drinks put this sports bar a notch or two above the usual venues where fried food and pitchers of beer rule. *6982 FM 1960 W, FM 1960, 281/537–0691.*

9 c-1

2517 Gessner, Richmond Strip, 713/952–1999.

14 c-3

TEXADELPHIA SANDWICHES & SPORTS

"More than 100 beers" are advertised. The list includes imports from the usual places, Belgium, Germany, Great Britain, Holland, Ireland, and the United Kingdom. They also have suds from Peru, and a fine selection of watery old-fashioned brews like Pearl and Lone Star. Suitably lubed sports fans can chew on greasy cheese steaks and watch sports on the big screen. *2420 Rice Blvd., Rice University Village, 713/522–8588.*

9 g-1

6025 Westheimer, Galleria/Post Oak, 713/785–6700.

WINE BARS

 12 *g-8*

BOULEVARD BISTRO

Chef-owner Monica Pope built the cellar to complement the food in her restaurant, but the not-so-hungry are more than welcome to savor vintage wines at the vast, dark, hardwood bar. *4319 Montrose, Montrose, 713/524–6922.*

12 *g-8*

ZIMM'S COFFEE & WINE BAR

Indoor and outdoor seating makes it easy to spend any afternoon slugging down lattes—rain or shine. When you're tired of vibrating in the sun, step inside to slow down with wine. *4321 Montrose, Montrose, 713/521–2002.*

chapter 6

HOTELS

lthough business gatherings book up large halls like the George R. Brown Convention Center, the Astroarena, and the Astro Hall most weeks, Houston doesn't have a major convention that eats up room availability, and the city is not a major tourist destination. It's difficult to predict when occupancy in a particular area will be high or low, which means you can usually find a deal if you try. If you need to be in the Galleria area, and it's booked solid, you might find a deal Downtown, or near the Dome. Typically, the rates quoted at the front desk, by 800-number operators, and on hotel and reservations Web sites differ, so check all your options for the best rate.

Houston's nearly 50,000 rooms typically come with coffeemakers, ironing boards, hair dryers, modem lines, and free parking. Hotels that don't have exercise rooms usually offer passes to nearby health clubs for $5 to $10 a day. The area hotel tax is a staggering 17%, the third highest in the nation, but at least most hotels offer shuttle service either directly to the airports or to transportation centers. However, Houston is not a public transportation town—guests who are not renting a car should plan to order a cab well ahead of departure time. Bear in mind that few Houston hotels are in the midst of a shopping area. If you need toiletries, books, or gym clothes, you'll probably have to depend on the gift shop or an excursion to a nearby strip center.

price categories

These categories are based on regular weekly rates for double occupancy. Many hotels, especially those catering to business travelers, offer deep discounts on weekends and during holidays. Also note that parking rates Downtown can add as much as $15 a day to your bill.

CATEGORY	COST
Very expensive	over $200
Expensive	$150–$199
Moderate	$100–$149
Budget	under $100

VERY EXPENSIVE LODGING

7 h-7

THE DOUBLETREE AT ALLEN CENTER

You can see the gleaming travertine marble lobby, the view of Buffalo Bayou to the west, and Downtown, but one of the most beautiful features is invisible—the soundproofing. All 350 thoroughly modern rooms are blissfully quiet. The hotel has a direct connection to the Downtown tunnels where quite a few restaurants and shops can be found. Travelers who don't mind an above-ground route will find Massas seafood and a Harlan's Barbecue nearby. Those who can't be bothered to leave the hotel have two options: the café-style Brasserie or formal dining in the Dover's restaurant. *400 Dallas St., Downtown, 77002, 713/759–0202, fax 713/759–1166. 350 rooms, 6 suites. 2 restaurants, in-room data ports, health club, meeting rooms. AE, D, DC, MC, V.*

13 G-4

FOUR SEASONS

Business travelers with spouses in tow would do well at this luxury hotel. Suites are decorated in colors and fabrics that are more country club than Continental, and the rooms are huge. Most of the bathrooms are large enough to park a compact car, not that guests here are likely to arrive with such a small vehicle. The Four Seasons has a pool area with a skyline view and is across the street from The Park Shops Downtown mall. Complimentary transportation is offered within the Downtown area. The dramatic staircase in the center of the main lobby is an attention-getter, but guests should focus on the DeVille restaurant. Travel and dining guides alike give its cuisine high marks. *1300 Lamar, Downtown, 77010, 713/650–1300, fax 713/652–6220. 399 rooms, 12 suites. 2 restaurants, lobby lounge, in-room data ports, no-smoking floors, room service, pool, health club, dry cleaning, laundry service, concierge, business center, parking (fee). AE, D, DC, MC, V.*

7 g-8

HILTON HOUSTON PLAZA

This small hotel in the midst of Downtown has one-bedroom suites. The thoroughly functional, unfussy decorating suits the academic types who stay here when consulting or attending conferences in the Medical Center. Guests enjoy 24-hour room service, access to a health club, jogging track, and outdoor heated pool. If a fear of heights, or simply a longing for green space, makes the rooftop jogging track unappealing, then get your laps around Rice University or in nearby Hermann Park. Complimentary transportation to area attractions, restaurants, and shopping is available. *6633 Travis, Downtown, 77030, 713/313–4000, fax 713/313–4660. 181 rooms, 141 suites. In-room data ports, room service, pool, hot tub, sauna, health club, jogging. Parking (fee). AE, D, DC, MC, V.*

9 *C-1*
HILTON HOUSTON WESTCHASE
At the center of a landscaped lawn, the building looks more like an office complex than a hotel. However, the 13-story hotel makes a cozy home for the business traveler. Curl up in a guest bathrobe, order room service, and indulge in cable or use the dual phone lines to work late into the night. Complimentary transportation is provided within 3 mi. The top four floors comprise the "towers." *9999 Westheimer, Memorial/Spring Branch, 77042, 713/974–1000, fax 713/974–2108. 298 rooms, 38 suites. Restaurant, bar, lounge, in-room data ports, laundry service, dry cleaning, concierge, business center, meeting rooms. AE, D, DC, MC, V.*

7 *a-7*
THE HOUSTONIAN
The initial expansive lobby has the clubby, wood-beam look of an expensive lodge. Other floors have well-appointed lounges and meeting rooms. The hotel's health club facilities have everything, including a rock-climbing wall. Although many formal exercise classes are offered, some may choose to simply stroll the wooded grounds. There is complimentary transportation to and from the Galleria. *111 N. Post Oak La., Galleria/Post Oak, 77024, 713/680–2626, fax 713/680–2992. 276 rooms, 9 suites. 5 restaurants, bar, in-room data ports, room service, spa, health club, golf privileges, dry cleaning, laundry service, concierge, business services, meeting rooms. AE, D, DC, MC, V.*

7 *g-8*
HYATT REGENCY HOUSTON
This elegant tower has nearly a thousand rooms, many looking out into the vast multistory lobby. The revolving roof restaurant is named Spindletop after the first gusher. More intense entertainment is within walking distance: Bayou Place, the Alley Theatre, the Wortham, and Jones Hall are all a few blocks north. *1200 Louisiana, Downtown, 77002, 713/654–1234, fax 713/951–0934. 963 rooms, 32 suites. 3 restaurants, 2 lounges, in-room data ports, no-smoking rooms, laundry service, dry cleaning, concierge, meeting rooms. AE, D, DC, MC, V.*

7 *f-8*
LA COLOMBE D'OR
This exclusive, European-style hotel, originally the W. W. Fondren mansion, has lost some exterior charm to the addition of a banquet facility, but the rooms, lounge, and restaurant still draw the rich and famous (and discreet). Genuine antiques, usually dark woods with luxe brocades, do much to complete the hotel's successful attempt at old-world charm. The tiny, but warm, bar and a small library room are both perfect spots for a cozy drink. The bar might hold 10 people, the library, half that. *3410 Montrose, Montrose, 77006, 713/524–7999, fax 713/524–8923. 15 suites. Restaurant, bar, in-room data ports, in-room fax, library, laundry service, dry cleaning. AE, D, DC, MC, V.*

7 *h-6*
LANCASTER HOTEL
The rooms are small and packed with exactly what it takes to make anyone feel pampered and secure. Overstuffed sofas and chairs, fat pillows, and thick curtains that effectively shut out both light and noise make a homey, yet elegant retreat. If we all had wealthy, kindly aunts with well-appointed guest rooms, then there would be no need for hotels like the Lancaster. Although the hotel is just steps from Jones Hall, the Alley Theatre, the Wortham Center, Bayou Place, and the Angelika cinema, you might elect to stay in. If you do, don't worry about room service: When you order tea, a full selection of teas and a carafe of water arrives so you can sit and sip in leisure. Town car transportation to Downtown is available. *701 Texas, Downtown, 77002, 713/228–9500, fax 713/223–4528. 93 rooms, 9 suites. Restaurant, in-room data port, in-room fax, in-room VCRs, minibars, no-smoking floors, room service, health club, dry cleaning, laundry service, concierge, meeting rooms. AE, D, DC, MC, V.*

7 a-7

OMNI HOUSTON HOTEL

Rock stars and men who make the pages of Forbes can ogle Air France hostesses at the huge pool. And they needn't worry about privacy. Despite its Galleria area location, the hotel is secluded and surrounded by grassy lawns. The furnishings in suites and rooms are well-maintained and frequently refurbished, and the bathrooms are done in marble. For room service, you can call the desk and have a masseuse, manicurist, or Grand Marnier soufflé sent up. Although the pool, grounds, and basic decor tend toward the modern and austere, the Omni's La Reserve restaurant is genteel and jackets are required. Tableside carving and a wealth of Continental sauces are always part of the dining experience. Complimentary transportation is provided to the Galleria. *4 Riverway, Galleria/Post Oak, 77056, 713/871–8181, fax 713/871–0719. 345 rooms, 33 suites. 2 restaurants, pub, in-room data ports, in-room safes, minibars, room service, 2 pools, health club, dry cleaning, laundry service, concierge, business services, meeting rooms, free parking. AE, D, DC, MC, V.*

GREAT HOTELS FOR CELEBRITY SPOTTING

Allen Park Inn (Moderate)
Midlevel rock and rollers on tour and supporting actors filming in Houston almost always stay here, with legions of roadies and gaffers.

La Colombe d'Or (Very Expensive)
Perhaps overwhelmed by the Old World charm, Ted Danson proposed to Mary Steenburgen here. Hundreds of stars have patiently sat for interviews in the bar and tearoom.

Omni Hotel Houston (Very Expensive)
Air France stewardesses are usually sunning by the vast pool. On occasion, physical specimens such as Flea, of the Red Hot Chili Peppers, splash around in the sparkling water.

Park Plaza Warwick Hotel (Very Expensive)
The A-list gravitates toward such baroque faux-European surroundings like ducks after June bugs.

14 g-1

PARK PLAZA WARWICK HOTEL

The Warwick has been through some major renovations since being celebrated on Lyle Lovett's first release, and the north side is now overwhelmed by the Museum of Fine Arts additions. The older rooms, which were in danger of becoming dowdy, are now refitted, and the glorious marble lobby, lavish Sunday brunch, views of Hermann Park, and proximity to the Museum District are unchanged. *5701 Main, Museum District, 77005, 713/526–1991, fax 713/639–4545. 308 rooms, 74 suites. 2 restaurants, in-room data ports, no-smoking rooms, dry cleaning, laundry service, health club concierge, business services. AE, D, DC, MC, V.*

7 a-8

SHERATON SUITES HOUSTON

Between the Super Mario Brothers on in-room Nintendo and full concierge service, you'll be well cared for. Certainly, this location puts you in easy reach of fine restaurants such as the Capital Grille and rowdier nightspots such as Joe's Crab Shack and Chuy's. However, if you choose to stay in counting up your Starpoints and enjoying R&R in your jammies, the hotel has many amenities and services to make your secluded stay perfect. Complimentary transportation is provided within a 3-mi radius. *2400 West Loop S, Galleria/Post Oak, 77027, 713/586–2444, fax 713/586–2445. 286 suites. Restaurant, lounge, in-room data ports, room service, pool, health club, dry cleaning, laundry service, concierge, business services, meeting rooms. No pets. AE, D, DC, MC, V.*

7 e-8

ST. REGIS

Wealthy locals and well-heeled travelers enjoy the centrally located hotel's plush accommodations and thorough service (including butlers on some floors). Rooms feature trademarked "Heavenly Beds" with duvet covers—if you're really impressed by a good night's sleep you can even order a bed through the hotel. Luxuries such as orchid plants come in each room, but thought goes into practicalities as well—like written instructions for the CD clock-radio. High tea is served in the small lounge, and a spectacular (and expensive) buffet brunch is served on Sunday, complete with ice

When it Comes to Getting Cash at an ATM,

Same Thing.

Whether you're in Yosemite or Yemen, using your Visa® card or ATM card with the PLUS symbol is the easiest and most convenient way to get cash. Even if your bank is in Minneapolis and you're in Miami, Visa/PLUS ATMs make getting cash so easy, you'll feel right at home. After all, Visa/PLUS ATMs are open 24 hours a day, 7 days a week, rain or shine. And if you need help finding one of Visa's 627,000 ATMs in 127 countries worldwide, visit **visa.com/pd/atm**. We'll make finding an ATM as easy as finding the Eiffel Tower, the Pyramids or even the Grand Canyon.

It's Everywhere You Want To Be.®

sculptures and clever arrangements. The Remington Grill serves American cuisine. Inquire if there are any upcoming package weekends, like 2000's Wildflower Weekend, which included a luxury car with which to explore the spring countryside. Town car transportation is provided within a 2-mi radius. *1919 Briar Oaks La., River Oaks, 77027, 713/840–8036, fax 713/840–8036. 180 rooms, 52 suites. Restaurant, lounge, in-room data ports, no-smoking floors, pool, health club, baby-sitting, dry cleaning, laundry service, concierge, meeting rooms, business center. No pets. AE, D, DC, MC, V.*

7 a-8

THE WESTIN GALLERIA AND OAKS HOTEL

These two hotels sit on the south side of the Galleria and offer every possible office or convention need (although video-conferencing facilities are extra). Although it may look as though the hotels have been encroached on by the expanding Galleria, the design always called for the hotels to be part of the center. And this proximity to shopping hasn't hurt business at all. According to local lore, wealthy wives from Mexico, Africa, the Middle East, and Asia check in, shop in the Galleria, and never set foot outdoors during their stay. The Westin Galleria is two floors taller, has 24-hour room service, and is closer to the Galleria skating rink than the Westin Oaks, but otherwise the hotels are essentially identical. *5060 W. Alabama, Galleria/Post Oak, 77056, 713/960–8100, fax, 713/960–6553. 485 rooms, 40 suites. Westin Oaks: fax 713/960–6554. 406 rooms, 11 suites. 3 restaurants, lounge, minibars, in-room data ports, no-smoking rooms, room service, 2 pools, concierge, business services, meeting rooms. AE, D, DC, MC, V.*

EXPENSIVE LODGING

2 d-5

ADAM'S MARK

The showcase feature of this hotel is the 10-story open-air lobby. The hive of rooms surrounding it are all efficient pods for the business traveler, but not unwelcoming. Where some hotels might try for a homey feel with warm cookies at turndown time or baskets of scented soaps, Adam's Mark depends on the staff to aid you in your comfort. The cheerful young men and women on staff

will treat you like a properly respected elder, whether you frantically check in at 9 AM or order a sandwich at 3 AM. *2900 Briarpark Dr., Memorial/Spring Branch, 77042, 713/978–7400, fax 713/735–2739. 604 rooms, 49 suites. Restaurant, lounge, sports bar, in-room data ports, no-smoking floors, room service, indoor-outdoor pool, sauna, health club, coin laundry, dry cleaning, laundry service, concierge, business services, meeting rooms, free parking. AE, D, DC, MC, V.*

9 b-7

EMBASSY SUITES

Nicely situated between the Galleria and Downtown areas and booming Sugar Land, this is an all-suite hotel with kitchenettes in every room. Smaller "suites" are like the smallest possible efficiency apartments. However, in that tight space, a consultant on a long-term assignment can cook, keep clothes clean (with the coin laundry), and stretch out on a big bed and watch TV. Larger suites are roomy enough for families in the midst of relocation. *9090 Southwest Fwy., Sharpstown, 77074, 713/995–0123, fax 713/779–0703. 243 suites. In-room data ports, kitchenettes, no-smoking rooms, refrigerators, indoor pool, hot tub, sauna, health club, coin laundry, dry cleaning, meeting rooms. AE, D, DC, MC, V.*

4 b-2

OMNI HOUSTON HOTEL WESTSIDE

Not as luxurious as the Omni Houston Hotel near the Galleria, this hotel still has attractive perks for the business traveler like a lush atrium lobby and access to outdoor green spaces. Work-weary guests can also use the hot tub. Guests who are still working on that deadline need other amenities, like laundry service and copier service. Complimentary transportation within a 1½-mi radius is available. *13210 Katy Fwy., Memorial/Spring Branch, 77079, 281/558–8338 or 800/228–9290, fax 281/558–4028. 400 rooms, 13 suites. Restaurant, coffee shop, lounge, in-room data ports, minibars, no-smoking rooms, pool, hot tub, 2 tennis courts, health club, dry cleaning, laundry service, business center, meeting rooms, free parking. AE, D, DC, MC, V.*

10 e-4

RADISSON HOTEL

Although the benefits of the location are immediately obvious, this Radisson is actually convenient to the Medical Center. Of course, if you're in town for pleasure, it's very near AstroWorld. Conventioneers and friends and family of those undergoing treatment in Houston stay at the hotel most of the year, and February and March is rodeo time. A light, slightly Southwestern look with oak and pine accents complementing iron bedposts and table legs is featured in many of the rooms. Complimentary transportation is available within 3 mi. *1400 Old Spanish Trail, Astrodome/Old Spanish Trail, 77054, 713/796–1000, fax 713/796–8055. 189 suites. Café, in-room data ports, no-smoking rooms, pool, health club, laundry service, dry cleaning, meeting rooms. AE, D, DC, MC, V.*

6 *a-5*
RADISSON SUITE HOTEL HOUSTON WEST
This simple 14-story tower with a dramatic logo was a bit more impressive before the Beltway obscured the bottom half of the building. Now, the hotel is crowded in at the corner of the two huge freeways. This diminishment of the exterior has not effected the efficient interior style. Rooms and suites offer that office-away-from-home feel with not just free coffee, but also microwave popcorn. Guests who need more than a snack can join Houstonians at the Radisson's popular Riviera Grill, which is also the setting for the free, full American breakfast buffet each morning. Just down the feeder road, is the Taste of Texas, a very deserving steak house. *10655 Katy Fwy., Memorial/Spring Branch, 77024, 713/461–6000, fax 713/467–2357. 92 rooms, 81 suites. 2 restaurants, piano bar, in-room data ports, no-smoking floors, no-smoking rooms, pool, laundry services.*

GREAT HOTELS FOR A DRINK

Allen Park Inn (Moderate)
At an time, any number of otherwise upright and hardworking Houstonians are considering turning to the life of a lush just so they can sit quietly at this unpretentious bar or on its lovely patio.

Hyatt Regency Houston (Very Expensive)
The brassy fern barn is not cozy or regal, but it is centrally located for terrific people-watching.

1 *d-1*
WOODLANDS RESORT
All 364 rooms at this lakefront lodge have access to spas, an Olympic-size pool, 21 lighted tennis courts, and two golf courses, one of which is the Tournament Players Course, one of the Houston area's finest and home to the Shell Houston Open. Designed by and for the sort of people who attended school with Dubya (George W. Bush, Jr.), attend fundraisers for Dubya, and want their boys to grow up to be like Dubya, this wooded resort is quiet and lovely. Should all that peace and quiet and impeccable lawns get to you, cab it to nearby Tinseltown 17 (1600 Lake Robins Drive) and enjoy a Hollywood movie and the neon glare of a contemporary movie palace. *2301 N. Millbend Dr., The Woodlands, 77380, 281/367–1100, fax 281/364–6345. 364 rooms, 82 suites. 4 restaurants, bar, lounge, in-room data ports, 1 indoor and 1 outdoor pool, beauty salon, spa, sauna, steam room, 2 18-hole championship golf courses, 21 tennis courts, health club, basketball, volleyball, business services, meeting rooms. AE, D, DC, MC, V.*

MODERATE LODGING

7 *g-6*
ALLEN PARK INN
Rooms resemble highway hotel accommodations, but the benefits of location are an overwhelming draw. An easy drive from Downtown, the Galleria area, and many points on I–10, the Inn is across the street from Buffalo Bayou. Enjoy the views or the jogging trail. *2121 Allen Pkwy., River Oaks, 77019, 713/521–9321, fax 713/521–9321. 242 rooms, 3 suites. Restaurant, bar, no-smoking rooms, room service, pool, health club, dry cleaning, laundry service, meeting rooms, free and fee parking. AE, D, DC, MC, V.*

14 *f-5*
BRAESWOOD HOTEL
Although close to the Medical Center and Downtown, this quiet hotel is surrounded by 10 acres of landscaped courtyards. There are several pools, including one that's Texas-shaped. Complimentary transportation to the Medical Center is provided. *2100 S. Braeswood, Astrodome/Old Spanish Trail, 77030, 713/797–9000, fax 713/799–8362. 331 rooms, 4 suites. Restaurant, lounge,*

no-smoking rooms, pool, health club, dry cleaning, laundry service, business services, meeting rooms. AE, D, DC, MC, V.

7 *a-7*

CROWNE PLAZA HOTEL

Many of the rooms in this 23-story tower have fax machines, along with a data port, voice mail, and other business traveler amenities. Special "Crowne Plaza Club" details include oversized TVs, oversized workstations, cognac with bedtime chocolates, and wine and hors d'oeuvres each evening. *2222 West Loop S, Galleria/Post Oak, 77027, 713/ 961–7272, fax 713/961–3327. 476 rooms, 15 suites. Restaurant, bar, in-room data ports, room service, pool, business services. AE, D, DC, MC, V.*

14 *e-3*

CROWNE PLAZA MEDICAL CENTER

This well-appointed, 10-story hotel seems very professional and tasteful, but one of its most important luxuries is Blue Bell ice cream. Confections from the little creamery in Brenham are included on all menus, including room service. If a sweet treat doesn't relax you, maybe the on-site masseuse can. Room decor is early American. None of the room furnishings are genuine Ethan Allan, but the look is very much in that conservative tradition. The Scoops Diner restaurant has a "Happy Days" soda fountain. *6701 Main, Medical Center, 77030, 713/797– 1110, fax 713/796–8291. 293 rooms, 5 suites. Restaurant, bar, no-smoking rooms, pool, health club, laundry services, business services. No pets. AE, D, DC, MC, V.*

7 *a-8*

DOUBLETREE AT POST OAK

Nearly half of the hotel's height is devoted to the open space of a six-story atrium lobby. If you are not in the mood to take advantage of the various "office away from office" amenities, find live entertainment in the lounges every day except Monday. There's complimentary transportation within a 3-mi radius. *2001 Post Oak Blvd., Galleria/Post Oak, 77056, 713/961–9300, fax 713/623–6685. 449 rooms, 37 suites. 2 restaurants, bar, lounge, in-room data ports, no-smoking rooms, room service, pool, beauty salon, sauna, health club, dry cleaning, laundry service, business services, free and fee parking. AE, D, DC, MC, V.*

4 *e-4*

FAIRFIELD INN HOUSTON WESTCHASE

This modest 82-room hotel has wide work desks for each guest, and the hotel staff can provide cribs for travelers on family trips. Guests who are bunked in this Beltway-area hotel can choose a room with one big bed and one big sofa for a civilized home away from home. Families can settle for two big beds, a sleeper sofa, and that crib. Take advantage of the white-and-blue-tiled pool fit for Jay Gatsby and Daisy. *2400 W. Sam Houston Pkwy., Memorial/Spring Branch, 77042, 713/334–2400, fax 713/334–2400. 82 rooms, 8 suites. In-room data ports, indoor pool, hot tub. AE, D, DC, MC, V.*

10 *e-6*

HOLIDAY INN ASTRODOME

This well-regarded hotel near AstroWorld doesn't win those points for anything swanky; this Holiday Inn simply delivers with reliable comforts. Big ol' slabs of beef, with baked potato or fries, are served in the Kirby Grille, and big-screen TVs blast pro and college games in the Sports Page Lounge. *8111 Kirby Dr., Astrodome/Old Spanish Trail, 77054, 713/790–1900, fax 713/799–8574. 235 rooms, 6 suites. Restaurant, sports bar, in-room data ports, pool, spa, health club, meeting rooms. AE, D, DC, MC, V.*

10 *c-1*

HOLIDAY INN SELECT

This particular stripe of Holiday Inn is up a few notches from the roadside motels. Instead of being a cut above Ramada Inn, this brand is set to grab a more demanding business market. In-room coffee and date ports allow the target customer to work all night, and on-site fitness options let him or her keep in shape while on the road. The full-service hotel is convenient to the Compaq Center, the Galleria area, Downtown, and AstroWorld. *2712 Southwest Fwy., Greenway Plaza, 77098, 713/ 523–8448, fax 713/526–7948. 355 rooms, 32 suites. Restaurant, bar, in-room data ports, no-smoking rooms, room service, pool, hot tub, health club, coin laundry, dry cleaning, business services, meeting rooms, free parking. AE, D, DC, MC, V.*

14 *g-1*

HOUSTON MARRIOTT MEDICAL CENTER

An in-house computer center helps workers on the road stay in touch and enables family members visiting the Medical Center to post the latest updates to family home pages. Another family bonus: it's within skipping distance of Hermann Park. Complimentary transportation is provided within a 1-mi radius. *6580 Fannin, Medical Center, 77030, 713/796–0080 or 800/228–9290, fax 713/770–8028. 386 rooms, 22 suites. 2 restaurants, bar, lounge, no-smoking rooms, room service, indoor pool, health club, dry cleaning, laundry service, concierge, business services, meeting rooms. AE, D, DC, MC, V.*

7 *a-8*

HOUSTON MARRIOTT WEST LOOP

Well aware that many business travelers are women, all 300 rooms are stocked with warm fluffy bathrobes. Those who choose to go out should take advantage of complimentary shuttle service, which offers free rides to nightclubs and restaurants in the Galleria area (as well as to the Galleria). *1750 West Loop S, Galleria/Post Oak, 77027, 713/960–0111, fax 713/624–1560. 302 rooms, 2 suites. Restaurant, lounge, sports bar, in-room data ports, no-smoking floors, indoor pool, hot tub, sauna, health club, dry cleaning, laundry service, concierge, business services, meeting rooms, free and fee parking. AE, D, DC, MC, V.*

4 *a-2*

LA QUINTA PARK 10 WEST

There's always a free light breakfast (muffins, cereal, juice, coffee, tea) in the lobby, and all La Quinta locations have a pool and offer suites. For in-room entertainment there's video games—one business traveler here rang up a three-figure Donkey Kong bill in one night. The early nineties Santa Fe décor, complete with pale pink and turquoise accents, seems charming instead of dated, and adds to the overall warm, but not overly friendly, mood of this tidy hotel chain. *15225 Katy Fwy., Memorial/Spring Branch, 77094, 281/646–9200, fax 281/646–9201. 96 rooms, 4 suites. In-room data ports, pool, spa, health club, video games, dry cleaning, laundry service, meeting rooms. AE, D, MC, V.*

7 *e-8*

LOVETT INN

It's possible that this quaint inn is more often host to receptions than to overnight guests. The grounds, gazebo, and pool area can accommodate up to 200 people. If you're planning a romantic stay in a main house room with a balcony, first check what the reception schedule is. A quiet drink on your balcony at sunset loses something if the "garden view" is 150 uncomfortably dressed kids from a children's cotillion squealing all over the landscaping. By the way, you are welcome to have a bottle of wine, or chilled champagne, but remember the inn is BYOB. In any case, those who do stay in the eight guest rooms can walk to any of the fine restaurants in the area or take advantage of health club facilities at Fitness Exchange. Guest usually choose to stay in, however, enjoying the quaint décor and modern appliances like coffeemakers and microwaves. And there's no hurry for the Continental breakfast—it's served until noon. *501 Lovett Blvd., Montrose, 77006, 713/522–5224, fax 713/528–6708. 8 private rooms with baths, 2 rooms with shared bath. Pool, spa, meeting rooms. AE, D, MC, V.*

10 *c-1*

RENAISSANCE HOUSTON HOTEL

At first glance, this tower in an office complex may seem all business, but it's attached to Greenway Plaza shops, which include the Landmark Greenway Cinema. If the Greenway's art-house fare doesn't suit you, Edward's 24-screen multiplex is a short walk away, and you're practically on top of the Compaq Center. The rooms, all the way up to the top of the tower, are gracious and offer expansive views of the city. However, a few guests always forsake the comfort of their rooms for the weirdly vacant rooms of Jason's sports bar on the ground floor. Typically, the TVs here outnumber the patrons. *6 Greenway Plaza E, Greenway Plaza, 77046, 713/629–1200, fax 713/629–4702. 389 rooms, 9 suites. Restaurant, lobby lounge, sports bar, in-room data ports, in-room fax, in-room safes, no-smoking rooms, room service, pool, health club, dry cleaning, laundry service, meeting rooms, airport shuttle, parking (fee). AE, D, DC, MC, V.*

11 *f-4*

SHERATON BROOKHOLLOW

The suburban locale lowers the prices at this well-designed, full-service hotel. Rooms have a clubby, masculine decor with wood accents, overstuffed chairs, and earth-tone wall coverings and drapes. The grounds are lovely, and an on-site Mailboxes Etc. offers office service. Complimentary transportation within a 5-mi radius (includes Galleria) is based on availability. *3000 North Loop W, Memorial/Spring Branch, 77092, 713/688–0100, fax 713/688–9224. 382 rooms, 14 suites. Restaurant, 2 bars, no-smoking floors, room service, pool, hot tub, sauna, health club, dry cleaning, laundry service, concierge, business center, meeting rooms, free parking. AE, D, DC, MC, V.*

2 *h-7*
SOUTH SHORE HARBOUR RESORT
Even if you're traveling on business, a swim-up bar says vacation loud and clear—and in this climate you can swim almost any time of year. The conference-ready hotel has 18 meeting rooms, including a ballroom with a maximum capacity of 1,000. There are also outdoor reception and meeting areas. *2500 S. Shore Blvd., Clear Lake/Bay Area, 77573, 281/334–1000, fax 281/334–1157. 250 rooms, 10 suites. 2 restaurants, in-room data ports, no-smoking floors, 27-hole golf course, health club, dry cleaning, laundry service, business services, meeting rooms, airport shuttle, free parking. AE, D, DC, MC, V.*

2 *d-3*
WYNDHAM GREENSPOINT
Checking in, you'll notice the 45-ft-high skylight arcing over the lobby. In-room amenities include Bath and Body Works gels and lotions and wet bars. The hotel has 50 luxury suites and a half dozen rooms specially equipped for guests with disabilities. Complimentary transportation is provided to Intercontinental Airport. *12400 Greenspoint Dr., North, 77060, 281/875–2222, fax 281/875–1652. 472 rooms, 50 suites. 2 restaurants, sports bar, lobby lounge, in-room data ports, no-smoking floors, room service, pool, health club, coin laundry, dry cleaning, business center, meeting rooms, parking (fee). AE, D, DC, MC, V.*

BUDGET LODGING

3 *f-2*
ECONO LODGE NORTH FREEWAY
Dark-wood molding, very '70s ceiling fans, and plaid coverlets give this relatively recent structure a folksy feel. Instead of the musty scent, and unpredictable plumbing of a country inn, this tidy motel has the roadside service modern travelers expect, including a

pool. *7447 Hwy. 45 N, North, 77076, 713/699–3800, fax. 713/699–3349. 50 rooms. Pool. AE, D, DC, MC, V.*

6 *b-7*
DRURY INN
The same college students and recent grads who dis this chain as the "Dreary Inn" are also the first to take advantage of low rates. After a long day on the road, all you really need is a hot bath and a clean bed. Above the basics are the whirlpool and free breakfast. *1000 Hwy 6 N, Memorial/Spring Branch, 77079, 281/558–7007. 120 rooms. Indoor pool. AE, D, DC, MC, V*

9 *e-4*
HAWTHORN SUITES
This hotel is equipped for family trips. The outdoor pool and basketball court, along with picnic and barbecue areas, give car-weary kids a chance to blow off steam. There's complimentary transportation within a 5-mi radius. *6910 Southwest Fwy., Sharpstown, 77094, 713/785–3415, fax 713/785–1130. 151 suites. In-room data ports, kitchenettes, no-smoking rooms, refrigerators, pool, dry cleaning, laundry service, meeting rooms. AE, D, DC, MC, V.*

4 *b-3*
MOTEL 6 KATY
This no-frills bunk is clean, cozy and willing to allow small pets with reservations. Caveat: rooms may have showers only, not tub. *14833 Katy Fwy., Katy/Bear Creek, 77094, 281/497–5000, fax 281/497–1472. 135 rooms. In-room data ports, pool, coin laundry. AE, D, DC, MC, V.*

9 *b-1*
RED ROOF INN
Obviously, the Red Roof Inn is not the swankiest spot. However, in recent years the chain has dolled up most locations, and newer establishments, like this one, are as nice, if not as large, as most mid-rate motels. King-size beds and desks, not features in Red Roof Inns of the past, are standard now. Rooms have pay-per-play Nintendo games, and in the morning there's free coffee to send you off. *2960 W. Sam Houston Pkwy. S, Memorial/Spring Branch, 77042, 713/785–9909, fax 713/785–6162. 135 rooms. Pool, business services. AE, D, DC, MC, V.*

9 f-2

SHONEY'S INN

Cross-country drivers are accustomed to Shoney's being on the outskirts of cities, with a whopping big buffet in the restaurant. In this case, the family-friendly inn is well inside the city, along the freeway sharing its feeder road space with strip centers and car dealerships. All five floors, including the ground, have hallways, not open air walkways, so that once you check in, you have full privacy. Morning perks are free coffee, breakfast, and a newspaper. *6687 Southwest Fwy., Sharpstown, 77060, 713/776–2633, fax 713/776–0326. 115 rooms. Pool, free coffee and breakfast, free newspaper, fax available. AE, DC, MC, V.*

HOSTELS

14 h-1

HOUSTON INTERNATIONAL YOUTH HOSTEL

The cheery house, a two-story, looks much like the other residences in the neighborhood, except for the array of flags waving from the front porch. Reservations are usually not needed, but since large groups sometimes fill all 30 spots, they're recommended. *5302 Crawford, Medical Center, 77004, 713/523–1009, fax 713/526–8618. 30 rooms. Coin laundry, kitchenette. No credit cards.*

HOTELS NEAR THE AIRPORT

very expensive lodging

2 e-3

HYATT REGENCY HOUSTON AIRPORT

One advantage to a sprawling city is that we care enough about space to have an airport hotel centered on a 5-acre plot. Although only a mile from George Bush Intercontinental Airport/Houston, this hotel and conference center has lush grounds and views of the nearby World Houston Golf Course. Guests seeking more challenging links can take a 20-minute ride to several elite golf courses, including Tour 18. Complimentary transportation to Intercontinental Airport or Greenspoint Mall is included. *15747 John F. Kennedy Blvd., North, 77032, 281/987–1234, fax 281/590–8461. 314 rooms, 11 suites. Restaurant, bar, lobby lounge, in-room*

data ports, in-room safes, no-smoking rooms, room service, pool, hot tub, health club, dry cleaning, laundry service, business services. Free parking. AE, D, DC, MC, V.*

expensive lodging

2 e-3

COMFORT SUITES/ INTERCONTINENTAL PLAZA

Like any Intercontinental Airport hotel, the Comfort Suites offers a free shuttle to the terminals. Each suite has three phones, the work desks have data ports and voice mail, and a call to the front desk will procure a fax or copier. Guests who prefer to relax can take advantage of an exercise room and whirlpool, or satellite TV. *15555 John F. Kennedy Blvd., North/George Bush Intercontinental Airport/Houston, 77032, 281/442–0600, fax 281/442–0606. 57 suites. In-room data ports, no-smoking rooms, refrigerators, outdoor hot tub, health club, coin laundry, dry cleaning, business services, meeting rooms, airport shuttle, free parking. AE, D, DC, MC, V.*

2 f-6

RADISSON HOTEL AND CONFERENCE CENTER, HOBBY AIRPORT

The hotel has an indoor heated pool and an outdoor tanning patio for the best of both worlds. If you must stay in your room and work, then the staff can provide secretarial service. Shuttle service to nearby Hobby Airport runs around the clock. *9100 Gulf Fwy., South Houston/Hobby Airport, 77017, 713/943–7979, fax 713/943–1621. 288 rooms. Restaurant, piano bar, in-room data ports, room service, indoor pool, hot tub, sauna, health club, dry cleaning, laundry service, business services, meeting rooms, airport shuttle, free parking. AE, D, DC, MC, V.*

moderate lodging

2 f-6

BEST WESTERN HOBBY AIRPORT INN

In-room microwaves and a Jacuzzi make it easy to kick back at this small, two-story chain motel. The multilingual staff offers another type of comfort for those using Hobby to hop between the United States and South-of-the-Border destinations. Why subject yourself to the dreary mood of airport bars when you can check in, make sure you have fresh clothes for the flight out, and just soak in relative privacy. *8600 Gulf Fwy., South Houston/Hobby Airport, 77017, 713/910–8600, fax 713/910–8600. 50 rooms, restaurant, pool, hot tub, laundry service, free parking. AE, D, DC, MC, V.*

2 *d-3*

DAYS INN

You're in, you're out, and you're 1 mi from the airport and on the freeway for quick trips to Greenspoint Mall or the myriad area fast-food joints. *12500 North Fwy., North, 77060, 281/876–3888, fax 281/876–1524. 172 rooms. Pool, laundry service, airport shuttle, free parking. AE, D, DC, MC, V.*

budget lodging

2 *e-3*

HAWTHORN SUITES, LTD.

For a room rate that is frequently less than $100 a night, guests have a good location 5 mi from the airport and on the Beltway for quick access to many parts of the city. Some rooms have kitchenettes; ten have full kitchens. *702 N. Sam Houston Pkwy. E, North/George Bush Intercontinental Airport/Houston, 77060, 281/999–9942, fax 281/591–1215. 110 rooms, 92 suites. In-room data ports, no-smoking rooms, pool, dry cleaning, laundry service, business services, meeting rooms, airport shuttle, free parking. AE, D, DC, MC, V.*

EXTENDED STAY

6 *a-5*

CANDLEWOOD SUITES

Candlewood makes a point of setting rates at least $20 lower than the competition. For the price, guests get free 24-hour fitness centers, laundry facilities, and budget snacks from the "Candle-wood Cupboard" system—a minibar expanded to include food. *10503 Town and Country Way, Memorial/Spring Branch, 77024, 713/464–2677, fax 713/464–1185. 122 rooms, 24 suites. In-room data ports, in-room VCR, kitchenettes, no-smoking rooms, health club, coin laundry. AE, D, DC, MC, V. $$$*

2 *d-2*

HOMESTEAD VILLAGE GUEST STUDIOS

The downside to a longer stay is weekly maid service instead of daily. The upside is a home away from home with a close-to-complete kitchen with everything except a stocked spice rack, private phones, and a laundry room. Rates average $400–$500 a week. *220 Bammel Westfield Rd., FM 1960 area, 77090, 281/580–2221. In-room data ports. AE, D, DC, MC, V. $*

B&B RESERVATION SERVICES

10 *g-1*

BED & BREAKFAST RESERVATION SERVICE OF TEXAS/PATRICIAN BED & BREAKFAST

Pat Thomas can book you for lodging, weddings, or murder mystery dinners in her three-story Colonial Revival mansion. Or, she can help you with B&B reservations throughout the state. *1200 Southmore Blvd., Museum District, 77004, 713/523–1114 or 800/553–5797, fax 713/523–0790. 5 rooms. AE, D, DC, MC, V.*

chapter 7

CITY SOURCES

getting a handle on the city

basics of city life

Houston and the various incorporated cities, villages, and bedroom communities that fall into the metro mix can be a confusing sprawl. The other chapters help you explore; this one directs you to basic things you need. With this slice of civic sources, you can get a license for your car or pet, register to vote, and find the agencies you need in a crisis.

All transportation issues are covered from car registration and parking to toll-road tags and public transportation. You'll also find ways to make life at home a little cozier. Hire a maid, subscribe to a newspaper, and sign up for the Internet. If you're not a homebody, look for classes, dance groups, and cooking schools to fill your leisure hours.

BANKS

Between direct deposit and ATMs, you barely need to visit a bank. For those rare occasions, know that most lobbies are open from 9 until 4 weekdays. Drive-through windows may be open as late as 6, and many branches open their drive-through windows from 9 to noon on Saturday. The following banks have multiple locations in the area: **Bank of America** (713/247–6000); **Bank One** (713/659–1111); **Compass Bank** (713/968–8200); **Guaranty Federal Bank** (713/759–1576)—most branches of this Texas-based bank are outside the Loop; **Wells Fargo Bank** (713/319–1753).

DRIVING

Driving is a necessity in Houston. Between sprawl and traffic, you'll spend a lot of time in your car. You will not, however, have to worry about getting up early to move your car. Many apartment complexes provide not one, but two designated parking spaces for each apartment. When you're on the road, look for posted speed limits. For instance, the

current official speed limit for FM (Farm to Market) roads is 70 mph, but many still have 55 mph signs and law enforcement officers who catch you speeding on such roads will not be impressed with your knowledge of Texas Department of Transportation policy, they will be offended by your disregard for posted speed limits. Highway speed limits range from 55 to 70 mph for passenger cars, although limited-access or controlled highways may have a lower speed limit. Toll roads have a 55 mph speed limit. There's a base speed limit of 30 mph on urban streets, but throughout Houston are roadways with speed limits of 35, 40, 45, and even 50 mph. School zone speed limits also vary, from 20 to 35 mph, but they are always enforced during posted hours, whether or not the flashing lights are working. When and wherever you see the bright orange "Give Us A Brake!" signs, slow down. Speeds are always lower in construction areas, and often, traffic fines are doubled for offenses in a construction area. Right turn on red is legal.

licenses

Drivers must apply for a Texas driver's license within 30 days of moving to the state. When applying, be sure to have proof of car registration, copy of your birth certificate or a valid out-of-state driver's license, your social security number, and proof of insurance. If you do not own a car, you will be required to complete an affidavit of non-ownership. Be prepared to pass a vision test, written exam, and driver's test if your driver's license has expired. You also must register your car within 30 days. You will need the following: title, sales or tax use affidavit, current driver's license, and vehicle identification certificate indicating your car has passed a safety inspection. All vehicles must have a safety inspection every 12 months. Inspections are available at many gas stations, service centers, and dealers. Cost varies by year and make. Texas requires that all drivers have liability insurance, available from a wide range of insurance companies.

Department of Motor Vehicles: There is much mythology about which driver's license office has the shortest lines. Just ignore this wishful thinking and go to the office nearest your home or office. Houston has four DMV driver's license offices: **Dacoma** (4545 Dacoma, 713/957–6144); **Dover** (3502 Dover, 713/643–

ESSENTIAL NUMBERS

Houston Chronicle Info Source (713/220–2000).
Houston Public Library (713/236–1313).
Moviefone (281/444–3456).
Ticketmaster (713/629–3700).

7501); **Gessner** (12220 Gessner, 713/
773–3334); and **Grant** (10503 Grant Rd.,
281/890–5440).

traffic

Because Houstonians spend so much
time in traffic, the city thoughtfully deco-
rates many major thoroughfares with
bright orange cones and jolly yellow
machinery, and the festivities are made
more exciting by the element of surprise. It's impossible to predict where
the cones and backhoes will appear
next, although it may seem the freeways
are simply under perpetual construction. Adventurous motorists strike off
on shortcuts, which can be foolhardy
because Houston is not, by any stretch
of the imagination, laid out on a grid.
(Even Downtown, which has square
blocks, is canted slightly off a north–
south axis because it was built to follow
Buffalo Bayou.) Kirby comes so darn
near to wrapping around that the 1300
block is nearly parallel to the 3900
block. Spring Cypress Road (which is
also Riley Ruzzel Road) and Fry Road
also wander like ant trails. Because the
Houston area is filled with and surrounded by cities and villages, street
signs may suddenly change color (and
traffic cops from small police forces
may suddenly materialize).

Keep a Key Map street-finder in the car
and listen for traffic updates on the
radio, and you'll find your way anywhere
pretty easily. If you get lost, drive as
straight a route as possible until you hit
a freeway or major road such as
Almeda, West Little York, or Houston's
20-mi main drag, Westheimer. Get on
the major thoroughfare and you'll soon
see a sign or cross street to help you get
your bearings. When signs and cross
streets disappear, that means you're in
the country, probably northwest of the
city. Street names can be misleading as
well. For instance, West Main Street is
not an extension of Main Street; in fact,
it runs perpendicular to it. East Cowen
and West Cowen are two parallel streets
running north/south.

If you plan to spend a lot of time on the
Sam Houston Parkway or the Hardy Toll
Road, get an EZ Tag, a windshield
sticker that never has to be replaced. As
long as your account balance is high
enough, the scanner will let you through
and deduct the amount from your
account. When you have used up the

balance, you can simply pay again
unless you've set up an automatic
billing with a credit card, in which case
you are effectively charged for use. To
get one, call 281/875–3279 or stop by an
EZ Tag store. The Southwest store is on
Beltway 8, just east of Highway 59. The
Northwest EZ Tag store is at 330 Mead-
owfern. To complicate life for commuters, the EZ Tag stores are open from
7:30 to 5:30. If you want to pay as you
go, have plenty of nickels, dimes, and
quarters. Toll rates vary from toll plaza
to toll plaza, but the most you can pay
for a full trip is about $4.

GEOGRAPHY

Houston developed along Buffalo
Bayou, and the oldest neighborhoods
are in the wards, the Heights, and Eastside. As you head west from Downtown,
you can (roughly) follow the waterway
through established neighborhoods like
Memorial and Spring Branch and communities like Bunker Hill and Piney
Point. To the east, neighborhoods housing ship channel and refinery workers
developed, such as Galena Park. Houston really began to grow in the 1960s,
the era of planned communities, and
soon developments like Sharpstown
and Meyerland in Southwest Houston
were shoulder to shoulder with what
had once been bedroom communities
like Sugar Land and Alief. And, of
course, the space program fueled
tremendous growth in Houston.

Each time the population moves outward, businesses follow . . . and then
people move farther out, and business
follows. This trend was exacerbated with
communities like The Woodlands and
First Colony, which were designed with
business parks baked in. As you drive
through Houston, you'll pass through
bands of commerce, community, decay,
commerce, and community, and decay.
Because Houston has little zoning and a
prevailing entrepreneurial attitude, few
barriers prevent folks from moving into
a falling-down neighborhood and bringing it back up. A good example is West
Gray east of River Oaks. Ten years ago,
many homes were deserted and the
neighborhood was generally one to be
avoided. Now, those deserted homes
are restaurants and businesses, and the
houses behind them are remodeled or
refurbished.

Despite the often-discussed "messiness" of Houston, there are several major arteries. The 610 Loop and Beltway 8 circle the city. Highway 45 stretches from Galveston's beaches to Dallas. Highway 290 carries Houstonians from central Houston to northwestern suburbs. And Highway 59, perhaps the busiest of Houston's burdened freeways, is the route to and through Southwest Houston.

Every neighborhood has a wealth of shops and restaurants, but perhaps the Montrose-River Oaks shopping area, Rice University Village, and the Heights have the most quaint, villagelike personalities. The picture-book look of these shopping areas is a credit to rare—for Houston—neighborhood planning.

HOLIDAYS

The city of Houston holidays are New Year's Day, Martin Luther King Day, Presidents Day, Go Texan Day (an unofficial holiday, each February, the Friday before the Houston Livestock Show and Rodeo begins), Memorial Day, Juneteenth (June 19, an unofficial holiday), Independence Day, Labor Day, Veterans Day, Thanksgiving Day, and Christmas Day.

LIQUOR LAWS

Twenty-one is the legal drinking age. Those who can drink will be cut off at 2 AM every night of the week, and liquor stores are closed on Sunday (although you can buy beer and wine at many grocery and convenience stores).

NO SMOKING

The image of the cigar-chomping Texan or the lean Clint Eastwood cowboy sneering through the smoke of his cheroot is no longer accurate. Like most major cities, Houston largely requires its smokers to huddle outside when they indulge. Livelier bars and nightclubs do not treat the smoker as a pariah, but even in restaurants and bars with posted smoking sections, you would be wise to assess the climate before lighting up. Even at parties in the homes of smokers, guests who want a cigarette break will step outside.

PARKING

rules and enforcement

There are few parking meters in Houston. Most are Downtown or in the Medical Center. This makes it easy for meter maids to keep tabs, so don't push your luck. Houston has a great deal of on-street parking, but there is little rhyme or reason as to what kind of parking is allowed where. Some zones are always no-parking, some are posted hours—only parking, and the rules for parking can change even in mid-block. Always look carefully for no-parking signs before you leave your car. If you don't see signs, make sure you park facing the direction of traffic. Violate parking regulations and you will be ticketed. Rack up enough unpaid tickets and your car will be booted.

parking lots

Throughout the city, you'll find large and usually free parking lots. The Galleria has some valet parking, but most is free. Downtown has many lots, with rates varying from 75¢ to $1.75 per hour for the first two to four hours. Once you exceed the minimum hourly rate, you pay the "daily" or "evening rate," which ranges from $5 to $15 depending on location. The Theater District has a large, convenient underground parking lot. Theater District parking is a flat fee, typically $4, which seems reasonable for safe, lighted parking at night.

PERSONAL SECURITY

When it comes to safety, use your common sense, even if you are a big, burly man. In a city as disorganized as Houston, a "nice, quiet street" can be around the corner from a seedy area. Houston's low crime rate will be little comfort if you end up the victim of crime, especially if you can look back and kick yourself for taking a foolish chance.

PUBLIC TRANSPORTATION

Private transportation, in the form of massive sport utility vehicles, is the preferred way to travel. However, every weekday almost 300,000 Houstonians make use of the city's 1,300 Metro buses. Metro has a Park & Ride program, with lots as far away as Victoria.

metro

Most bus routes run from approximately 5 AM to midnight. The 14 transit centers are clean, and well-lighted; do be aware they don't have rest rooms. Except for Park & Ride, adult fares are $1 for local routes and $1.50 on express routes. However, you can save money with passes and SVC cards. A $2 adult-fare day pass is good for all travel during one day, a weekly pass is $9, a monthly pass is $35, and an annual pass is $315. Senior fares are discounted, so much that an annual pass for seniors, students, travelers with disabilities, or Medicare cardholders is $52. Discounts are available on a per-fare basis, but you must obtain a Metro ID card to benefit. SVC cards also offer a volume discount. For instance, if you pay $15 for your card, you can use it for up to $18.75 in fares—and more than one person can use the card. For $150, you can get an SVC card worth $204.50. You can get transfers with your card; just tell the driver before swiping the card in the fare box. All transfers are good for three hours.

Metro has a guaranteed ride home program. Those who register can count on quick service if they have a midday emergency and there is no regular bus service to get them home, or to the hospital or other destination. Only circumstances you could not have foreseen such as an accident, sudden illness, or a death in the family meet program requirements. Metro will send a cab to pick you up and take you to your destination. The cab ride is free, but tips are your responsibility.

Several routes are part of the Bikes on Buses program (bikes ride free, the fares on these routes are $1), and all transit centers have bike racks. For schedules, to obtain an ID card, to find a Metro Ride store near you, or other information, call 713/635–4000 or go to www.metroride.org.

metro park & ride

There are more than 20 park-and-ride locations in and surrounding Houston. A lot of riders tried Park & Ride once, while their car was in the shop, and have commuted by bus ever since. The Park & Ride program provides free lots (some

of which fill up fast), and the buses whiz commuters from the lot to central Houston. The lowest rate is Zone 1, $1.50 per trip. Zone 4 is $3.50. Monthly and annual passes offer savings.

metro trolley

Metro's Downtown trolleys are a cute and convenient way to get around during the business day and early evening, and they're free. Trolleys come along about every seven minutes. The "old-time" decor of the trolleys includes hard wooden seats.

taxis

Although you can't hail them on the street or find them at stands (except at some shopping malls), **Yellow Cabs** (713/236–1111), **United Cab** (713/699–0000), and others are 10 to 25 minutes away by phone. Airport hotels and some downtown hotels will call cabs for guests, and most restaurant hosts and bartenders are happy to call cabs for patrons.

PUBLICATIONS

Houston Chronicle (713/220–7211): Houston's only daily newspaper puts out a Sunday edition that's as big as a hay bale. Circulars and new home and car ads make up a hefty portion of the Sunday paper, and the editorial and metro sections run longer commentary on the newsworthy events of the past week. Breaking news, sports scores, and good ol' Ann Landers are featured in weekday editions. Julie Mason and Jane Ely write thoughtful and refreshing columns about the deeds and misdeeds of local pols, and these columnists' independent spirit is a nice contrast to the big business boosterism of the paper. (Survey results showing that most Houstonians were foursquare against a new football stadium were reported not as an indicator of popular opinion but as proof of the average person's failure to understand the issue.)

Doug Pike's outdoorsman column is one of the paper's most popular features, and untold numbers of Houston men have Walter Mitty dreams based on Pike's engaging and informed writing about the sporting life. Subscribers can also take advantage of the Chron's lively Web site, www.chron.com. (Some parts of the Web site are accessible to surfers, but to reach many pages you must either be a print paper subscriber or buy a Qpass for access.)

Houston Business Journal (713/688–8811): This lively business-news magazine features lifestyle stories, too. The weekly is especially helpful for small-business owners.

Houston Defender (713/663–6996): Houston's leading black newspaper was founded in 1930 and has been a force in the community every decade since. Publisher Sonny Messiah Giles offers readers a mix of local news and tightly focused lifestyle features. While other local papers cover prominent minister and civic leader Kirbyjon Caldwell and successful African-American business people such as Harlon Brooks, Mayor Lee Brown, and other newsmakers, they are not as likely to position such achievers as role models, or to take such role models to task.

Houston Press (713/280–2400): Houston's New Times weekly has some delicious crime reporting, intriguing features, and a hefty live-music and movies section.

Inside Houston (713/784–7575): This free weekly has a bit of politics and news along with its entertainment coverage.

Outsmart (713/520–7237): Houston's gay and lesbian monthly offers features on the local life and issues.

RADIO STATIONS

fm
KJIC 88.1 Gospel

KUHF 88.7 Classical

KSBJ 89.3 Christian

KACC 89.7 Alvin Community College

KPFT 90.1 Pacifica and National Public Radio programming

KTSU 90.9 Texas Southern University radio, blues, jazz, gospel, hip-hop

KPVU 91.3 Prairie View A&M University radio

KTRU 91.7 Rice University radio

KRTS 92.1 Classical

KKBQ 92.9 Country

KKRW 93.7 Classic rock

KLDE 94.5 Oldies

KIKK 95.7 Country

KHMX 96.5 Top 40

KKTL 97.1 Alternative

KBXX 97.9 Rap, R&B, soul

KHYS 98.5 Dance

KODA 99.1 Easy listening, jazz

KILT 100.3 Country

KLOL 101.1 Rock

KMJQ 102.1 Contemporary

KKPN 102.9 Spanish

KRBE 104.1 Top 40

KMPQ 104.9 Spanish

KHCB 105.7 Christian

KQQK 106.5 Spanish

KKHT 106.9 Talk

KTBZ 107.5 Top 40

KKTJ 107.9 Tejano

am
KILT 610 Sports

KIKK 650 Country (simulcast with KIKK-FM)

KSEV 700 News, sports, talk

KTRH 740 News, sports, talk

KBME 790 Easy listening

KEYH 850 Spanish

KJOJ 880 Christian

KYST 920 Spanish

KPRC 950 Talk

KMPQ 980 Spanish

KLAT 1010 Spanish

KENR 1070 Talk

KTEK 1110 Christian

KSSQ 1140 Gospel

KGOL 1180 Christian

KQUE 1230 Easy listening

KXYZ 1320 Spanish

KWWJ 1360 Gospel

KCOH 1430 R&B

KLVL 1480 Spanish

KYND 1500 Christian

KYOK 1590 Radio Disney

RECYCLING

Curbside recycling is not available throughout the city. For more information on pick-up service, call the hot line (713/837–9103). Houston has two recycling centers for glass, paper, plastic, and aluminum. One is off Highway 59 at Fountainview (entrance on Westpark), and one is off Highway 3 at Beltway 8 (on Brantley). For more information on city recycling, call 713/868–8369.

TAX & TIP

sales tax and beyond

Though Texas does not have a state income tax, and no city in Texas has a local income tax, estate property, or unitary tax, and there is no tax on groceries—you still got to pay the man. In the city of Houston proper, sales tax is 8.25%. Sales tax may be lower in other area towns. All lodging in Houston has a 17% hotel tax.

tipping

Generally, waiters expect between 15% and 20% of the bill (many restaurants automatically add a gratuity for large parties), ditto hairdressers, manicurists, cab drivers, and dog groomers. Minor players in the service industries, such as shampoo girls, expect a couple of bucks. The average valet tip, and valets are everywhere, seems to be rising from $2 to $3.

TELEVISION

network

Local network channels in Houston are ABC, Channel 13; CBS, Channel 11; FOX, Channel 26; NBC, Channel 2; PBS, Channel 8; Telmundo, Channel 48; UPN, Channel 20; WB, Channel 39.

cable

There are several local cable companies, and to make it even harder to keep up with what's on channel 42, Warner Cable regularly reshuffles the service package. Check your Southwestern Bell Yellow Pages for the latest cable company listings.

Kingwood Cablevision (281/360–7500).

Warner (713/341–1000).

VOTER REGISTRATION

Because this is a state of iconoclasts, Texas voters do not register by party but as a Texan from a certain precinct. No party affiliation is included in your registration unless you vote in a primary. Party stamps, applied when you vote in a primary, are used to keep people from voting in both Republican and Democratic primaries. The **Harris County Tax Assessor-Collector's Office** (1001 Preston, 2nd floor, 713/224–1919) and several substations handle voter registration. For more information, call the **League of Women Voters** (713/784–2923) or the state election commission (800/252–VOTE).

WEATHER

Houston weather is very simple, really: February has a damp cold that sinks into your bones no matter how warmly you dress; the rest of the year is blistering hot, even when it rains. And rain is common. Houston has a 1 in 10 chance of receiving 3½ inches of rain in any hour. Naturally, it doesn't work out so that we have hour-long rains. Some days see sudden storms that blow over in a half hour, other days see slow steady drizzle from dawn to dark. Average annual rainfall is 45 inches, but more than 60 inches annually is not unheard of. Even when it's not raining, you'll often feel like you're wrapped in a damp wool blanket. Thanks to the combination of warmth and water, even finicky annuals bloom three and four times a year.

With the exception of flooding, Houston weather is largely irrelevant. People drive in their climate-controlled cars to climate-controlled buildings. (Some office workers would like a little less AC—clerical workers commonly keep space heaters hidden under their desks to protect them from 62° air blasting from air-conditioning vents.) For breaking weather, there's always TV. If you think the Weather Channel is boring, tune in during hurricane season. Cable channels are as follows: most Warner Cable systems, 27; Optel, 67; Westchase Interactive, 29; Houston Skyline, 24; Peoples Choice, 37; Houston Home Theater, 24; Phonoscope, 23. Heat alerts, issued in triple-digit weather, usually come with the advice to go somewhere air-conditioned; libraries and malls are specifically suggested. But we've noticed that sports bars seem to be where people end up during a heat wave. Apparently, the medical community has failed in its attempts to educate the public about the dehydrating effect of cold beer.

resources for challenges & crises

BABY-SITTING SERVICES

Caretemps (713/263–9440): licensed and bonded agency that can be reached any hour of the day.

Morningside Nanny (713/526–3989, www.morningsidenannies.com): member of International Nanny Association and venerable child-care agency. Like the Hair Club for Men president Sy Sperling, Morningside Nanny owner Pat Cascio uses her own services. Her four daughters had nannies.

Nannykins (713/777–4949): bonded referral service. Nannykins does a thorough background check on all caregivers.

CATERING

grown-up parties

Abbey Party & Tent Rentals (7930 Blankenship Dr., 713/957–4800): Pretty much everything but your guests can be hired through Abbey. Rent a 40-ft by 80-ft tent with a chandelier, heated or cooled, and tables, chairs, and table settings. It may seem like a big deal to you, but it's all in a day's work for Abbey.

Chamber Music Unlimited (FM 1950, 14303 Hargrave Rd., 281/469–2496): DJs, your younger brother's band, a party CD—these are all background music possibilities for your next party, but a better bet is live professional musicians. Despite the name, this ensemble plays both pop and classical.

Creative Catering Innovations (281/482–5132): Who has time to throw a party? Invitations, a menu, decorations—leave all the details to this group.

Ethel Houston Catering Service (3722 Zephyr St., 713/748–2563): Ethel's favorite food to cook is "Whatever I want to cook." If you're lucky, what she wants to cook might be her baked chicken in lemon or stuffed potatoes with Cornish hens, or some other seemingly ordinary dish. In Ethel's hands, Southern and country-style food, and even Continental dishes, are extraordinary. One day soon, Emeril Lagasse is going to stumble across Ethel, and when he does they'll write a cookbook together and she'll be a star. Oh, Ethyl will do any kind of menu, she's not fussy about what she wants to cook. Speak up if you get her on the phone.

Jackson Hicks Catering (707 Hawthorne, 713/523–5780): If the event wasn't held in Tony's wine cellar, then Jackson Hicks probably catered any soiree described in Maxine Mesinger's page-one Chronicle gossip column, and any fete touted in Shelby Hodge's Chronicle society column (which, currently, runs a few pages into the lifestyle section). Hicks's talented crew can prepare a conservative roast beef buffet or a lavish spread featuring the latest fusion fare. Through the years, though, chic Oscetra caviar and bite-sized lemon tarts with a Southern sensibility have been unfailing staples of the Hicks kitchens.

kids' parties

Animal Parties (281/354–6001): The company does provide kiddy party standards like a moonwalk, Ferris wheels, and space balls, but the real deal is critters. If your nerves and your yard can stand it, Animal Parties will bring llamas, deer, pygmy goats, potbellied pigs, giant land tortoises (30 pounds each), a wallaby, and up to 20 ponies. Not that you have to order all 20 ponies. The Birthday Special package is a full petting zoo, 25 to 30 animals, and one pony for rides.

The cost is $275 for a two-hour party, with $50 extra for each additional pony. Animal Parties doesn't do food, or catering referrals, but they do feel after 28 years of giving parties in Houston that kids are perfectly happy with a pizza delivery or hot dogs catered from James Coney Island. Because few people have a garage large enough for an Animal Party party, they do have contingency plans for inclement weather. They can reschedule for a rain date, although there is a $75 trip charge if the crew leaves the ranch before the rain cancellation.

CHARITIES

Goodwill Industries (2500 Jensen, 713/692–6221): accepts donations at several locations throughout the city. If you don't have time to drop off old clothes or household goods, you can unload them at a garage sale and send a check to the **Red Cross** (2700 Southwest Fwy., 713/526–8300).

CHILD CRISIS

Child Abuse Hotline (713/626–5701).

L.I.F.E., Local Infant Formula for Emergencies, (713/528–6044).

CITY GOVERNMENT

Citizen's Assistance Division Office (713/247–1888): offers "coaching" for any complaints or civic projects a citizen might have. The staff will help you direct your complaints to the proper office in the proper form, and follow through for resolution. If you have an idea, the Citizen's Assistance office will steer you around to meet with the city offices equipped to help with research for your project. If you want to make a presentation at a city council meeting, the office will guide you so that your time, and the council's, is well spent.

Mayor's office (713/247–2200).

COAST GUARD

Houston Coast Guard (9640 Clinton Dr., 713/671–5100): call to report accidents and crime on the water.

CONSUMER PROTECTION

Attorney General—Consumer Protection (713/223–5886).

Better Business Bureau (713/868–9500).

Consumer Products Safety Commission (281/324–6900).

COUNSELING & REFERRALS

Family Service Center (713/861–4849).

aids advice
AIDS Foundation Houston (713/623–6796).

Ryan White Planning Council Harris County (713/572–3724).

alcoholism treatment
Alcoholics Anonymous (4140 Director's Row, 713/686–6300): more than 2,000 meetings a week in Houston.

Houston Council on Alcoholism and Drug Abuse (303 Jackson Hill, 713/942–4100).

crime victims
Attorney General of Texas (800/983–9933).

Houston Police Hate Crimes Hotline (713/308–8737).

drug abuse treatment
Houston Council on Alcoholism and Drug Abuse (303 Jackson Hill, 713/942–4100).

mental health information & referral
Mental Health & Mental Retardation Authority of Harris County (713/970–7070).

rape victims
Houston Area Women's Center Rape Crisis Hotline (713/528–7273).

DOCTOR & DENTIST REFERRALS

Eldercare Referrals (281/397–9997).

UTMB Physician Referral (888/488–3627).

EMERGENCIES

ambulance
City of Houston EMS (911).

Cypress Creek EMS (281/440–9650).

hospital emergency rooms
Ben Taub (1504 Taub Loop, 713/793–2000).

Columbia/HCA Spring Branch Medical Center (8850 Long Point, 713/467–6555).

Columbia/HCA West Houston Medical Center (12141 Richmond, 281/558–3444).

Columbia Kingwood Medical Center (22999 Hwy. 59, 281/359–7500).

Houston Northwest Medical Center (710 FM 1960, 281/440–1000).

Memorial Healthcare System Southwest (7600 Beechnut, 713/776–5000).

Memorial Hermann Hospital (6411 Fannin St., 713/704–4000).

Memorial Hermann Hospital Southeast (11800 Astoria Blvd., 281/929–6100).

Methodist Sugar Land (16655 Southwest Fwy., 281/274–7000).

Tomball Regional Hospital (605 Holderrieth, Tomball, 281/351–1623).

poison control center
Poison Control Center (713/654–1701 or 800/764–7661).

suicide prevention
Suicide Prevention Hotline (713/790–0949, 713/222–2121, or 800/SUICIDE).

FAMILY PLANNING

Planned Parenthood (713/522–6363).

GAY & LESBIAN CONCERNS

Dignity Gay and Lesbian Hotline (713/880–2872): offers people who are no longer involved in the church of their upbringing with spiritual referrals and support.

Gay and Lesbian Switchboard (713/529–3211): The Houston Lesbian and Gay Community Center maintains this line to offer community support and resource information to the gay and lesbian and transgender community. AIDS help agency referrals and information about various community groups are offered.

HOUSE-CLEANING HELP AGENCIES

Maid Brigade (713/664–7740).

Maid in the Shade (713/665–6243).

Westside Maids (281/855–9212).

INTERIOR DESIGNER & ARCHITECT REFERRALS

ImproveNet (888/424–1220).

LANDLORD/ TENANT ASSISTANCE

If you rent, please understand that your deposit is not your last month's rent; if you move without paying the last month's rent, assuming the deposit will cover it instead of getting an agreement in writing, your former landlord can sue you, and will very likely win.

HUD Homebuyers and Renters Counseling (713/313–2274): A HUD counseling officer will help if you feel you have been discriminated against, and can also talk to you about your other housing rights.

LEGAL SERVICES

ACLU Houston (713/942–8146): The ACLU is not a legal service. Rather, it's a nonprofit concerned with the rights of all citizens. When the ACLU determines that basic rights such as freedom of speech, freedom of the press, freedom of religion and separation of church and state, due process, and proper treatment by law enforcement officials may be in jeopardy, the ACLU may take the case on as a test case to set a precedent. All issues brought before the Houston chapter will be reviewed by the state office.

LULAC District 18 (713/223–5510): The now national League of United Latin American Citizens was founded in south Texas. Much like the NAACP or Urban League, LULAC is organized to fight discrimination and to enrich a particular community.

Texas Bar Association (800/252–9690 or 877/9TEXBAR): Houstonians can call the Texas bar for legal referrals.

LOST & FOUND

Local police precincts do not maintain lost and found areas.

at airlines & airports
If you lose something on a flight, you need to contact the airline (see Airlines, below) and the airports you visited. George Bush Intercontinental Airport/Houston lost and found (713/230–3100, press 5); Hobby Airport lost and found (713/640–3000).

on other public transportation
BUSES
Metro (713/658–0854).

LONG-DISTANCE BUSES
Greyhound (713/759–6530).

TAXICABS
If you've left a bag in a cab, or like Yo-Yo Ma, your cello on top of one, you must call the cab company's dispatch office (see Public Transportation, above).

TRAINS
Amtrak (800/872–7245).

lost animals
First, know that cats rarely go far and dogs usually head into the wind. If you cannot find your pet, contact all the animal shelters daily; call area vets; put up posters in your neighborhood; and lay out clothes in parks and open areas near your home, especially in places

your pet has been taken for walks. If your pet finds something that smells like you, your pet will stay with the scent. (When you are reunited with your pet, report back to the shelters and vets you've called.)

Citizens for Animal Protections (11925 Katy Fwy., 281/497–0591).

Harris County Rabies and Animal Control (612 Camino, 281/999–3191).

Houston Humane Society (14700 Almeda, 713/433–6421).

SPCA (900 Portway Dr., 713/869–7722).

lost credit cards
American Express (800/528–4800).

Discover (800/347–2683).

MasterCard (800/307–7309).

Visa (800/336–8472).

lost traveler's checks
American Express (800/221–7282).

ON-LINE SERVICES

In addition to the multitude of national Internet service porviders, some local companies provide Houstonians with access to the Internet.

Blackbox (281/480–2684).

Insync (713/407–7000).

Neosoft (713/968–5800).

PDQ.net (713/830–3100).

PETS

adoptions
Citizens for Animal Protections (11925 Katy Fwy., 281/497–0591).

Harris County Rabies and Animal Control (612 Camino, 281/999–3191).

Houston Humane Society (14700 Almeda, 713/433–6421).

SPCA (900 Portway Dr., 713/869–7722).

grooming

Animal Inn (10339 Farm Road, 281/277–2727).

Club Pet (1703 West Gray, 713/942–8448).

training

Houston Clickers dog training club (www.homestead.com/HoustonClickers).

Houston Obedience Training—HOT Dog Club (713/694–7446; www.flash.net/~hotdc).

Lone Star Search and Rescue Dog Association (281/322–0163; www.lonestarsarda.org).

Man's Best Friend (1511 Upland, 713/932–6709).

Southwest Tracking Association of Metro Houston (www.epick9.com/sta).

Westkoak Dog Training Center (281/376–9061).

veterinary hospitals

Animal Emergency Clinic (1111 West Loop S, 713/693–1100).

Low Cost Spay & Neuter Clinic (14700 Almeda, 713/433–6453).

Sunset Boulevard Animal Clinic (2525 Sunset Blvd., 713/526–5881).

PHARMACIES OPEN 24 HOURS

Twelve **Eckerd Drugs** (800/325–3737) and 26 **Walgreen's** (713/247–4400) never close. Call to locate the closest 24-hour store.

POLICE

In the city of Houston proper, the non-emergency number is 713/247–4400. In an emergency, dial 911.

stations/patrol divisions

Central (6100 Riesner, 713/247–4400).

Clear Lake (2855 Bay Area Blvd., 281/218–3800).

Eastside (7525 Sherman, 713/928–4600).

Fondren (11168 Fondren, 713/773–7900).

North (9455 W. Montgomery, 281/405–5300).

Northeast (8301 Ley, 713/635–0200).

Northwest (6000 Teague, 713/744–0900).

Southeast (8300 Mykawa, 713/731–5000).

South Central (2202 St. Emanuel, 713/651–8100).

Southwest (4503 Beechnut, 713/666–8806).

Westside (3203 S. Dairy Ashford, 281/584–4700).

storefronts

Storefront stations aim to make Houston Peace Officers community fixtures like Mayberry's Andy Taylor and Barney Fife. The storefronts are typically in strip centers and other neighborhood areas. The officers also take extra time to speak at school and churches and various community meetings.

Acres Homes (6719 W. Montgomery, 713/699–9591).

Aldine (10966 Aldine, 281/272–4784).

Broadway Square (8751 Broadway, 713/847–4155).

Clarkcrest (8940 Clarkcrest, 713/952–0182).

Downtown (1415 Fannin, 713/308–8000).

Fifth Ward (4300 Lyons Ave., 713/672–5890).

Gessner (1331 Gessner, 713/722–7691).

Greenspoint (Greenspoint Mall, 281/875–6155).

Gulfton (5980 Renwick, 713/668–4141).

Heights (357 W. 19th St., 713/863–7233).

Hiram Clark (14723 Hiram Clark, 713/433–2720).

Independence Heights (803 Crosstimbers, 713/742–1491).

Irvington Village (2901 Fulton, 713/222–3325).

Jensen Street (9211 Jensen, 713/742–1406).

Kingwood (23910 Eastex Fwy., 281/359–6761).

Lyons Avenue (6702 Lyons, 713/672–5809).

Neartown (802 Westheimer, 713/284–8604).

Near North (1335 W. 43rd St., 713/956–3140).

Northline Park (7208 Nordling, 281/272–4250).

Palm Center (5300 Griggs, 713/845–2488).

Ripley House (4401 Navigation, 713/238–2283).

Southmore (3711 Southmore, 713/526–1255).

Spring Branch (8400 Long Point, 713/464–6901).

Sunnyside (3511 Reed Rd., 713/732–5132).

Telephone (10201 Telephone Rd., 713/991–3504).

Wesley House (1410 Lee, 713/228–9168).

Westbury (5550 Gasmer, 713/728–2424).

Willowbrook (12932 Willowchase, 281/807–9054).

POSTAL SERVICES

There are almost 200 post offices in the Houston area. A list of the major neighborhoods follow. Houston post offices are open 8 to 5 weekdays. The main post office and many other post offices have lobbies open 24 hours with stamp machines. There is mail pick up on the weekends at all post offices. For general information, mail rates, and zip code information, call 800/275–8777. Also, many of the branches can be reached through this number.

Albert Thomas (14917 El Camino Real, 281/488–8013).

Almeda (3030 W. Fuqua, 713/433–3511).

Addicks Barker (16830 Barker Springs, 281/492–6162).

Astrodome/Old Spanish Trail (8205 Braesmain Dr., 713/665–1141).

Baytown (601 W. Baker Rd., 281/420–2508).

Bear Creek (16015 Cairnway Dr., 281/855–2556).

Beechnut (11703 Beechnut, 281/498–0672).

Bellaire (5350 Bellaire, 713/668–0521).

East Houston (9604 Mesa Rd., 713/631–4835).

Eastwood (5415 Lawndale, 800/275–8777).

Fairview (1315 Hyde Park, 713/522–3897).

First Colony (3130 Grants Lake Blvd., 281/494–3130).

Fleet Wood (315 Addicks Howell, 281/759–7860).

Galleria (5015 Westheimer, 713/622–0764).

Garden Oaks Finance (3816 N. Shepherd, 713/694–0111).

Greenbriar (3740 Greenbriar, 713/528–2283).

Greens North (1530 Greensmark, 800/275–8777).

Long Point (1702 Hillendahl, 713/468–1581).

Main Post Office (401 Franklin, 713/226–3452).

Medical Center (7205 Almeda, 713/741–5537).

Memorial Park (10505 Town and Country Way, 800/275–8777).

North Shepherd (7511 N. Shepherd, 281/447–4086).

Oak Forest (2499 Judiway, 713/686–2575).

River Oaks (1900 W. Gray, 713/528–3366).

South Post Oak (5505 Belrose, 713/723–3563).

Spring Klein (7717 Louetta, 281/251–8000).

Sugar Land (225 Matlage Way, 281/494–2042).

Willow Place (12955 Willow Place, 281/890–9416).

Westfield (17119 Red Oak, 281/444–7295).

SENIOR-CITIZEN SERVICES

Houston/Harris County Area Agency on Aging (713/794–9001).

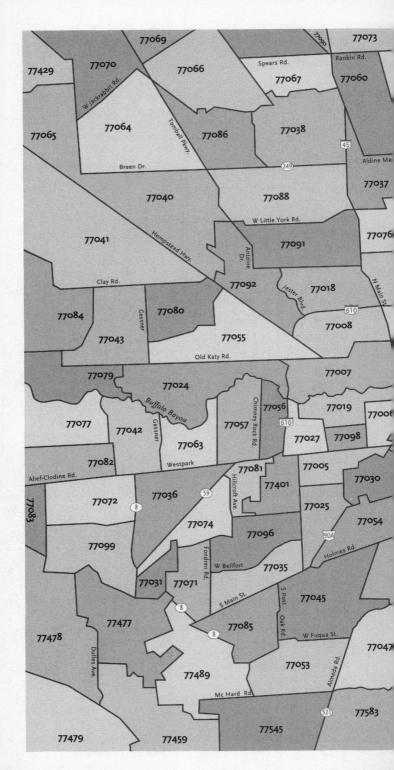

Houston Zip Codes

77032
77396
77338
77346
77532
Lake Houston
Aldine-Bender Rd.
Lee Dr.
77039
77050
77044
Mt Houston Rd.
Sheldon Reservoir
77093
77016
77078
Green's Bayou
Hardy Toll Rd.
Hirsch Rd.
Beaumont Hwy.
77028
Mesa
77049
022
77026
77013
Carpenter Bayou
7009
610
77530
77015
10
77002
77020
77029
Hunting Bayou
Buffalo Bayou
77003
77010
77011
77547
South St.
77536
7004
77023
77506
Bray's Bayou
Griggs
77012
225
77503
77021
77017
Southmore Ave.
Preston Rd.
77087
77502
77033
45
Spencer Hwy.
051
77587
77061
77504
77505
Sims Bayou
865
Genoa-Red Bluff Rd.
Cullen Blvd.
Mykawa Rd.
77048
77075
77034
Kings Point Rd.
77059
3
77062
77089
865
77581
Clear Creek
77598
Dixie Farm Rd.
77581
77584

207

Houston Junior Forum Senior Guidance Program Referral Service (713/529–9991): Seniors and their caregivers can turn to the Junior Forum on advice about area programs for the elderly.

Meals on Wheels (713/794–9001).

UTILITIES

When Reliant Energy, a deregulated electric company, merged our gas and electric providers into one company, without the convenience of one bill, people grumbled. When Reliant announced plans for a Power of Houston laser-fireworks-concert extravaganza, people grumbled, but those murmurings turned to cheers when the event kicked off in September 1997. For one, it was amazing—the night sky and Downtown buildings were lighted, there was music and more than 10 tons of fireworks to burst eardrums well outside the Beltway, and a genuine sense of festivity. Second, it engendered community. People from outlying areas came in for tailgate parties at private parking lots, and nobody minded. In fact, many area businesses volunteered their rest rooms for tailgaters. The Power of Houston celebration was exciting, beloved, and one of the few annual events that Houstonians celebrated with civic pride (as distinguished from the unlocalized spirit of fun we usually enjoy). Yet after four years the Power of Houston was canceled. Reliant's PowerPage customer newsletter is not, despite impressive graphics and a dramatic black and gold cover, as exciting as a four-hour fireworks and laser show.

gas
Reliant Energy (713/654–5100).

electric
Reliant Energy/HL&P (713/207–7777).

telephone
Southwestern Bell (800/464–7928).

water
Houston Public Utilities (713/371–1400).

VOLUNTEERING

For a general overview of opportunities in Houston, call **United Way** (713/685–2300). You can also check with community theaters and programs, nature centers, and museums in your neighborhood. For a unique volunteering experience with your pet, contact **Caring Critters** (713/812–4322, www.caringcritters.org), which visits hospitals and people who appreciate a furry friend's company.

ZONING & PLANNING

Houston is not big on zoning and planning, but there is a city **Department of Planning and Development** (713/837–7707).

learning

ACTING SCHOOLS

TUTS' Humphrey's School of Musical Theatre (2600 Southwest Fwy., 713/558–2600): plenty of singing and dancing, and sometimes a chance to be a supernumerary on stage with a real star.

Unicorn School of Acting (15037 Delaney Rd., LaMarque, 409/935–3002): children get the thespian basics in *Our Town, The Wizard of Oz, Godspell*, and other classics of the stage.

University of Houston (713/743–3000): offers degree programs.

ART & PHOTOGRAPHY SCHOOLS

Art League of Houston (1953 Montrose, 713/523–9530): without much attitude or fanfare, the hub of Houston art.

Houston Center for Photography (1441 W. Alabama, 713/529–4755): classes in the art and technique of photography, and art appreciation.

Glassell School of Art (5101 Montrose, 713/639–7500): Studio School and Junior School offer both art history and instruction in various disciplines. Expensive and, at some levels, competitive.

Watercolor Art Society Houston (1601 Alabama, 713/942–9966): technique classes, demonstrations, and lectures.

University of Houston (713/743–3000): offers degree programs only.

BALLROOM DANCING

1960 Whip Club (281/655–5309).

Barbara King's Houston Center of Dance (5700 S. Rice, 713/667–3890).

Bay Area Whip Dance Club (281/480–9447).

Discover Dance (14520 Memorial Dr., 281/558–0369).

Fred Astaire Dance Studio (12649 G1 Memorial Dr., Suite 59, 713/827–8084).

Houston Swing Dance Society (713/662–3861).

Houston Argentine Tango Association (3618 Glen Haven, 713/665–3812).

Victor Collin's Studio at Bella Terrazza (2840 Chimney Rock, 281/443–3322).

BOOKBINDING

Glassell School of Art (5101 Montrose, 713/639–7500).

COMMUNITY COLLEGES

North Harris College (2700 W. W. Thorne Dr., 281/618–5400).

San Jacinto College (4624 Fairmont Pkwy., Pasadena, 281/998–7100).

San Jacinto College South (13735 Beamer Rd., 281/484–1900).

COMPUTER TRAINING

ExecuTrain (5051 Westheimer, Suite 500, Galleria, 713/626–4546).

HAL PC (4543 Post Oak Pl., 713/993–3300).

Learning Edge (1020 Holcombe, Bank of America, 713/794–0100).

COOKING SCHOOLS

Alain & Marie LeNotre Culinary Institute (7070 Allensby, 713/629–0077).

Art Institute of Houston (1900 Yorktown, 800/275–4344).

Le Panier (7275 Brompton Rd., 713/664–9848).

Texas Chefs Association (19826 Atascocita Dr., Humble, 281/459–7150).

DANCE

Houston Ballet Academy (1921 West Bell, 713/523–6300): no experience required. Anyone over the age of 14 with an interest in ballet is welcome to sign up for classes.

LANGUAGE SCHOOLS

Berlitz Language Center (520 Post Oak Blvd., 713/626–7844): language instruction in English as a second language, French, German, Italian, Russian, Spanish, and many other languages.

chinese
Institute of Chinese Culture (10550 Westoffice, 713/339–1992).

esl
Bilingual Education Institute (8401 Westheimer, 713/789–4555).

Houston Community College System Places to Go, Schools).

french
Alliance Francaise de Houston (427 Lovett Blvd., 713/526–1121).

german
Goethe Institut (3120 Southwest Fwy., 713/528–2787).

One World Language Solutions (600 Jefferson, 713/650–3133).

italian
Italian Cultural and Community Center (1101 Milford, 713/524–4222).

japanese
Japanese Language Instruction (281/920–1338).

korean
Korean Translation & Counseling (6100 Hillcroft, 713/541–3100).

russian
Russian Language Connection (713/663–7086).

spanish
Bilingual Institute of Houston (8401 Westheimer, 713/789–4555).

Conversational Spanish Center (3327 Woods Edge, 281/651–8290).

Spanish Language Institute (337 Sawdust Rd., The Woodlands, 281/367–4006).

MUSIC SCHOOLS

Houston Music Institute (14511 Memorial, 281/556–1644).

Rockin' Robin Guitars & Music (3619 Shepherd, 713/529–5442).

West Oaks Music Studio (2305 Hwy. 6, 281/531–5560).

vacation & travel information

AIRLINES

Aero Mexico (800/237–6639).

Air Canada (800/776–3000).

Air France (800/237–2747).

Air Tran (800/825–8538).

America West (800/235–9292).

American Airlines/American Eagle (800/433–7300).

Atlantic Southeast Airlines (800/282–3424).

Aviasca (713/266–6653).

British Airways (800/247–9297).

Cayman Airways (800/422–9626).

Continental Airlines (800/525–0280).

Delta (800/221–1212).

KLM Royal Dutch Airlines (800/374–7747).

Lufthansa German Airline (800/645–3880).

Northwest Airlines (800/225–2525).

Southwest Airlines (800/435–9792).

Sun Country Airlines (800/359–5786).

TACA International Airlines (800/535–8780).

Trans World Airlines (800/221–2000).

United Airlines (800/241–6522).

US Air (800/428–4322).

AIRPORTS

The Houston Airport System comprises **George Bush Intercontinental Airport/Houston** (281/230–3100), **Hobby Airport** (713/640–3000), and **Ellington Field** (713/847–4200). The TDD number for all is (800/735–2988). Bush and Hobby's combined traffic is more than 1,500 flights arriving and departing every day. *See* Lost & Found, *above,* for how to inquire about lost items.

getting there by public transportation
Metro has bus service from Downtown to both Bush and Hobby, and some transit centers, such as the Greenspoint transit center in the Greenspoint Mall parking lot, have routes to Bush. Rates are standard fare ($1 for local, $1.50 for express). A variety of shuttles offer airport service at $12 to $20 depending on pickup site. Call **Express Shuttle USA** (713/523–8888) for details.

Cab rates to the airport are based on zones. The lowest rate is $17 for travel between Downtown and Hobby. High rates are $38 between Bush and several outside-the-Loop zones. The zone rate for a trip from Downtown to Bush is $33.50. You may find that a town car will be cheaper than a cab, especially if you or your company has frequent bookings. All major car rental companies have pick up and drop off at the airports, but in many cases, the cars are at outlying lots, so you need to factor in extra time for shuttle to or from the lot.

getting there by car

You can reach Bush from Highway 59 north or Highway 45 north, and if you are coming from Downtown or the Loop, you may want to use the traffic-free Hardy toll road. The Gulf Freeway is the route for Hobby. Do not make the mistake of thinking that you can pick up Airport Boulevard off Highway 288 south and cut east.

CAR RENTAL

The state's car rental tax is 15%, but the number of taxes and fees levied on your rented car will depend on whether you rent it at an airport or neighborhood location.

Here's a tip for any rental agency in the country—if you want a special car, like a convertible or a Chrysler PT Cruiser, call agents at the pickup location and ask if they actually have that specific car on the lot. Be as charming and respectful as possible. Ask them if they can hold your dream car. Often, kindly agents will do what they can to make sure you get exactly what you want instead of the standard rental agreement's "or similar."

Alamo-Rent-A-Car (800/327–9633): Our own homegrown agency has low rates. Even without coupons or special offers, you can get a Gran Prix for less than $200 a week. But, like most budget rental agencies, Alamo saves on operating costs by putting parking lots farther from the airport, so be sure to calculate extra shuttle time into your trip when you rent from Alamo.

Avis (800/831–2847): The feel is all American-made cars. The stable, conservative image put forth by the cars carries over to the counter service. The company would rather be considered dependable than exciting, and their specials are more likely to be simple percentage-off deals than discount theme-park packages.

Budget (713/988–7300): Hey, it's not just about your budget. If you're willing to spend extra, Budget has a few Jaguars in its rental fleet.

Dollar (713/641–2806): During these days of a thriving economy, Dollar has left behind its cut-rate attitude and become just another rental car company. However, in nostalgia for their origins, the company has a special "Silver Dollar" club for senior renters.

Hertz (713/941–6821): Catering to the business traveler, Hertz does not have friendly rates. However, frequent renters get a lovely packet of coupons each month. One day free or upgrades are frequent specials, and a special that can put you in a convertible Chrysler Sebring at midsize car rates is special indeed.

National (713/641–0533): American, Continental, Delta, and Northwest all have arrangements with National, so if your business requires you to fly one of their major routes, you could end up saving a lot of time and money by joining the Emerald Club. You can also earn American West miles by renting with National.

Thrifty (713/442–5000): Reasonable rates are the only reason for twentysomething travelers to take advantage of Thrifty savings—the agency has special rates for college students. Perfect for road trips, the college plan has no fee for additional drivers. Four kids can pick into a no-frills four-door for $200 a week, including gas.

CURRENCY EXCHANGE

American Express Travel Agency (1200 McKinney, The Park Shops, 713/658–1114).

International Money Exchange (1130 Travis, 713/654–1900).

Thomas Cook Currency (10777 Westheimer, 713/782–8092).

EMBASSIES & CONSULATES

Argentina Consulate General (3050 Post Oak, 713/871–8935).

Austrian Consulate (230 Westcott, 713/723–9979).

Bolivian Consulate General (800 W. Sam Houston Pkwy. S, 713/977–2344).

British Consulate (1000 Louisiana, Suite 1900, 713/659–6270).

Chilean Consulate (1360 Post Oak, 713/621–5853).

Consulado General de Nicaragua (2825 Wilcrest, 713/953–0237).

Consulate General Guatemala (3600 Gessner, 713/953–9531).

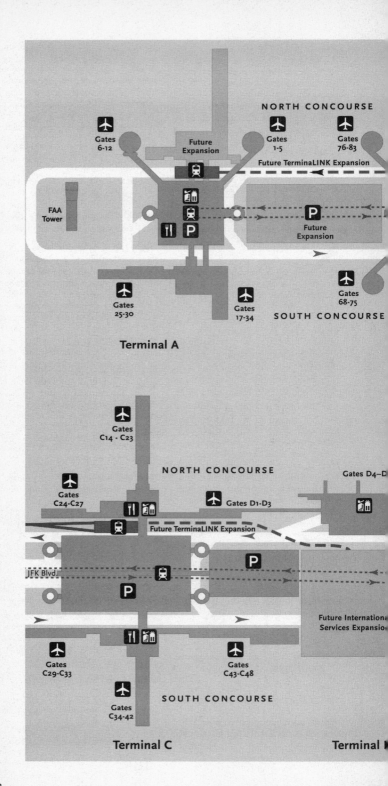

NORTH CONCOURSE

Gates
6-12

Future
Expansion

Gates
1-5

Gates
76-83

Future TerminaLINK Expansion

FAA
Tower

P

Future
Expansion

Gates
68-75

Gates
25-30

Gates
17-34

SOUTH CONCOURSE

Terminal A

Gates
C14 - C23

NORTH CONCOURSE

Gates D4–D

Gates
C24-C27

Gates D1-D3

Future TerminaLINK Expansion

JFK Blvd.

P

P

Future Internationa
Services Expansio

Gates
C29-C33

Gates
C43-C48

Gates
C34-42

SOUTH CONCOURSE

Terminal C

Terminal I

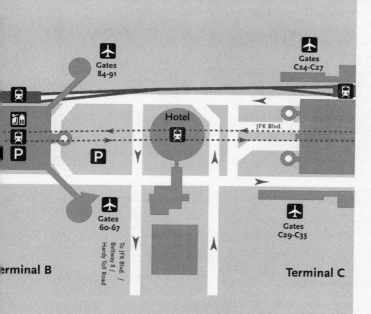

George Bush Intercontinental Airport/Houston

Gates
84-91

Gates
C24-C27

Hotel

JFK Blvd.

P

P

Gates
60-67

Gates
C29-C33

To JFK Blvd. /
Beltway 8 /
Hardy Toll Road

Terminal B

Terminal C

P

To Will Clayton Pkwy.

Airline	Phone	Terminal
AeroMexico	800-237-6639	D
Air Canada	800-776-3000	D
Air France	800-237-2747	D
America West	800-235-9292	A
American Airlines	800-433-7300	A
Atlantic Southeast Airlines	800-221-1212	A
Aviacsa	800-237-6396	D
British Airways	800-247-9297	D
Canadian Airlines	800-426-7000	D
Cayman Airways	800-422-9626	D
Comair	800-354-9822	A
Continental Airlines	800-523-3273	C,D
Continental Express	800-523-3273	B
Delta Air Lines	800-221-1212	A
KLM Royal Dutch Airlines	800-374-7747	D
Lufthansa	800-645-3880	D
Northwest Airlines	800-225-2525	B
Southwest Airlines	800-435-9792	A
Sun Country Airlines	800-752-1218	A
TACA	800-535-8780	D
Trans World Airlines	800-221-2000	A
United Airlines	800-241-6522	A
US Airways	800-428-4322	A

Consulate General of Brazil (1700 West Loop S, Suite 1450, 713/961–3063).

Consulate General of Colombia (2990 Richmond Ave., Suite 200, 713/527–8919).

Consulate General of Haiti (6310 Auden, 713/661–8275).

Consulate General of Japan at Houston (1000 Louisiana St., Suite 5300, 713/652–2977).

Consulate General of Senegal (3602 MacGregor Way, 713/747–4711).

Consulate General of Spain (1800 Bering, 713/783–6200).

Consulate General of the State of Qatar (1990 Post Oak Blvd., Suite 810, 713/355–8221).

Consulate General of Switzerland (1000 Louisiana, Suite 5670, 713/650–0000).

Consulate of Costa Rica (3000 Wilcrest, Suite 112, 713/266–0484).

Consulate of Sweden (2401 Fountain View, 713/953–1417).

Cypriot Consulate (320 S. 66th St., 713/928–2264).

Danish Consulate for Houston (4545 Post Oak, 713/622–9018).

El Salvador Consulate General (6420 Hillcroft, 713/270–6239).

French and Monacan Consulate (777 Post Oak Blvd, Suite 600, 713/572–2799).

Germany Consulate General (1330 Post Oak Blvd., Suite 1850, 713/627–7770).

Greece Consulate General (1360 Post Oak, 713/840–7522).

Honduran Consulate (4151 Southwest Fwy., 713/622–4572).

Honorary Consulate of Belgium (2929 Allen Pkwy., Suite 2222, 713/224–8000).

Hungarian Consulate (713/529–2727).

Indian Consulate (1990 Post Oak Blvd., 713/626–2148).

Indonesian Consulate (10900 Richmond, 713/785–1691).

Israeli Consulate (24 Greenway Plaza, 713/627–3780).

Italian Consulate General (1300 Post Oak Blvd., 713/850–7520).

Korean Consulate General (1990 Post Oak Blvd., 713/961–0186).

Mexican Consulate General (10103 Fondren, 713/271–6800).

Mongolian Consulate (1221 Lamar, 713/759–1922).

Netherlanders Consulate (2200 Post Oak Blvd., Suite 610, 713/622–8000).

Norwegian Consulate (2777 Allen Pkwy., 713/521–2900).

Panamanian Consulate (24 E. Greenway Plaza, 713/622–4451).

Peruvian Consulate (5177 Richmond, 713/355–9517).

The Republic of China-Taiwan (11 Greenway Plaza, 713/626–7445).

Republic of Egypt Consulate General (1990 Post Oak Blvd., 713/961–4915).

Thai Consulate (600 Travis, 713/229–8241).

Turkish Consulate General (1990 Post Oak, 713/622–5849).

Venezuelan Consulate (2925 Briar Park, 713/974–0028).

INOCULATIONS, VACCINATIONS & TRAVEL HEALTH

Diagnostic Clinic of Houston (713/797–9191): Dr. Travis will give you all the sticks you need for anywhere on earth. Think you picked up a funny intestinal flora in Bora Bora? The clinic has doctors of internal medicine seeing and testing patients on an outpatient basis. If your health care plan does not cover your visit, cash at time of service is preferred.

PASSPORTS

The main passport office is in the **Mickey Leland Federal Building** (1919 Smith St., Suite 1100). Call the automated appointment system before you go (713/751–0294). The main office will mail your passport within 14 business days, and the extra expedite charge is $35. You must be able to prove your expedite need either with an airline itinerary or letter from your employer. If you do not require visa processing, you may apply at designated post offices, clerks of court, and municipal offices. You will normally receive your passport within 25 business days. If you have expedited, the official time is 10 days, although they often arrive in a week. Applicants must have proof of citizenship (certified birth certificate, previous U.S. passport, or naturalization certificate), valid identification (such as a driver's license), two identical passport-size photographs (2 by 2 inches), and a completed passport application.

passport photo agencies

Two identical photos are required. Many Kinko's and photography shops offer instant passport photos.

Passport Agency Services (1903 Louisiana, 713/650–9900) Photos, expediting and renewal services, international driver's licenses, and fingerprinting are among the services offered right across the street from the passport office in the Mickey Leland building. When you've submitted your info and paid your fee to the expediters, they save you the trouble of standing in line.

TOURIST INFORMATION

local information

The **Houston Visitors Center** downtown (in City Hall, 901 Bagby) is open from 9 until 4 daily. It's a minimuseum of Houston history, and video screens run "previews" of area attractions. The number for all visitors' information is 800/4-HOUSTON.

statewide information

The State of Texas maintains a well-organized and comprehensive Web site, www.state.tx.us. (There's a special travel section for snowbirds.) You can also order a CD "virtual tour of Texas" travel brochure (800/252–9600).

travel planning

Several offices in Houston can help you plan.

Aruba Tourism Authority (12707 North Fwy., 281/872–7822).

Austria Ski (1535 West Loop S, 713/960–0900).

British Tourist Authority (800/462–2748).

Fox Travel (25701 Hwy. 45 N, 281/363–0573).

Mexican Government Tourism Office (10103 Fondren, 713/772–2581).

TRAVELER'S AID

George Bush Intercontinental Airport/Houston (281/230–3032).

William P. Hobby Airport (713/640–3000).

U.S. CUSTOMS

The general number for local customs offices is 281/985–6700.

VISA INFORMATION & TRAVEL ADVISORIES

You can always contact the consulate or national tourism office of the place you plan to visit for detailed information. The Office of the **United States State Department** in Houston also maintains and issues travel advisories, 713/209–3482. Find out about vaccinations and health issues from the **Centers for Disease Control and Prevention's** international travelers' hot line, 888/394–8747.

The Houston office of **Immigration and Naturalization** (126 Northpoint, 281/847–7900) serves 30 Texas counties: Angelina, Austin, Brazoria, Chambers, Colorado, Fort Bend, Galveston, Grimes, Hardin, Harris, Jasper, Jefferson, Liberty, Madison, Matagorda, Montgomery, Nacogdoches, Newton, Orange, Polk, Sabine, San Augustin, San Jacinto, Shelby, Trinity, Tyler, Walker, Waller, Washington, and Wharton.

DIRECTORIES

alphabetical listing of resources & topics

restaurants by neighborhood

shops by neighborhood

resources & topics

Baba Yega (vegetarian), 34
Barnaby's Café (American casual), 4
Black Labrador Pub (English), 14
Blue Agave (Tex-Mex), 30
Café Noche (Mexican), 22
Churrascos (Latin), 21
Daily Review Café (contemporary), 9
Damian's (Italian), 17
El Pueblito Café (Mexican), 22–23
Fox Diner (American), 3
Fusion Café (Eclectic), 13
Golden Room (Thai), 32
La Colombe D'Or (French), 14
La Mora Cucina Toscana (Italian), 18
La Strada (Italian), 18
Mark's (contemporary), 10
Mo Mong (Vietnamese), 34
Niko Niko's (Greek), 15
Nino's (Italian), 18–19
Paulie's (delicatessen), 13
Ruggles Grill (Southwestern), 28
Thai Pepper (Thai), 33
Tony Ruppe's (contemporary), 10–11
Urbana (eclectic), 13–14

MONTROSE/ MUSEUM DISTRICT

Boulevard Bistrot (contemporary), 9
Redwood Grill (contemporary), 10

MUSEUM DISTRICT

Raven Grill (Southwestern), 27
Sierra Grill (Southwestern), 28

NEARTOWN

Merida (Mexican), 23–24

NORTH

Roznovsky's Hamburgers (American casual), 5

NORTHWEST

Red Onion (Caribbean), 8
Vung Thai (Thai), 33

POST OAK

Beck's Prime (American casual), 4

RICE UNIVERSITY VILLAGE

Benjy's (contemporary), 9
Collinas (Italian), 16–17
Jax Grill (American), 3
Mi Luna (Spanish), 28
Miss Saigon Café (Vietnamese), 34
Nit Noi (Thai), 33
Prego (Italian), 19
Sabroso Grill (Latin), 22
Shiva (Indian), 16

RICHMOND STRIP

Chuy's (Tex-Mex), 30–31
Copeland's of New Orleans (Cajun/Creole), 7
Pappasito's Cantina (Tex-Mex), 32
Simposio (Italian), 19
Taquería la Tapatia (Mexican), 24–25

RIVER OAKS

Anthony's Restaurant (continental), 11
Avalon Drug Co. and Diner (American casual), 4
Backstreet Café (American casual), 4
Berryhill Hot Tamales (Mexican), 22
Chuy's (Tex-Mex), 30–31
Da Marco (Italian), 17
Grotto (Italian), 17–18
La Griglia (Italian), 18
Mesa Grill (Southwestern), 27
Ouisie's Table (American), 3
Rainbow Lodge (continental), 11–12
River Oaks Grill (continental), 12
Taco Milagro (Mexican), 24
Tila's (Mexican), 25
Vallone's (steak), 30

SHARPSTOWN

Super Rico (Peruvian), 26

SOUTH DOWNTOWN

Brennan's (Cajun/ Creole), 7

SOUTHWEST

Annie's Hamburgers (American casual), 4
Fung's Kitchen (Chinese), 8–9

Garson Restaurant (Middle Eastern), 25–26
Rio Ranch (Southwestern), 27

TANGLEWOOD

Carrabba's (Italian), 16
Grotto (Italian), 17–18
Scott Chen's (contemporary), 10

THIRD WARD

Drexler's Bar-B-Que (barbecue), 5–6

UPPER KIRBY DISTRICT

Beck's Prime (American casual), 4
Café Express (café), 6
Carrabba's (Italian), 16
Churrascos (Latin), 21
Cooke's Gourmet (meats & poultry), 76
Dimassi's Mediterranean Café (Middle Eastern), 25
El Tiempo (Mexican), 23
Khyber North Indian Grill (Indian), 15–16
Little Pappasito's Cantina (Tex-Mex), 32
Mission Burritos (Tex-Mex), 31–32
Taquería la Tapatia (Mexican), 24–25
Whole Foods (health food), 76

WEST

Denis' Seafood House (seafood), 26
Korea Garden (Korean), 21
Taste of Texas (steak), 30

WEST DOWNTOWN

Blue Orchid (Thai), 32

WEST UNIVERSITY PLACE

Bubba's Texas Burger Shack (American casual), 4
Dimassi's Mediterranean Café (Middle Eastern), 25
Elde Street Deli (delicatessen), 13
Fuzzy's Pizza (Italian), 17
Goode Company Bar-B-Que (barbecue), 6
Goode Company Hamburgers and Taquería (Tex-Mex), 31
Goode Company Seafood (seafood), 26

shops by neighborhood

RICHMOND STRIP AREA

RIVER OAKS

CITY NOTES

CITY NOTES

CITY NOTES

CITY NOTES

CITY NOTES